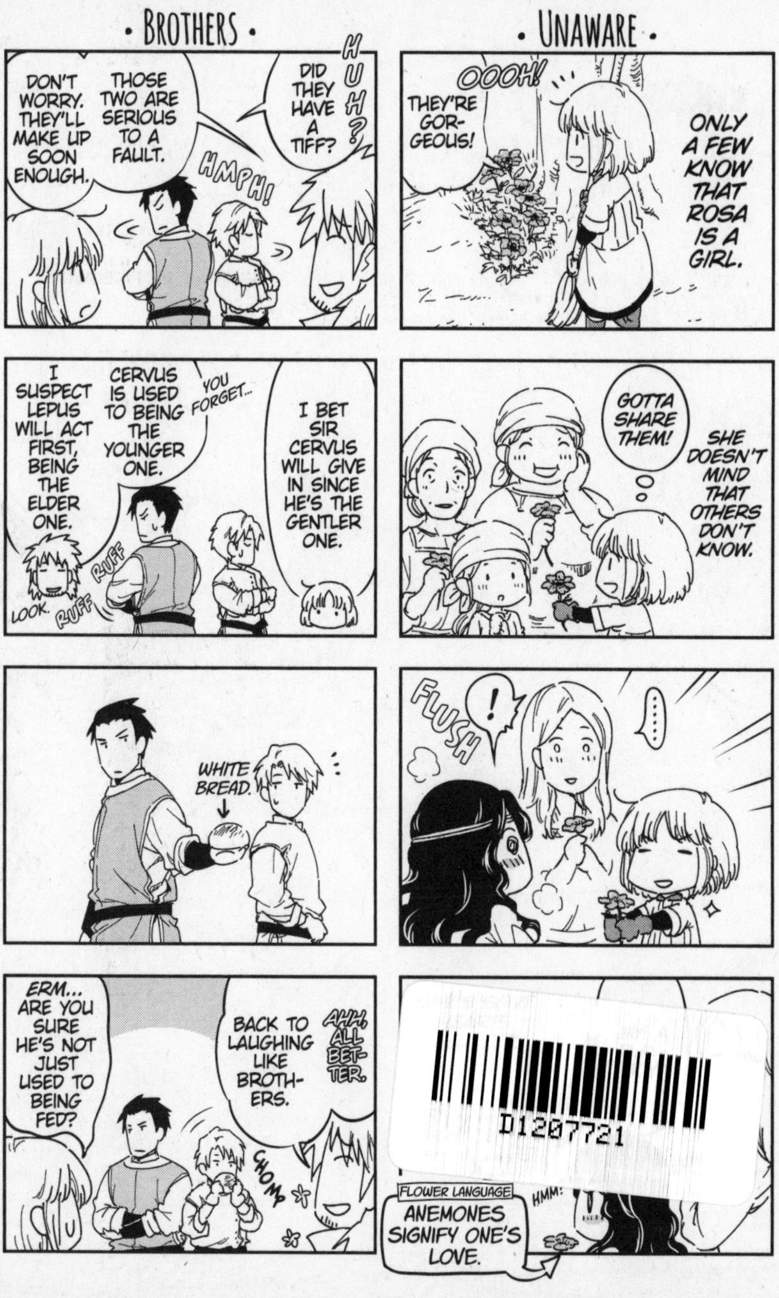
• UNAWARE •
ONLY A FEW KNOW THAT ROSA IS A GIRL.
OOOH!
THEY'RE GORGEOUS!
SHE DOESN'T MIND THAT OTHERS DON'T KNOW.
GOTTA SHARE THEM!
......
!
FLUSH
HMM?
FLOWER LANGUAGE
ANEMONES SIGNIFY ONE'S LOVE.
• BROTHERS •
HUH?
DID THEY HAVE A TIFF?
THOSE TWO ARE SERIOUS TO A FAULT.
DON'T WORRY. THEY'LL MAKE UP SOON ENOUGH.
HMPH!
I BET SIR CERVUS WILL GIVE IN SINCE HE'S THE GENTLER ONE.
YOU FORGET...
CERVUS IS USED TO BEING THE YOUNGER ONE.
I SUSPECT LEPUS WILL ACT FIRST, BEING THE ELDER ONE.
RUFF
RUFF
LOOK.
WHITE BREAD.
AHH, ALL BETTER.
BACK TO LAUGHING LIKE BROTHERS.
ERM... ARE YOU SURE HE'S NOT JUST USED TO BEING FED?
CHOMP

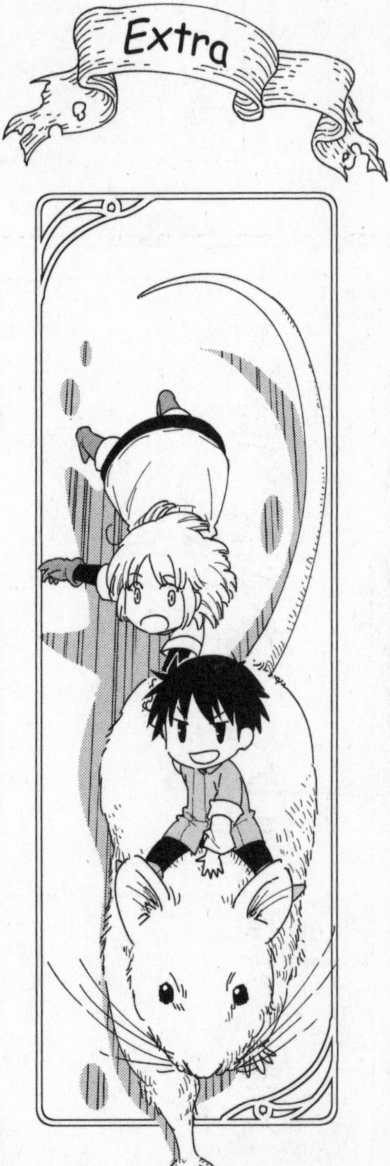
Extra

• PET...S? •

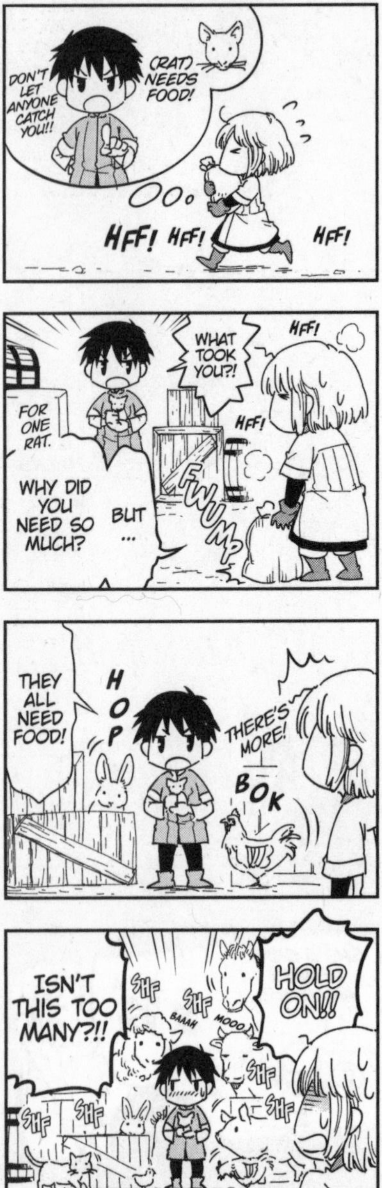
(RAT) NEEDS FOOD!
DON'T LET ANYONE CATCH YOU!!
HFF! HFF! HFF!
HFF!
WHAT TOOK YOU?!
HFF!
FOR ONE RAT. WHY DID YOU NEED SO MUCH? BUT ...
FWUMP
THERE'S MORE!
BOK
HOP
THEY ALL NEED FOOD!
HOLD ON!!
MOOO
SHF SHF
BAAAH
SHF SHF SHF SHF
ISN'T THIS TOO MANY?!!

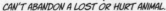

CAN'T ABANDON A LOST OR HURT ANIMAL.

SEVEN SEAS ENTERTAINMENT PRESENTS

THE KNIGHT BLOOMS
BEHIND CASTLE WALLS
story and art by MASANARI YUDUKA
VOL. 1

TRANSLATION
Margaret Ngo

LETTERING
Rai Enril

COVER DESIGN
Hannah Carey

LOGO DESIGN
George Panella

PROOFREADER
Krista Grandy

EDITOR
K. McDonald

PRODUCTION DESIGNER
George Panella

PRODUCTION MANAGER
Lissa Pattillo

PREPRESS TECHNICIAN
Melanie Ujimori
Jules Valera

EDITOR-IN-CHIEF
Julie Davis

ASSOCIATE PUBLISHER
Adam Arnold

PUBLISHER
Jason DeAngelis

The Knight Blooms Behind Castle Walls Vol. 1
© 2020 Masanari Yuduka
First published in Japan in 2020 by OVERLAP Inc., Ltd., Tokyo.
English translation rights arranged with OVERLAP Inc., Ltd., Tokyo.

Seven Seas press and purchase enquiries can be sent to Marketing Manager Lianne Sentar at press@gomanga.com. Information regarding the distribution and purchase of digital editions is available from Digital Manager CK Russell at digital@gomanga.com.

ISBN: 978-1-63858-956-3
Printed in Canada
First Printing: January 2023
10 9 8 7 6 5 4 3 2 1

//// READING DIRECTIONS ////

This book reads from *right to left*, Japanese style. If this is your first time reading manga, you start reading from the top right panel on each page and take it from there. If you get lost, just follow the numbered diagram here. It may seem backwards at first, but you'll get the hang of it! Have fun!!

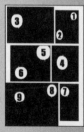

Follow us online: www.SevenSeasEntertainment.com

• AFTERWORD •

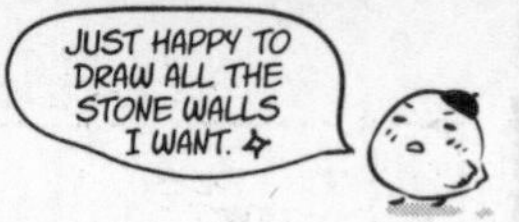
JUST HAPPY TO DRAW ALL THE STONE WALLS I WANT.

- THANK YOU SO MUCH FOR READING TO THE END!
- I REALLY HOPE YOU ENJOYED READING AS MUCH AS I'M ENJOYED DRAWING THIS MANGA FILLED WITH ALL MY WHIMSIES AND FAVORITE THINGS.
- I'D ENVISIONED A SERIES FOCUSED ON THE DAILY LIFE OF A KNIGHT(-IN-TRAINING) PROTAGONIST WITHOUT FIGHTING. BUT THAT OUTLINE HAD TO GO THROUGH MANY REVISIONS BEFORE IT WAS ALLOWED TO SEE THE LIGHT OF DAY.
- I'M ETERNALLY GRATEFUL TO MY EDITOR AND THE EDITORIAL DEPARTMENT FOR SHARING MY INTERESTS AND TAKING ME ON. EVERY DAY! FROM THE BOTTOM OF MY HEART!! I'M EXTREMELY THANKFUL TO YOU ALL!!!
- I HOPE TO HAVE YOUR CONTINUED SUPPORT AS THIS TALE GOES ON A LITTLE LONGER.
- LOOKING FORWARD TO SEEING YOU AGAIN!

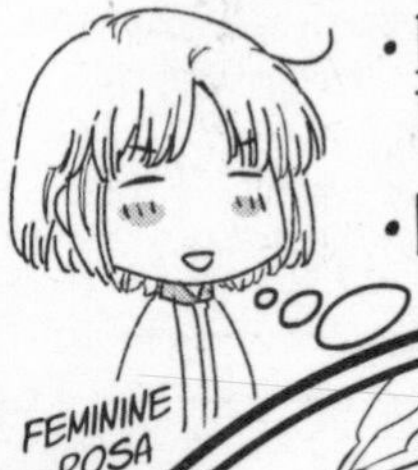
FEMININE ROSA

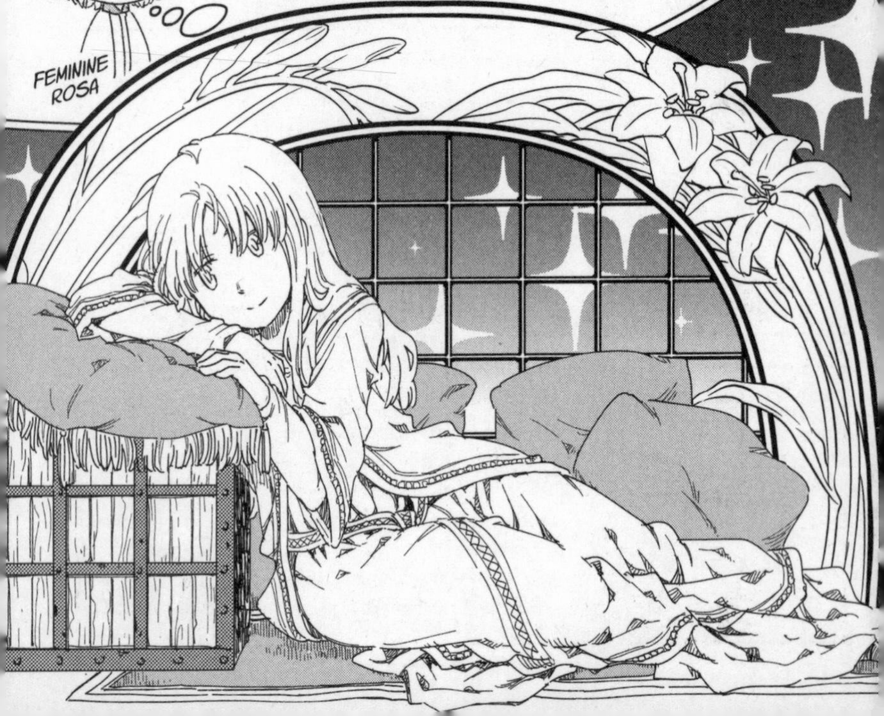

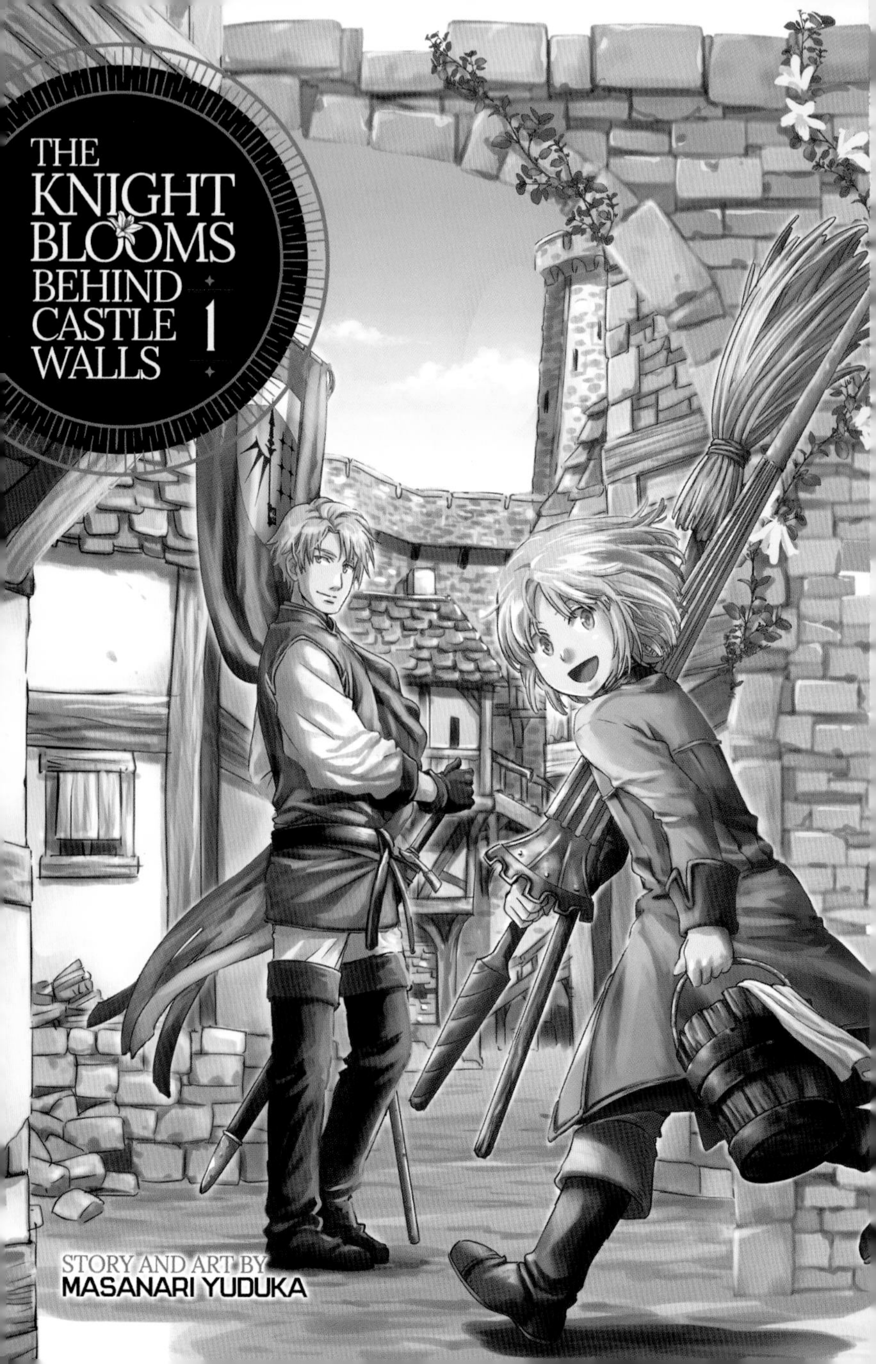
THE KNIGHT BLOOMS BEHIND CASTLE WALLS
1
STORY AND ART BY
MASANARI YUDUKA

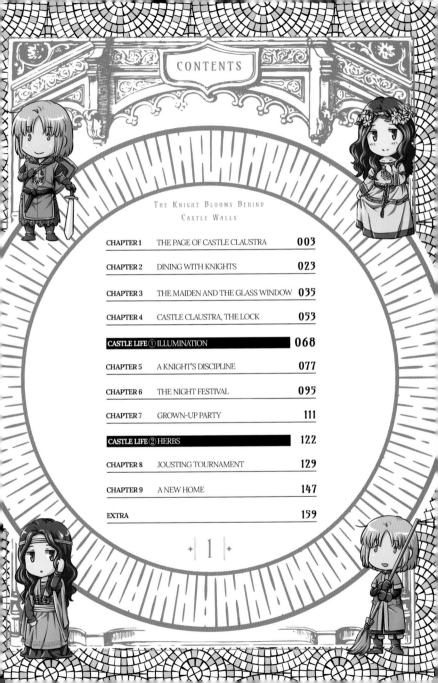

CONTENTS

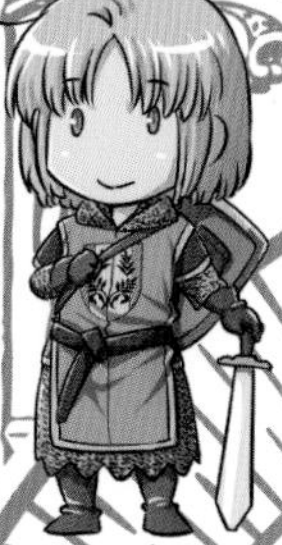

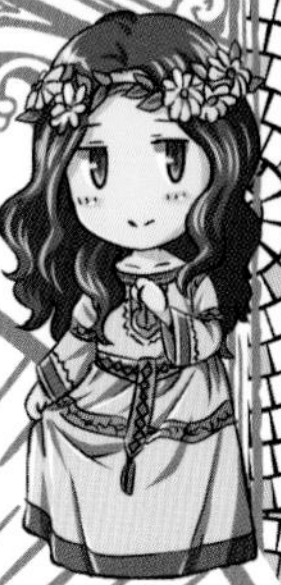

THE KNIGHT BLOOMS BEHIND CASTLE WALLS

1

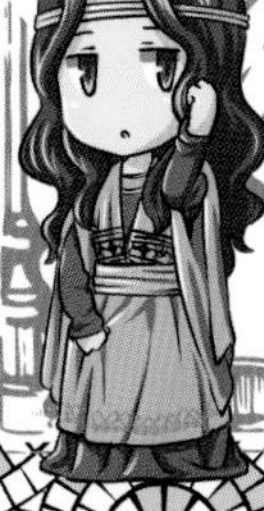

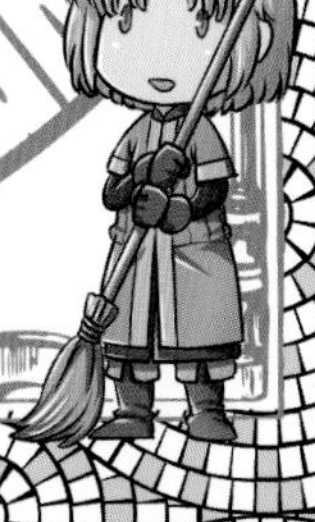

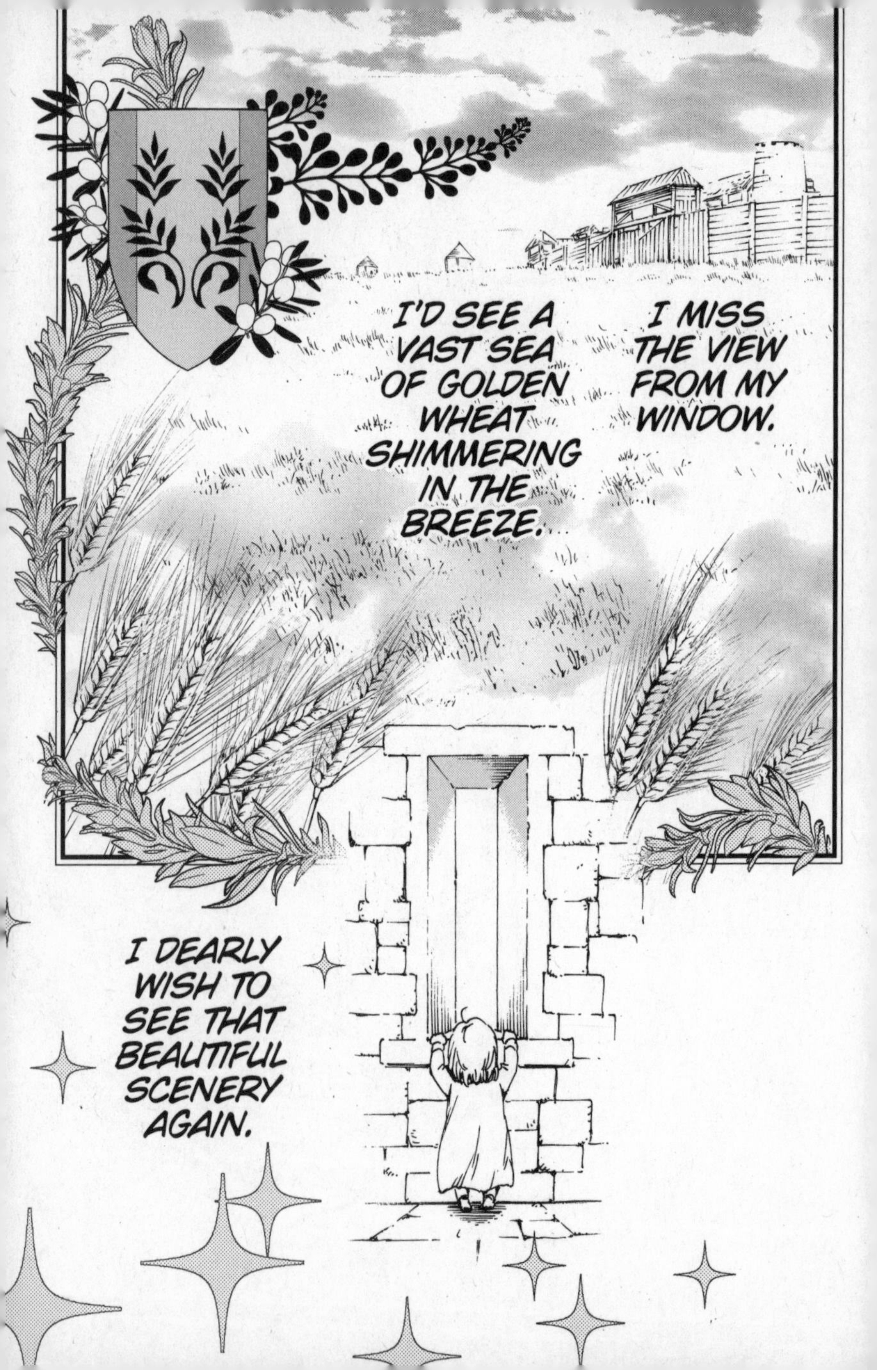
I MISS THE VIEW FROM MY WINDOW.
I'D SEE A VAST SEA OF GOLDEN WHEAT SHIMMERING IN THE BREEZE...
I DEARLY WISH TO SEE THAT BEAUTIFUL SCENERY AGAIN.

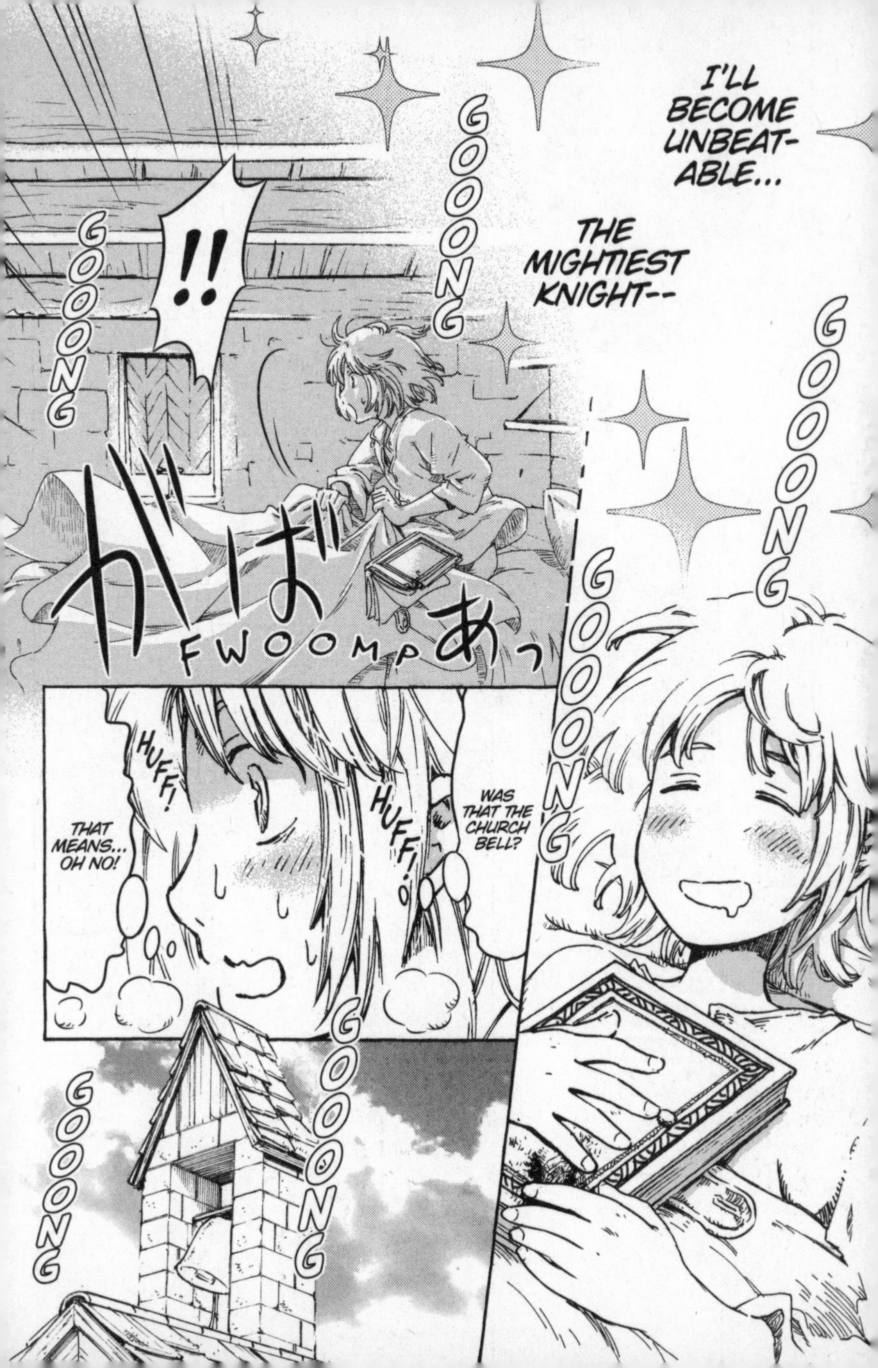
I'LL BECOME UNBEAT-ABLE...
THE MIGHTIEST KNIGHT--
GOOOONG
GOOOOONG
GOOOONG
!!
GOOOONG
がばあっ
FWOOMP
WAS THAT THE CHURCH BELL?
HUFF!
HUFF!
THAT MEANS... OH NO!
GOOOONG
GOOOONG

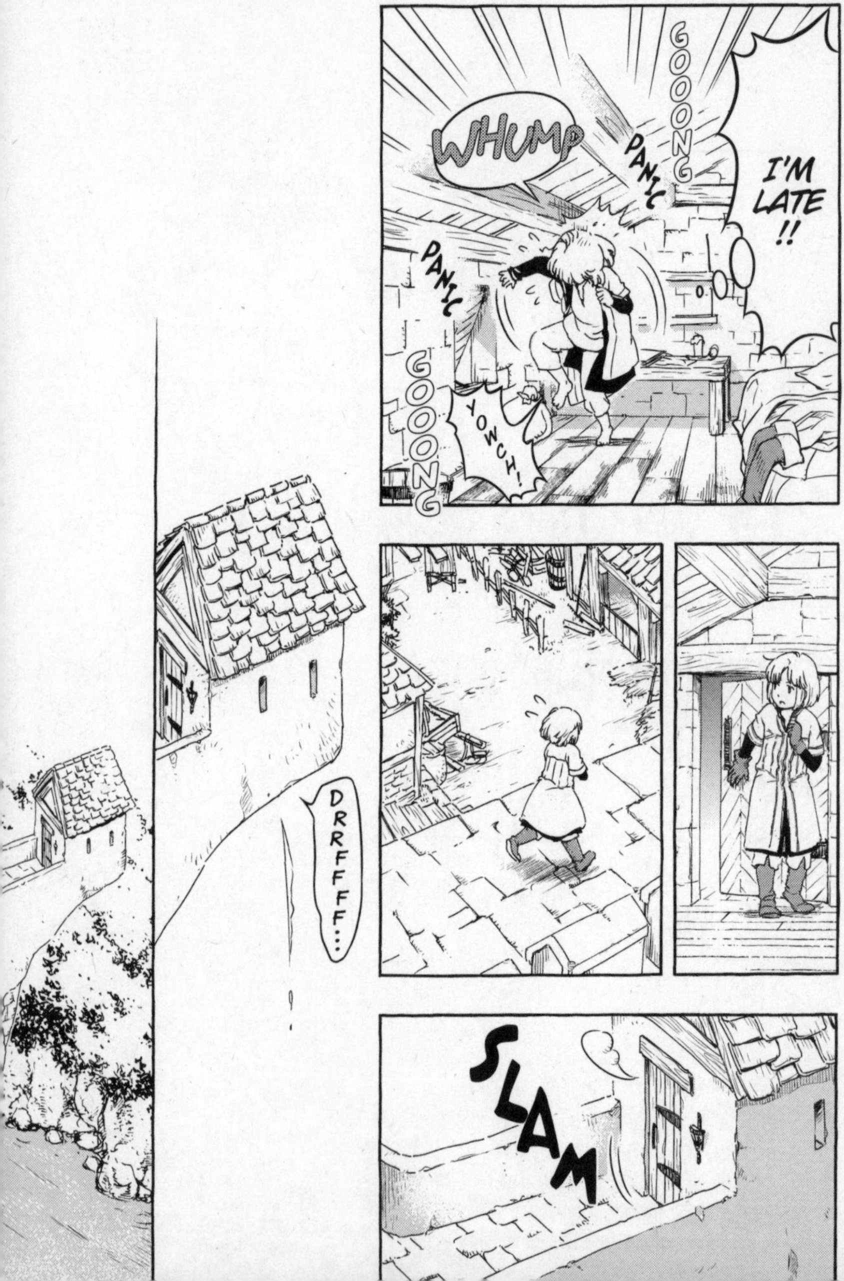
I'M LATE!!
GOOOONG
PANIC
WHUMP
PANIC
GOOOONG
YOWCH!
SLAM
DRRFFFF...

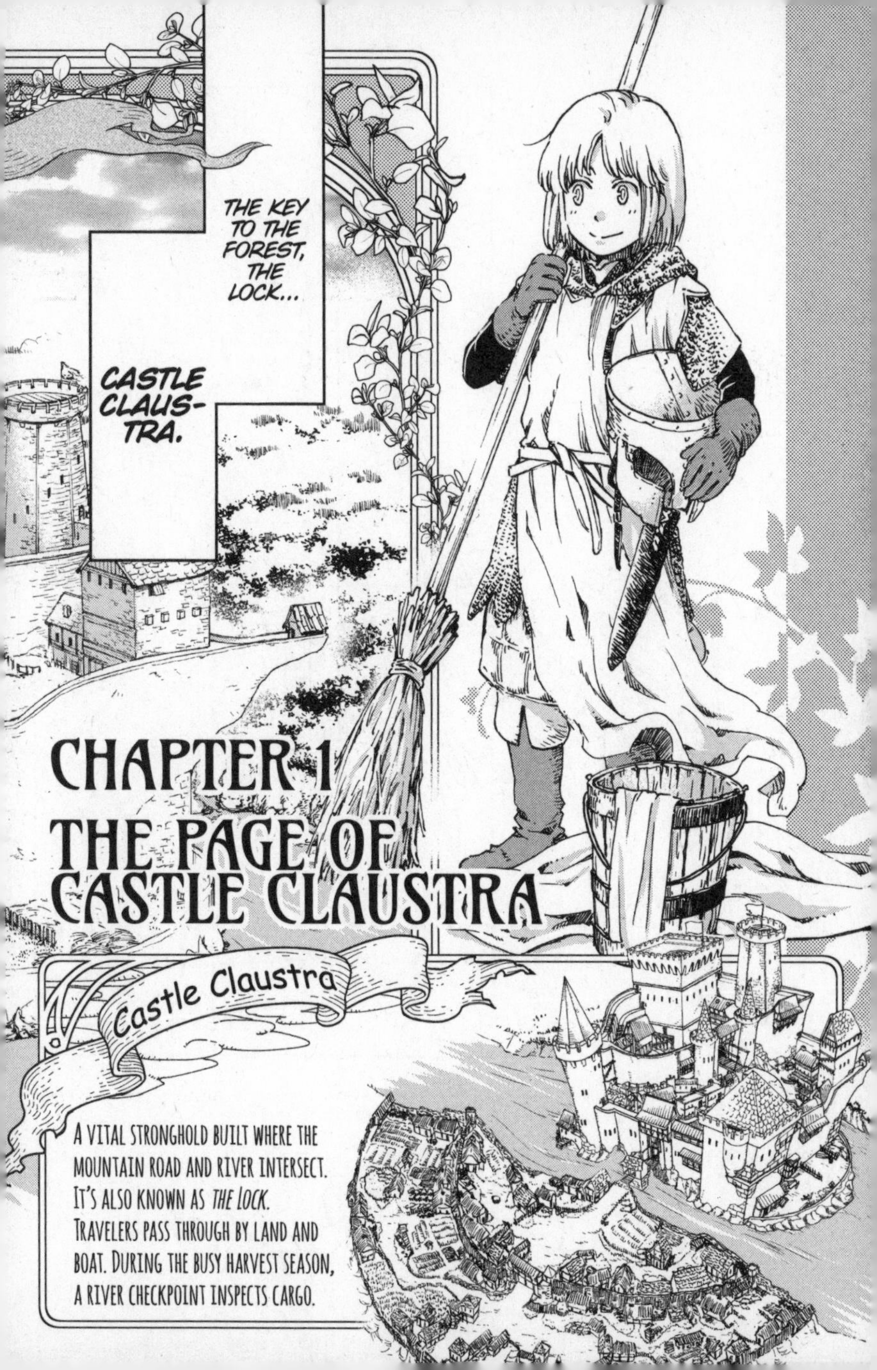
THE KEY TO THE FOREST, THE LOCK...
CASTLE CLAUS-TRA.
CHAPTER 1
THE PAGE OF CASTLE CLAUSTRA
Castle Claustra
A VITAL STRONGHOLD BUILT WHERE THE MOUNTAIN ROAD AND RIVER INTERSECT. IT'S ALSO KNOWN AS *THE LOCK*. TRAVELERS PASS THROUGH BY LAND AND BOAT. DURING THE BUSY HARVEST SEASON, A RIVER CHECKPOINT INSPECTS CARGO.

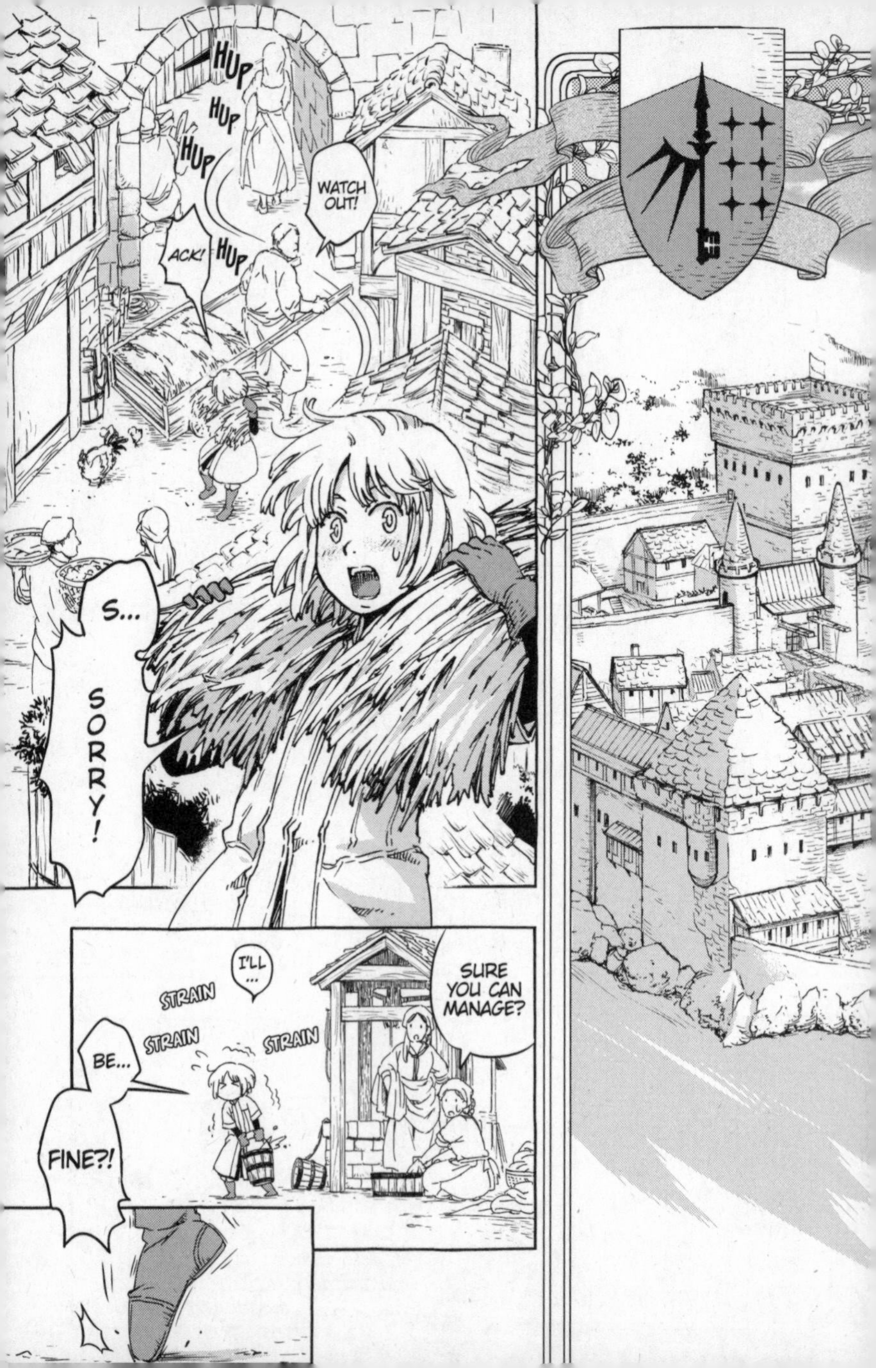
WATCH OUT!
HUP HUP HUP HUP
ACK!
S... SORRY!
SURE YOU CAN MANAGE?
STRAIN
I'LL...
STRAIN
STRAIN
BE... FINE?!

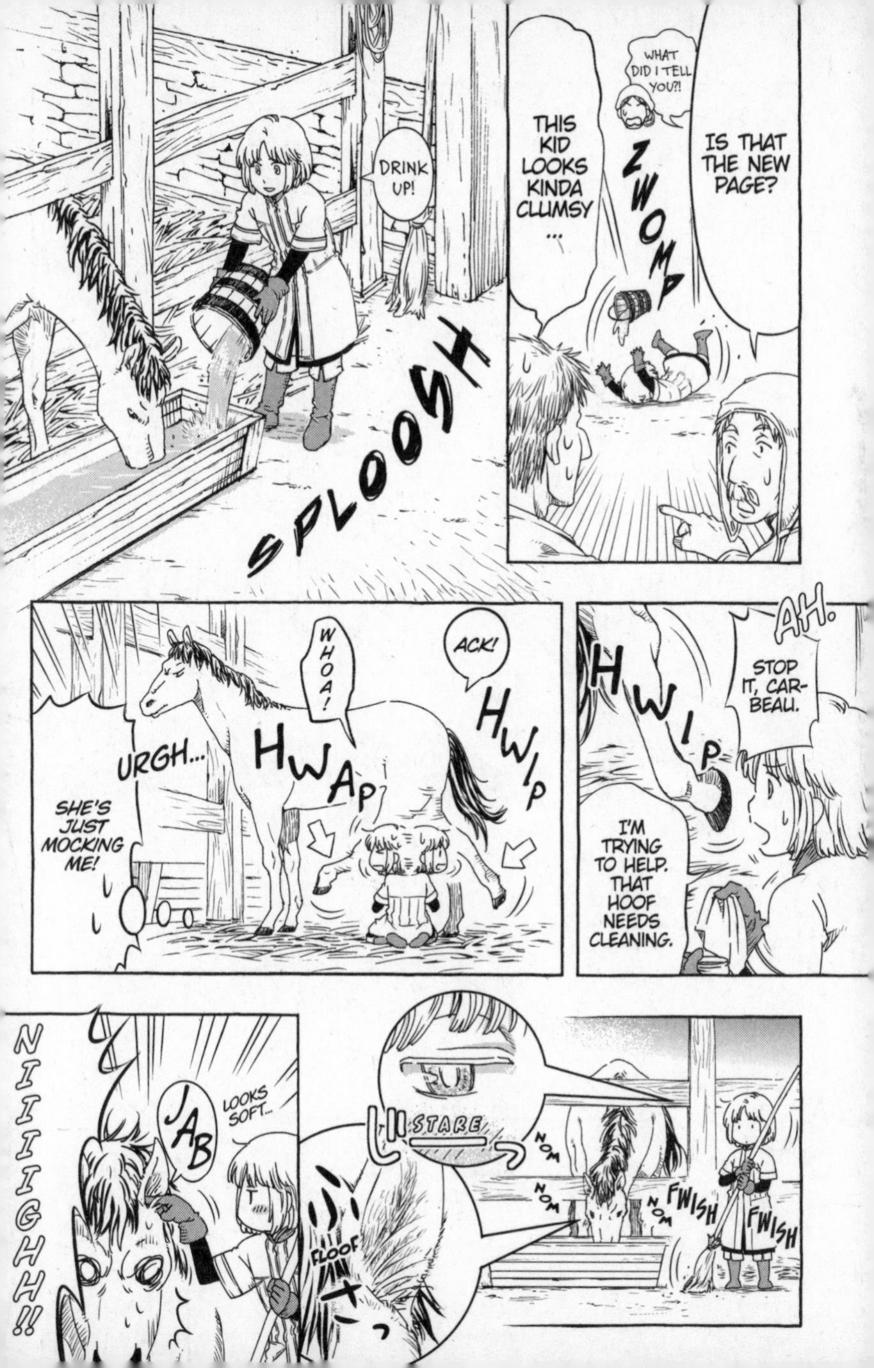
IS THAT THE NEW PAGE?
WHAT DID I TELL YOU?!
ZWOMP
THIS KID LOOKS KINDA CLUMSY ...
DRINK UP!
SPLOOSH
AH.
STOP IT, CAR-BEAU.
HWIP
I'M TRYING TO HELP. THAT HOOF NEEDS CLEANING.
ACK!
HWIP
WHOA!
HWAP
URGH...
SHE'S JUST MOCKING ME!
FWISH
FWISH
NOM
NOM
NOM
STARE
LOOKS SOFT...
JAB
FLOOF
NIIIIIGHH!!

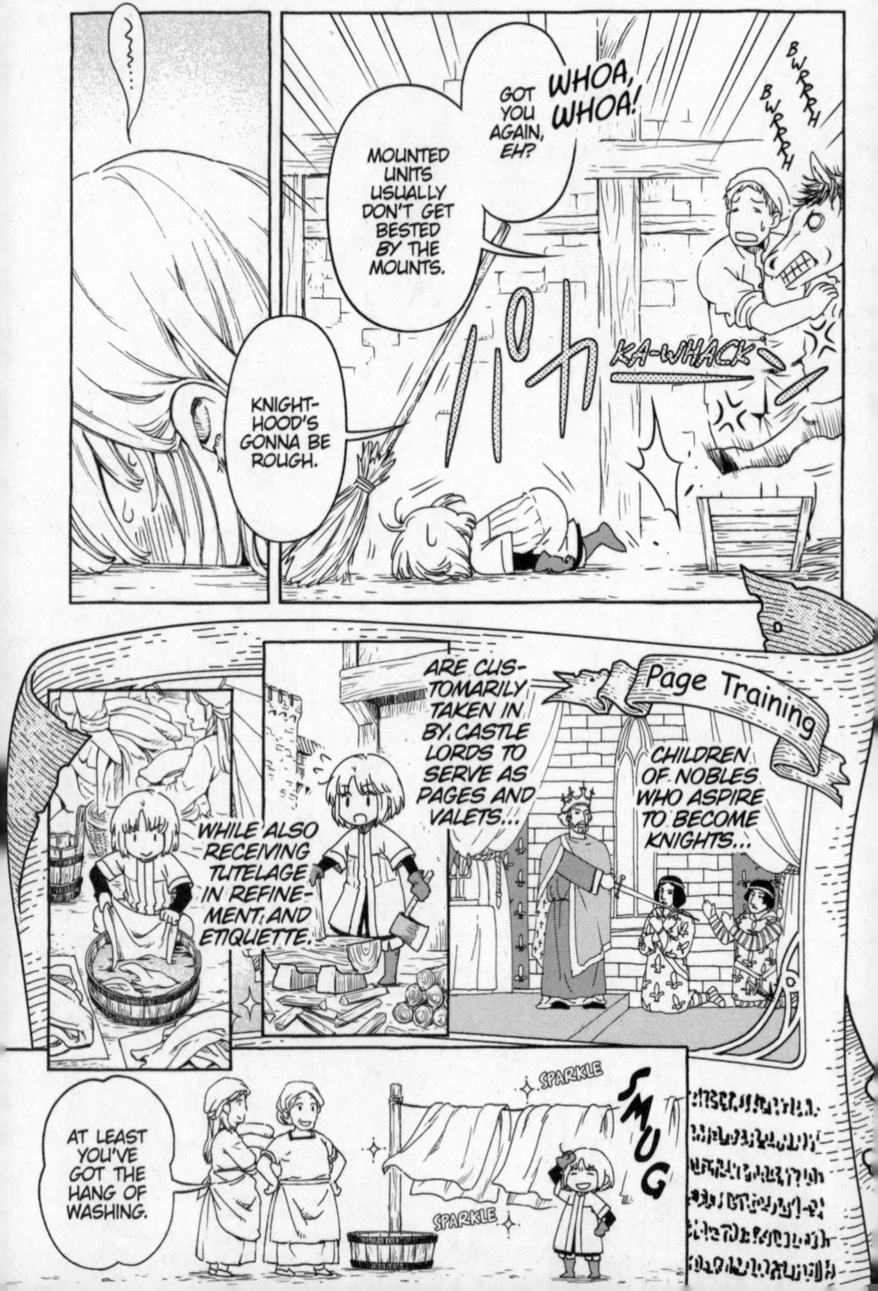

BWRRRH BWRRRH
WHOA, WHOA!
GOT YOU AGAIN, EH?
MOUNTED UNITS USUALLY DON'T GET BESTED BY THE MOUNTS.
KA-WHACK
KNIGHT-HOOD'S GONNA BE ROUGH.
......
Page Training
CHILDREN OF NOBLES WHO ASPIRE TO BECOME KNIGHTS...
ARE CUS-TOMARILY TAKEN IN BY CASTLE LORDS TO SERVE AS PAGES AND VALETS...
WHILE ALSO RECEIVING TUTELAGE IN REFINE-MENT AND ETIQUETTE.
SMUG
SPARKLE
SPARKLE
AT LEAST YOU'VE GOT THE HANG OF WASHING.

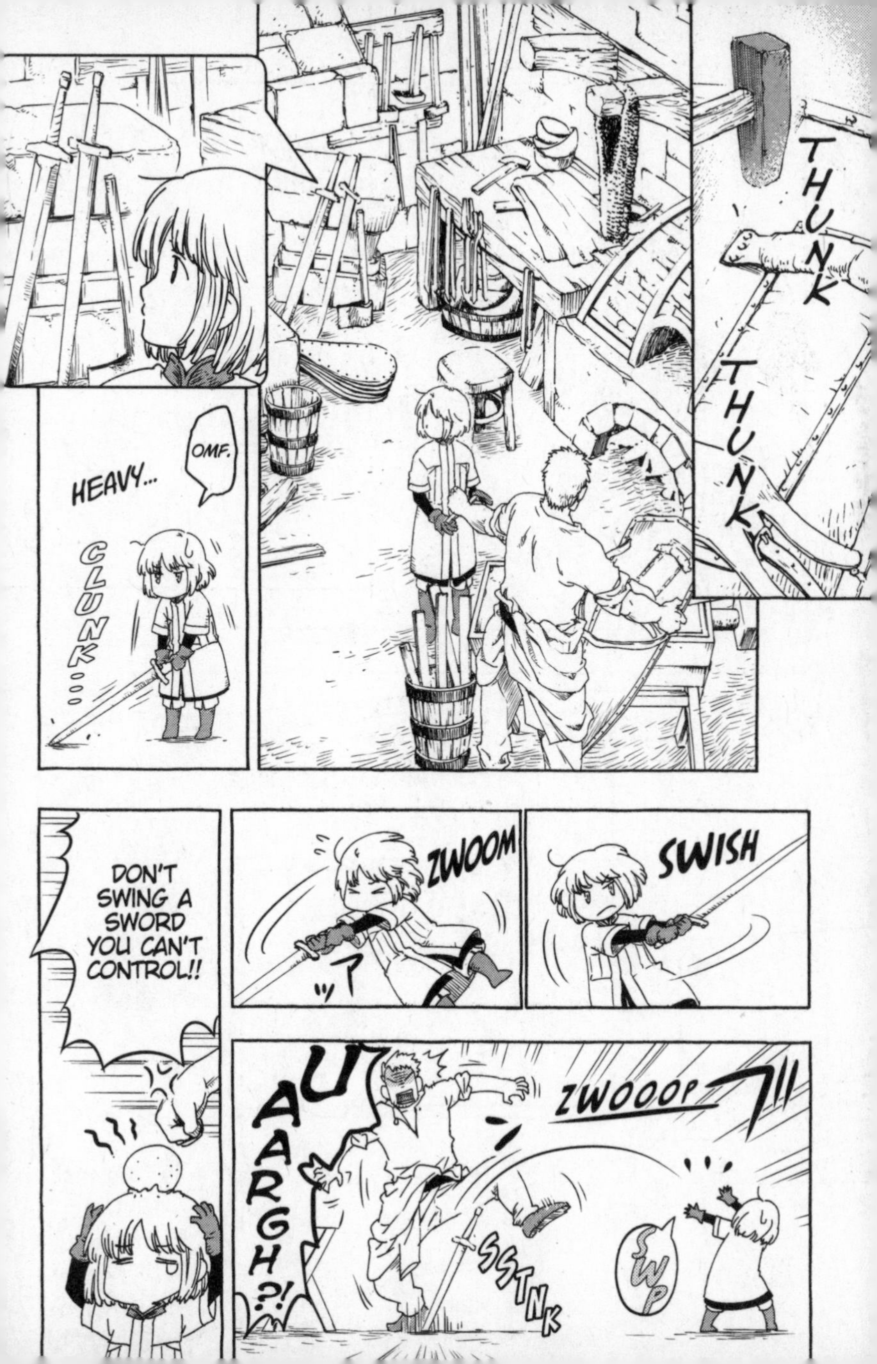
THUNK
THUNK
THUNK
OMF.
HEAVY...
CLUNK...
SWISH
ZWOOM
アッ
SWP
ZWOOOP
AARGH?!
SSTNK
DON'T SWING A SWORD YOU CAN'T CONTROL!!

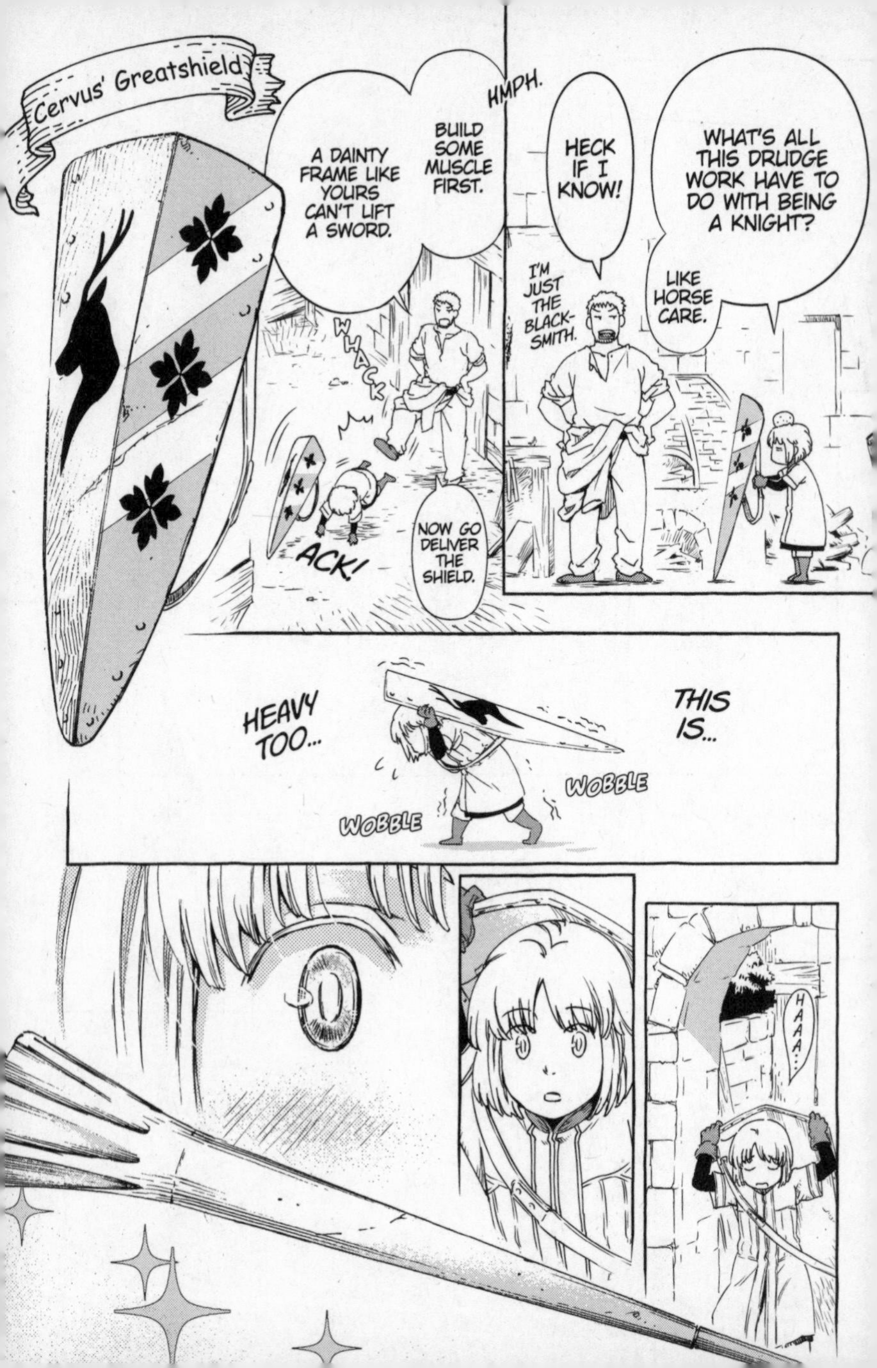
WHAT'S ALL THIS DRUDGE WORK HAVE TO DO WITH BEING A KNIGHT?
LIKE HORSE CARE.
HECK IF I KNOW!
I'M JUST THE BLACK-SMITH.
HMPH.
BUILD SOME MUSCLE FIRST.
A DAINTY FRAME LIKE YOURS CAN'T LIFT A SWORD.
WHACK
ACK!
NOW GO DELIVER THE SHIELD.
Cervus' Greatshield
THIS IS...
WOBBLE
HEAVY TOO...
WOBBLE
HAAA...

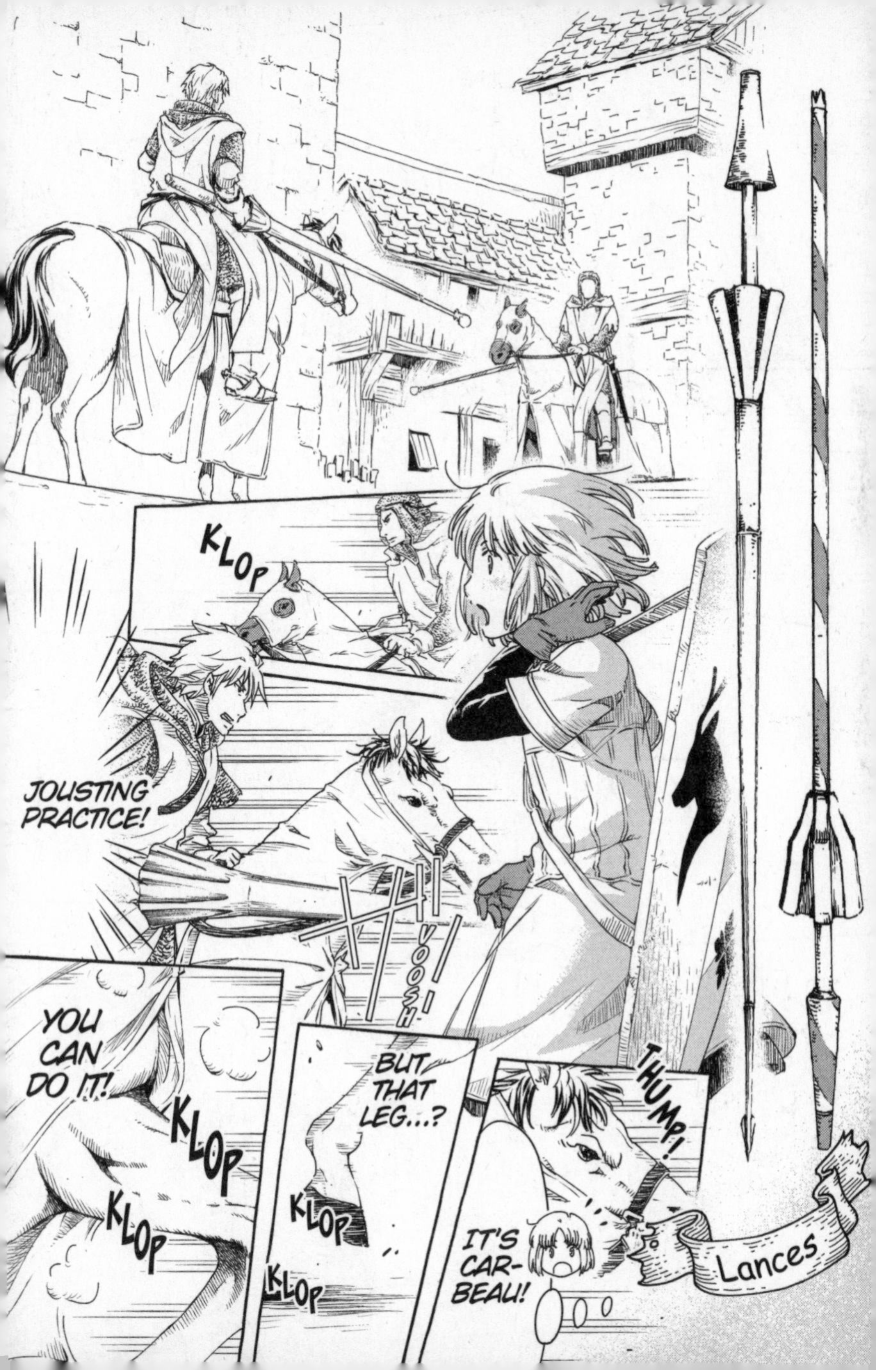
Lances
KLOP
JOUSTING PRACTICE!
VOOSH
THUMP!
IT'S CAR-BEAU!
BUT THAT LEG...?
KLOP
KLOP
YOU CAN DO IT!
KLOP
KLOP

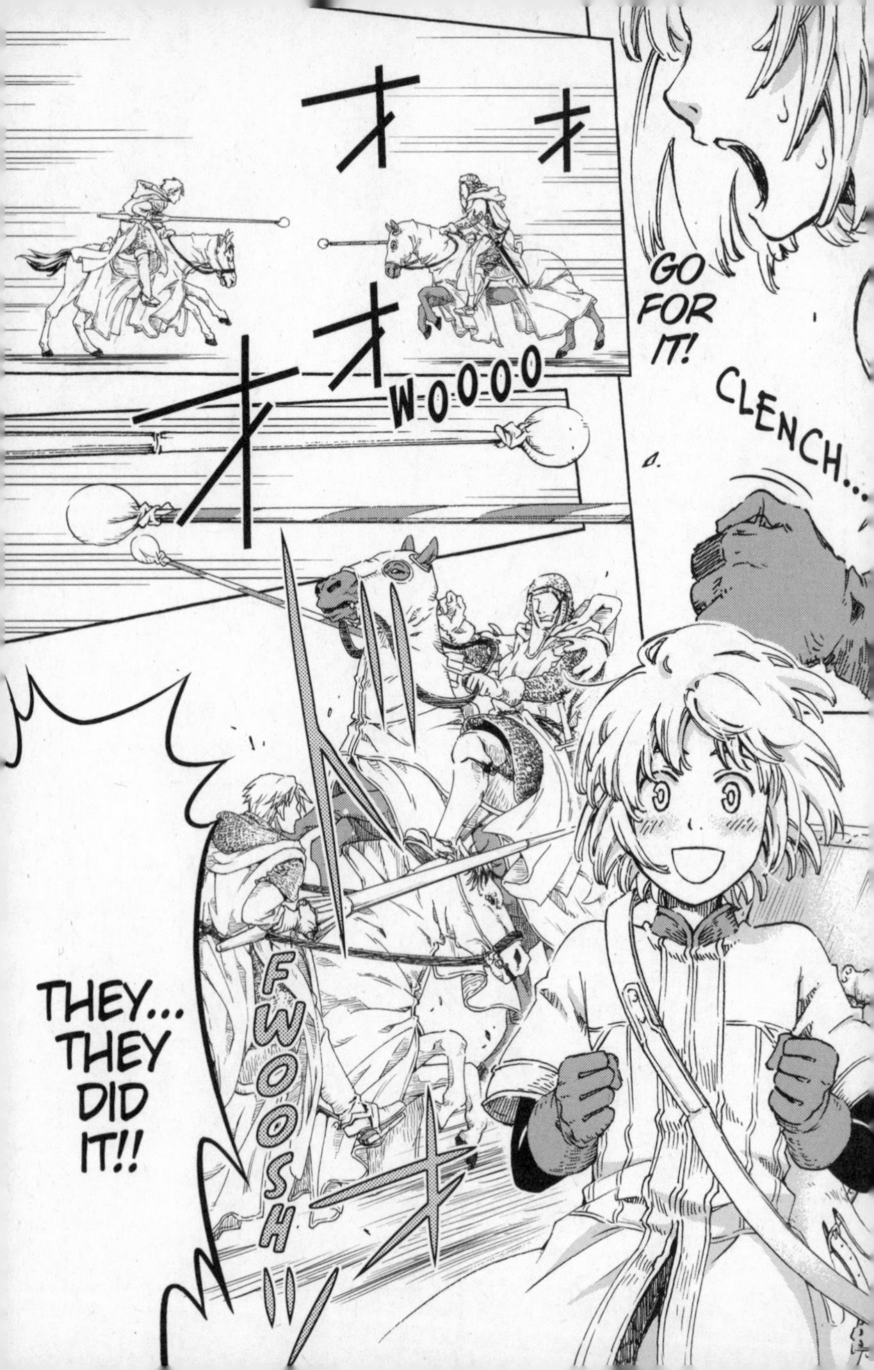
GO FOR IT!
CLENCH...
オオオオ
WOOOO
FWOOSH!!
オ
THEY... THEY DID IT!!

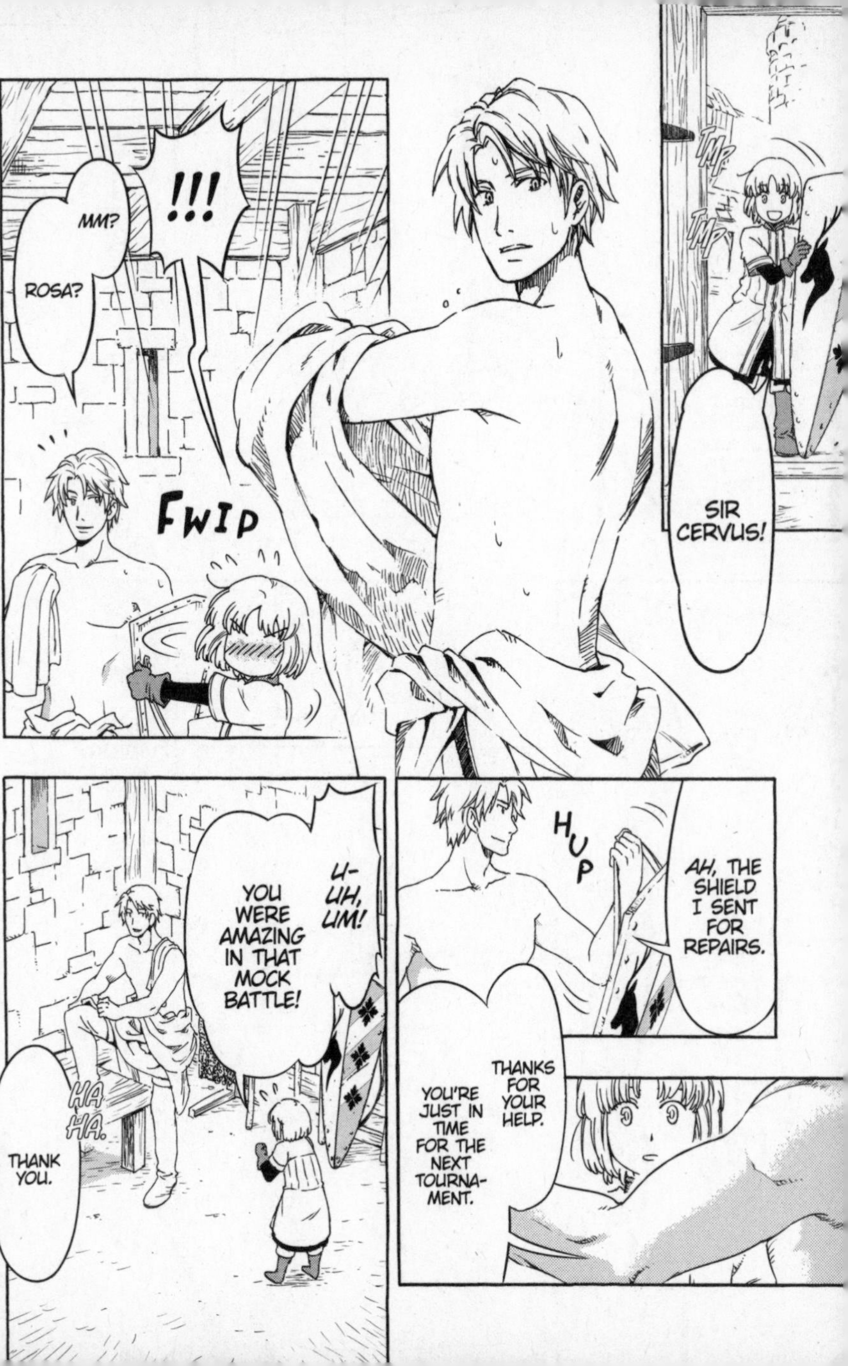
TMP
TMP
SIR CERVUS!
MM?
ROSA?
!!!
FWIP
HUP
AH, THE SHIELD I SENT FOR REPAIRS.
THANKS FOR YOUR HELP.
YOU'RE JUST IN TIME FOR THE NEXT TOURNAMENT.
U-UH, UM!
YOU WERE AMAZING IN THAT MOCK BATTLE!
HA HA.
THANK YOU.

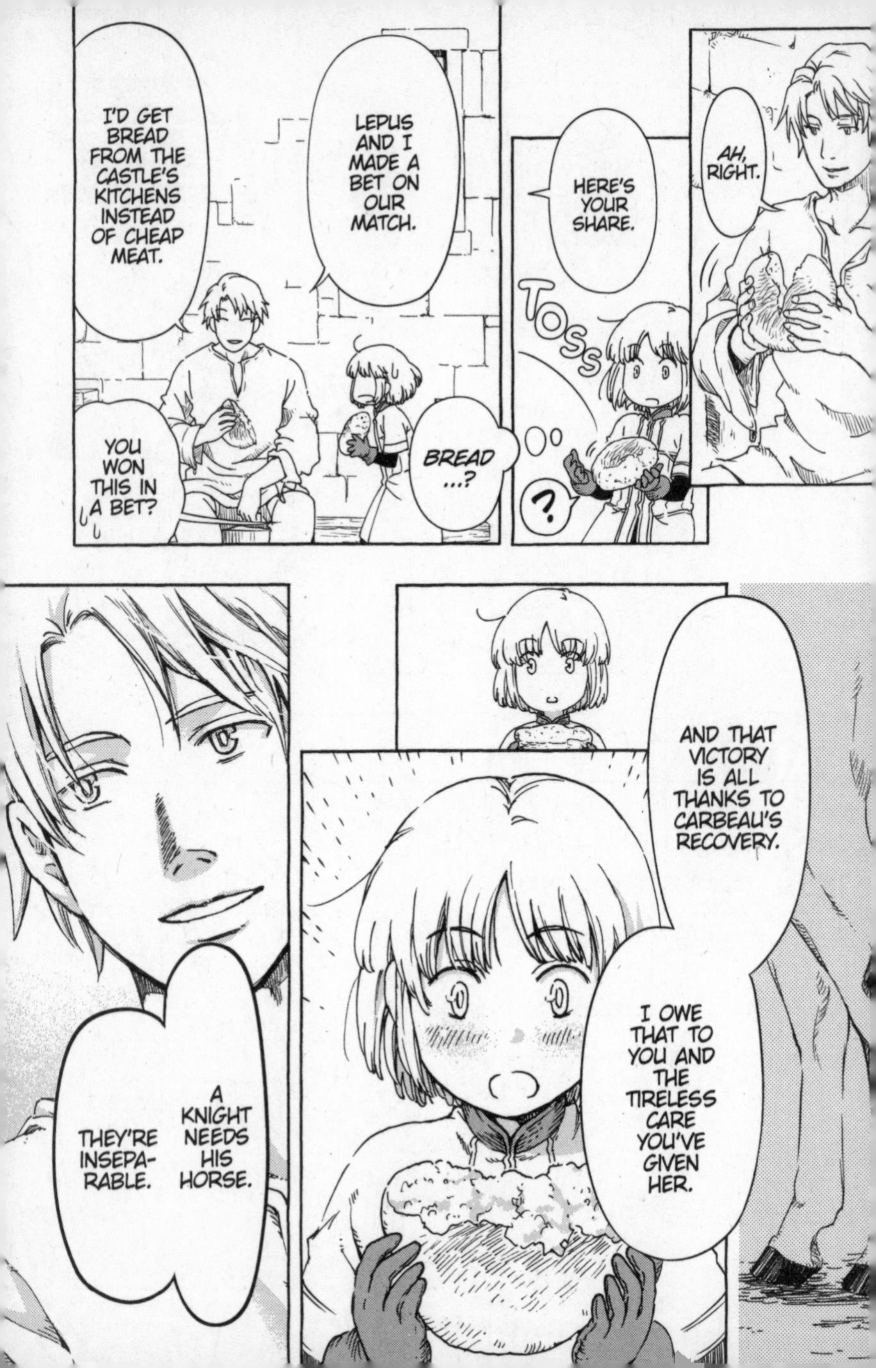
AH, RIGHT.
HERE'S YOUR SHARE.
TOSS
?
BREAD ...?
LEPUS AND I MADE A BET ON OUR MATCH.
I'D GET BREAD FROM THE CASTLE'S KITCHENS INSTEAD OF CHEAP MEAT.
YOU WON THIS IN A BET?
AND THAT VICTORY IS ALL THANKS TO CARBEAU'S RECOVERY.
I OWE THAT TO YOU AND THE TIRELESS CARE YOU'VE GIVEN HER.
A KNIGHT NEEDS HIS HORSE.
THEY'RE INSEPA-RABLE.

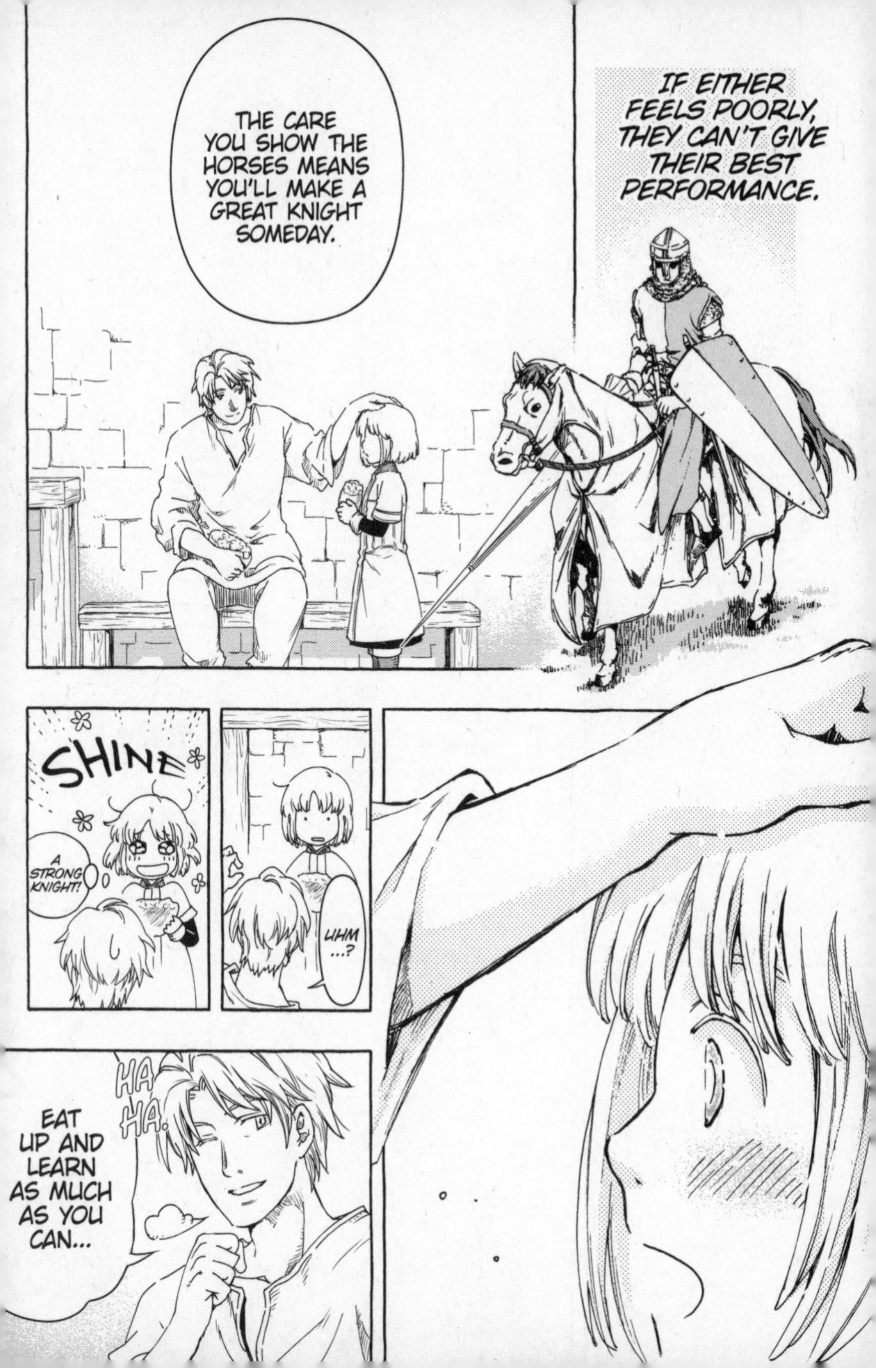
IF EITHER FEELS POORLY, THEY CAN'T GIVE THEIR BEST PERFORMANCE.
THE CARE YOU SHOW THE HORSES MEANS YOU'LL MAKE A GREAT KNIGHT SOMEDAY.
UHM ...?
SHINE
A STRONG KNIGHT!
HA HA.
EAT UP AND LEARN AS MUCH AS YOU CAN...

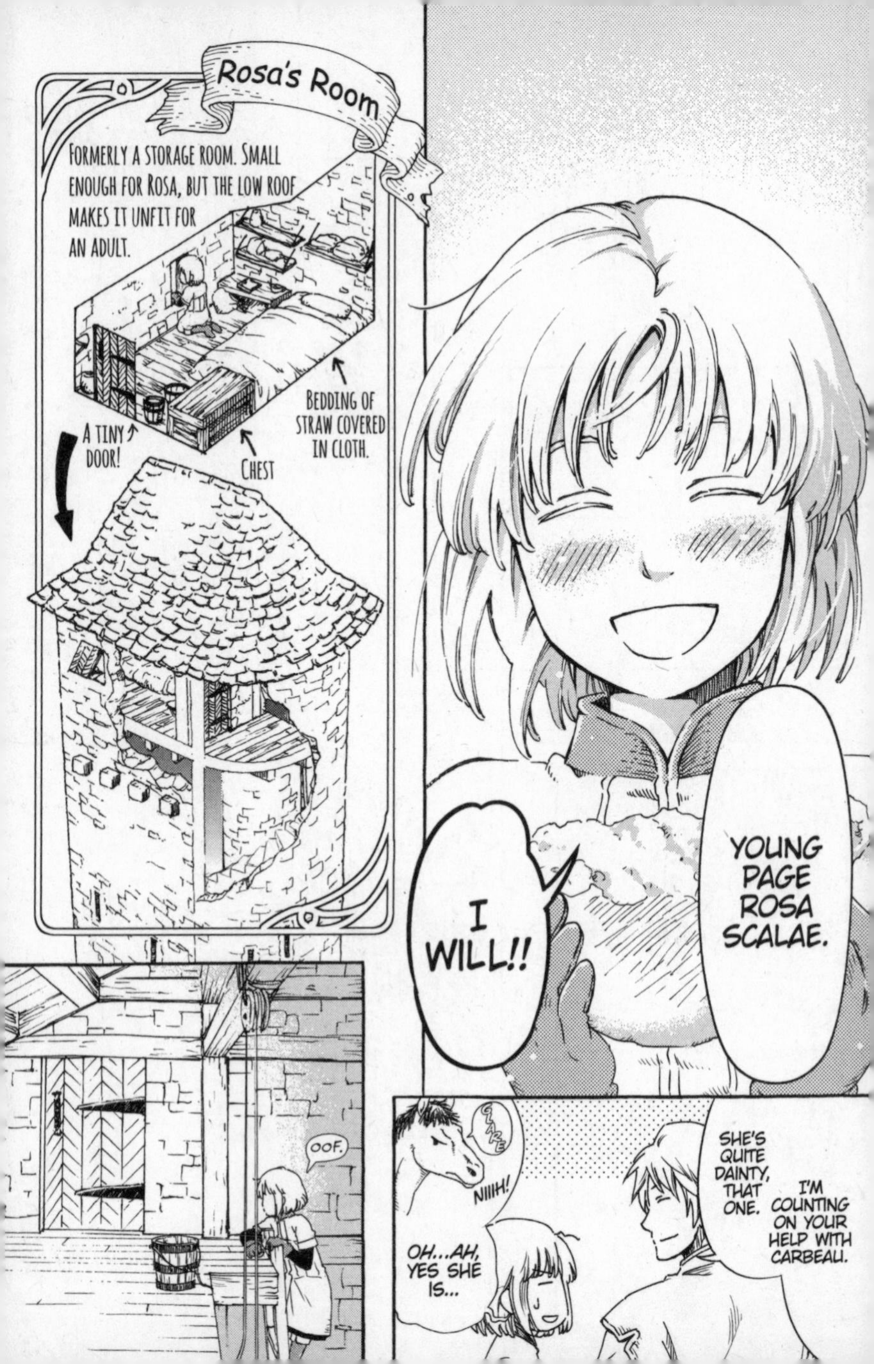
YOUNG PAGE ROSA SCALAE.
I WILL!!
SHE'S QUITE DAINTY, THAT ONE.
I'M COUNTING ON YOUR HELP WITH CARBEAU.
GLARE
NIIIH!
OH...AH, YES SHE IS...
Rosa's Room
FORMERLY A STORAGE ROOM. SMALL ENOUGH FOR ROSA, BUT THE LOW ROOF MAKES IT UNFIT FOR AN ADULT.
BEDDING OF STRAW COVERED IN CLOTH.
A TINY DOOR!
CHEST
OOF.

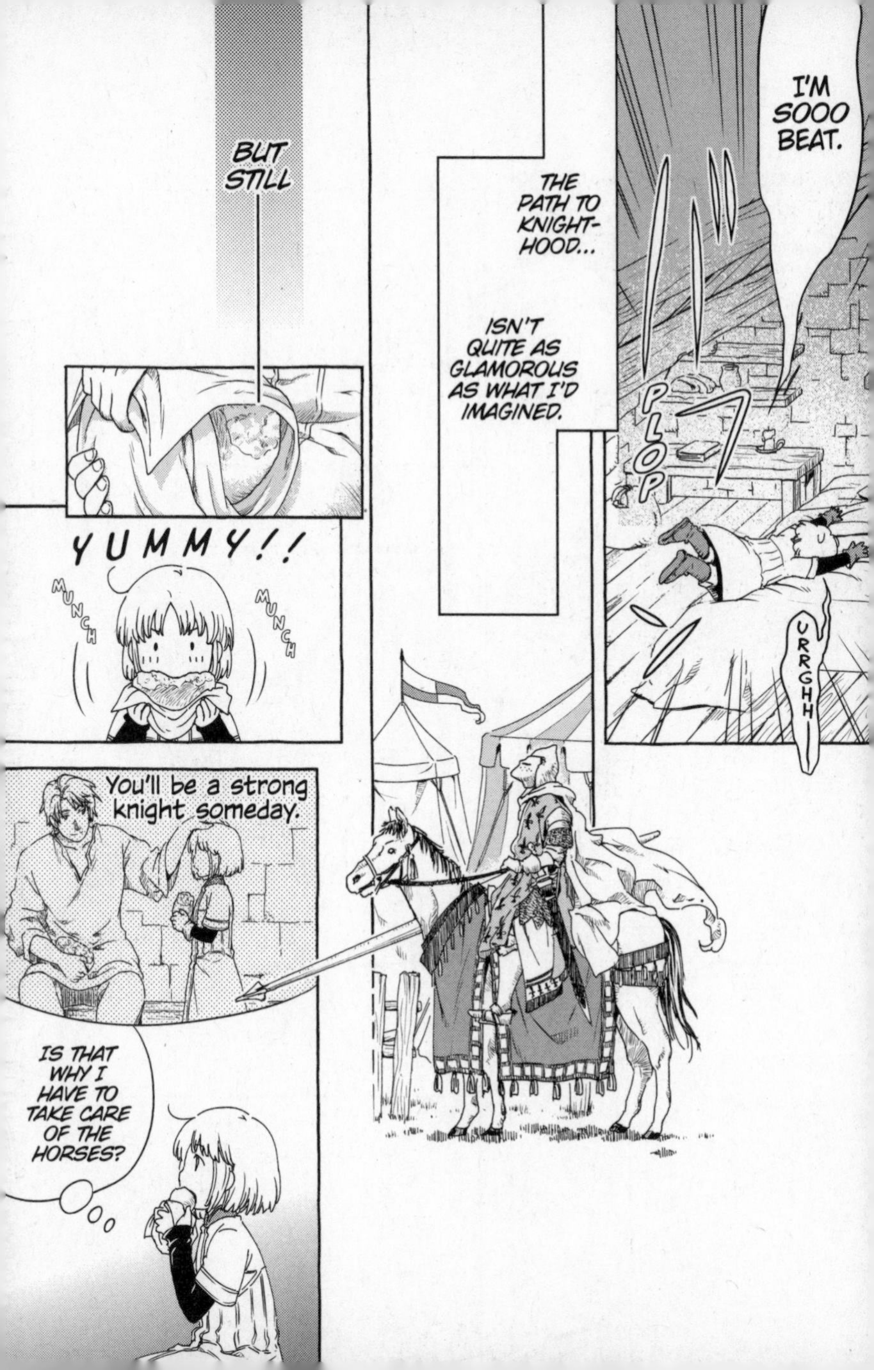
I'M SOOO BEAT.
PLOP
URRGH
THE PATH TO KNIGHT-HOOD...
ISN'T QUITE AS GLAMOROUS AS WHAT I'D IMAGINED.
BUT STILL
YUMMY!!
MUNCH
MUNCH
You'll be a strong knight someday.
IS THAT WHY I HAVE TO TAKE CARE OF THE HORSES?

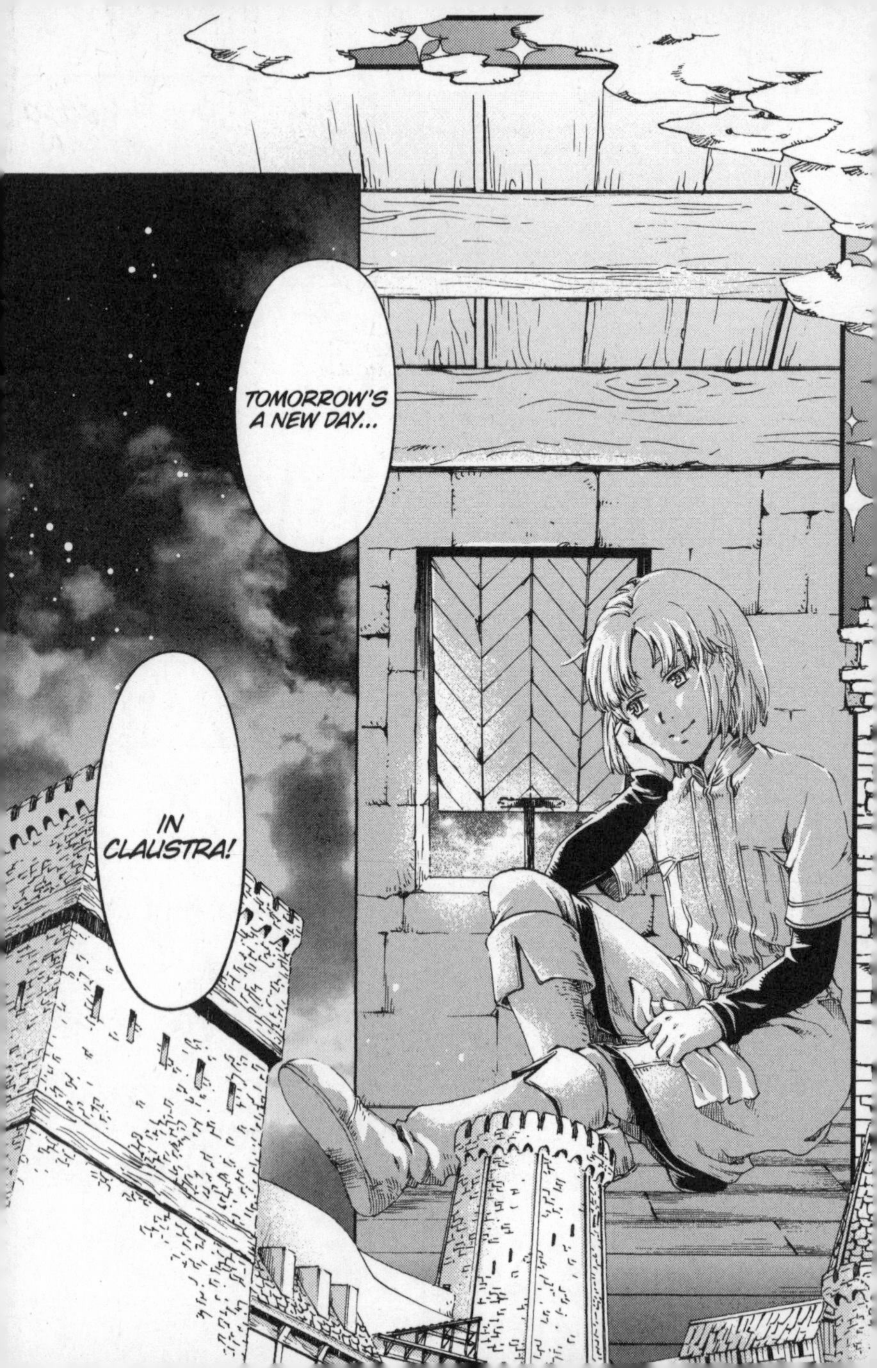
TOMORROW'S A NEW DAY...
IN CLAUSTRA!

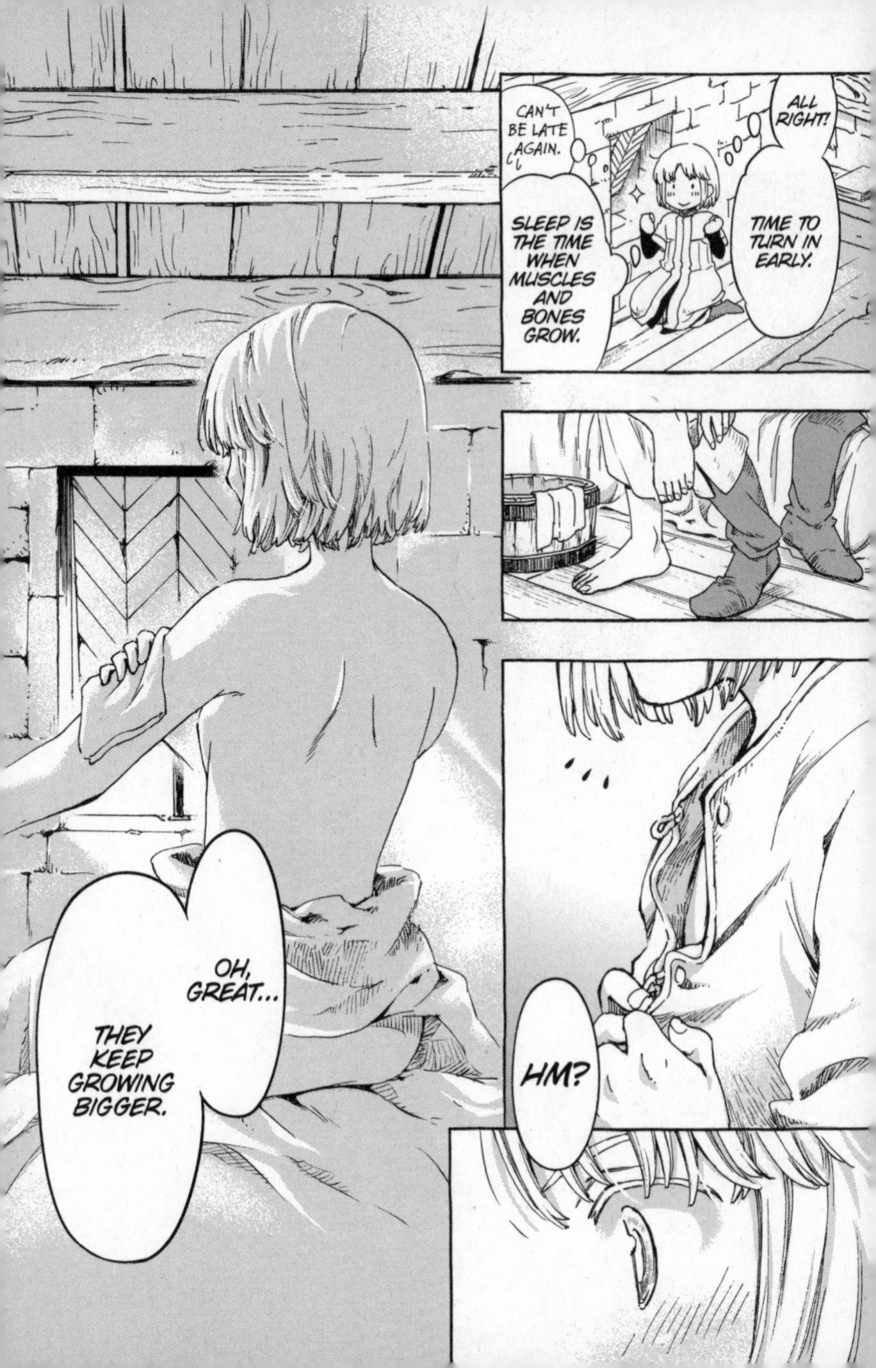
ALL RIGHT!
TIME TO TURN IN EARLY.
CAN'T BE LATE AGAIN.
SLEEP IS THE TIME WHEN MUSCLES AND BONES GROW.
HM?
OH, GREAT...
THEY KEEP GROWING BIGGER.

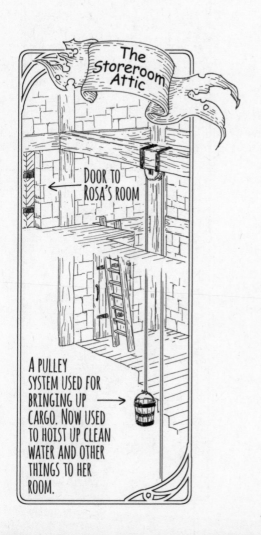

The
Storeroom
Attic

Door to
Rosa's Room

A Pulley
System used for
Bringing up
Cargo. Now used
to hoist up clean
water and other
things to her
room.

Rosa Scalae

Hailing from Castle Scalae, Rosa has left behind her home to become a page. She's a serene child who grew up in the idyllic countryside. However, she can be surprisingly hotheaded.

- Favorite Foods
  Poultry
  Fruits

- Least Favorite Foods
  Nothing in particular

- Talents
  A tough body
  (especially her head)
  Making dry flowers

- Weaknesses
  Weak core strength
  so she falls over
  a lot...

• Rosa

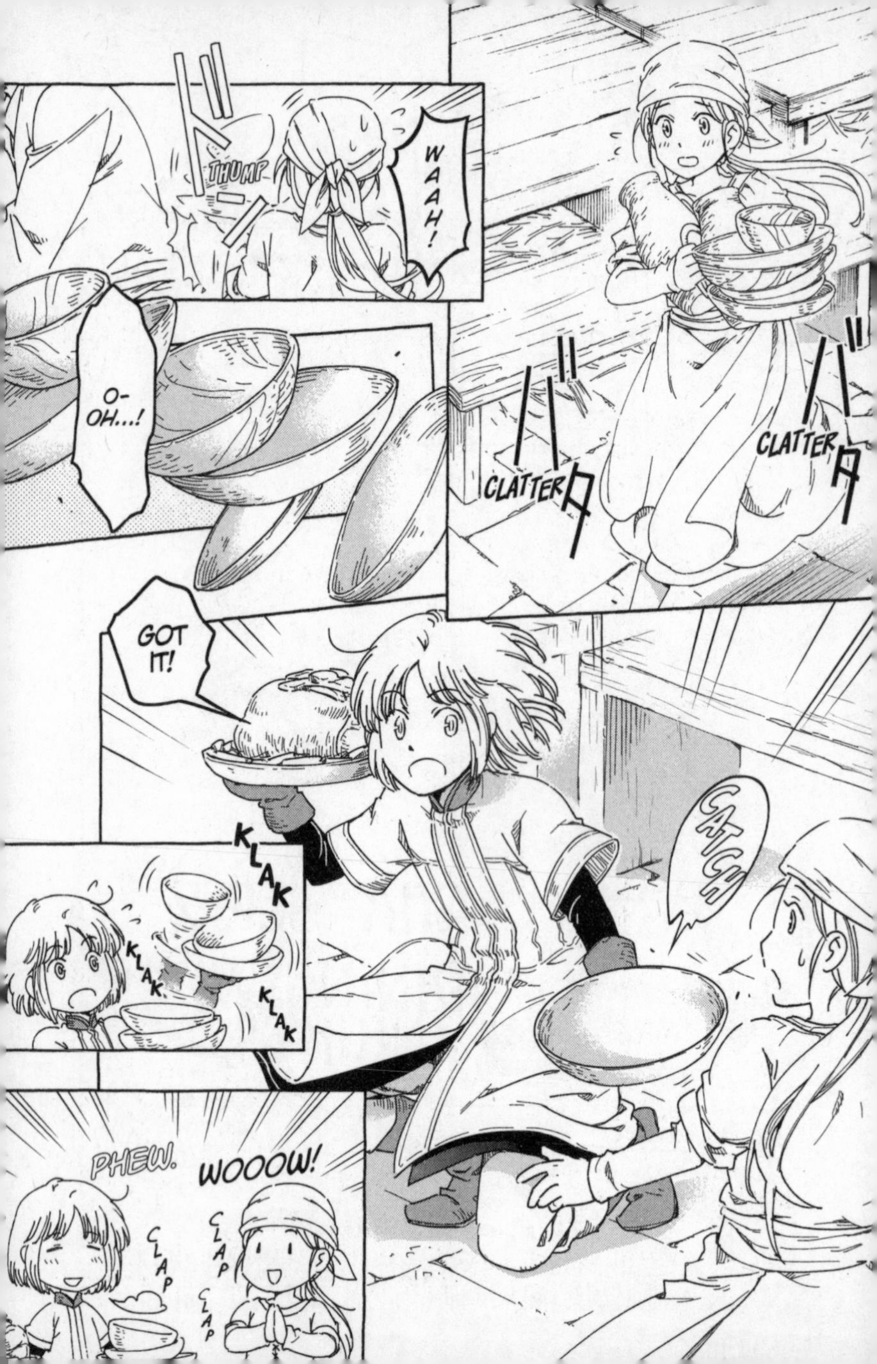
CLATTER
CLATTER
WAAH!
THUMP
O-OH...!
CATCH
GOT IT!
KLAK
KLAK
KLAK
WOOOW!
CLAP
CLAP
PHEW.
CLAP
CLAP

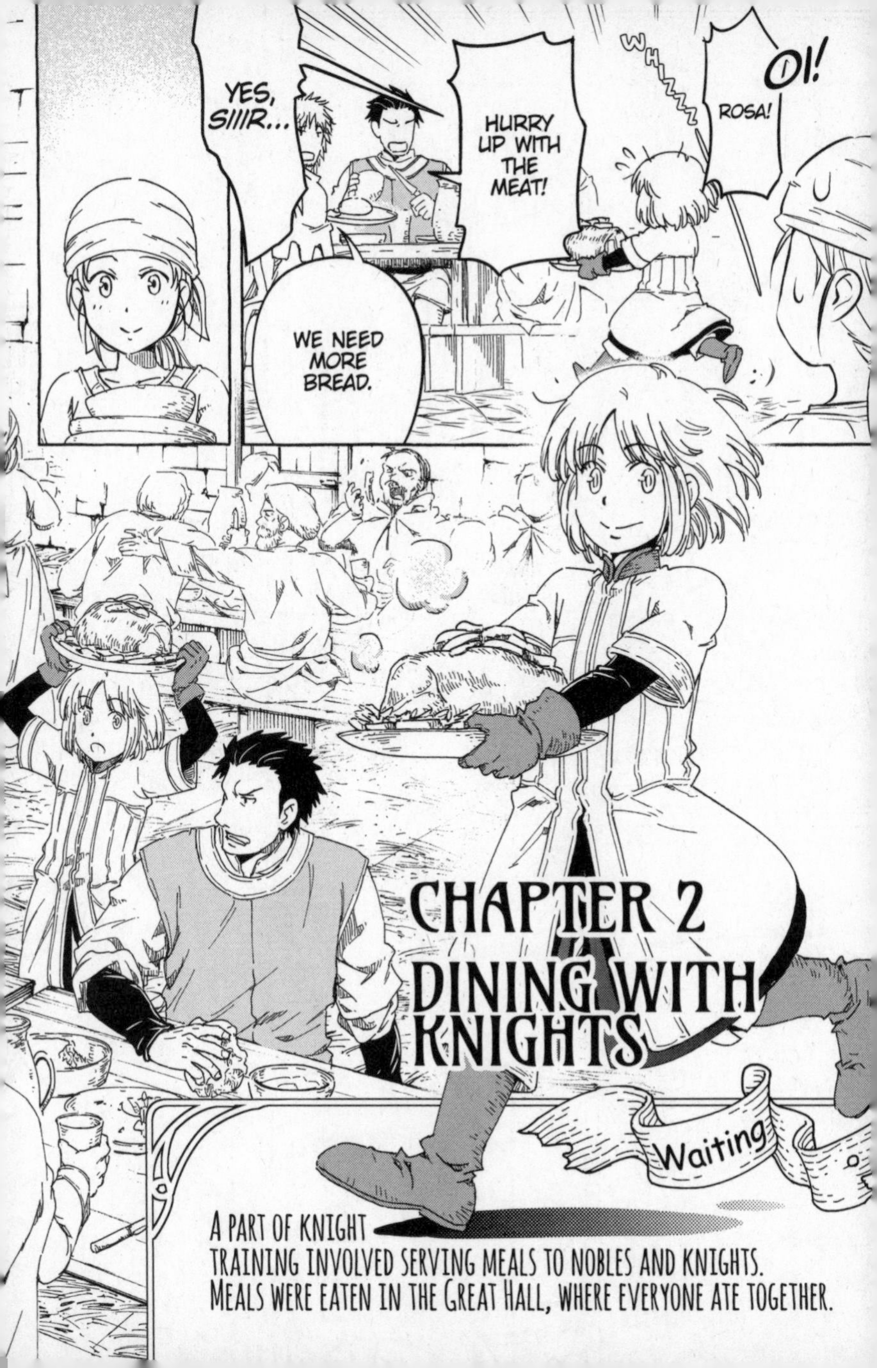
OI!
ROSA!
WHIZZZZ
HURRY UP WITH THE MEAT!
YES, SIIIR...
WE NEED MORE BREAD.
CHAPTER 2
DINING WITH KNIGHTS
Waiting
A PART OF KNIGHT TRAINING INVOLVED SERVING MEALS TO NOBLES AND KNIGHTS. MEALS WERE EATEN IN THE GREAT HALL, WHERE EVERYONE ATE TOGETHER.

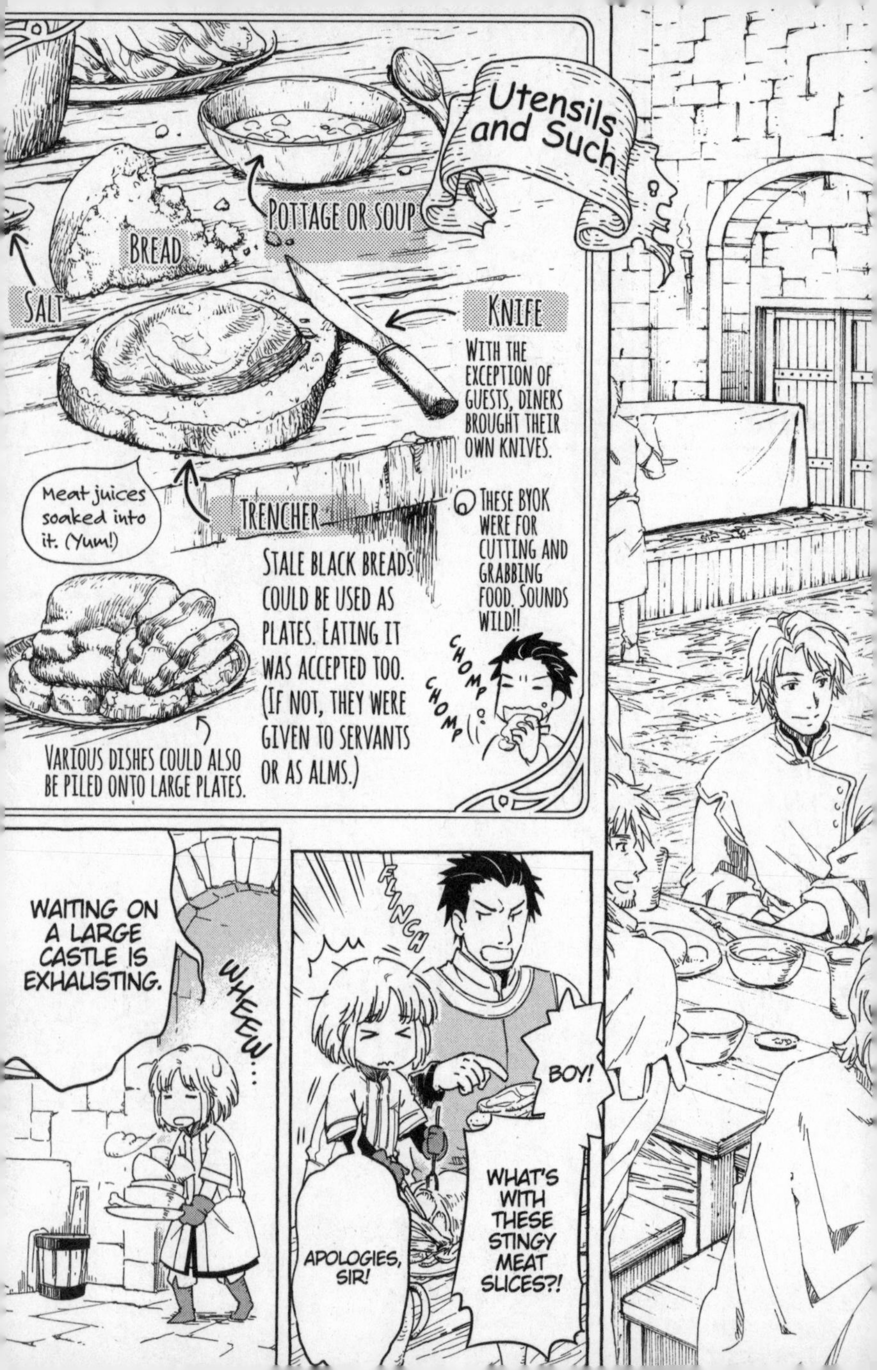

Utensils and Such
Pottage or soup
Bread
Salt
Knife
With the exception of guests, diners brought their own knives.
These BYOK were for cutting and grabbing food. Sounds wild!!
CHOMP CHOMP
Trencher
Meat juices soaked into it. (Yum!)
Stale black breads could be used as plates. Eating it was accepted too. (If not, they were given to servants or as alms.)
Various dishes could also be piled onto large plates.
FLINCH
BOY!
WHAT'S WITH THESE STINGY MEAT SLICES?!
APOLOGIES, SIR!
WAITING ON A LARGE CASTLE IS EXHAUSTING.
WHEEEW...

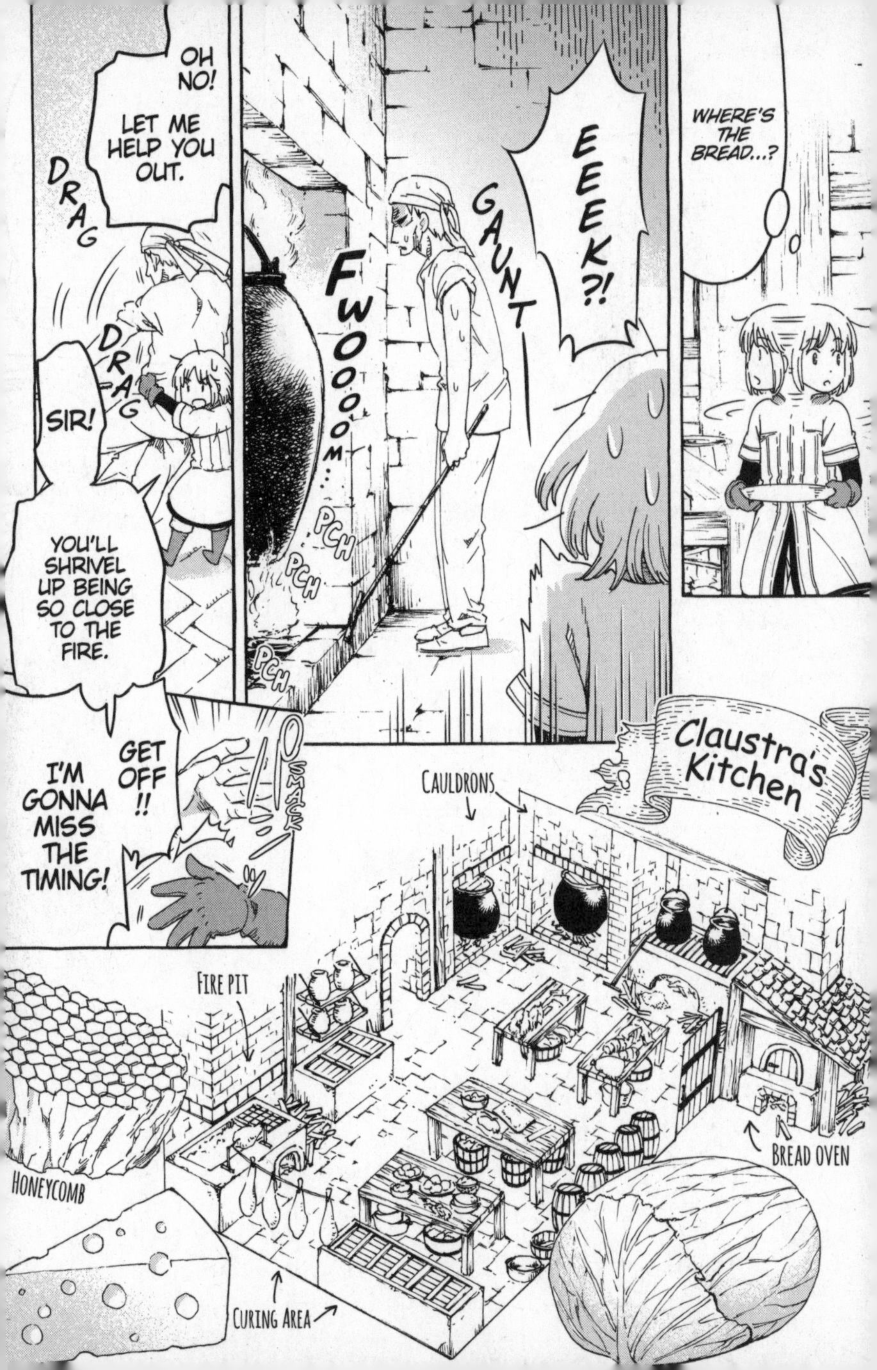
WHERE'S THE BREAD...?
EEEK?!
GAUNT
FWOOOOOOM...
PCH
PCH
PCH
OH NO!
LET ME HELP YOU OUT.
DRAG
DRAG
DRAG
SIR!
YOU'LL SHRIVEL UP BEING SO CLOSE TO THE FIRE.
SMACK
GET OFF!!
I'M GONNA MISS THE TIMING!
Claustra's Kitchen
CAULDRONS
BREAD OVEN
FIRE PIT
HONEYCOMB
CURING AREA

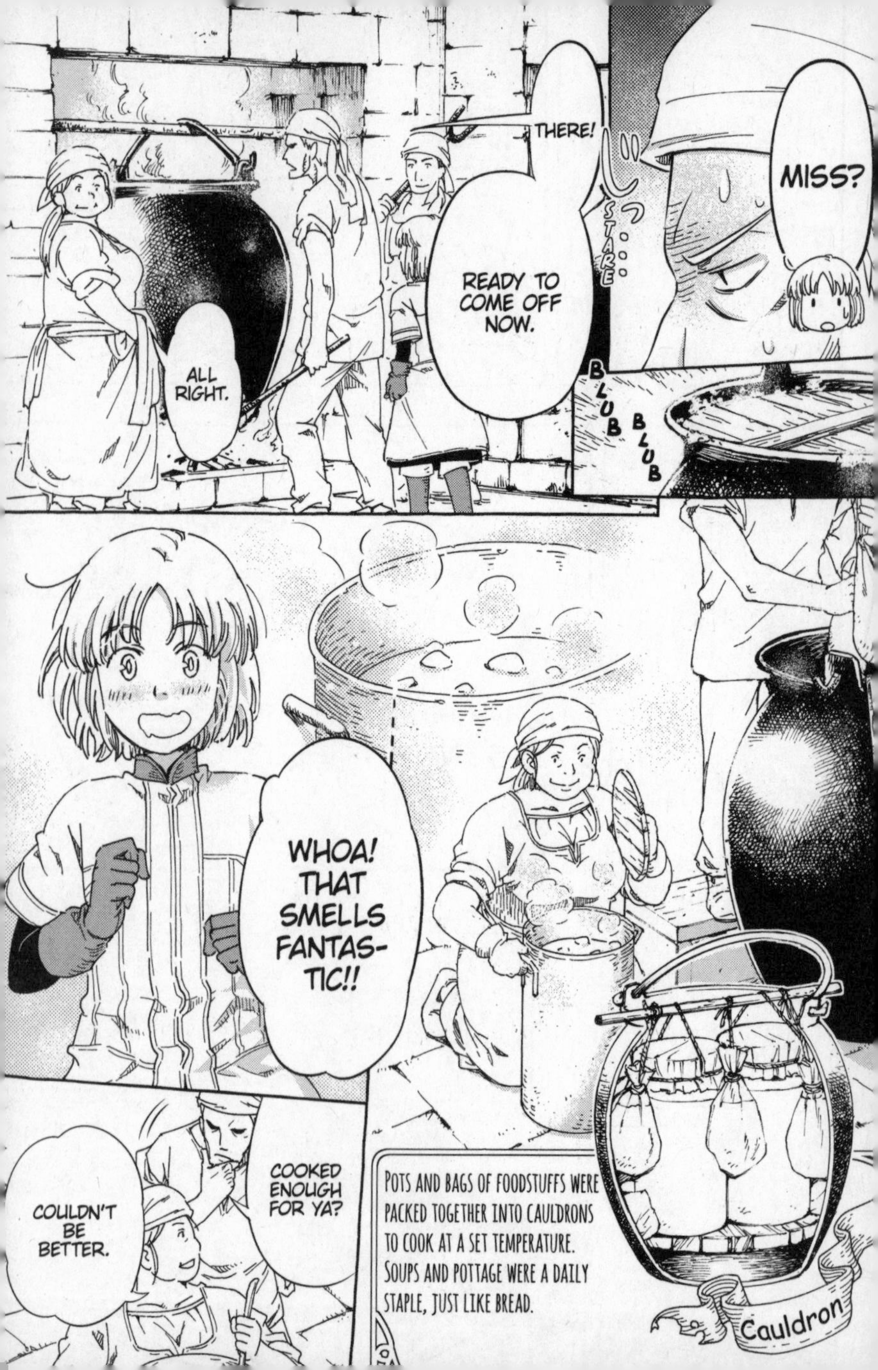
MISS?
STARE...
BLUB BLUB
THERE!
READY TO COME OFF NOW.
ALL RIGHT.
WHOA! THAT SMELLS FANTAS-TIC!!
POTS AND BAGS OF FOODSTUFFS WERE PACKED TOGETHER INTO CAULDRONS TO COOK AT A SET TEMPERATURE. SOUPS AND POTTAGE WERE A DAILY STAPLE, JUST LIKE BREAD.
Cauldron
COOKED ENOUGH FOR YA?
COULDN'T BE BETTER.

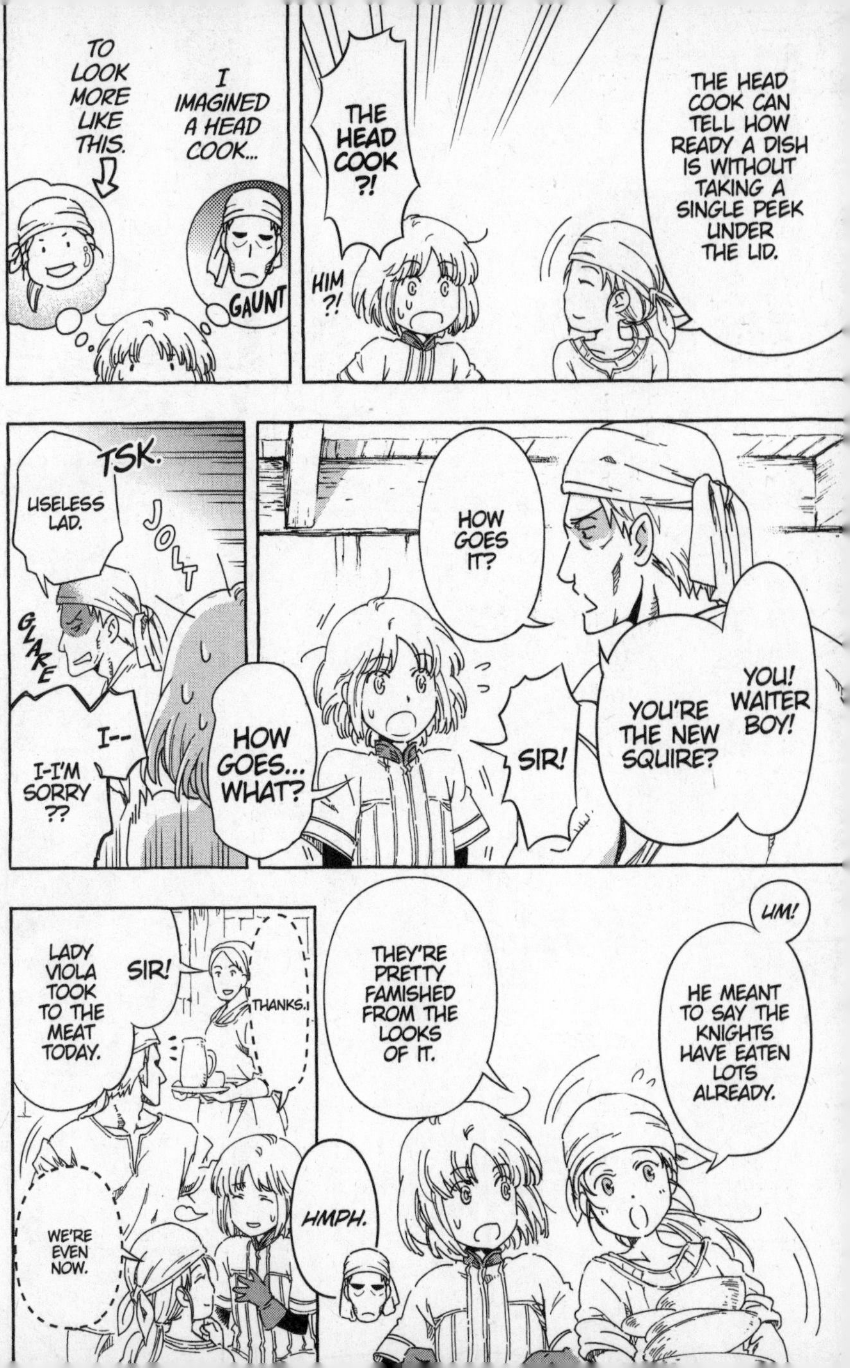
THE HEAD COOK CAN TELL HOW READY A DISH IS WITHOUT TAKING A SINGLE PEEK UNDER THE LID.
THE HEAD COOK ?!
HIM ?!
I IMAGINED A HEAD COOK...
TO LOOK MORE LIKE THIS.
GAUNT
HOW GOES IT?
YOU! WAITER BOY!
YOU'RE THE NEW SQUIRE?
SIR!
HOW GOES... WHAT?
TSK.
USELESS LAD.
JOLT
GLARE
I--
I-I'M SORRY ??
UM!
HE MEANT TO SAY THE KNIGHTS HAVE EATEN LOTS ALREADY.
THEY'RE PRETTY FAMISHED FROM THE LOOKS OF IT.
HMPH.
SIR!
LADY VIOLA TOOK TO THE MEAT TODAY.
THANKS.
WE'RE EVEN NOW.

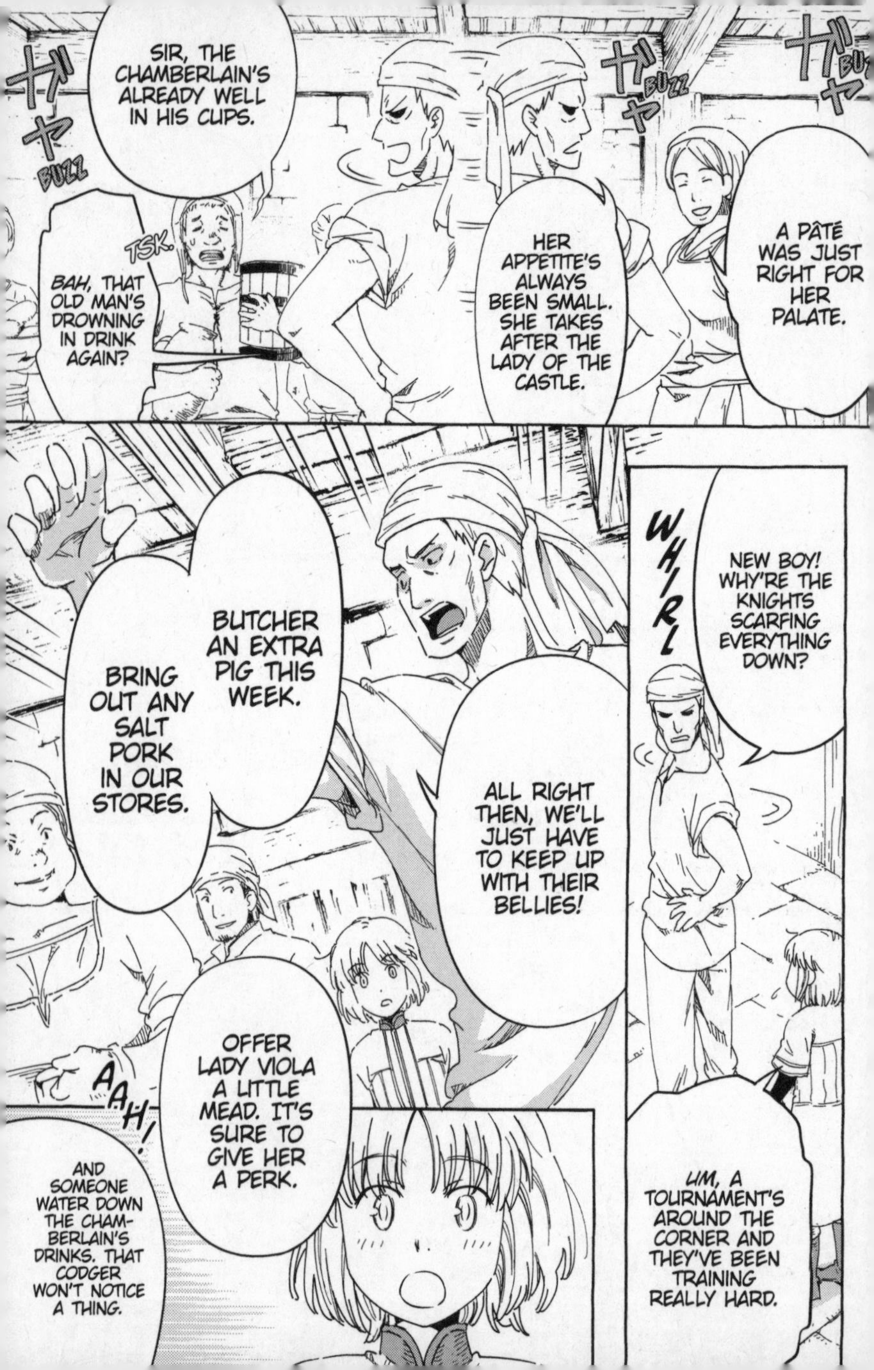

ガヤ BUZZ
A PÂTÉ WAS JUST RIGHT FOR HER PALATE.
ガヤ BUZZ
HER APPETITE'S ALWAYS BEEN SMALL. SHE TAKES AFTER THE LADY OF THE CASTLE.
SIR, THE CHAMBERLAIN'S ALREADY WELL IN HIS CUPS.
ガヤ BUZZ
TSK.
BAH, THAT OLD MAN'S DROWNING IN DRINK AGAIN?
NEW BOY! WHY'RE THE KNIGHTS SCARFING EVERYTHING DOWN?
WHIRL
UM, A TOURNAMENT'S AROUND THE CORNER AND THEY'VE BEEN TRAINING REALLY HARD.
ALL RIGHT THEN, WE'LL JUST HAVE TO KEEP UP WITH THEIR BELLIES!
BUTCHER AN EXTRA PIG THIS WEEK.
BRING OUT ANY SALT PORK IN OUR STORES.
OFFER LADY VIOLA A LITTLE MEAD. IT'S SURE TO GIVE HER A PERK.
AAH!
AND SOMEONE WATER DOWN THE CHAM-BERLAIN'S DRINKS. THAT CODGER WON'T NOTICE A THING.

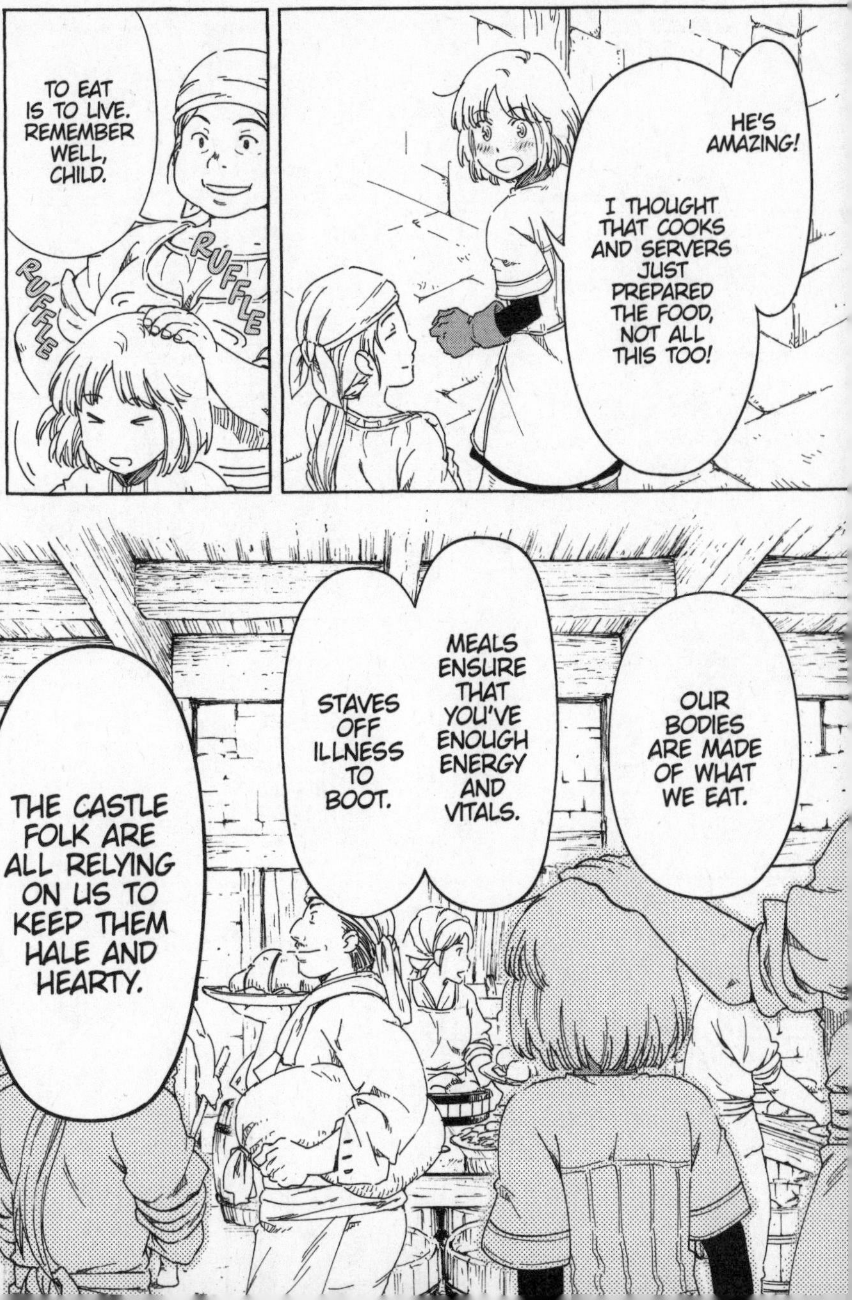
HE'S AMAZING!
I THOUGHT THAT COOKS AND SERVERS JUST PREPARED THE FOOD, NOT ALL THIS TOO!
TO EAT IS TO LIVE. REMEMBER WELL, CHILD.
RUFFLE
RUFFLE
OUR BODIES ARE MADE OF WHAT WE EAT.
MEALS ENSURE THAT YOU'VE ENOUGH ENERGY AND VITALS.
STAVES OFF ILLNESS TO BOOT.
THE CASTLE FOLK ARE ALL RELYING ON US TO KEEP THEM HALE AND HEARTY.

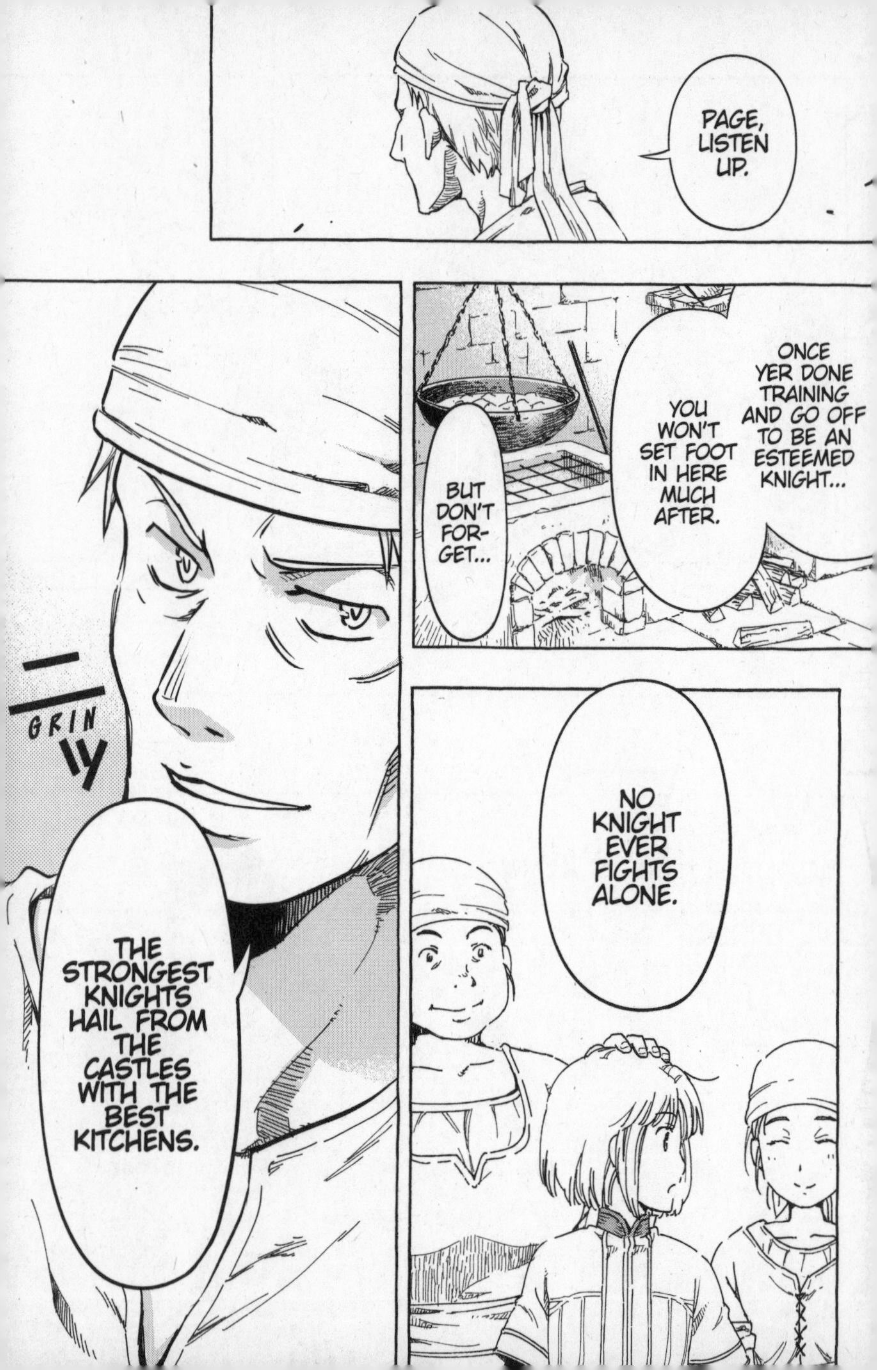
PAGE, LISTEN UP.
ONCE YER DONE TRAINING AND GO OFF TO BE AN ESTEEMED KNIGHT...
YOU WON'T SET FOOT IN HERE MUCH AFTER.
BUT DON'T FOR-GET...
NO KNIGHT EVER FIGHTS ALONE.
GRIN
THE STRONGEST KNIGHTS HAIL FROM THE CASTLES WITH THE BEST KITCHENS.

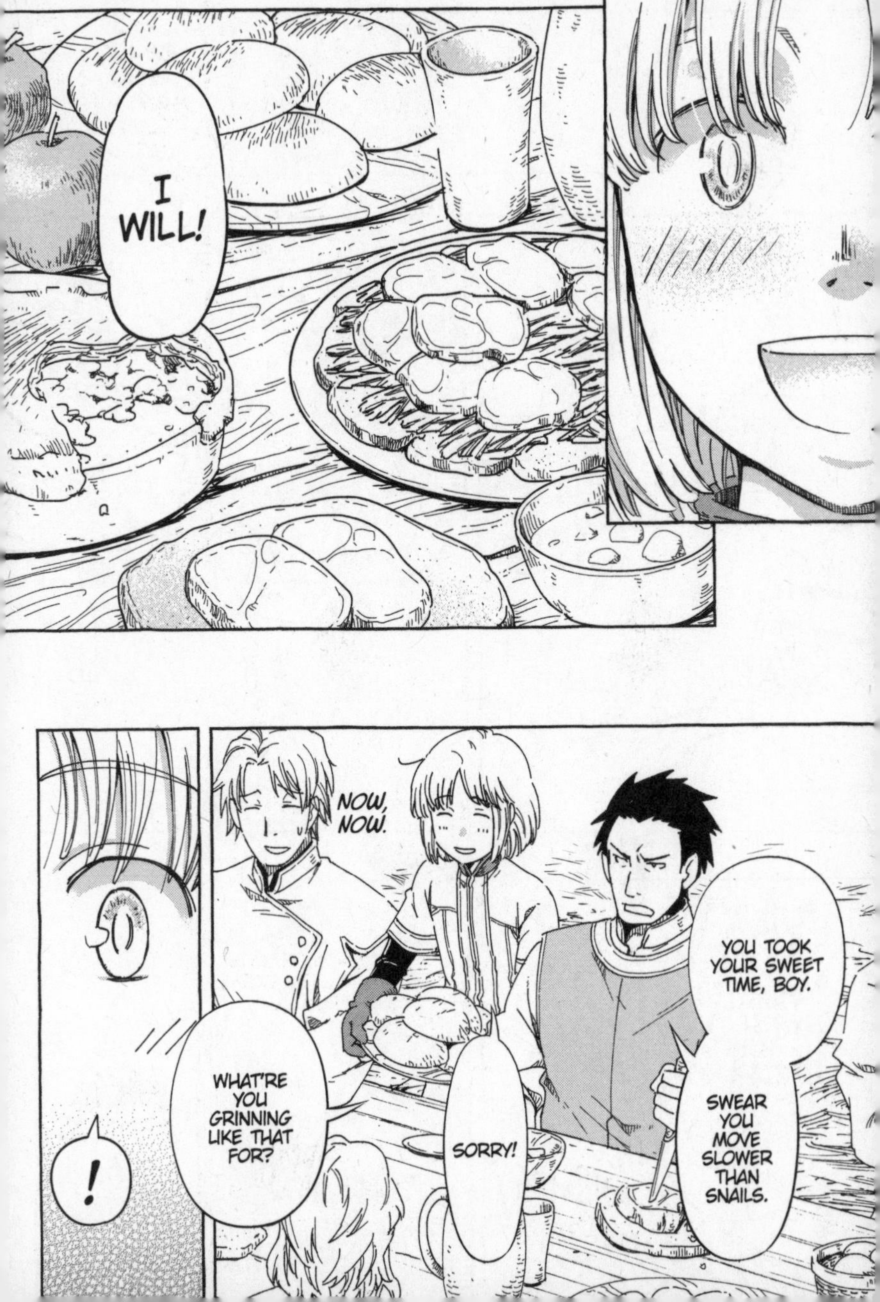
I WILL!
YOU TOOK YOUR SWEET TIME, BOY.
SWEAR YOU MOVE SLOWER THAN SNAILS.
NOW, NOW.
WHAT'RE YOU GRINNING LIKE THAT FOR?
SORRY!
!

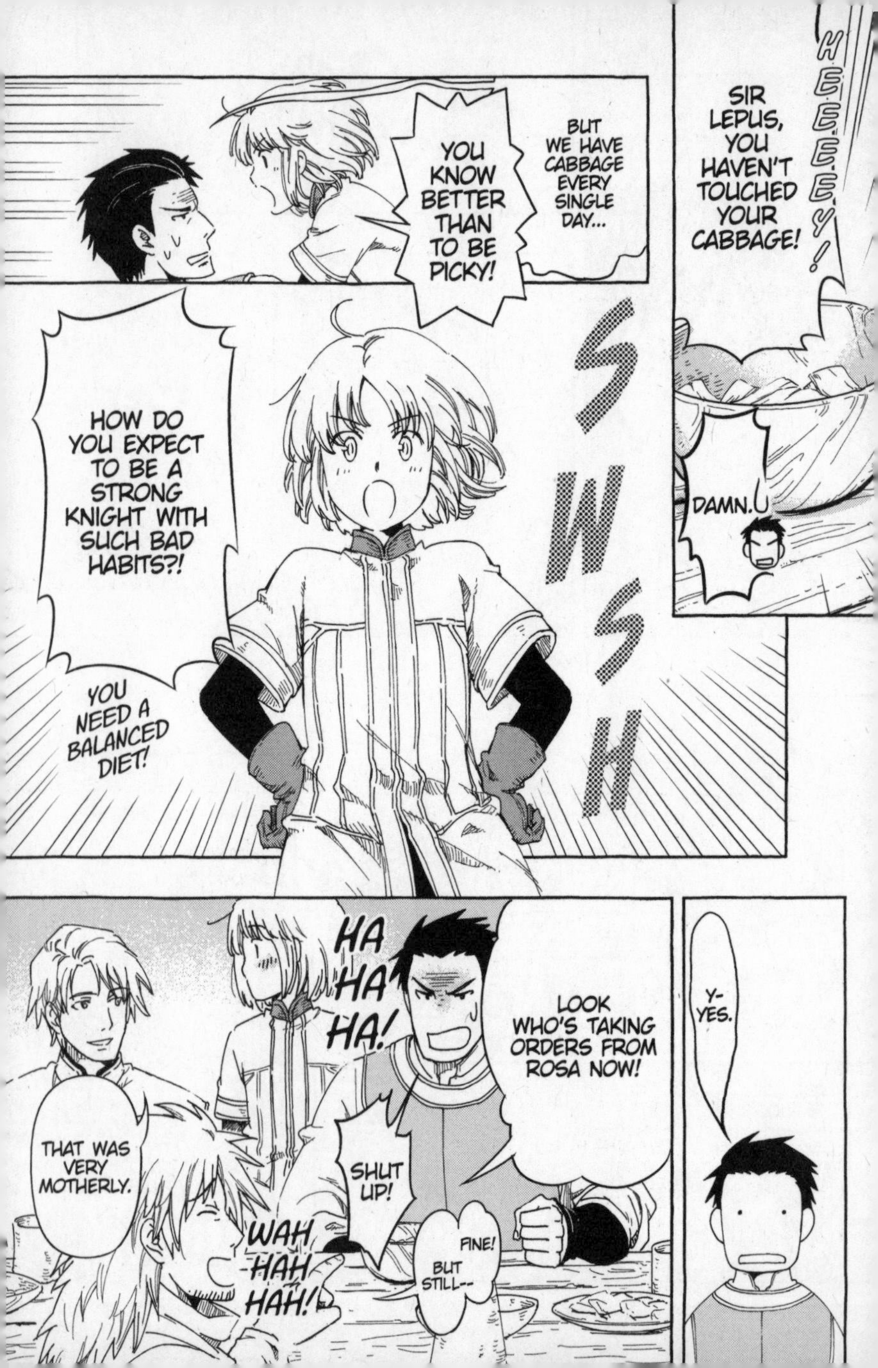
HEEEEY!
SIR LEPUS, YOU HAVEN'T TOUCHED YOUR CABBAGE!
DAMN.
BUT WE HAVE CABBAGE EVERY SINGLE DAY...
YOU KNOW BETTER THAN TO BE PICKY!
SWSH
HOW DO YOU EXPECT TO BE A STRONG KNIGHT WITH SUCH BAD HABITS?!
YOU NEED A BALANCED DIET!
Y-YES.
LOOK WHO'S TAKING ORDERS FROM ROSA NOW!
HA HA HA!
SHUT UP!
THAT WAS VERY MOTHERLY.
WAH HAH HAH!
FINE! BUT STILL--

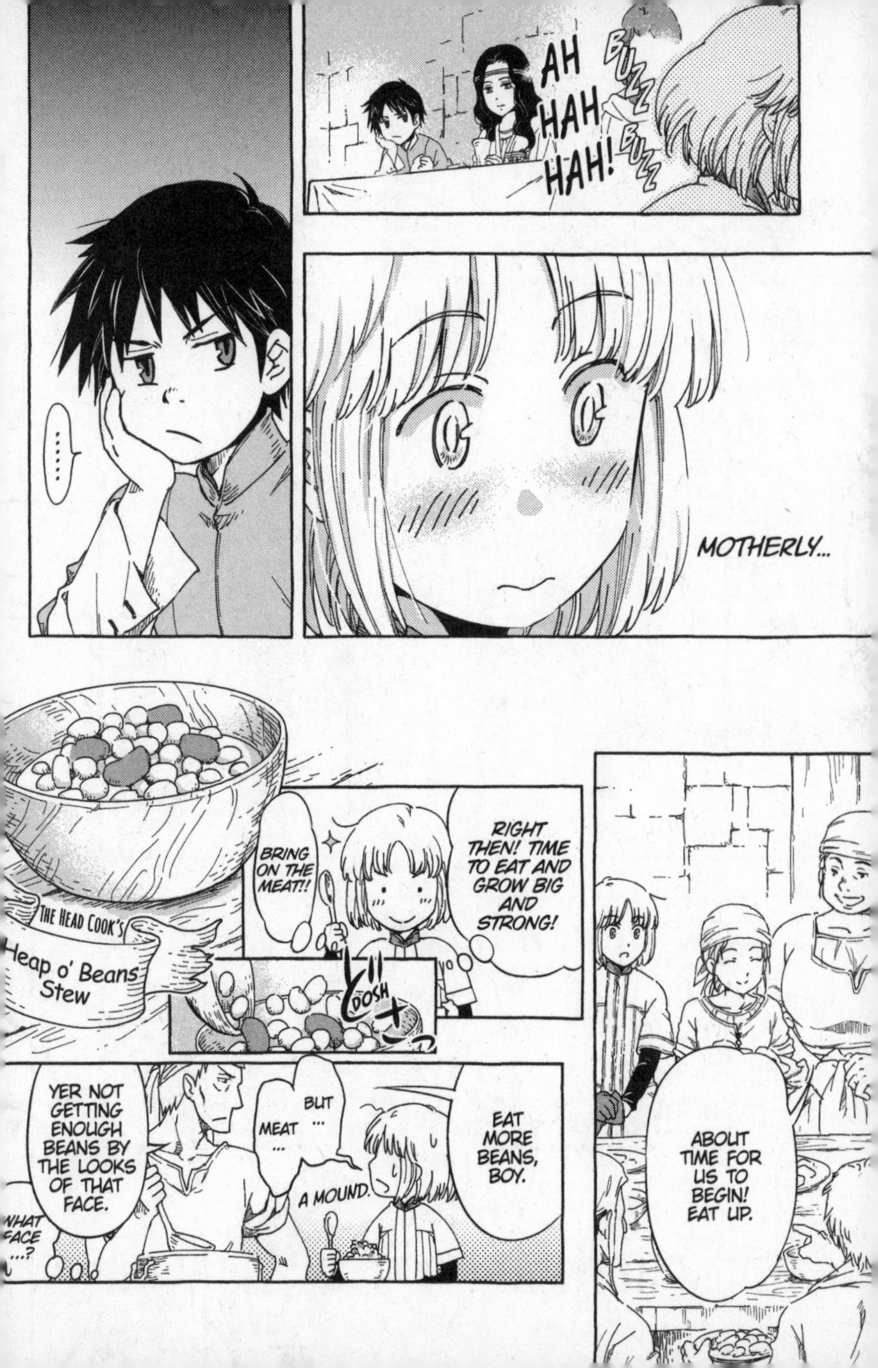
AH HAH HAH!
BUZZ BUZZ
MOTHERLY...
......
ABOUT TIME FOR US TO BEGIN! EAT UP.
RIGHT THEN! TIME TO EAT AND GROW BIG AND STRONG!
BRING ON THE MEAT!!
DOSH
THE HEAD COOK'S
Heap o' Beans Stew
EAT MORE BEANS, BOY.
BUT ...
MEAT ...
A MOUND.
YER NOT GETTING ENOUGH BEANS BY THE LOOKS OF THAT FACE.
WHAT FACE ...?

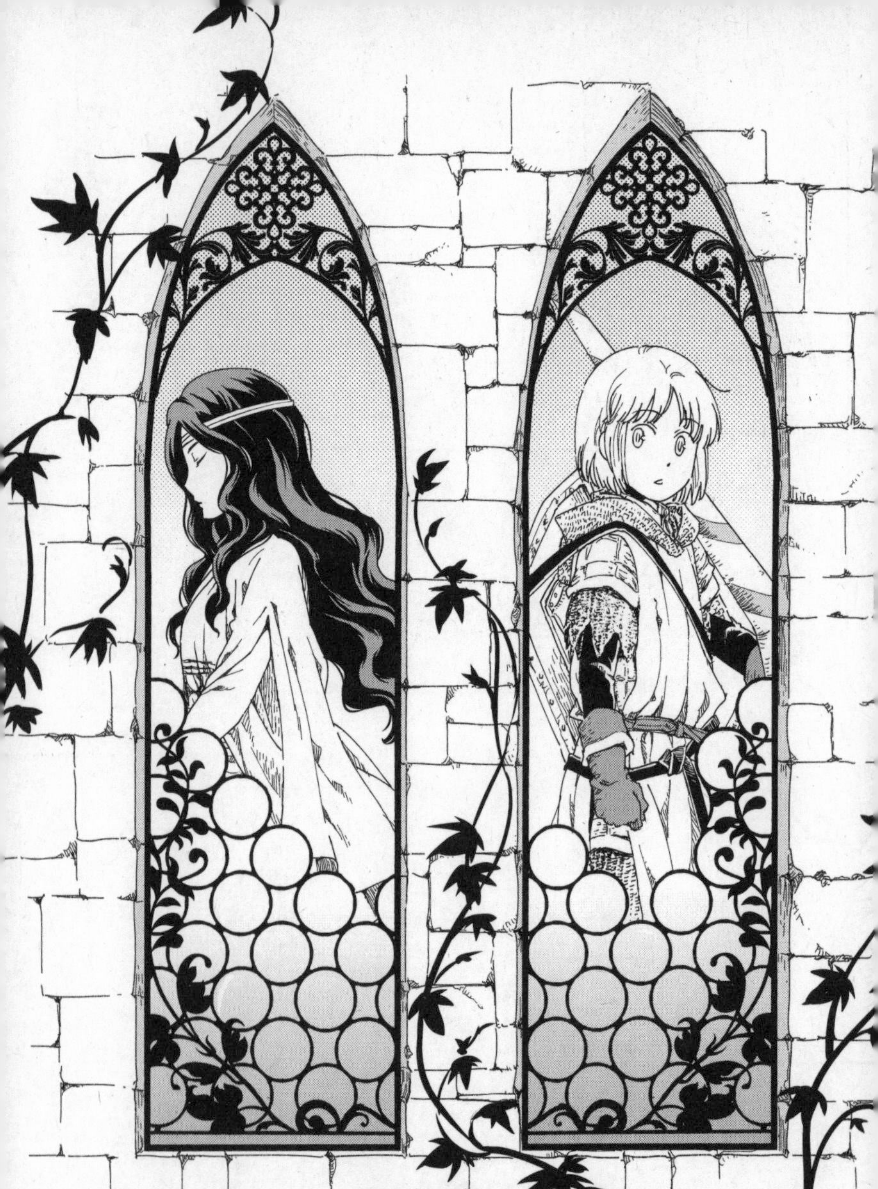

CHAPTER 3
THE MAIDEN AND THE GLASS WINDOW

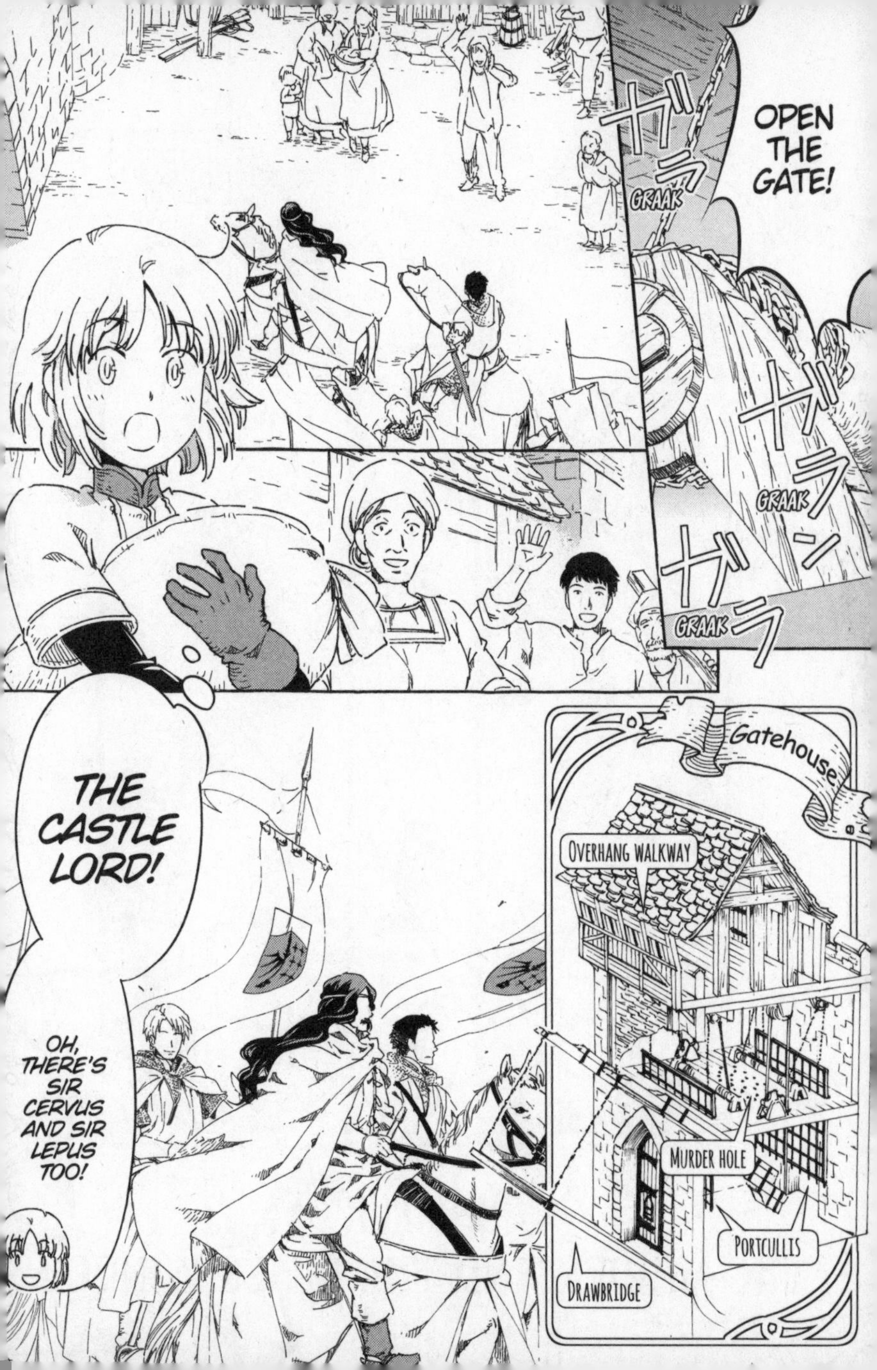

OPEN THE GATE!
ガラ
GRAAK
ガラン
GRAAK
ガラ
GRAAK
Gatehouse
Overhang walkway
Murder hole
Portcullis
Drawbridge
THE CASTLE LORD!
OH, THERE'S SIR CERVUS AND SIR LEPUS TOO!

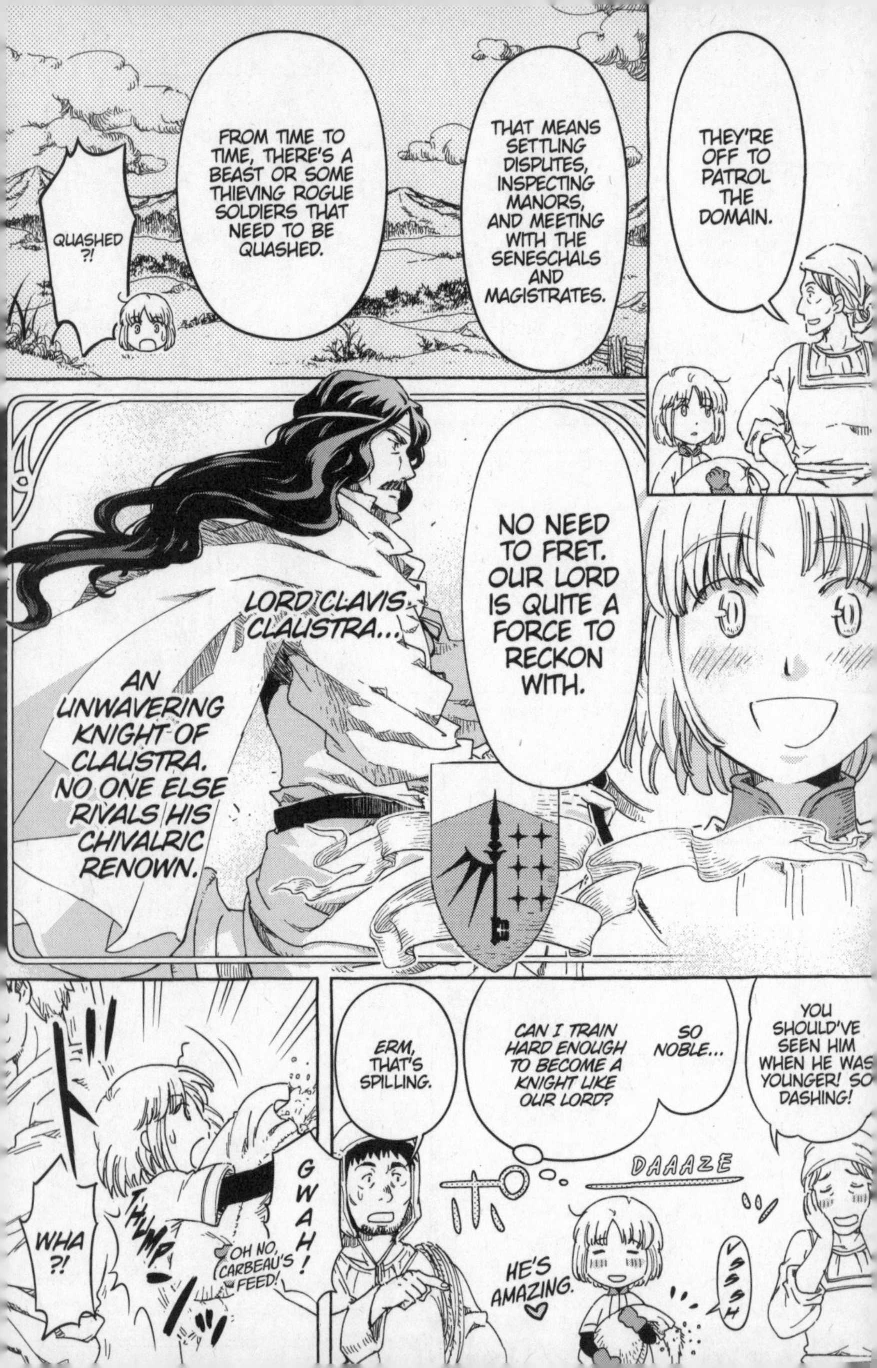
THEY'RE OFF TO PATROL THE DOMAIN.
THAT MEANS SETTLING DISPUTES, INSPECTING MANORS, AND MEETING WITH THE SENESCHALS AND MAGISTRATES.
FROM TIME TO TIME, THERE'S A BEAST OR SOME THIEVING ROGUE SOLDIERS THAT NEED TO BE QUASHED.
QUASHED ?!
NO NEED TO FRET. OUR LORD IS QUITE A FORCE TO RECKON WITH.
LORD CLAVIS CLAUSTRA...
AN UNWAVERING KNIGHT OF CLAUSTRA. NO ONE ELSE RIVALS HIS CHIVALRIC RENOWN.
YOU SHOULD'VE SEEN HIM WHEN HE WAS YOUNGER! SO DASHING!
SO NOBLE...
CAN I TRAIN HARD ENOUGH TO BECOME A KNIGHT LIKE OUR LORD?
DAAAZE
HE'S AMAZING. ♡
VSSSH
ERM, THAT'S SPILLING.
GWAH!
THUMP
OH NO, CARBEAU'S FEED!
WHA ?!

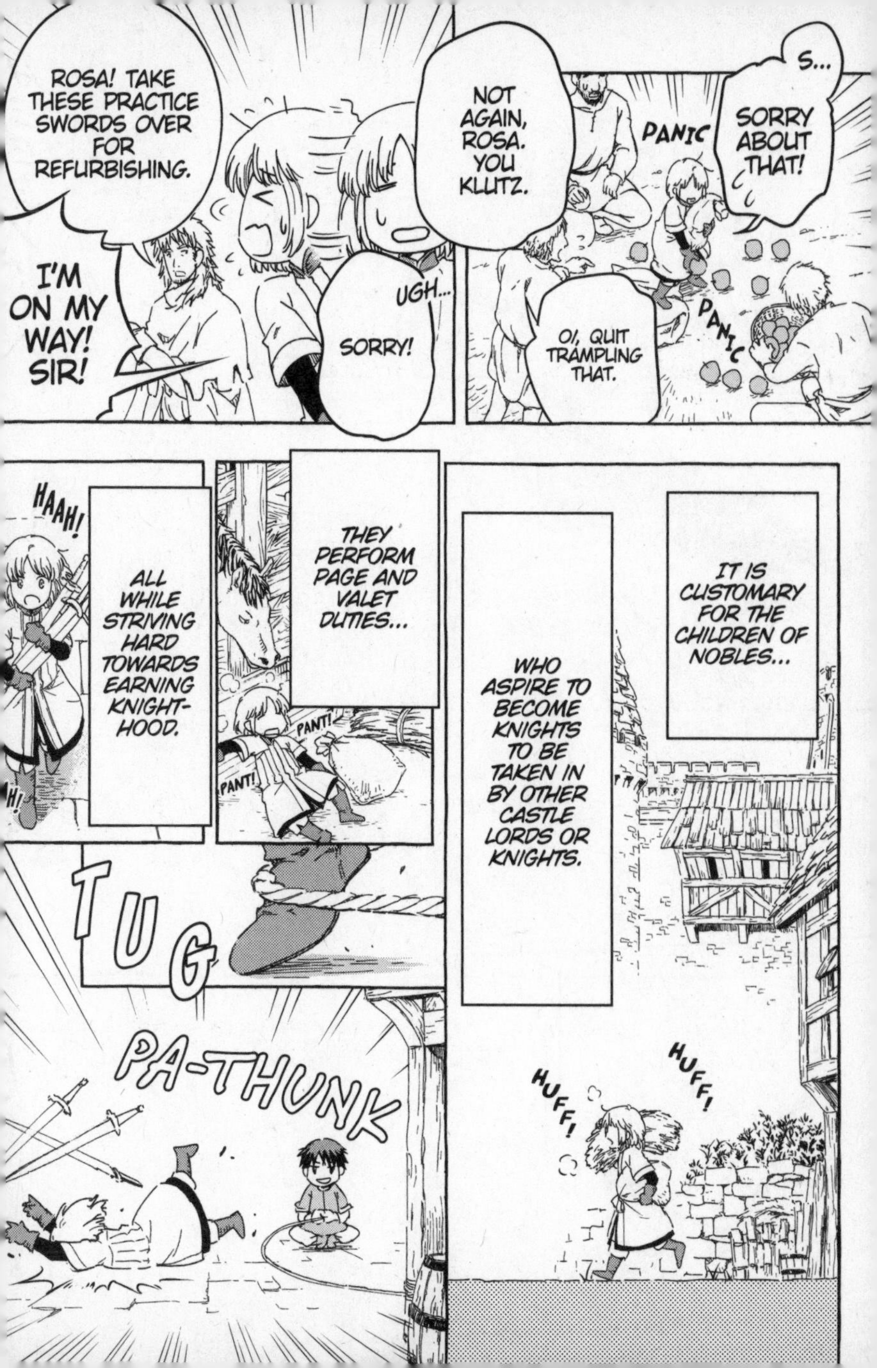
S...
SORRY ABOUT THAT!
NOT AGAIN, ROSA. YOU KLUTZ.
PANIC
PANIC
OI, QUIT TRAMPLING THAT.
ROSA! TAKE THESE PRACTICE SWORDS OVER FOR REFURBISHING.
UGH...
SORRY!
I'M ON MY WAY! SIR!
IT IS CUSTOMARY FOR THE CHILDREN OF NOBLES...
WHO ASPIRE TO BECOME KNIGHTS TO BE TAKEN IN BY OTHER CASTLE LORDS OR KNIGHTS.
HUFF!
HUFF!
THEY PERFORM PAGE AND VALET DUTIES...
PANT!
PANT!
ALL WHILE STRIVING HARD TOWARDS EARNING KNIGHT-HOOD.
HAAAH!
TUG
PA-THUNK

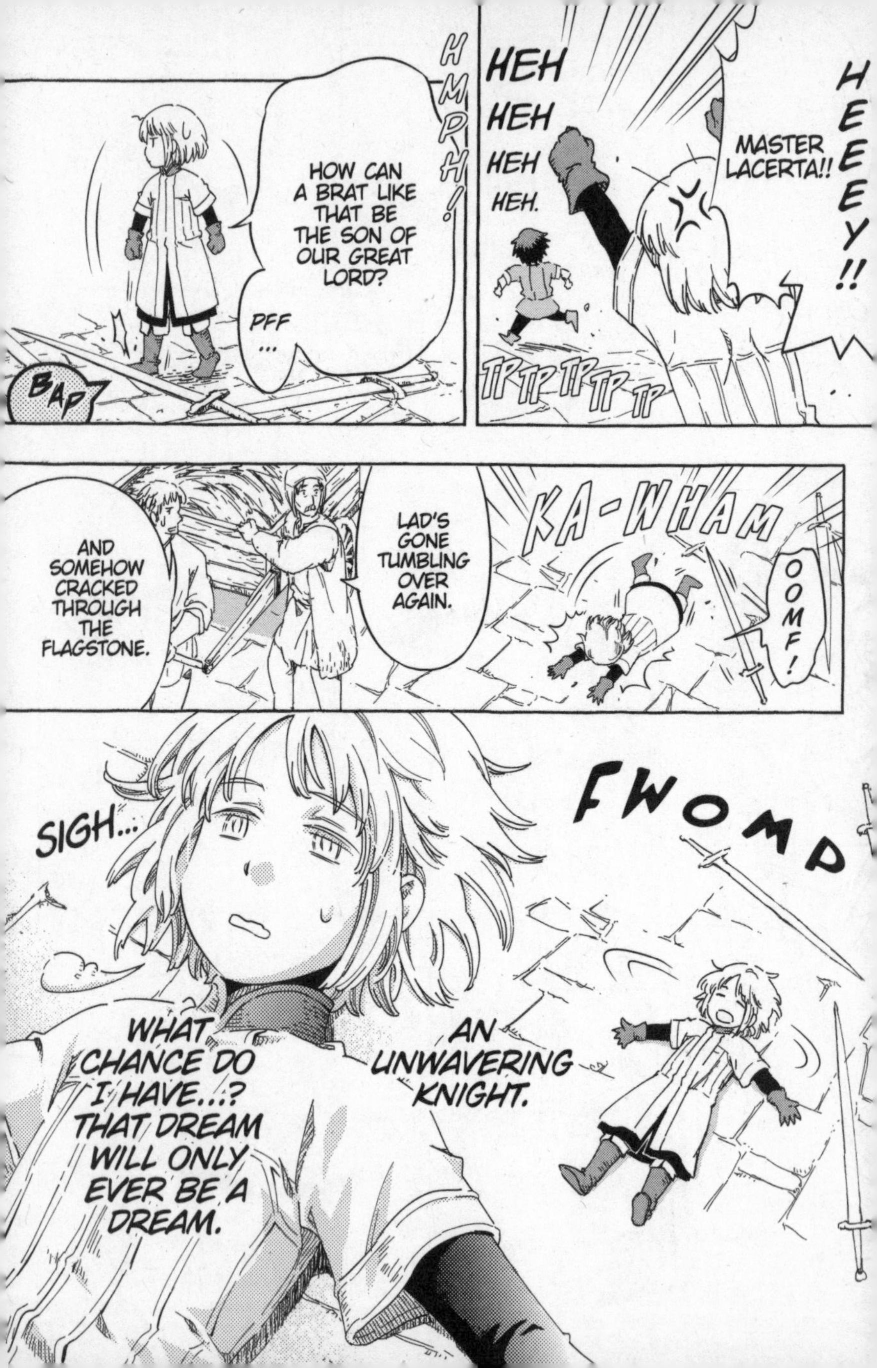
HEEEEY!!
MASTER LACERTA!!
HEH HEH HEH HEH.
TP TP TP TP TP
HMPH!
HOW CAN A BRAT LIKE THAT BE THE SON OF OUR GREAT LORD?
PFF ...
BAP
KA-WHAM
OOMF!
LAD'S GONE TUMBLING OVER AGAIN.
AND SOMEHOW CRACKED THROUGH THE FLAGSTONE.
FWOMP
SIGH...
AN UNWAVERING KNIGHT.
WHAT CHANCE DO I HAVE...? THAT DREAM WILL ONLY EVER BE A DREAM.

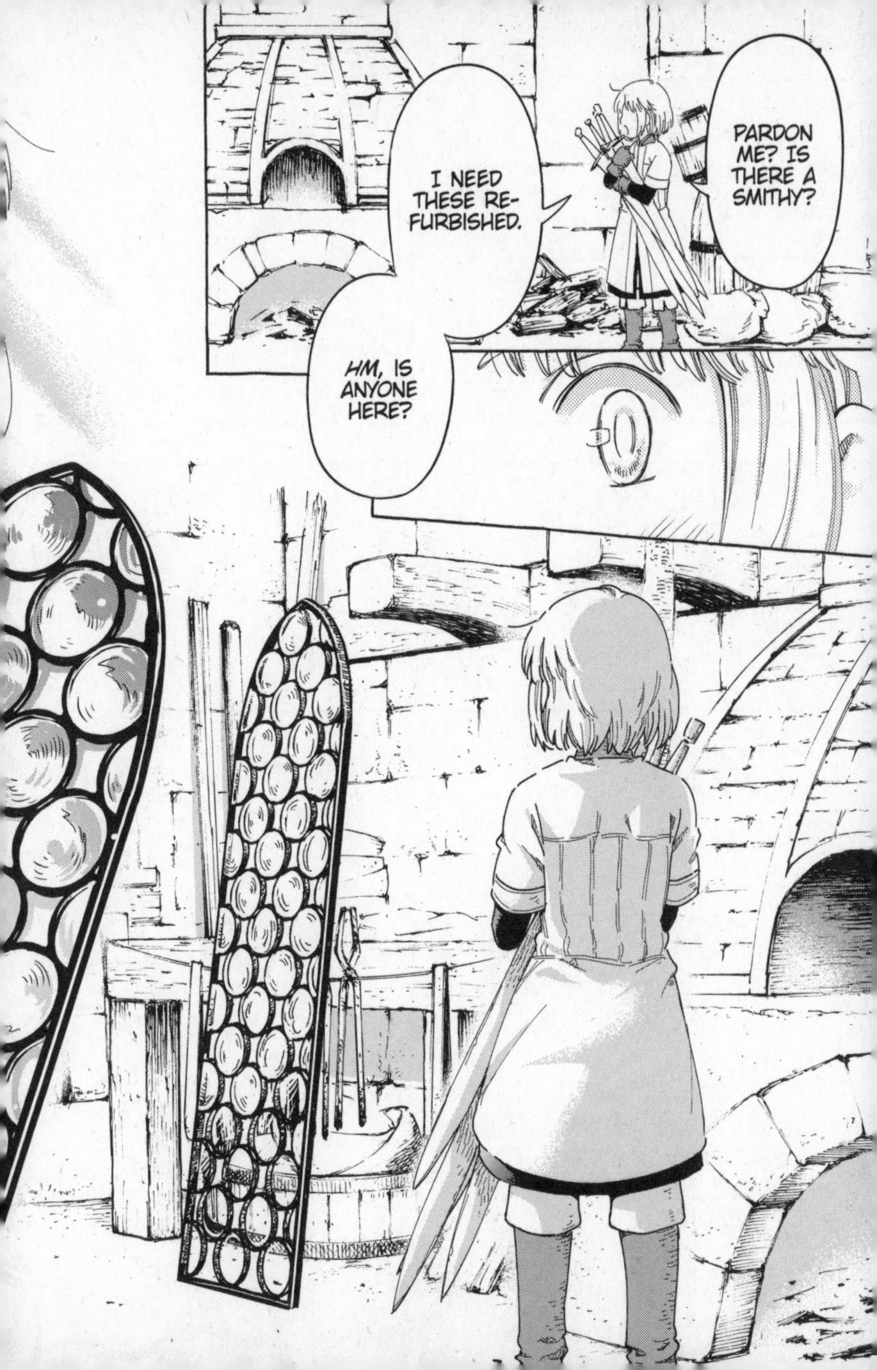
PARDON ME? IS THERE A SMITHY?
I NEED THESE RE-FURBISHED.
HM, IS ANYONE HERE?

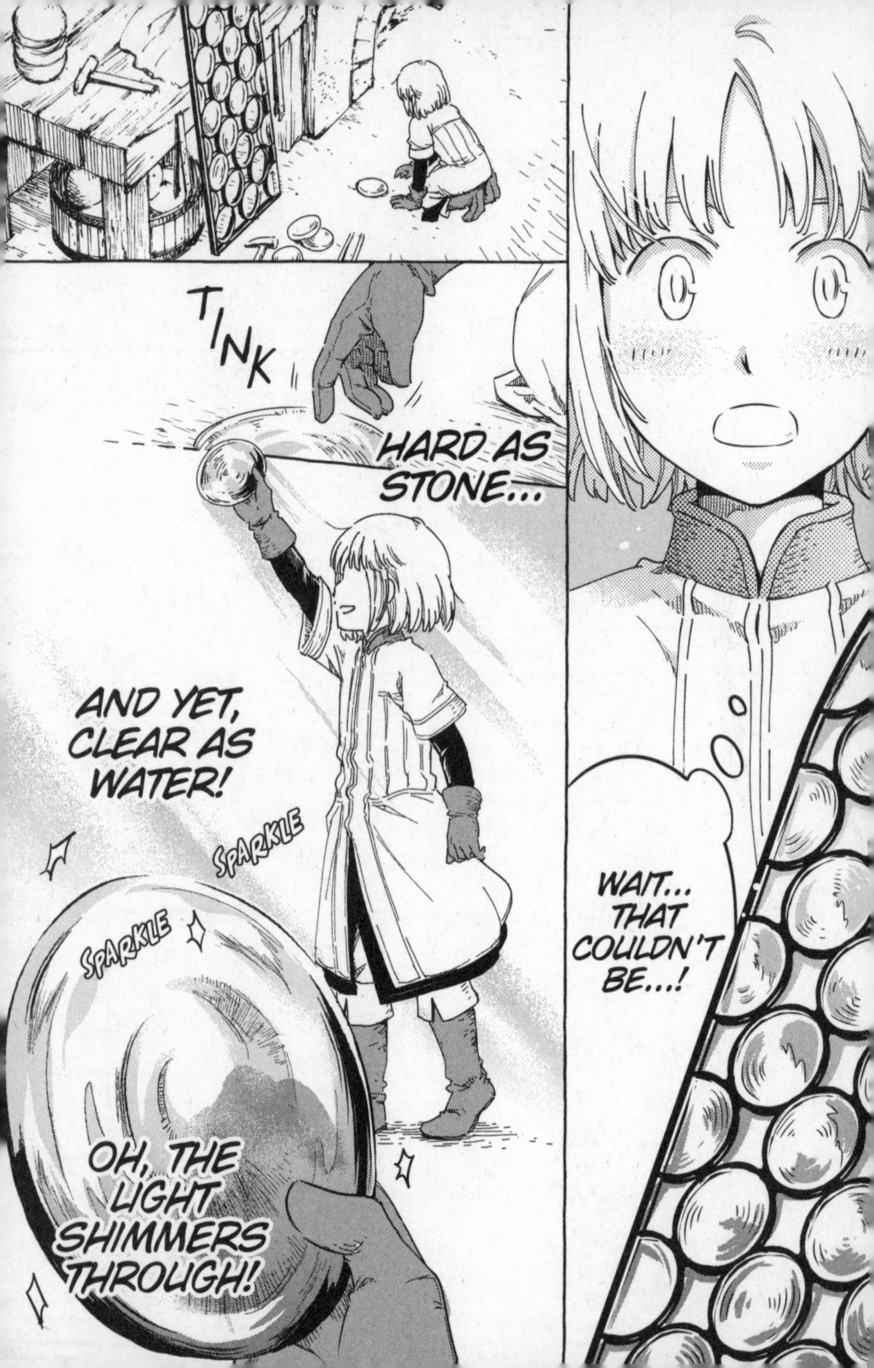
WAIT... THAT COULDN'T BE...!
TINK
HARD AS STONE...
AND YET, CLEAR AS WATER!
SPARKLE
SPARKLE
OH, THE LIGHT SHIMMERS THROUGH!

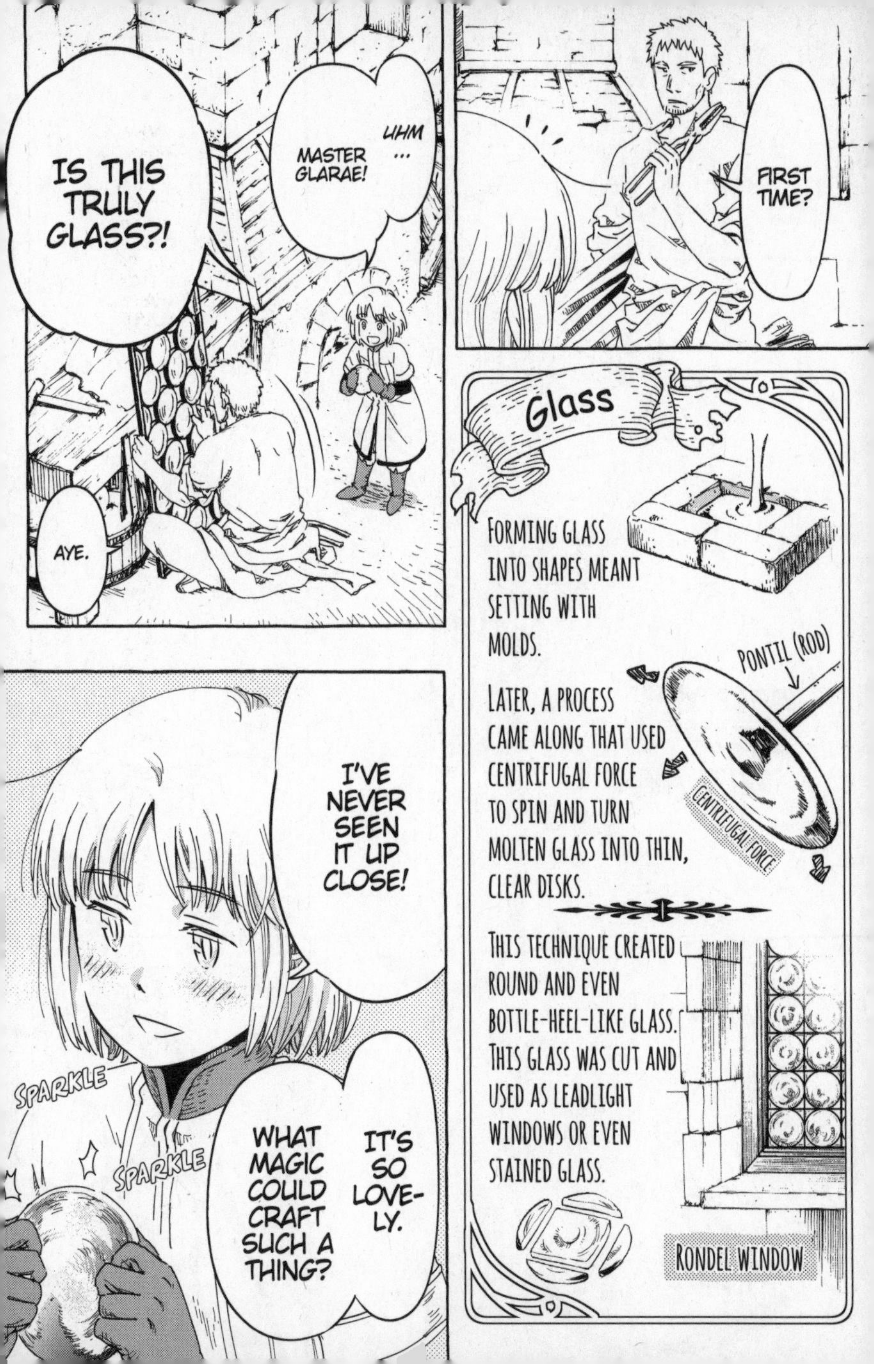
FIRST TIME?
UHM ...
MASTER GLARAE!
IS THIS TRULY GLASS?!
AYE.
Glass
FORMING GLASS INTO SHAPES MEANT SETTING WITH MOLDS.
PONTIL (ROD)
LATER, A PROCESS CAME ALONG THAT USED CENTRIFUGAL FORCE TO SPIN AND TURN MOLTEN GLASS INTO THIN, CLEAR DISKS.
CENTRIFUGAL FORCE
THIS TECHNIQUE CREATED ROUND AND EVEN BOTTLE-HEEL-LIKE GLASS. THIS GLASS WAS CUT AND USED AS LEADLIGHT WINDOWS OR EVEN STAINED GLASS.
RONDEL WINDOW
I'VE NEVER SEEN IT UP CLOSE!
IT'S SO LOVE-LY.
WHAT MAGIC COULD CRAFT SUCH A THING?
SPARKLE
SPARKLE

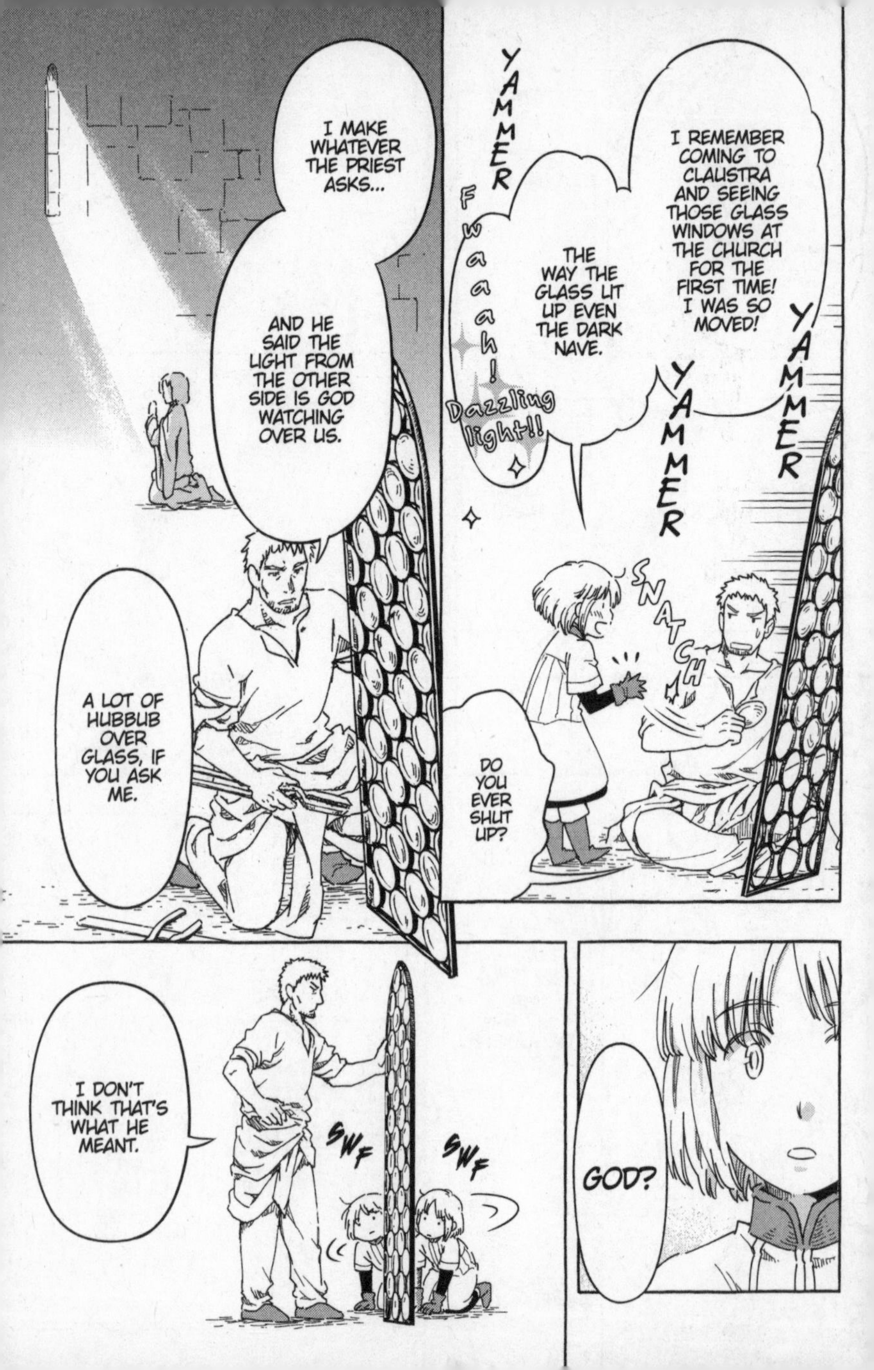
I REMEMBER COMING TO CLAUSTRA AND SEEING THOSE GLASS WINDOWS AT THE CHURCH FOR THE FIRST TIME! I WAS SO MOVED!
YAMMER
YAMMER
THE WAY THE GLASS LIT UP EVEN THE DARK NAVE.
YAMMER
Fwaaah! Dazzling light!!
SNATCH
DO YOU EVER SHUT UP?
I MAKE WHATEVER THE PRIEST ASKS...
AND HE SAID THE LIGHT FROM THE OTHER SIDE IS GOD WATCHING OVER US.
A LOT OF HUBBUB OVER GLASS, IF YOU ASK ME.
GOD?
I DON'T THINK THAT'S WHAT HE MEANT.
SWF
SWF

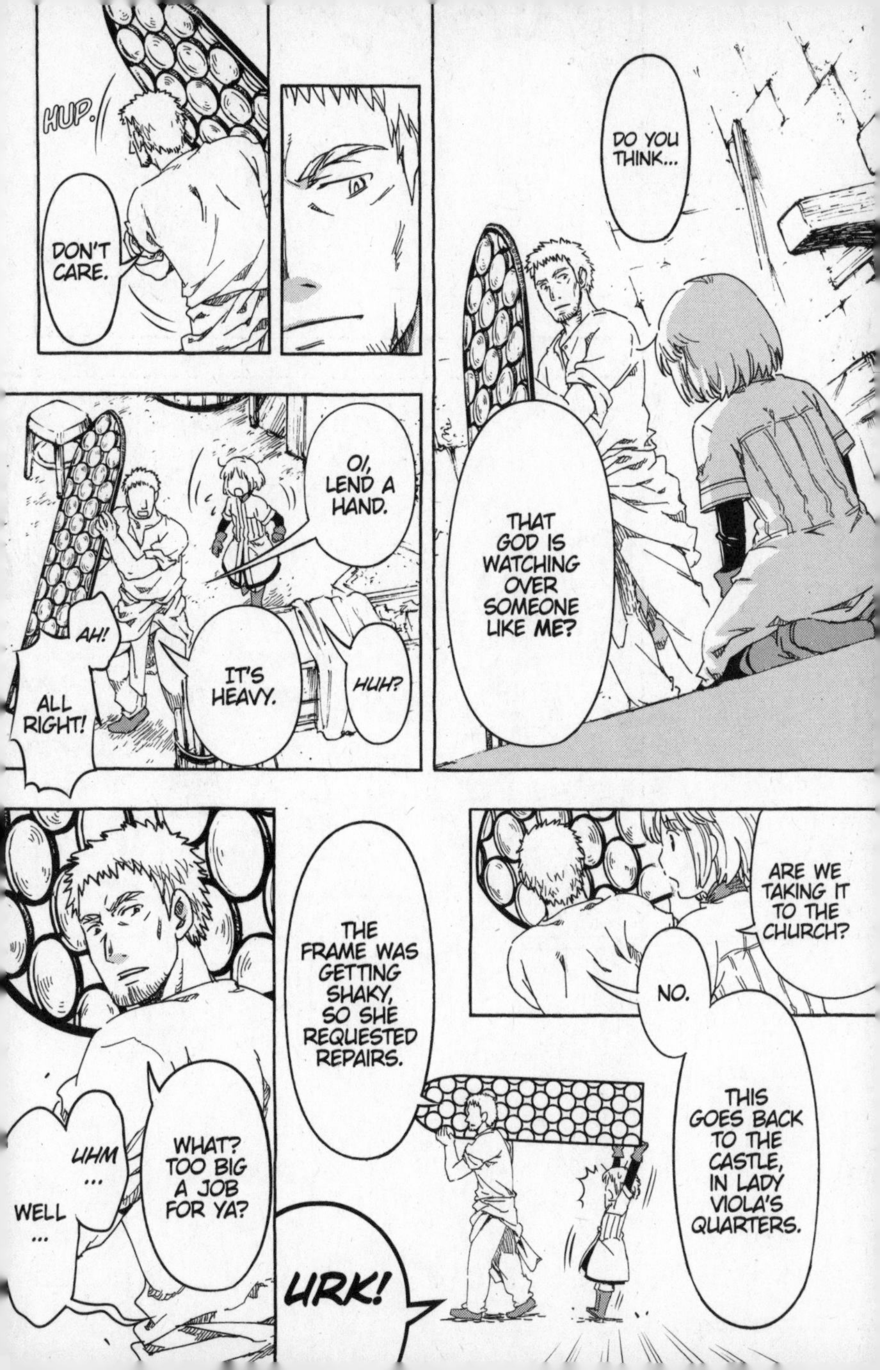
DO YOU THINK...
THAT GOD IS WATCHING OVER SOMEONE LIKE ME?
HUP.
DON'T CARE.
OI, LEND A HAND.
HUH?
IT'S HEAVY.
AH!
ALL RIGHT!
ARE WE TAKING IT TO THE CHURCH?
NO.
THIS GOES BACK TO THE CASTLE, IN LADY VIOLA'S QUARTERS.
THE FRAME WAS GETTING SHAKY, SO SHE REQUESTED REPAIRS.
URK!
WHAT? TOO BIG A JOB FOR YA?
UHM ...
WELL ...

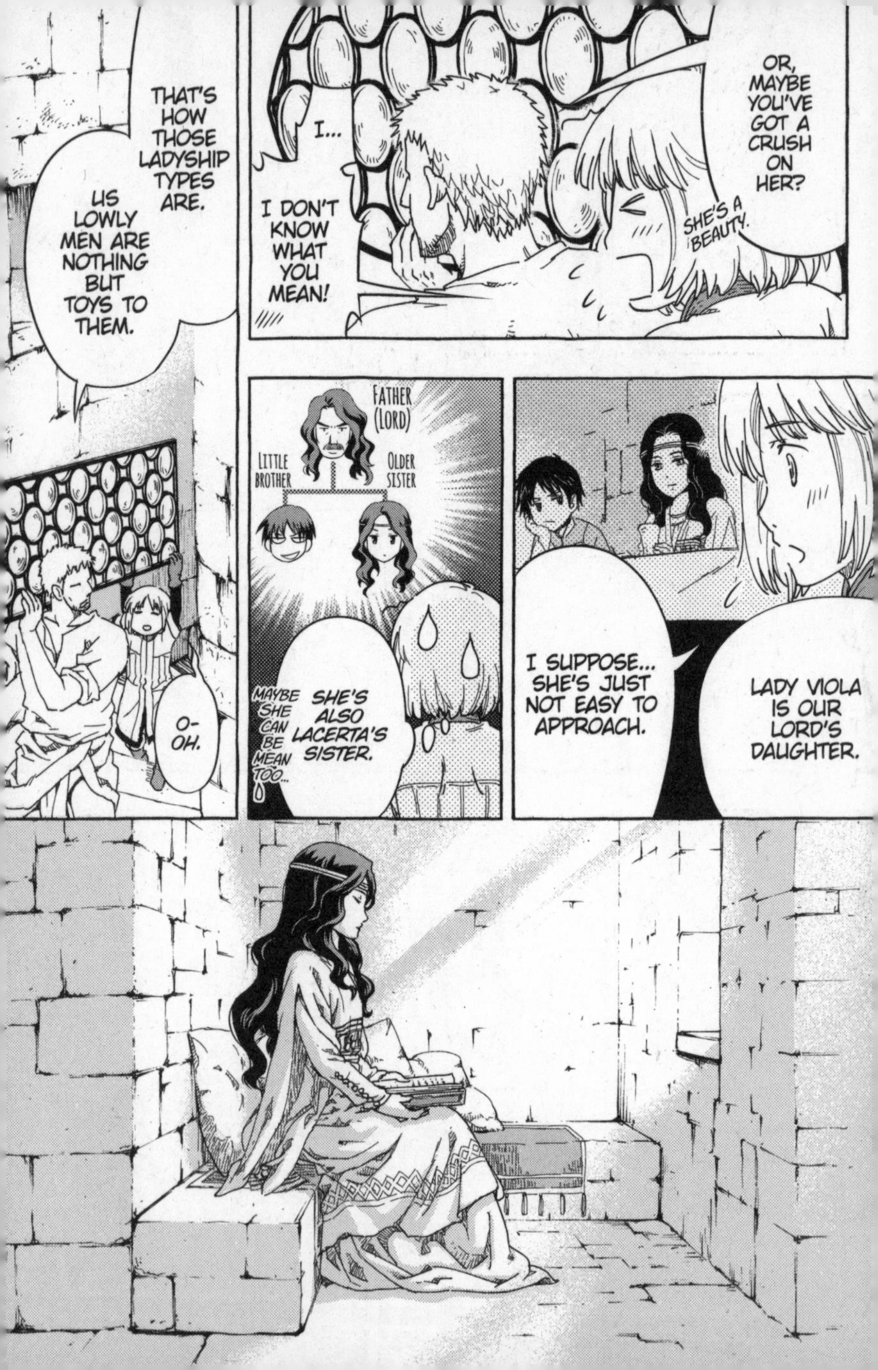
OR, MAYBE YOU'VE GOT A CRUSH ON HER?
SHE'S A BEAUTY.
I...
I DON'T KNOW WHAT YOU MEAN!
LADY VIOLA IS OUR LORD'S DAUGHTER.
I SUPPOSE... SHE'S JUST NOT EASY TO APPROACH.
FATHER (LORD)
LITTLE BROTHER
OLDER SISTER
SHE'S ALSO LACERTA'S SISTER.
MAYBE SHE CAN BE MEAN TOO...
THAT'S HOW THOSE LADYSHIP TYPES ARE.
US LOWLY MEN ARE NOTHING BUT TOYS TO THEM.
O-OH.

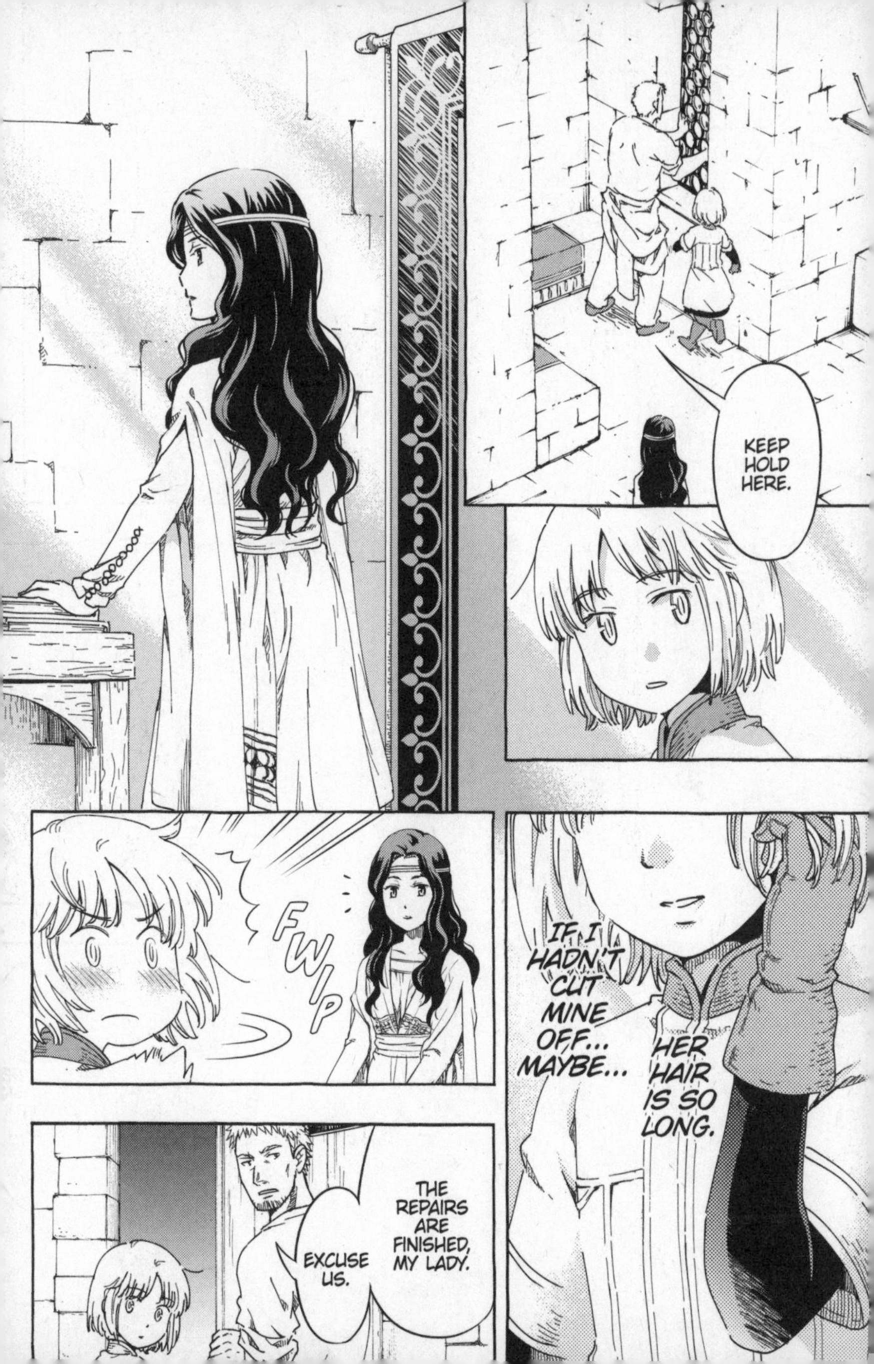
KEEP HOLD HERE.
HER HAIR IS SO LONG.
IF I HADN'T CUT MINE OFF... MAYBE...
FWIP
THE REPAIRS ARE FINISHED, MY LADY.
EXCUSE US.

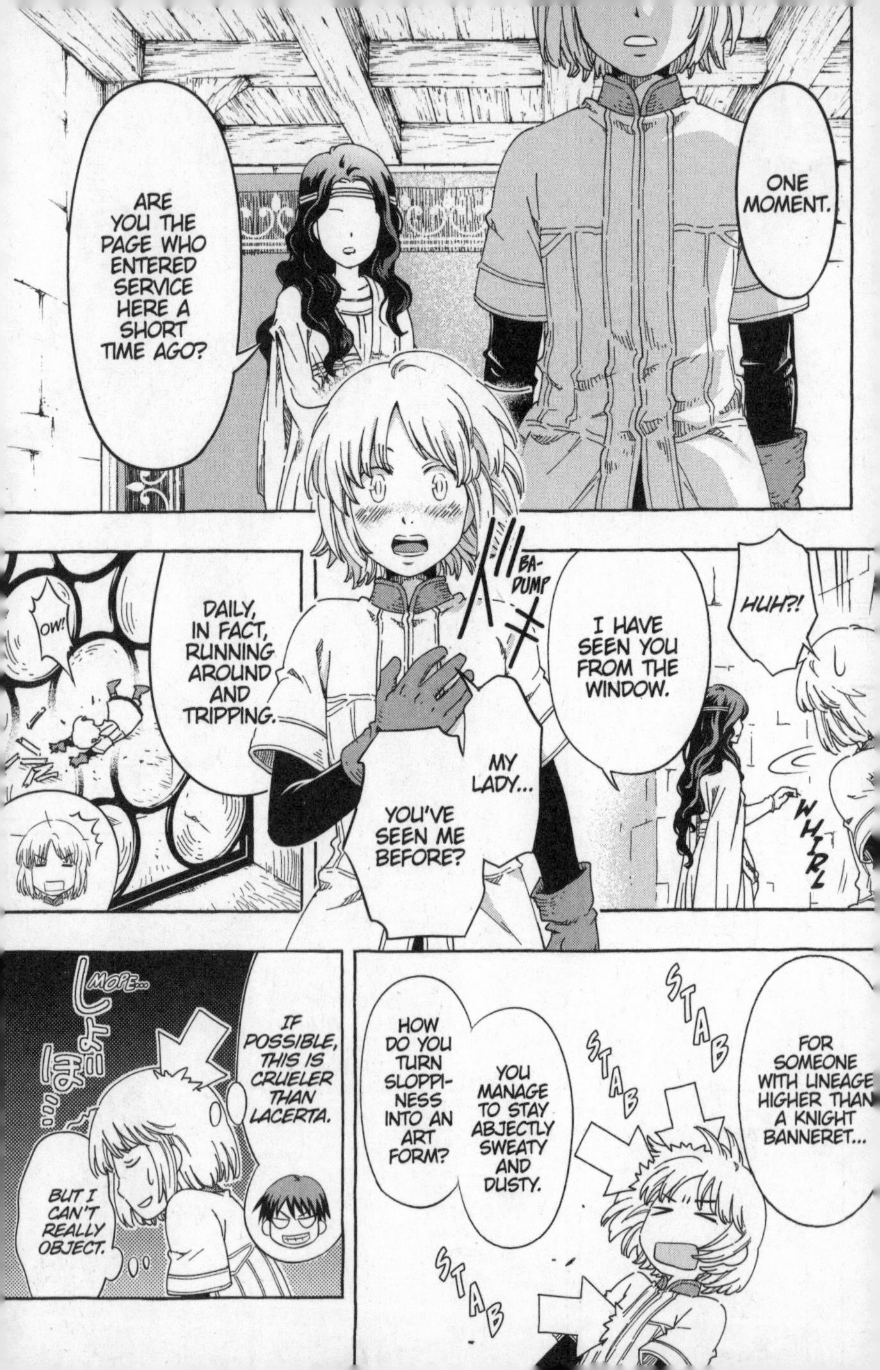
ONE MOMENT.
ARE YOU THE PAGE WHO ENTERED SERVICE HERE A SHORT TIME AGO?
HUH?!
WHIRL
I HAVE SEEN YOU FROM THE WINDOW.
BA-DUMP
MY LADY...
YOU'VE SEEN ME BEFORE?
DAILY, IN FACT, RUNNING AROUND AND TRIPPING.
OW!
FOR SOMEONE WITH LINEAGE HIGHER THAN A KNIGHT BANNERET...
STAB
STAB
YOU MANAGE TO STAY ABJECTLY SWEATY AND DUSTY.
HOW DO YOU TURN SLOPPI-NESS INTO AN ART FORM?
STAB
MOPE...
IF POSSIBLE, THIS IS CRUELER THAN LACERTA.
BUT I CAN'T REALLY OBJECT.

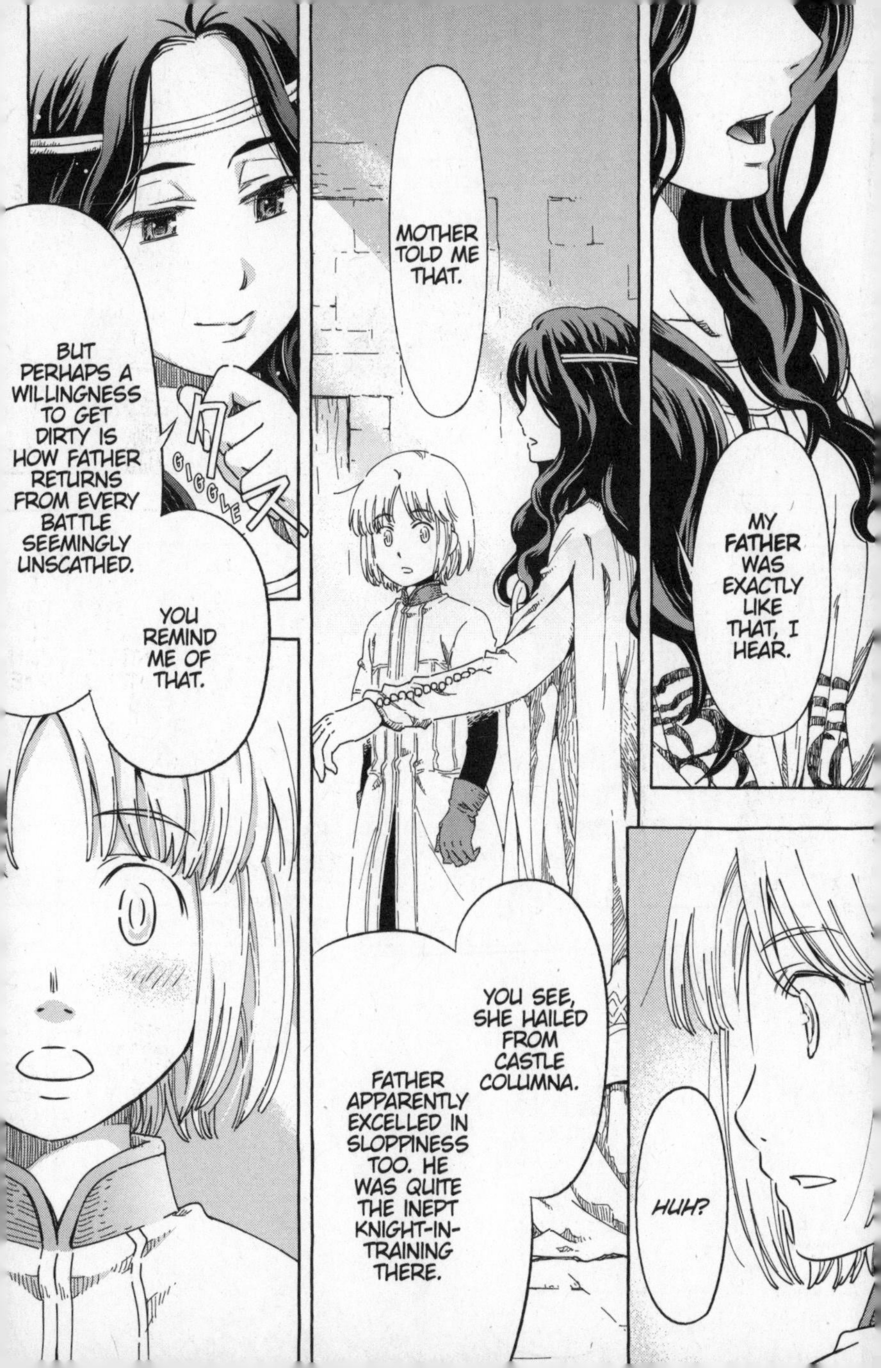

MY FATHER WAS EXACTLY LIKE THAT, I HEAR.
HUH?
MOTHER TOLD ME THAT.
YOU SEE, SHE HAILED FROM CASTLE COLUMNA.
FATHER APPARENTLY EXCELLED IN SLOPPINESS TOO. HE WAS QUITE THE INEPT KNIGHT-IN-TRAINING THERE.
BUT PERHAPS A WILLINGNESS TO GET DIRTY IS HOW FATHER RETURNS FROM EVERY BATTLE SEEMINGLY UNSCATHED.
GIGGLE
YOU REMIND ME OF THAT.

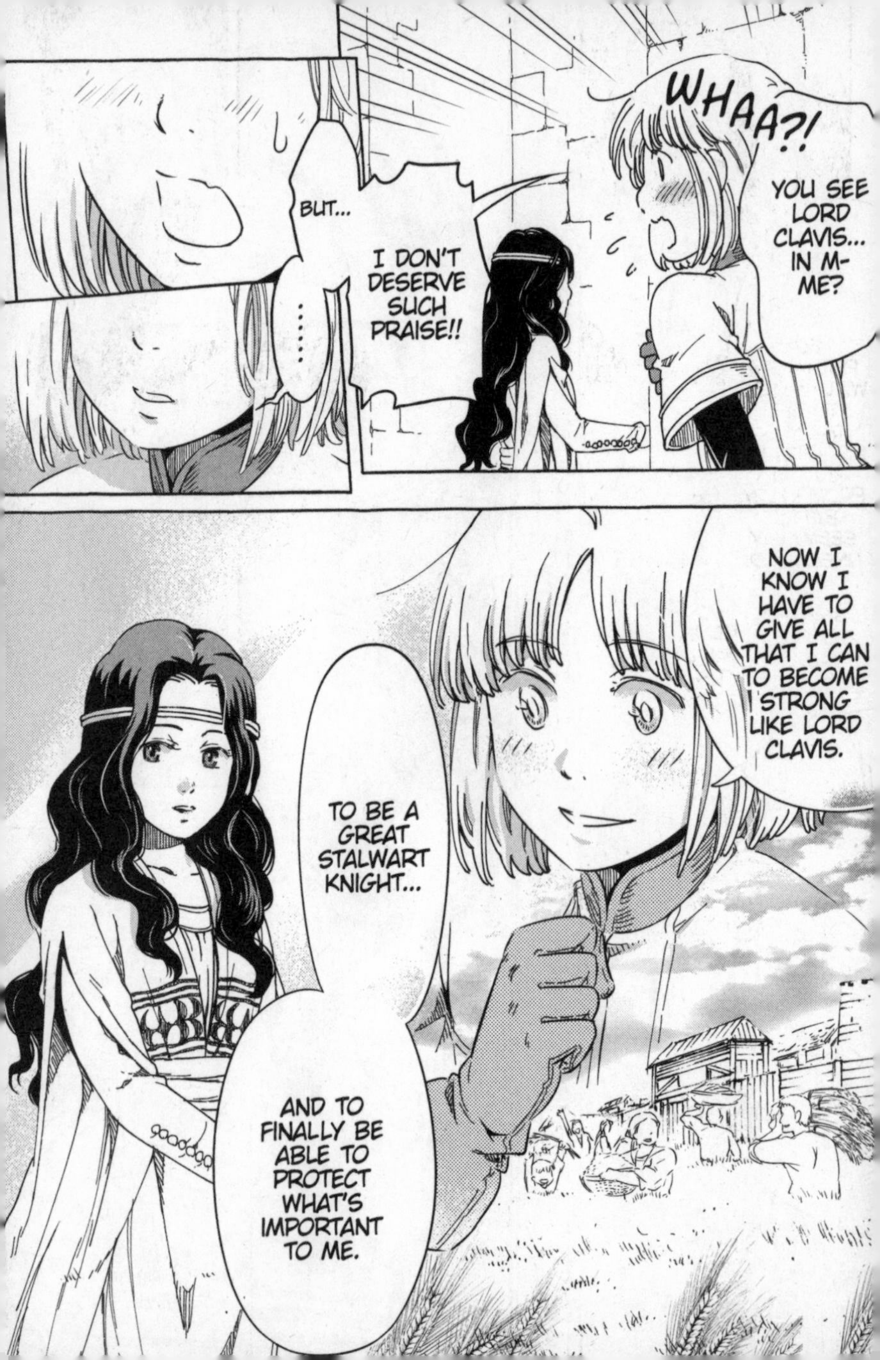
WHAA?!
YOU SEE LORD CLAVIS... IN M-ME?
I DON'T DESERVE SUCH PRAISE!!
BUT...
......
NOW I KNOW I HAVE TO GIVE ALL THAT I CAN TO BECOME STRONG LIKE LORD CLAVIS.
TO BE A GREAT STALWART KNIGHT...
AND TO FINALLY BE ABLE TO PROTECT WHAT'S IMPORTANT TO ME.

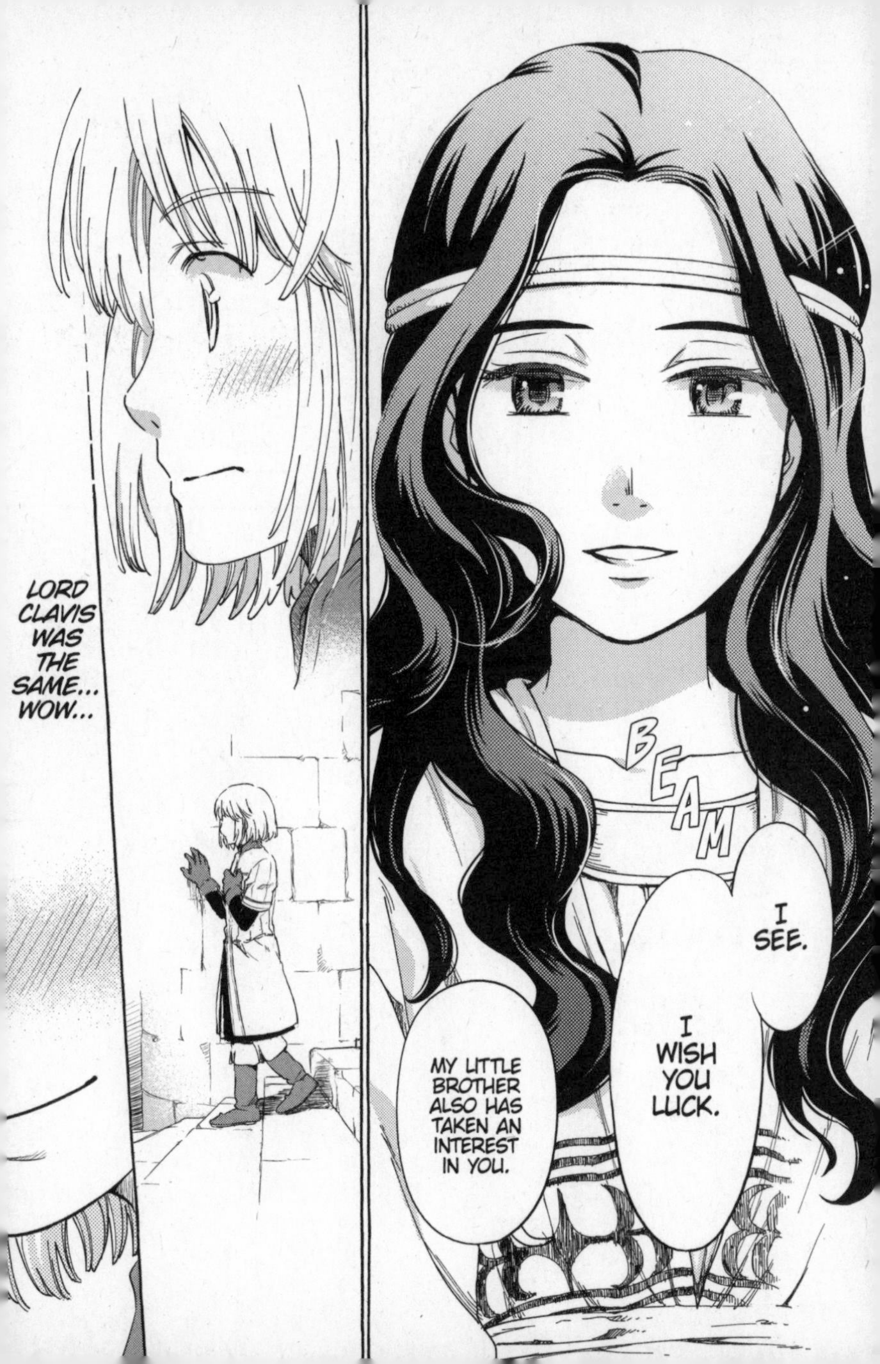
BEAM
I SEE.
I WISH YOU LUCK.
MY LITTLE BROTHER ALSO HAS TAKEN AN INTEREST IN YOU.
LORD CLAVIS WAS THE SAME... WOW...

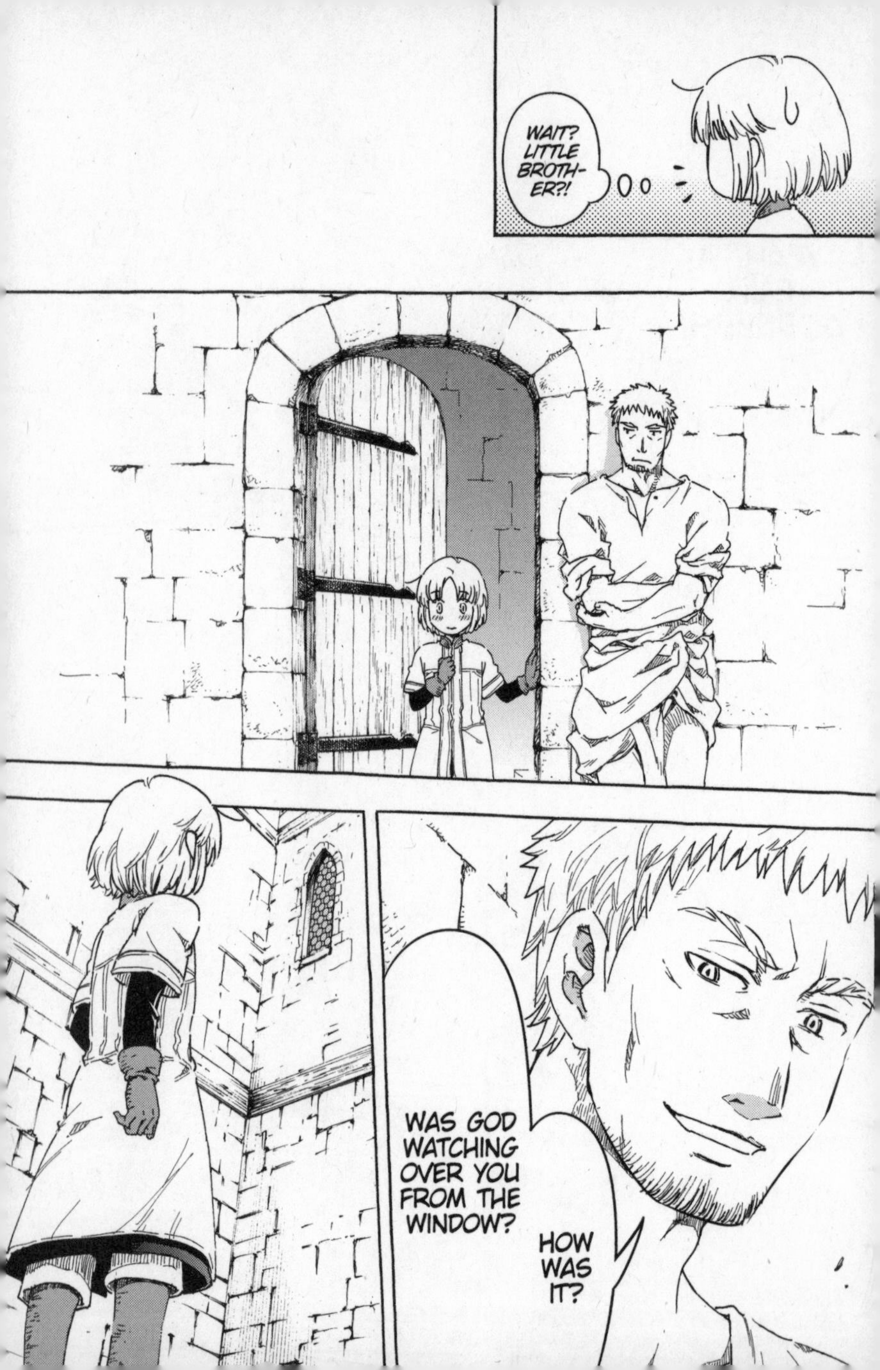
WAIT? LITTLE BROTH-ER?!
HOW WAS IT?
WAS GOD WATCHING OVER YOU FROM THE WINDOW?

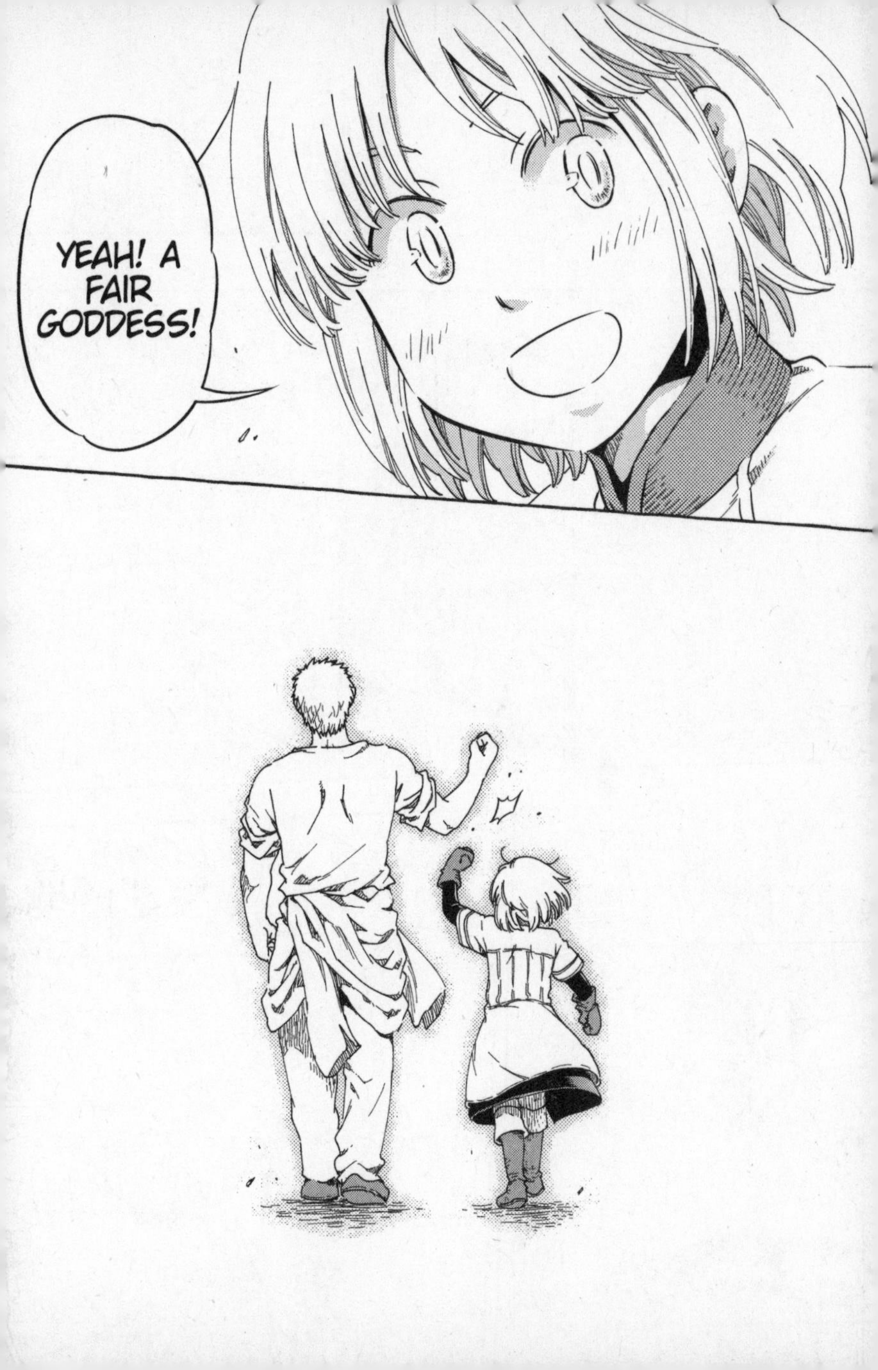
YEAH! A FAIR GODDESS!

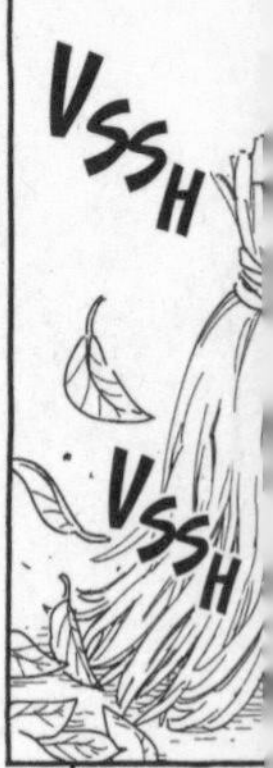
VSSH
VSSH
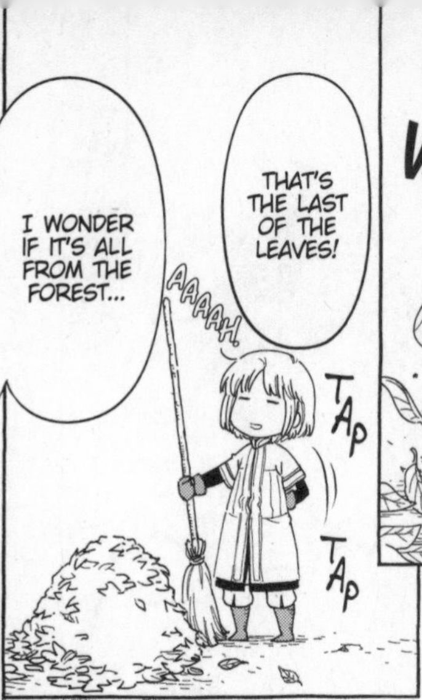
THAT'S THE LAST OF THE LEAVES!
AAAAAH!
TAP
TAP
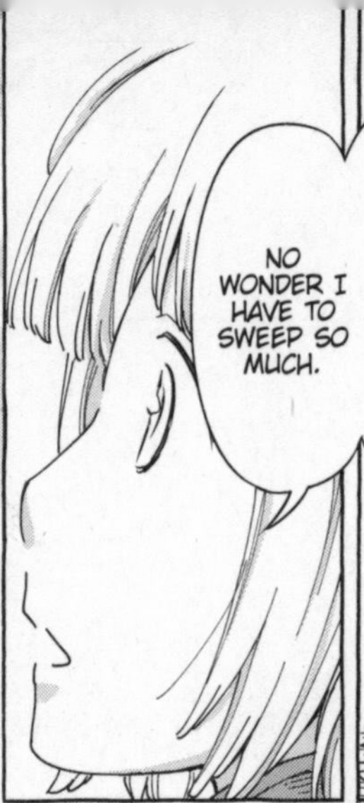
I WONDER IF IT'S ALL FROM THE FOREST...
NO WONDER I HAVE TO SWEEP SO MUCH.
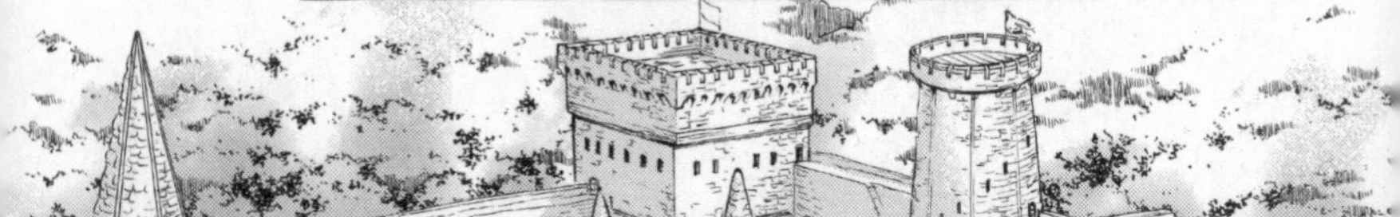
CHAPTER 4
CASTLE CLAUSTRA, THE LOCK
Castle Claustra
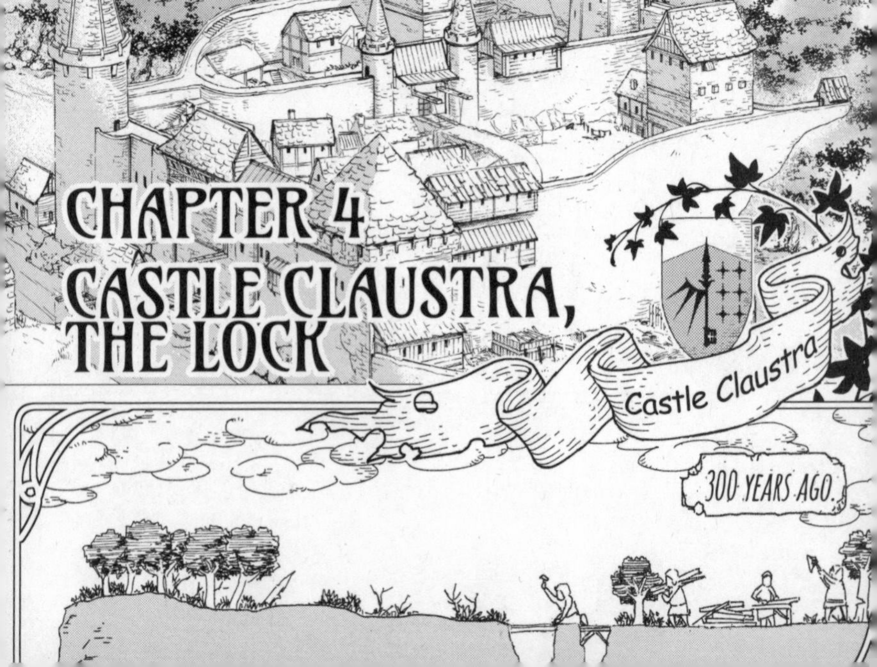
300 YEARS AGO.

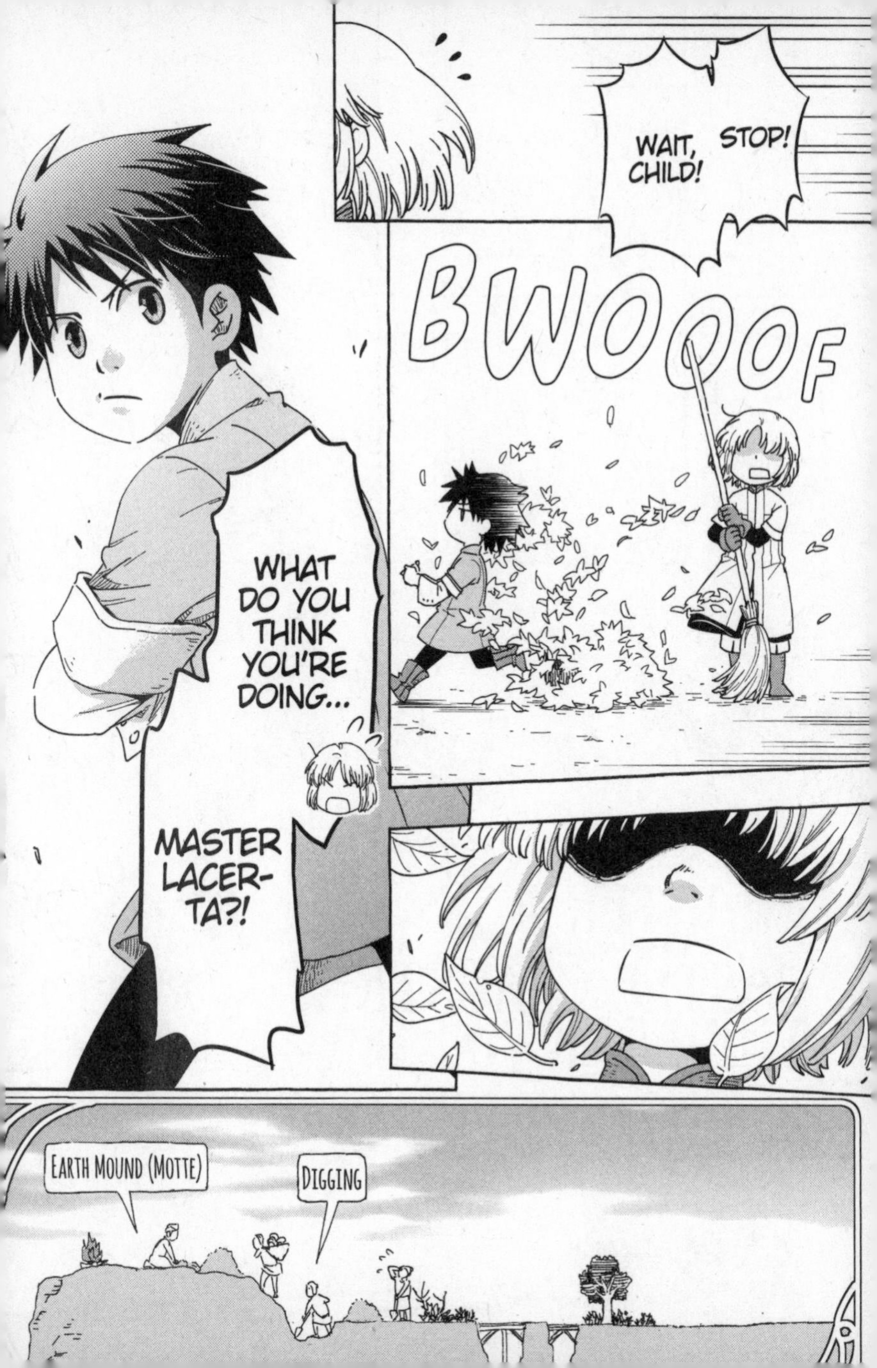
STOP!
WAIT, CHILD!
BWOOOF
WHAT DO YOU THINK YOU'RE DOING...
MASTER LACERTA?!
DIGGING
EARTH MOUND (MOTTE)

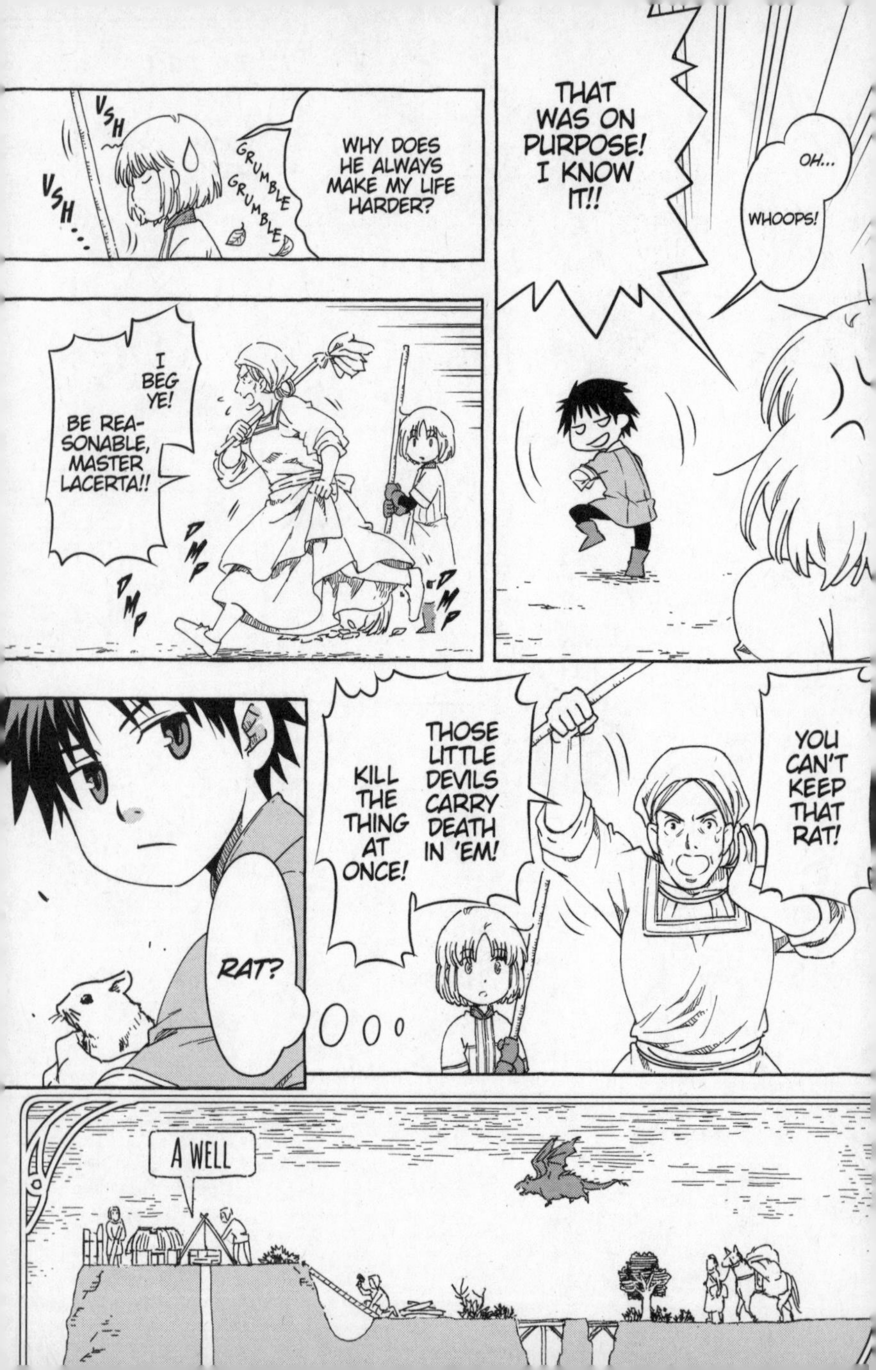
OH... WHOOPS!
THAT WAS ON PURPOSE! I KNOW IT!!
WHY DOES HE ALWAYS MAKE MY LIFE HARDER?
GRUMBLE GRUMBLE
VSH
VSH...
I BEG YE!
BE REA-SONABLE, MASTER LACERTA!!
DMP DMP
DMP DMP
YOU CAN'T KEEP THAT RAT!
THOSE LITTLE DEVILS CARRY DEATH IN 'EM!
KILL THE THING AT ONCE!
RAT?
A WELL

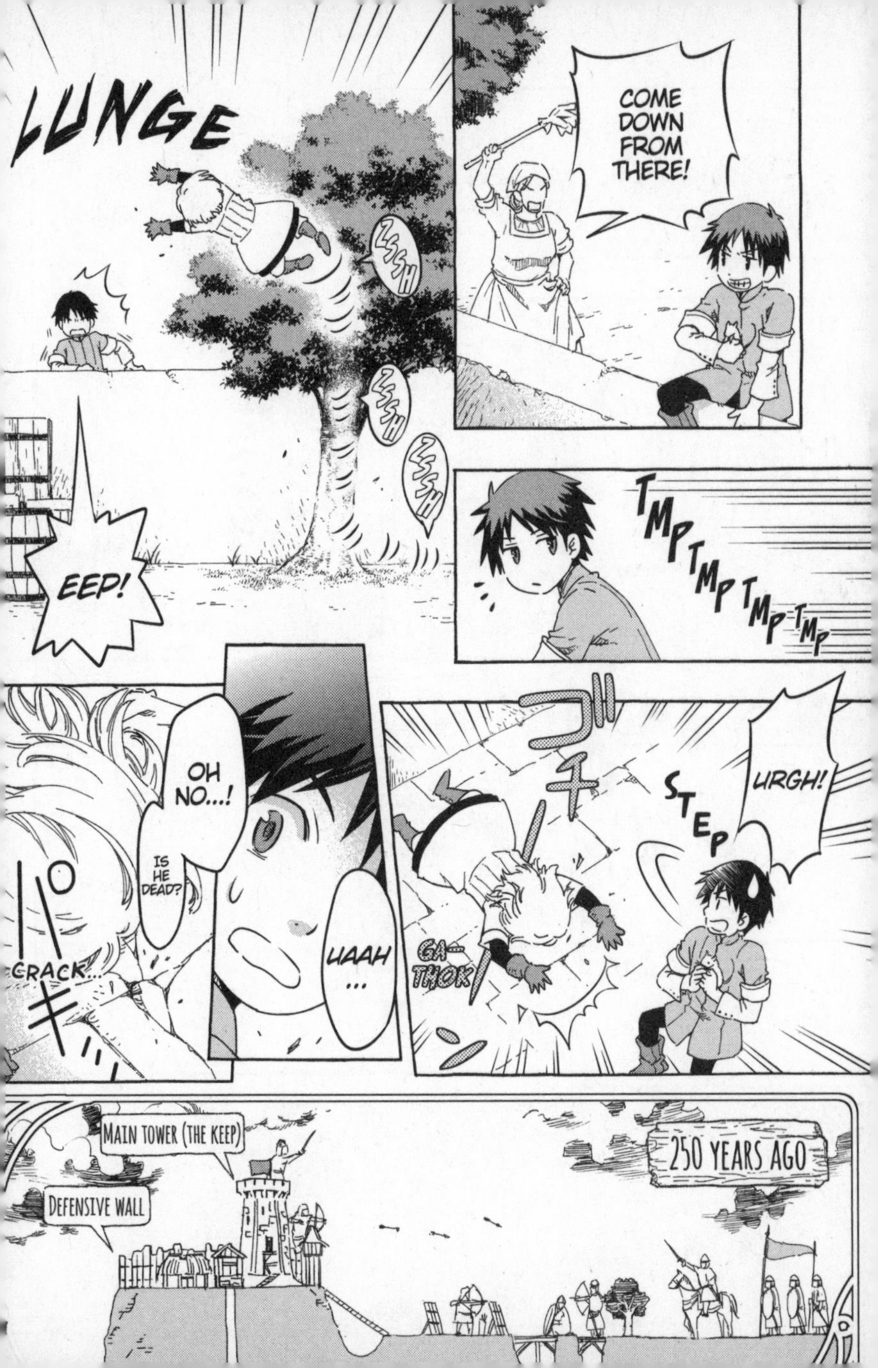
COME DOWN FROM THERE!
TMP TMP TMP TMP TMP
LUNGE
ZSSH
ZSSH
ZSSH
EEP!
ゴチ
URGH!
STEP
GA-THOK
OH NO...!
UAAH ...
IS HE DEAD?
CRACK...
250 YEARS AGO
MAIN TOWER (THE KEEP)
DEFENSIVE WALL

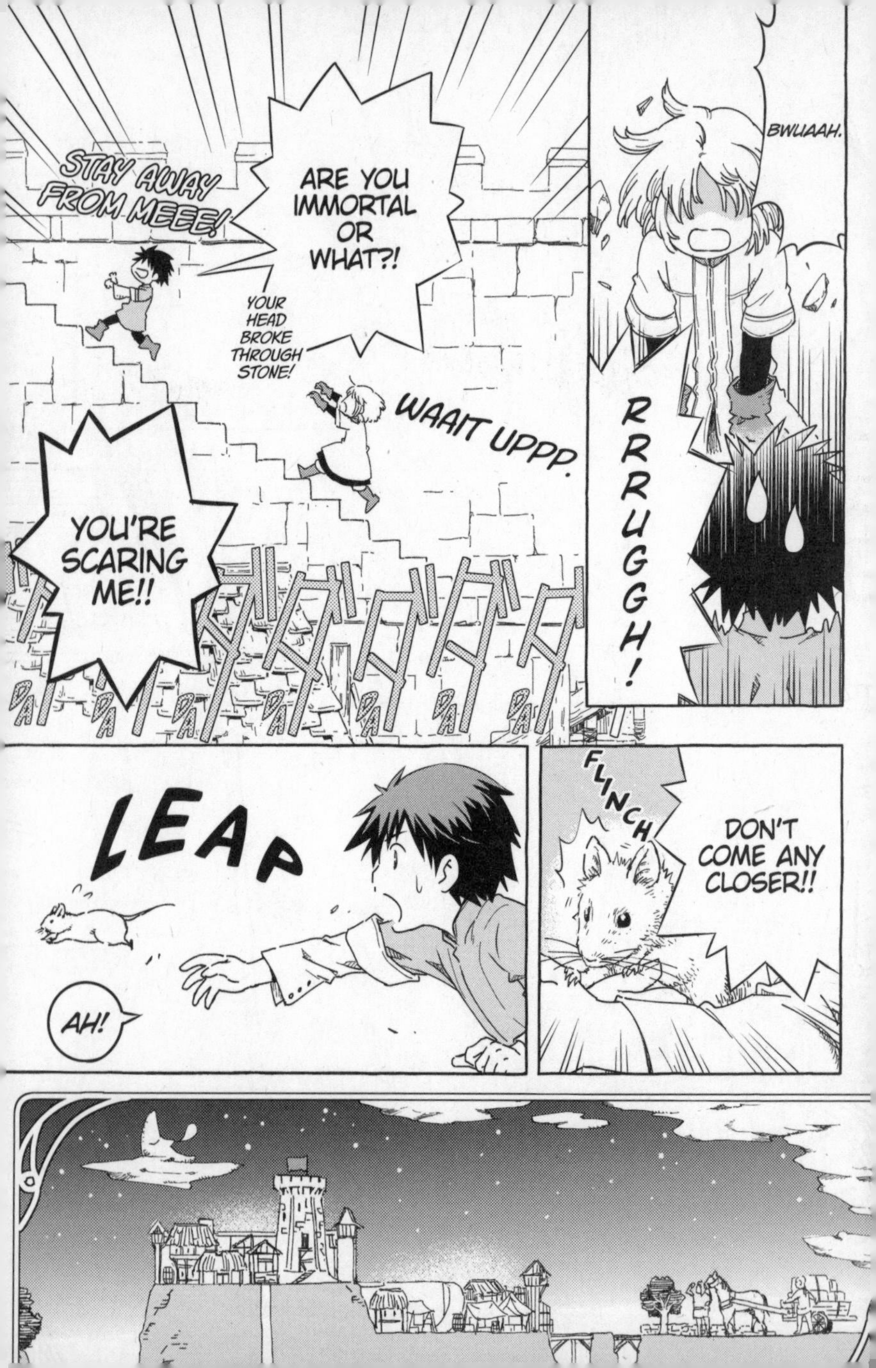
BWUAAH.
RRRUGGH!
STAY AWAY FROM MEEE!
ARE YOU IMMORTAL OR WHAT?!
YOUR HEAD BROKE THROUGH STONE!
WAAAIT UPPP.
YOU'RE SCARING ME!!
DA DA DA DA DA DA DA DA DA
FLINCH
DON'T COME ANY CLOSER!!
LEAP
AH!

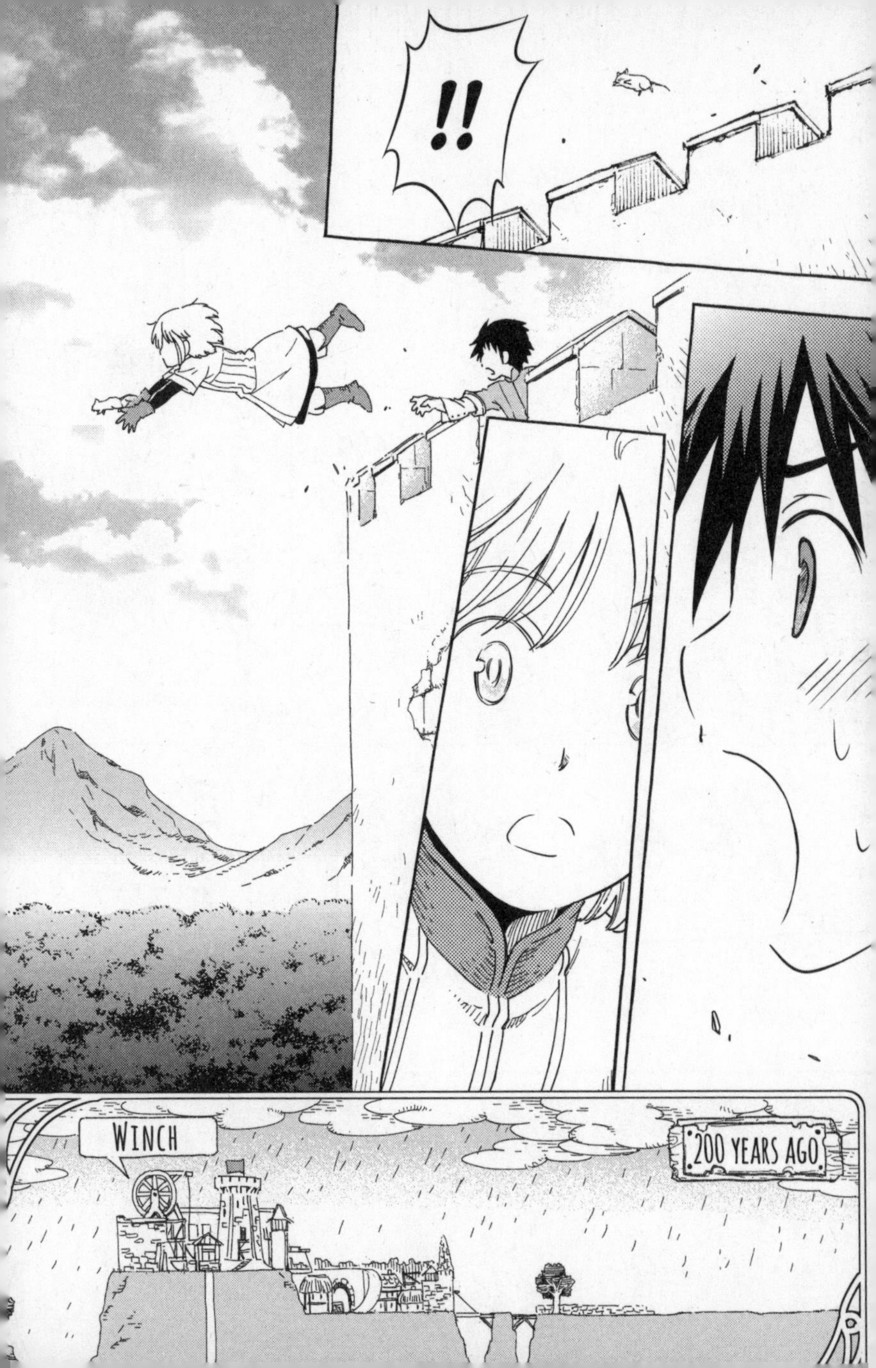
!!
200 YEARS AGO
WINCH

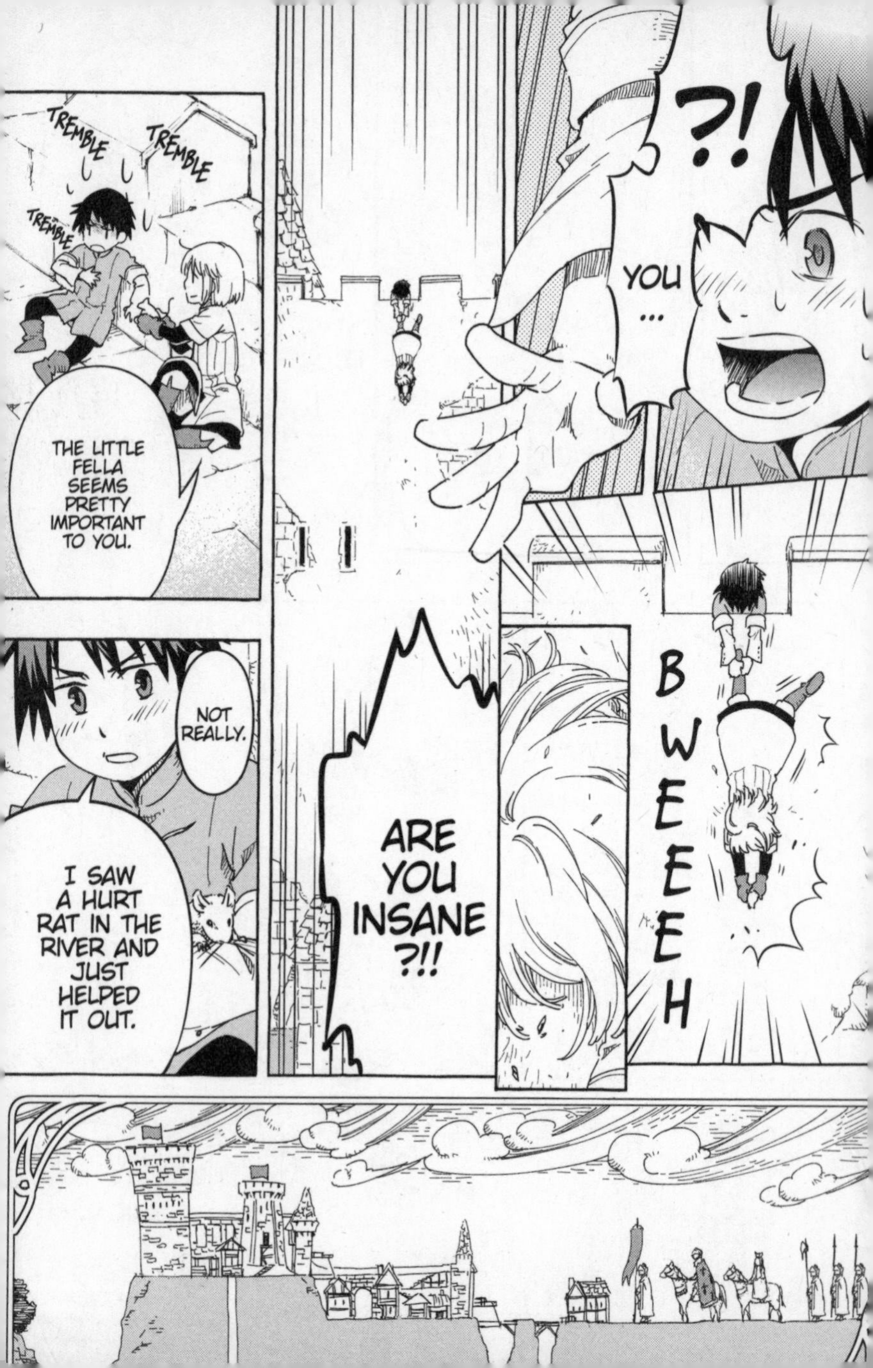
?!
YOU ...
B W E E E E H
ARE YOU INSANE ?!!
TREMBLE
TREMBLE
TREMBLE
THE LITTLE FELLA SEEMS PRETTY IMPORTANT TO YOU.
NOT REALLY.
I SAW A HURT RAT IN THE RIVER AND JUST HELPED IT OUT.

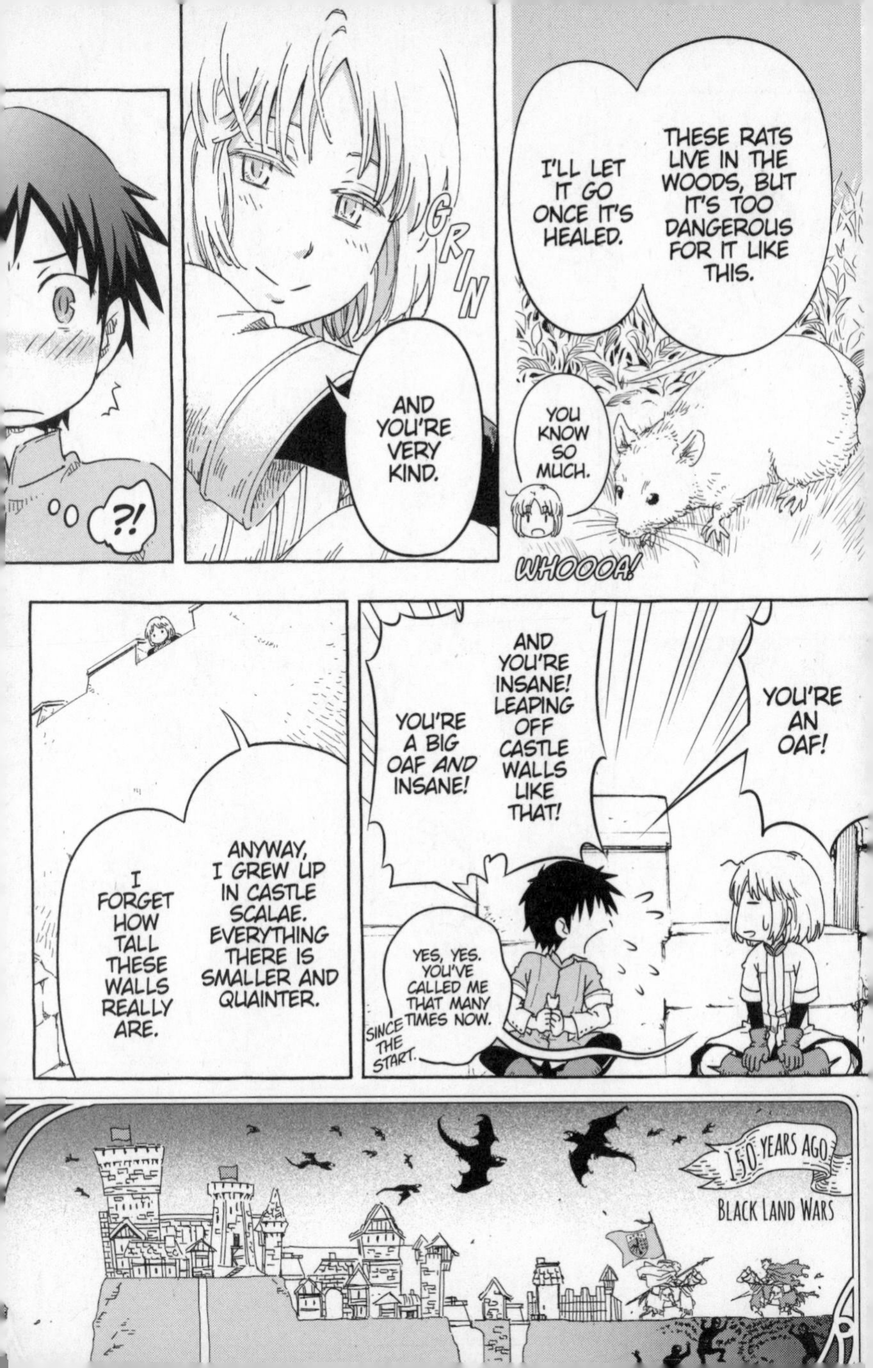
THESE RATS LIVE IN THE WOODS, BUT IT'S TOO DANGEROUS FOR IT LIKE THIS.
I'LL LET IT GO ONCE IT'S HEALED.
YOU KNOW SO MUCH.
WHOOOOA!
GRIN
AND YOU'RE VERY KIND.
?!
YOU'RE AN OAF!
AND YOU'RE INSANE! LEAPING OFF CASTLE WALLS LIKE THAT!
YOU'RE A BIG OAF AND INSANE!
YES, YES. YOU'VE CALLED ME THAT MANY TIMES NOW.
SINCE THE START.
ANYWAY, I GREW UP IN CASTLE SCALAE. EVERYTHING THERE IS SMALLER AND QUAINTER.
I FORGET HOW TALL THESE WALLS REALLY ARE.
150 YEARS AGO
BLACK LAND WARS

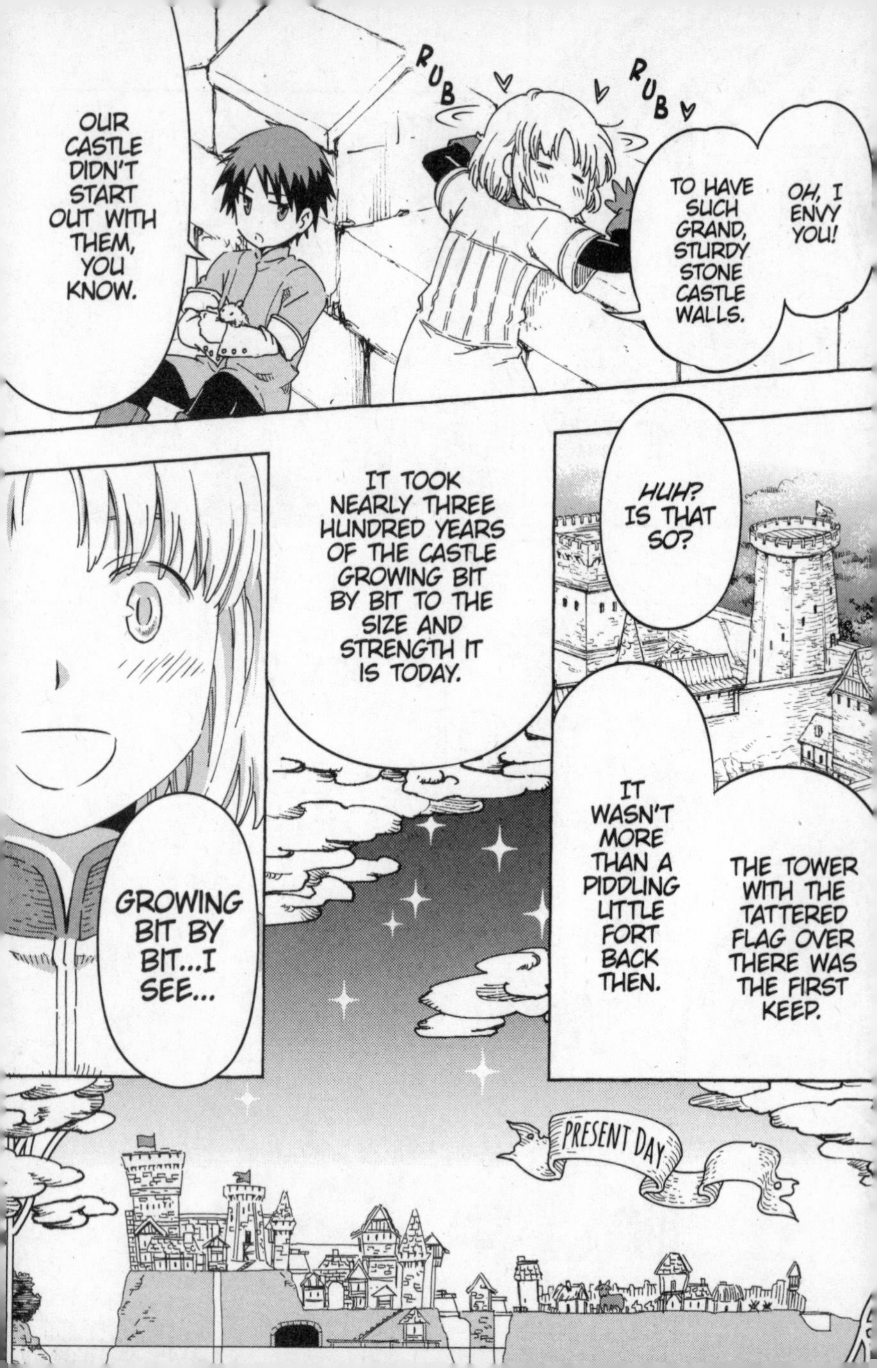
OH, I ENVY YOU!
TO HAVE SUCH GRAND, STURDY STONE CASTLE WALLS.
RUB
RUB
OUR CASTLE DIDN'T START OUT WITH THEM, YOU KNOW.
HUH? IS THAT SO?
THE TOWER WITH THE TATTERED FLAG OVER THERE WAS THE FIRST KEEP.
IT WASN'T MORE THAN A PIDDLING LITTLE FORT BACK THEN.
IT TOOK NEARLY THREE HUNDRED YEARS OF THE CASTLE GROWING BIT BY BIT TO THE SIZE AND STRENGTH IT IS TODAY.
GROWING BIT BY BIT...I SEE...
PRESENT DAY

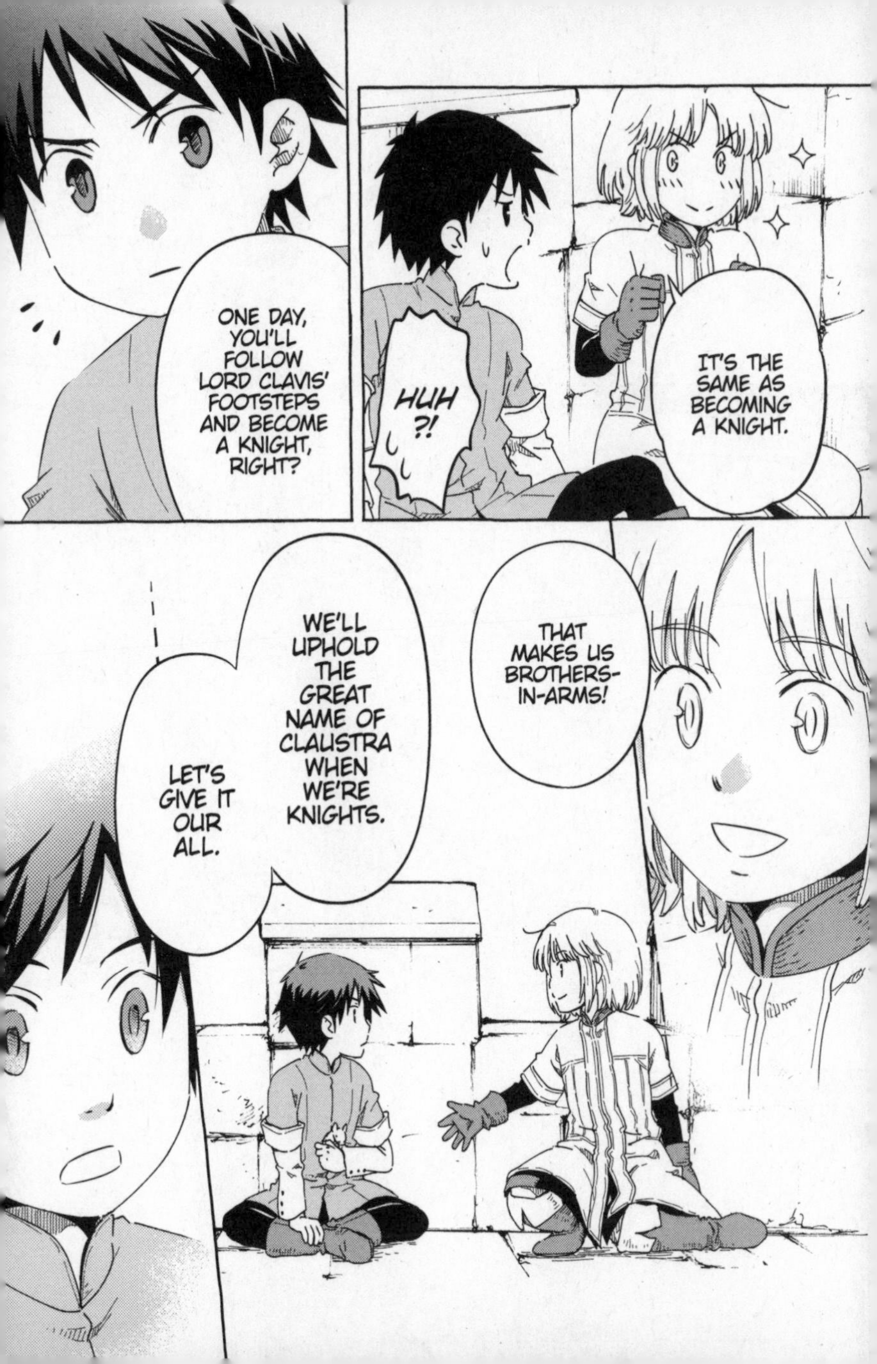
IT'S THE SAME AS BECOMING A KNIGHT.
HUH ?!
ONE DAY, YOU'LL FOLLOW LORD CLAVIS' FOOTSTEPS AND BECOME A KNIGHT, RIGHT?
THAT MAKES US BROTHERS-IN-ARMS!
WE'LL UPHOLD THE GREAT NAME OF CLAUSTRA WHEN WE'RE KNIGHTS.
LET'S GIVE IT OUR ALL.

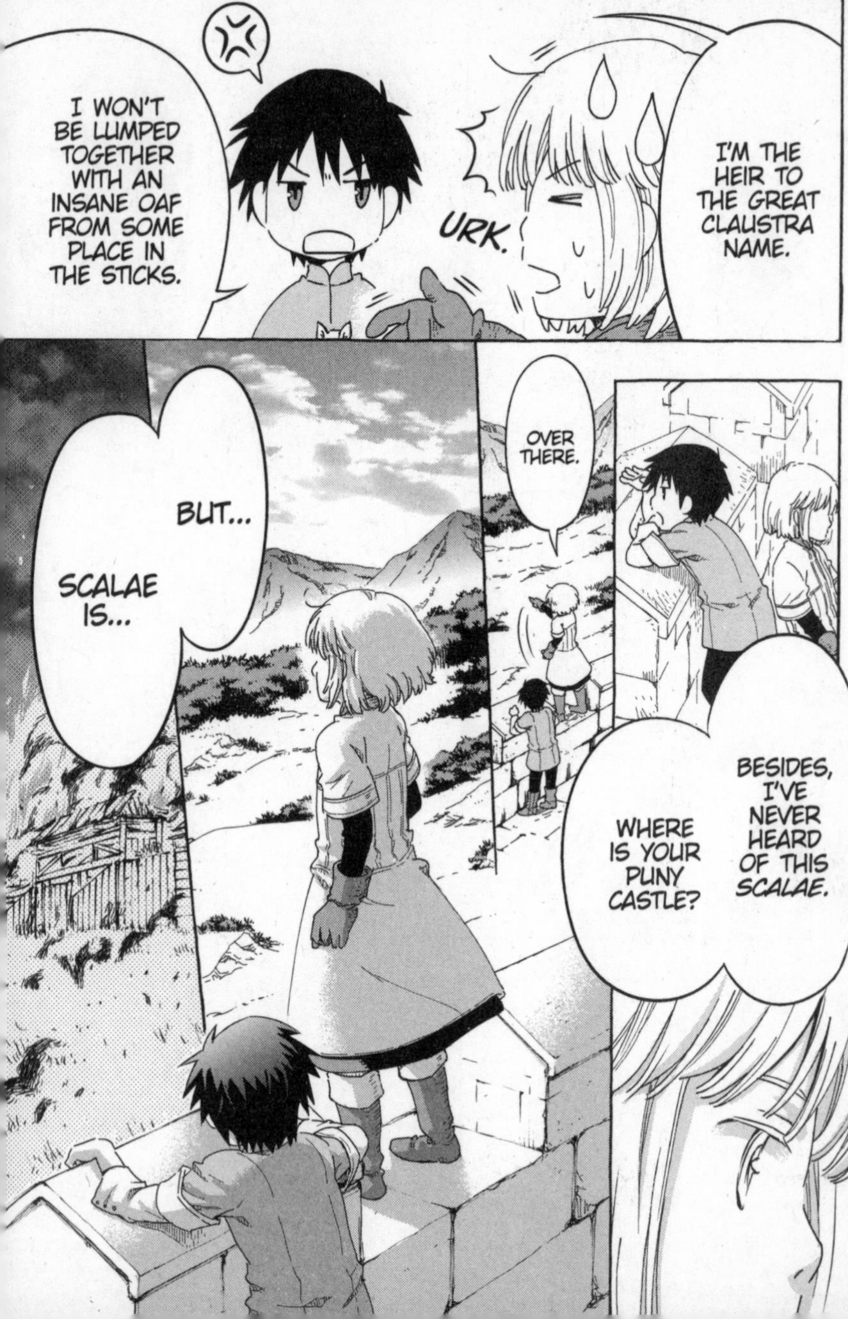
I'M THE HEIR TO THE GREAT CLAUSTRA NAME.
URK.
I WON'T BE LUMPED TOGETHER WITH AN INSANE OAF FROM SOME PLACE IN THE STICKS.
BESIDES, I'VE NEVER HEARD OF THIS SCALAE.
WHERE IS YOUR PUNY CASTLE?
OVER THERE.
BUT...
SCALAE IS...

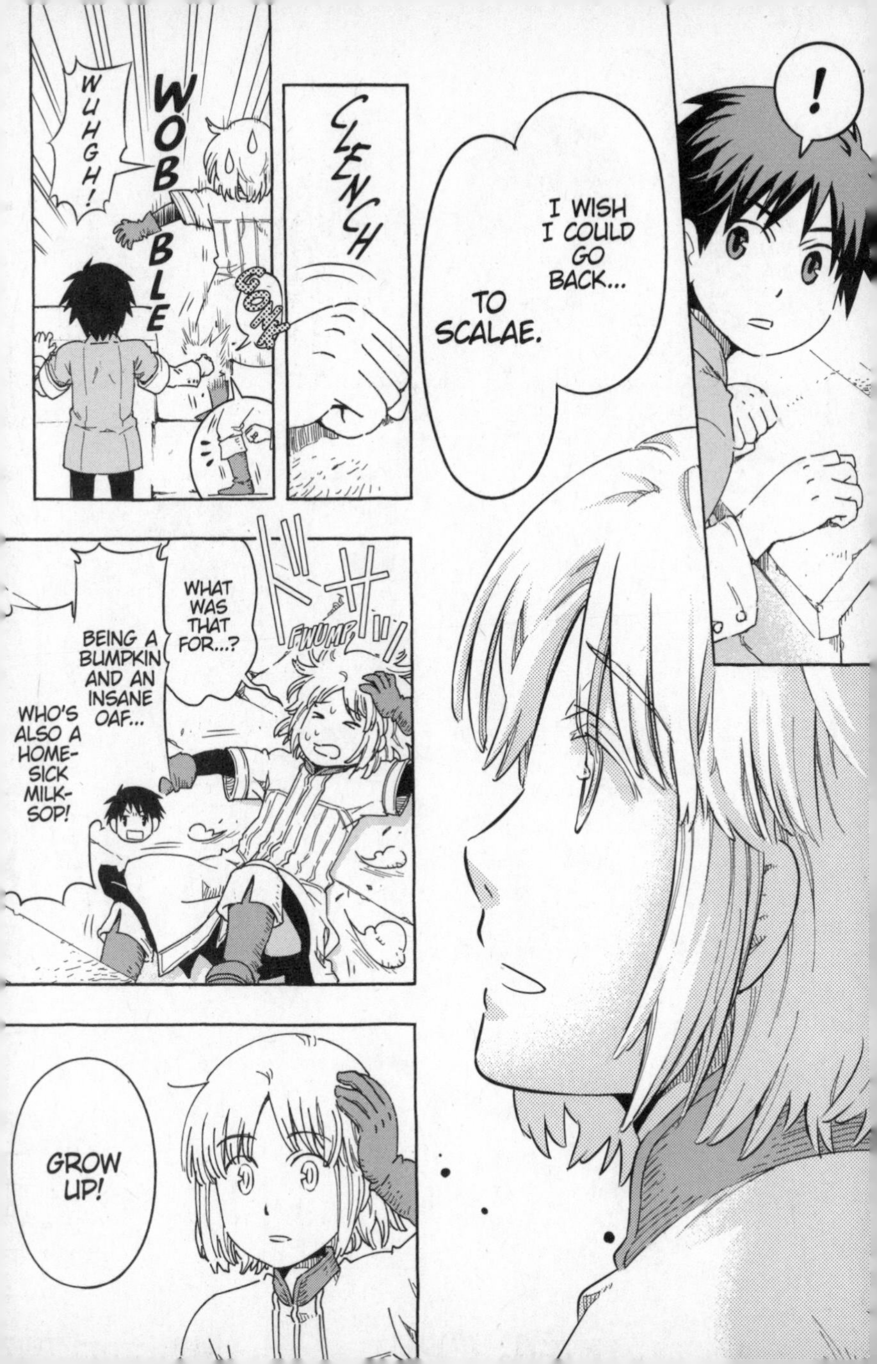
I WISH I COULD GO BACK...
TO SCALAE.
!
CLENCH
WUHGH!
WOBBLE
GONK
WHAT WAS THAT FOR...?
FWUMP
ドサッ
BEING A BUMPKIN AND AN INSANE OAF...
WHO'S ALSO A HOME-SICK MILK-SOP!
GROW UP!

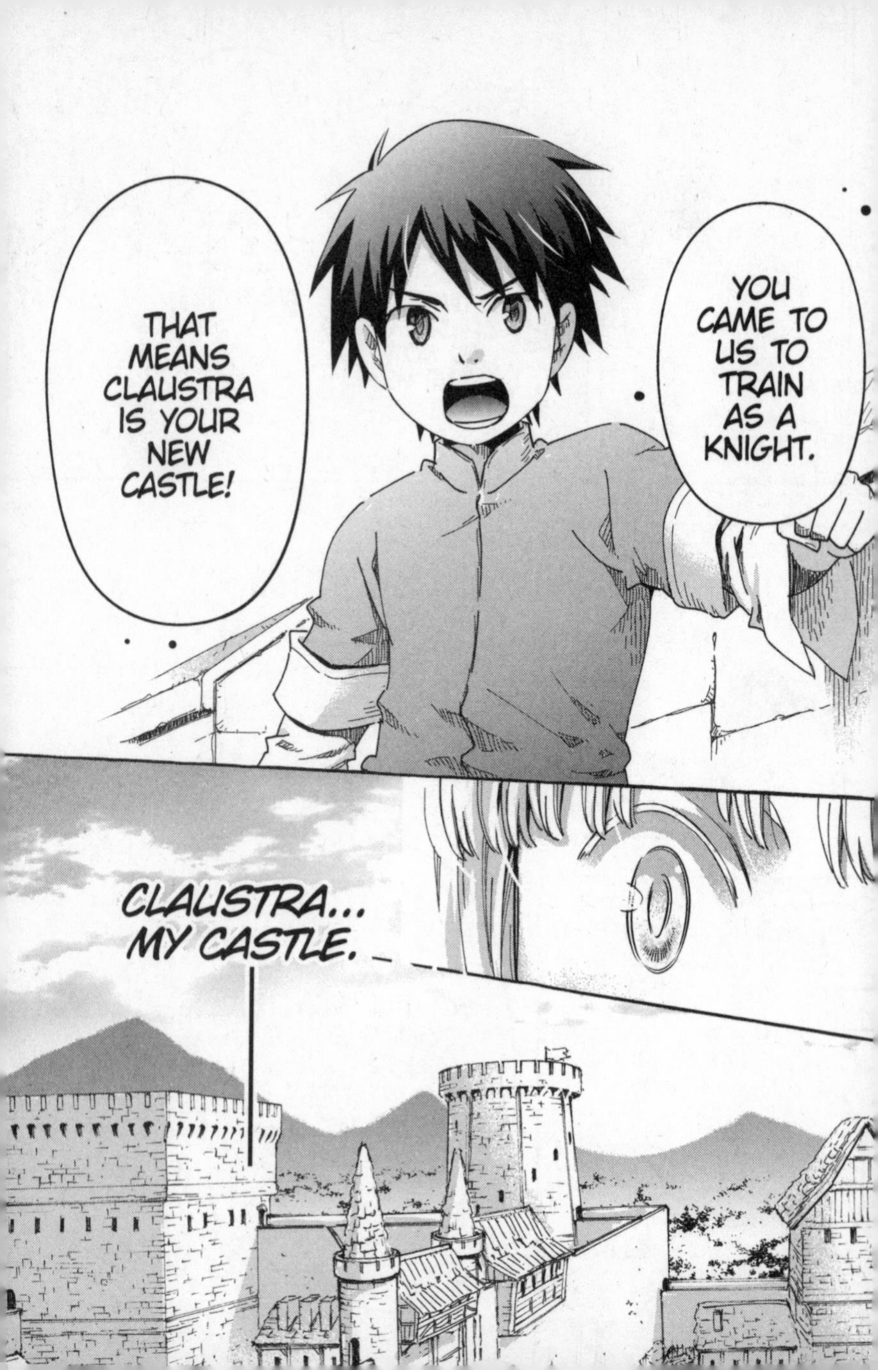
YOU CAME TO US TO TRAIN AS A KNIGHT.
THAT MEANS CLAUSTRA IS YOUR NEW CASTLE!
CLAUSTRA... MY CASTLE.

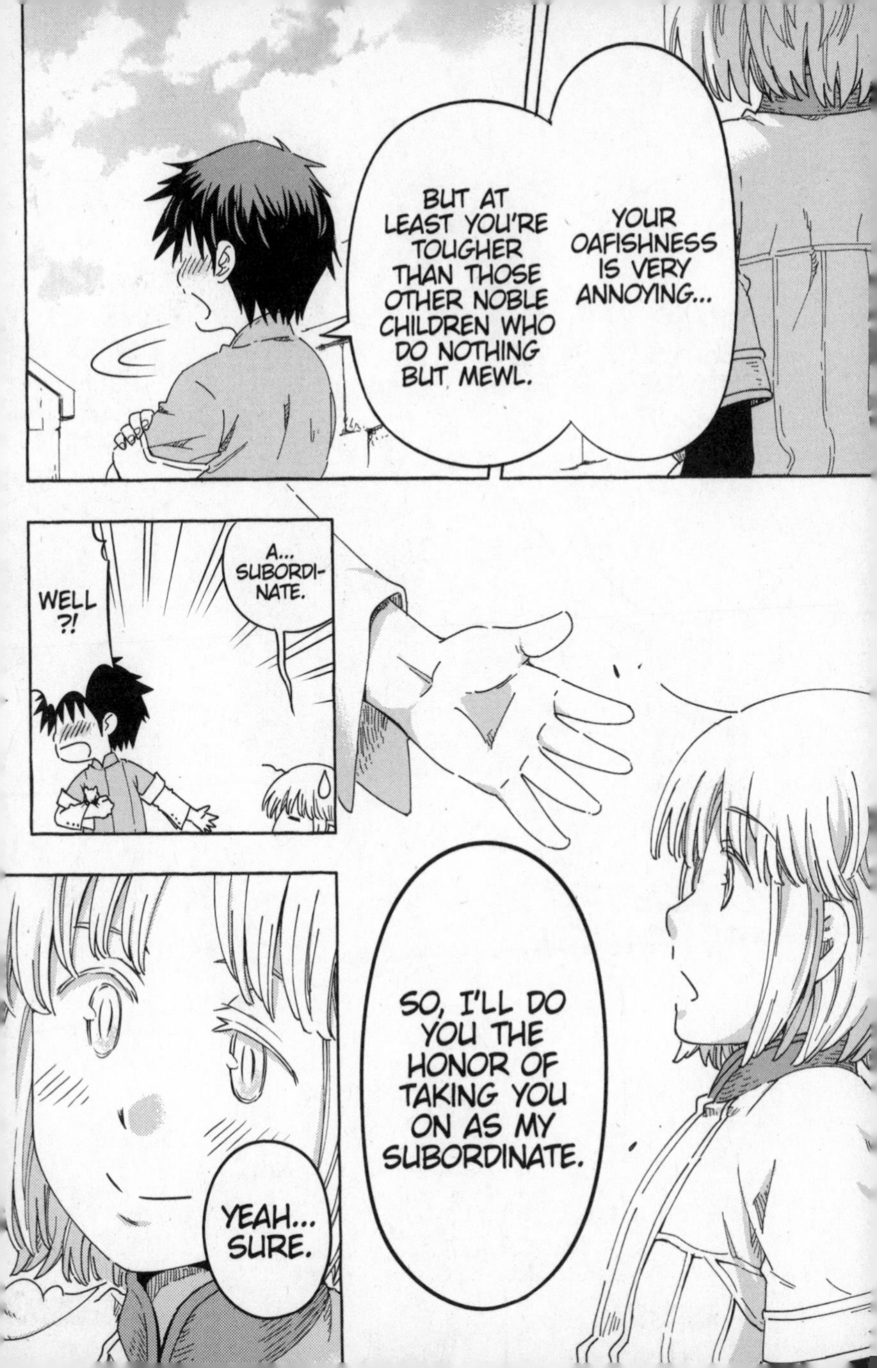
YOUR OAFISHNESS IS VERY ANNOYING...
BUT AT LEAST YOU'RE TOUGHER THAN THOSE OTHER NOBLE CHILDREN WHO DO NOTHING BUT MEWL.
SO, I'LL DO YOU THE HONOR OF TAKING YOU ON AS MY SUBORDINATE.
A... SUBORDI-NATE.
WELL ?!
YEAH... SURE.

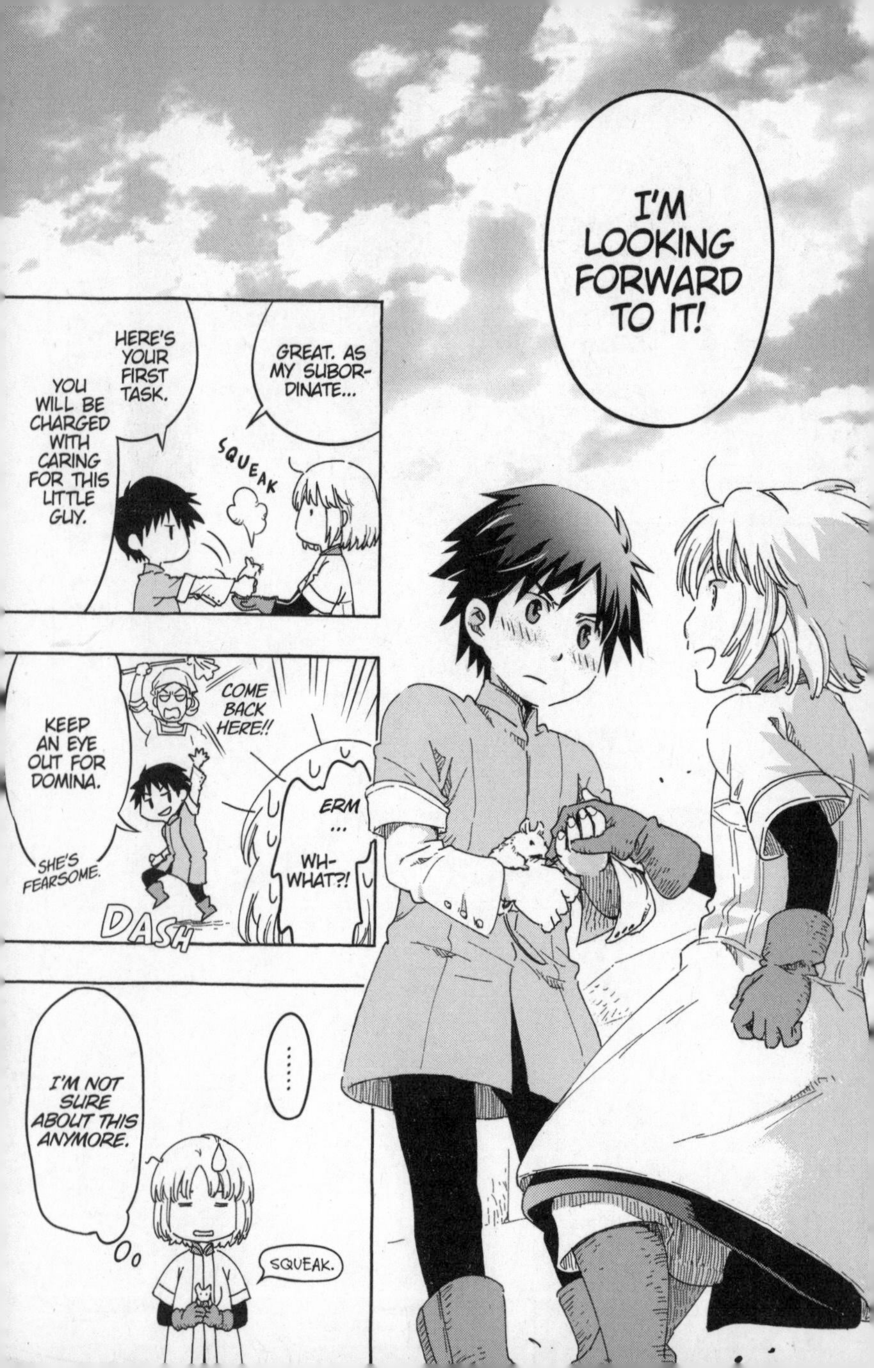
I'M LOOKING FORWARD TO IT!
GREAT. AS MY SUBOR-DINATE...
HERE'S YOUR FIRST TASK.
YOU WILL BE CHARGED WITH CARING FOR THIS LITTLE GUY.
SQUEAK
COME BACK HERE!!
ERM ...
WH-WHAT?!
KEEP AN EYE OUT FOR DOMINA.
SHE'S FEARSOME.
DASH
......
I'M NOT SURE ABOUT THIS ANYMORE.
SQUEAK.

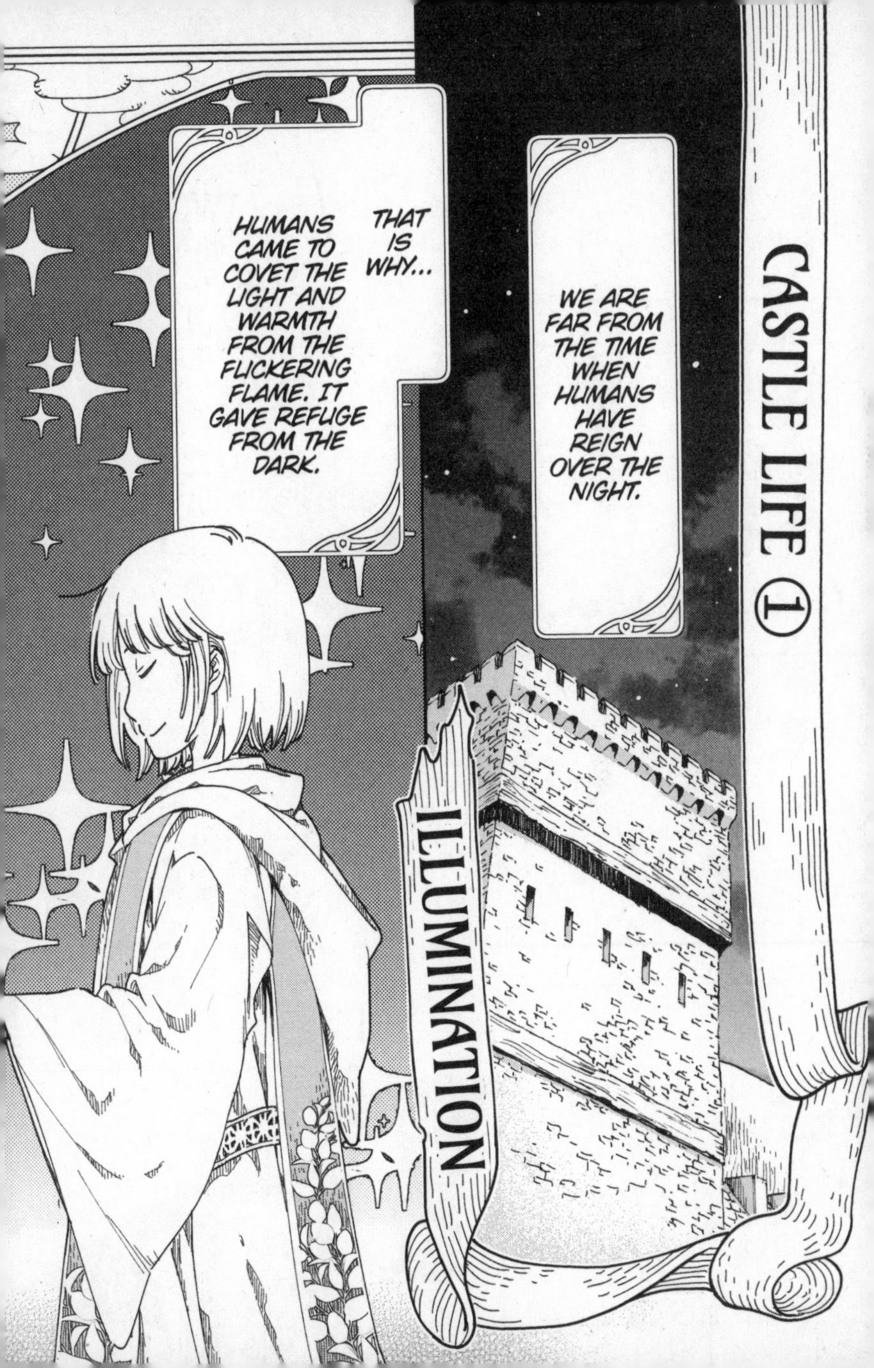

CASTLE LIFE ①
WE ARE FAR FROM THE TIME WHEN HUMANS HAVE REIGN OVER THE NIGHT.
THAT IS WHY...
HUMANS CAME TO COVET THE LIGHT AND WARMTH FROM THE FLICKERING FLAME. IT GAVE REFUGE FROM THE DARK.
ILLUMINATION

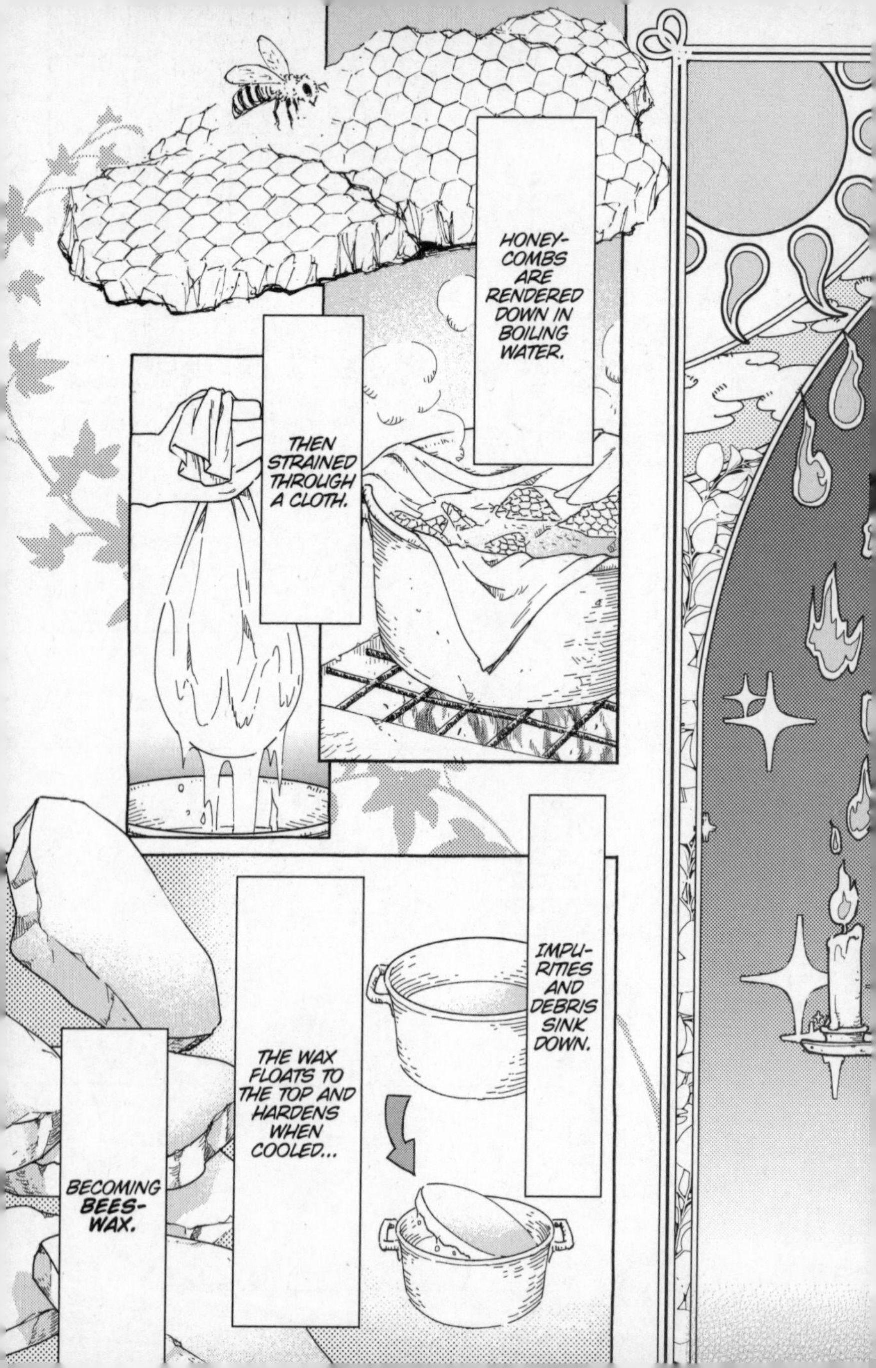
HONEY-COMBS ARE RENDERED DOWN IN BOILING WATER.
THEN STRAINED THROUGH A CLOTH.
IMPURITIES AND DEBRIS SINK DOWN.
THE WAX FLOATS TO THE TOP AND HARDENS WHEN COOLED...
BECOMING BEES-WAX.

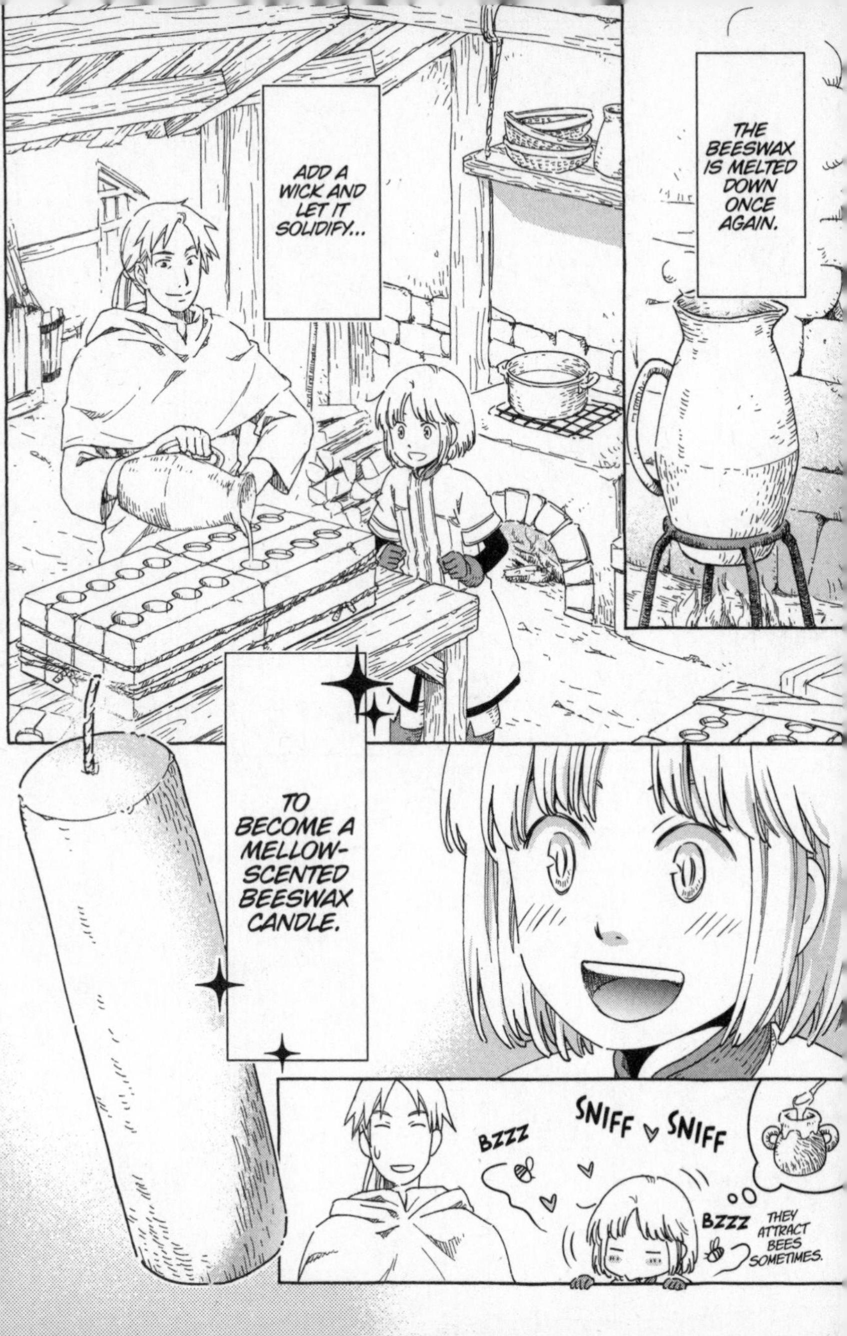
THE BEESWAX IS MELTED DOWN ONCE AGAIN.
ADD A WICK AND LET IT SOLIDIFY...
TO BECOME A MELLOW-SCENTED BEESWAX CANDLE.
SNIFF ♥ SNIFF
BZZZ
BZZZ
THEY ATTRACT BEES SOMETIMES.

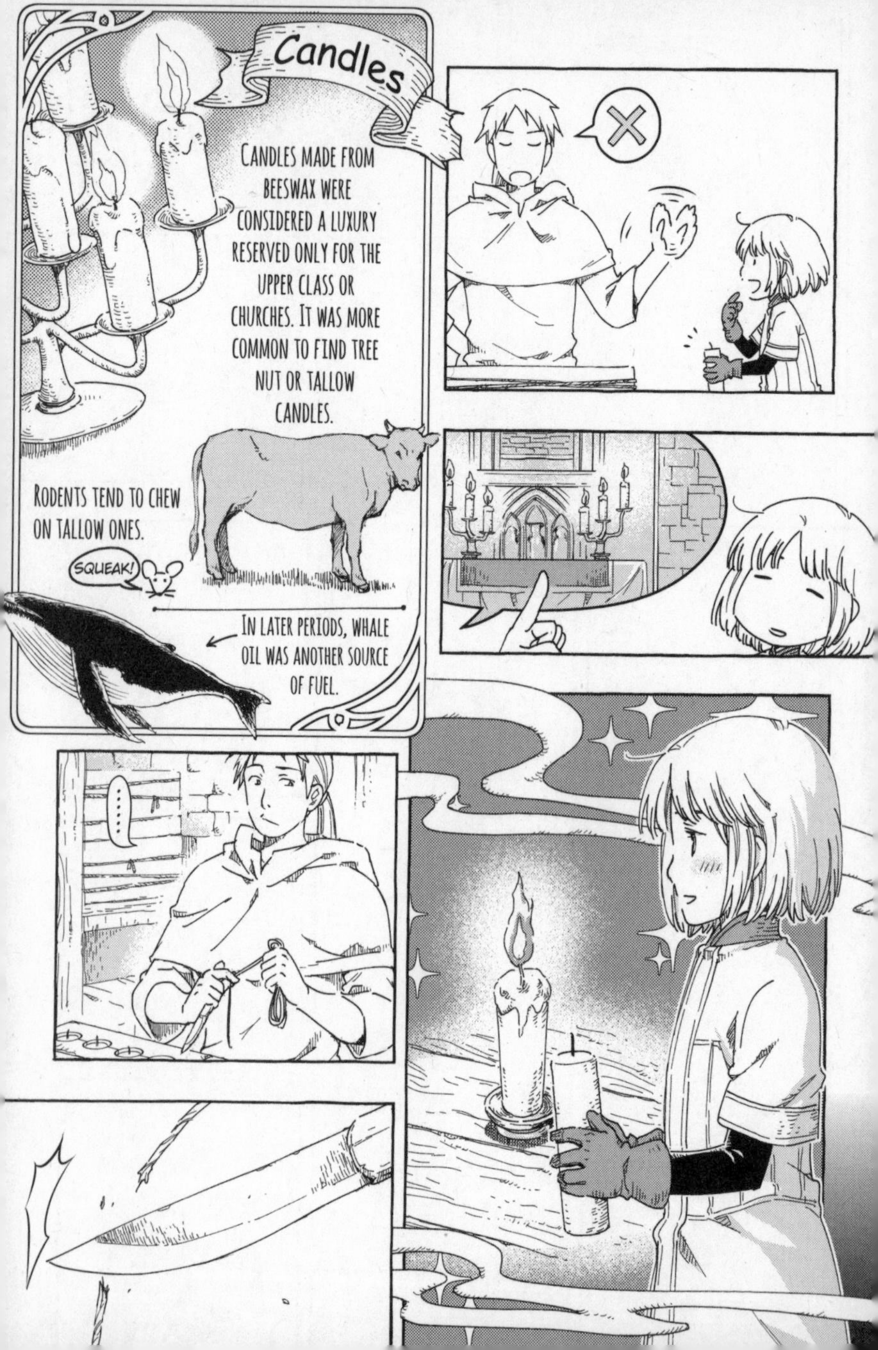

Candles
Candles made from beeswax were considered a luxury reserved only for the upper class or churches. It was more common to find tree nut or tallow candles.
Rodents tend to chew on tallow ones.
SQUEAK!
In later periods, whale oil was another source of fuel.

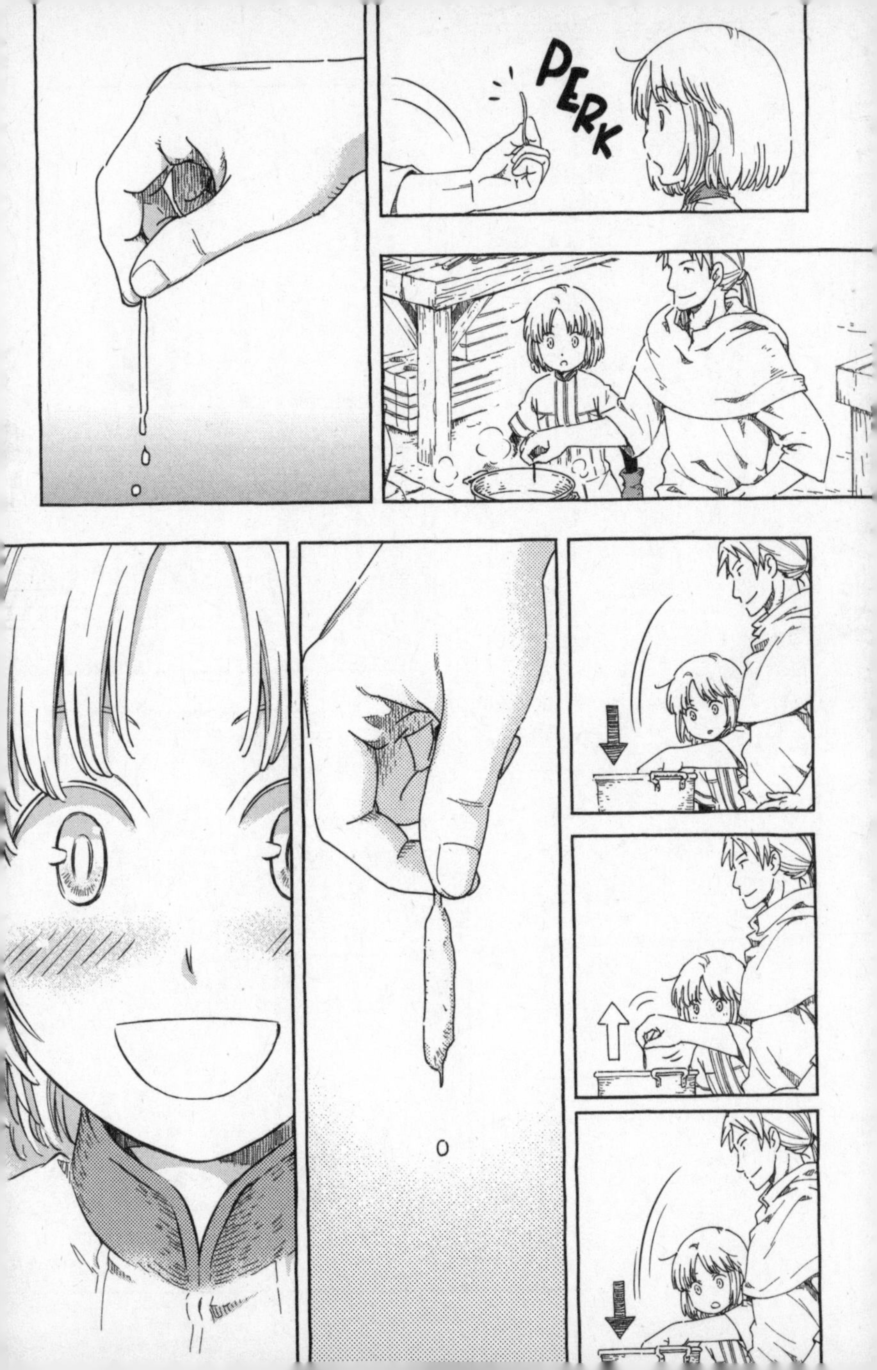
PERK

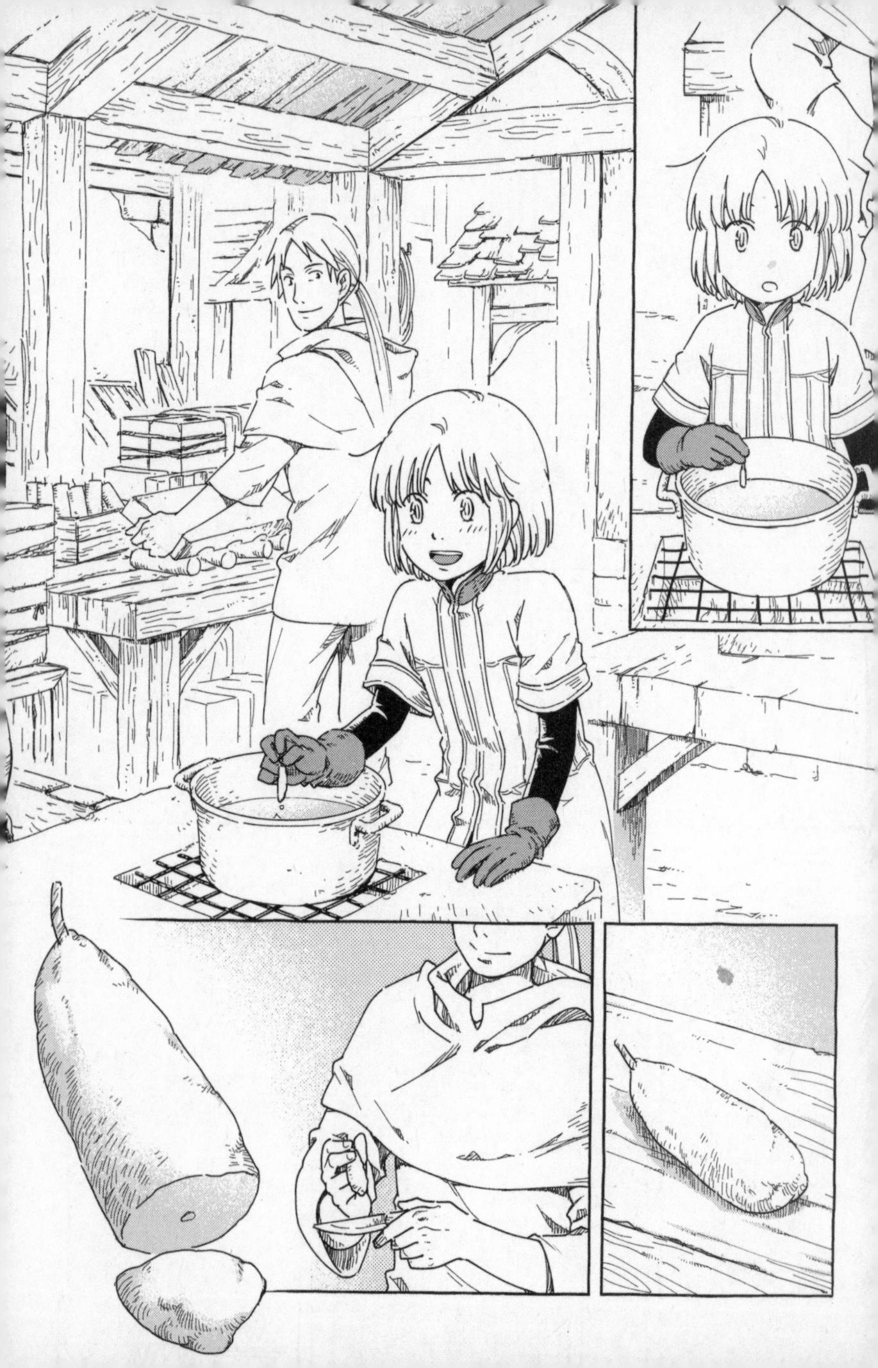

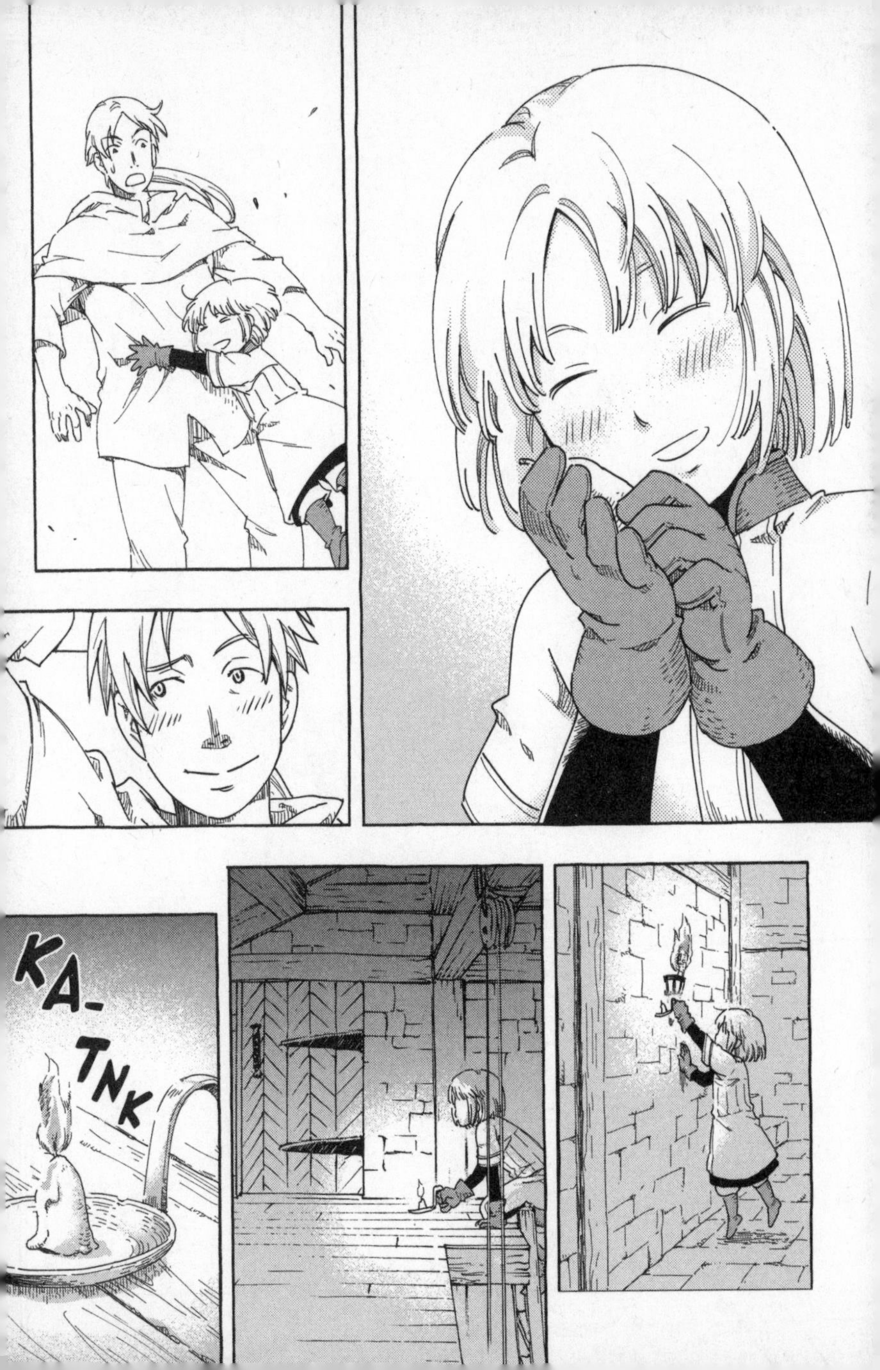
KA-TNK

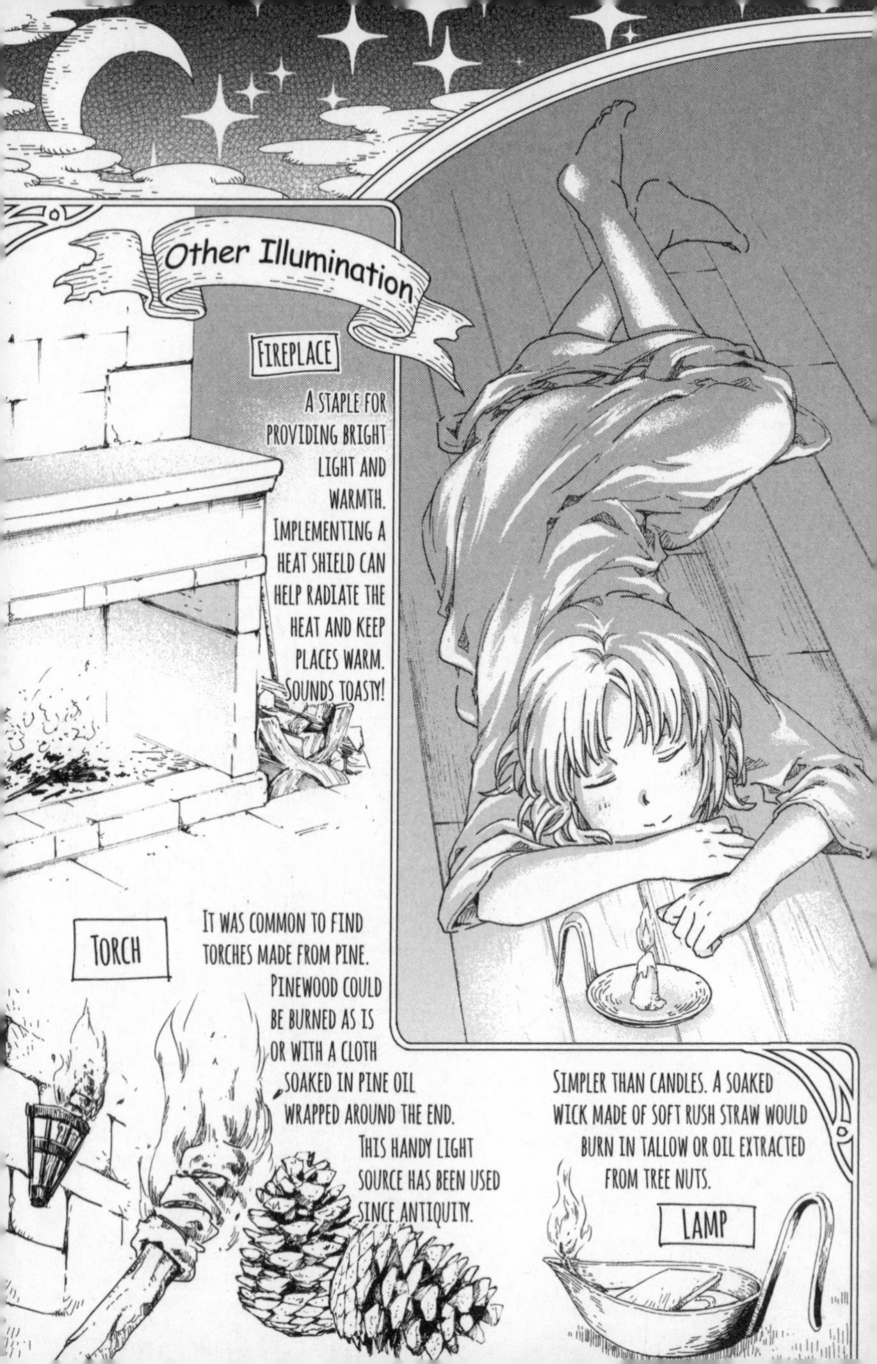
Other Illumination
FIREPLACE
A STAPLE FOR PROVIDING BRIGHT LIGHT AND WARMTH. IMPLEMENTING A HEAT SHIELD CAN HELP RADIATE THE HEAT AND KEEP PLACES WARM. SOUNDS TOASTY!
LAMP
SIMPLER THAN CANDLES. A SOAKED WICK MADE OF SOFT RUSH STRAW WOULD BURN IN TALLOW OR OIL EXTRACTED FROM TREE NUTS.
TORCH
IT WAS COMMON TO FIND TORCHES MADE FROM PINE. PINEWOOD COULD BE BURNED AS IS OR WITH A CLOTH SOAKED IN PINE OIL WRAPPED AROUND THE END. THIS HANDY LIGHT SOURCE HAS BEEN USED SINCE ANTIQUITY.

Candle Clock

CANDLES WERE WIDELY USED AS CLOCKS, BURNED TO INDICATE THE PASSAGE OF TIME. (ALTHOUGH THIS METHOD WASN'T PRECISE...) THERE WERE OIL LAMP CLOCKS TOO.

← EVEN MARKERS TO SHOW HOW MUCH TIME HAD PASSED.

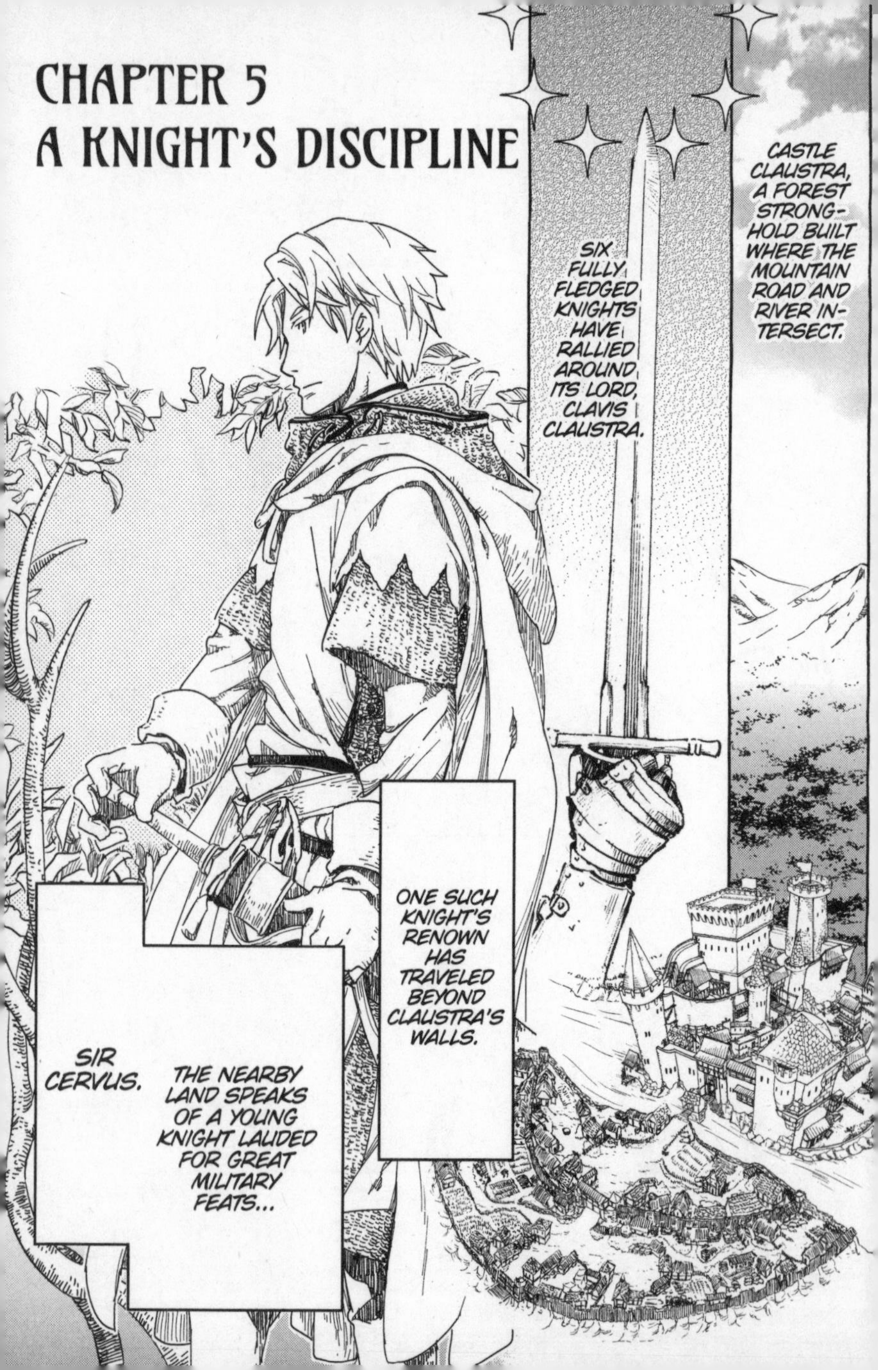
CHAPTER 5
A KNIGHT'S DISCIPLINE
CASTLE CLAUSTRA, A FOREST STRONG-HOLD BUILT WHERE THE MOUNTAIN ROAD AND RIVER IN-TERSECT.
SIX FULLY FLEDGED KNIGHTS HAVE RALLIED AROUND ITS LORD, CLAVIS CLAUSTRA.
ONE SUCH KNIGHT'S RENOWN HAS TRAVELED BEYOND CLAUSTRA'S WALLS.
THE NEARBY LAND SPEAKS OF A YOUNG KNIGHT LAUDED FOR GREAT MILITARY FEATS...
SIR CERVUS.

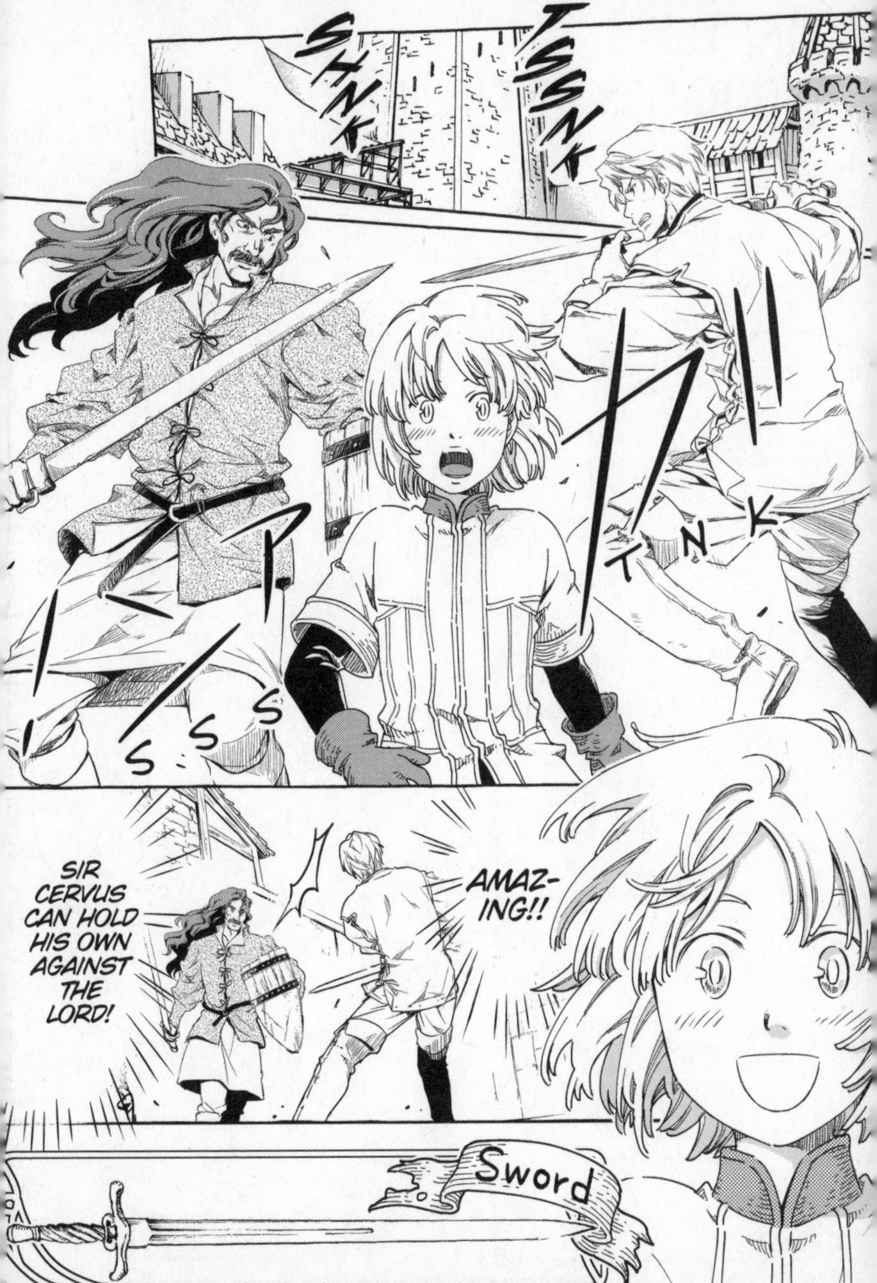
TSSNK
SHNK
TNK
SSS
AMAZ-ING!!
SIR CERVUS CAN HOLD HIS OWN AGAINST THE LORD!
Sword

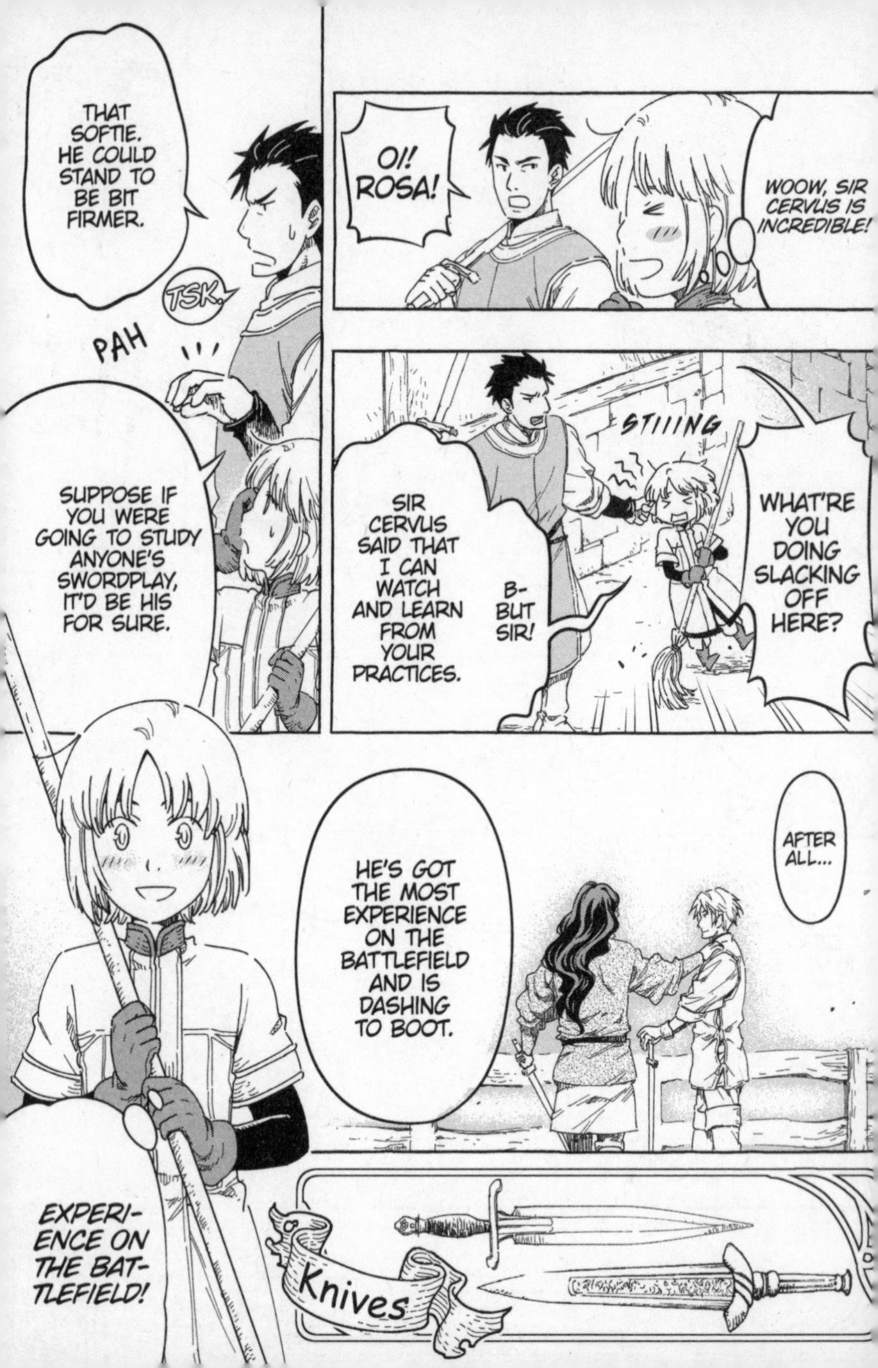
WOOW, SIR CERVUS IS INCREDIBLE!
OI! ROSA!
WHAT'RE YOU DOING SLACKING OFF HERE?
STIIING
B-BUT SIR!
SIR CERVUS SAID THAT I CAN WATCH AND LEARN FROM YOUR PRACTICES.
THAT SOFTIE. HE COULD STAND TO BE BIT FIRMER.
TSK.
PAH
SUPPOSE IF YOU WERE GOING TO STUDY ANYONE'S SWORDPLAY, IT'D BE HIS FOR SURE.
AFTER ALL...
HE'S GOT THE MOST EXPERIENCE ON THE BATTLEFIELD AND IS DASHING TO BOOT.
Knives
EXPERI-ENCE ON THE BAT-TLEFIELD!

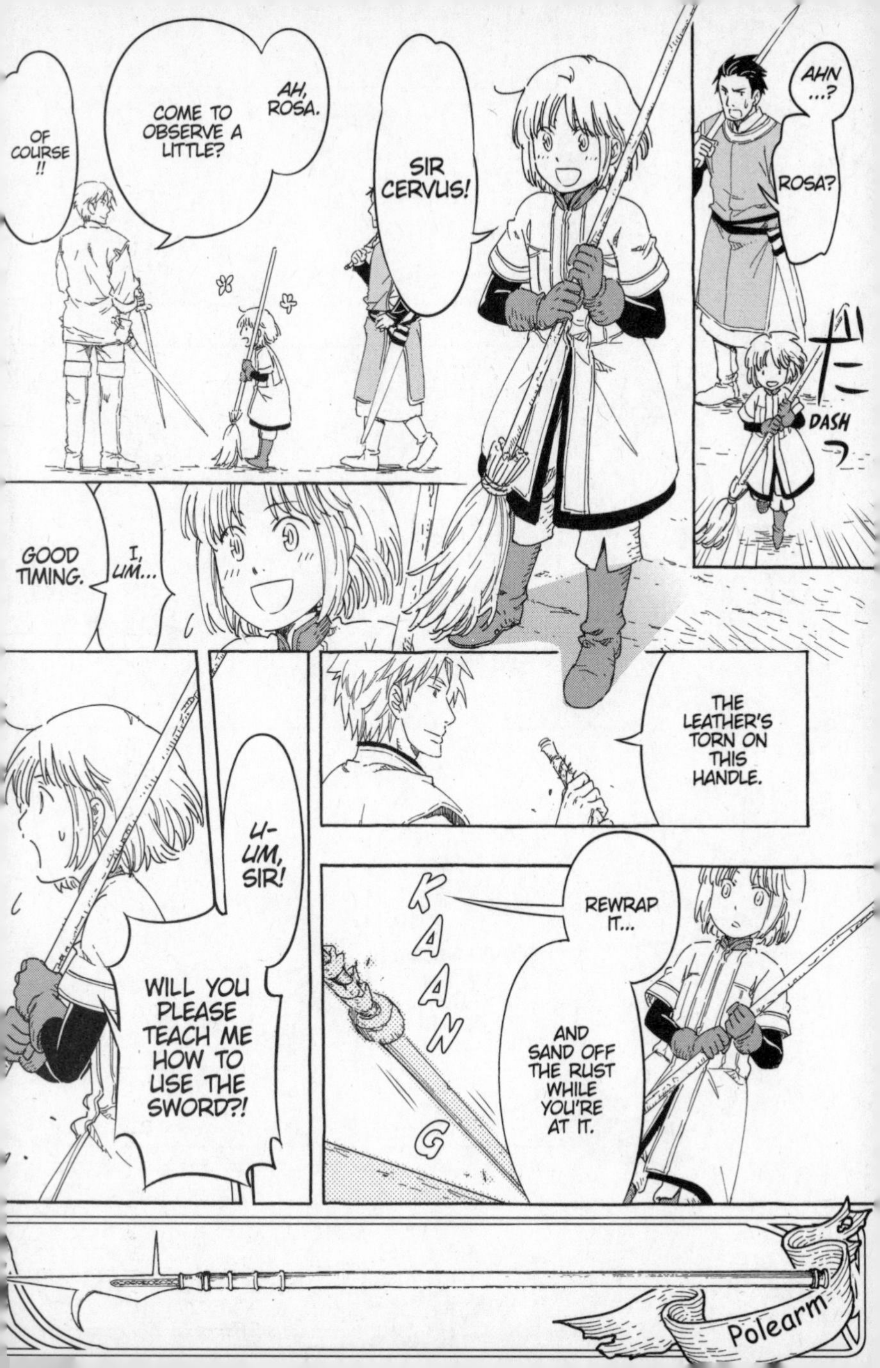
AHN ...?
ROSA?
DASH
SIR CERVUS!
AH, ROSA.
COME TO OBSERVE A LITTLE?
OF COURSE !!
I, UM...
GOOD TIMING.
THE LEATHER'S TORN ON THIS HANDLE.
REWRAP IT...
KAANG
AND SAND OFF THE RUST WHILE YOU'RE AT IT.
U-UM, SIR!
WILL YOU PLEASE TEACH ME HOW TO USE THE SWORD?!
Polearm

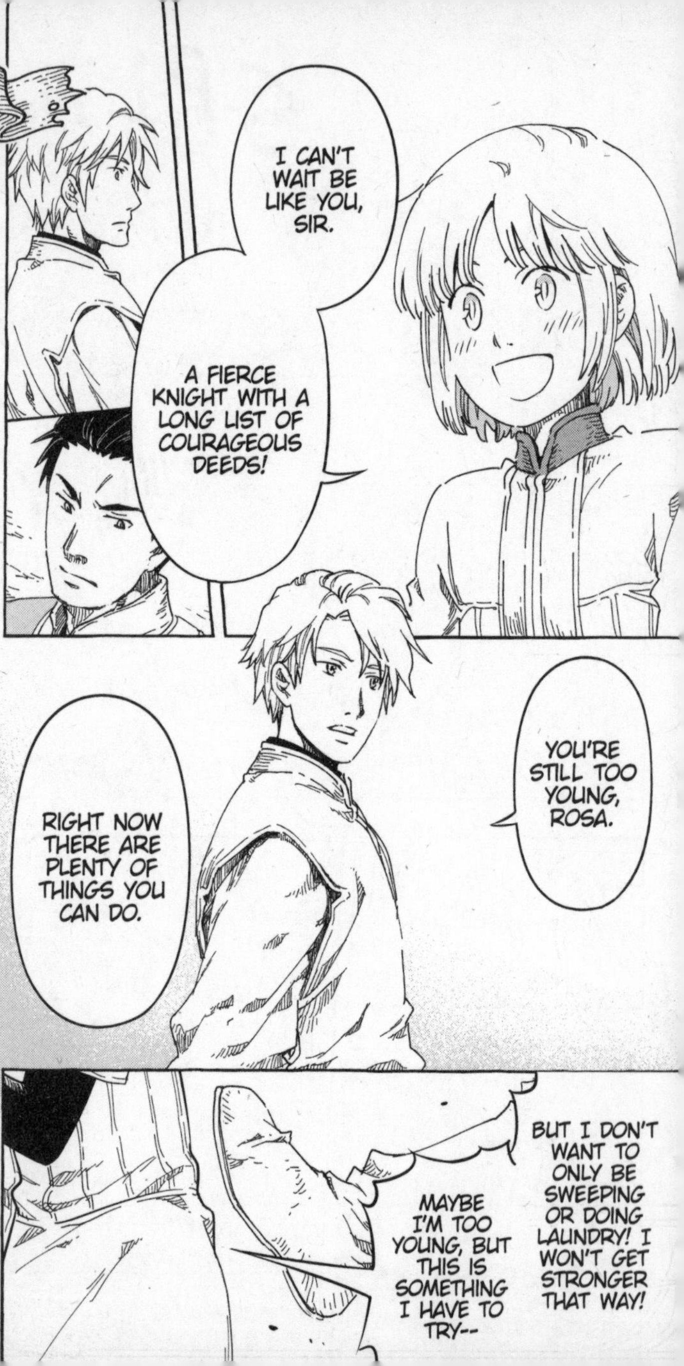
I CAN'T WAIT BE LIKE YOU, SIR.
A FIERCE KNIGHT WITH A LONG LIST OF COURAGEOUS DEEDS!
YOU'RE STILL TOO YOUNG, ROSA.
RIGHT NOW THERE ARE PLENTY OF THINGS YOU CAN DO.
BUT I DON'T WANT TO ONLY BE SWEEPING OR DOING LAUNDRY! I WON'T GET STRONGER THAT WAY!
MAYBE I'M TOO YOUNG, BUT THIS IS SOMETHING I HAVE TO TRY--

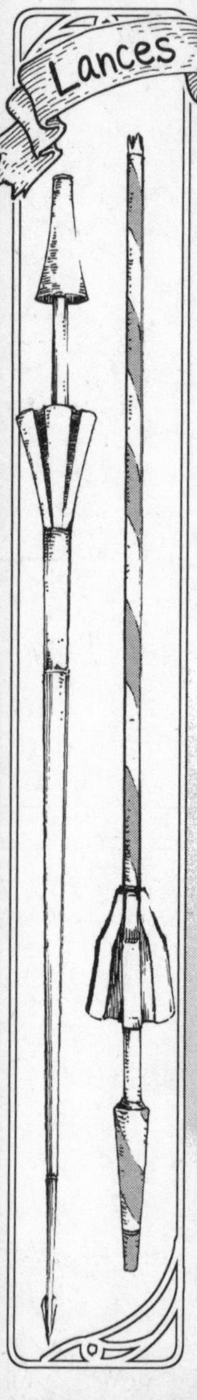
Lances

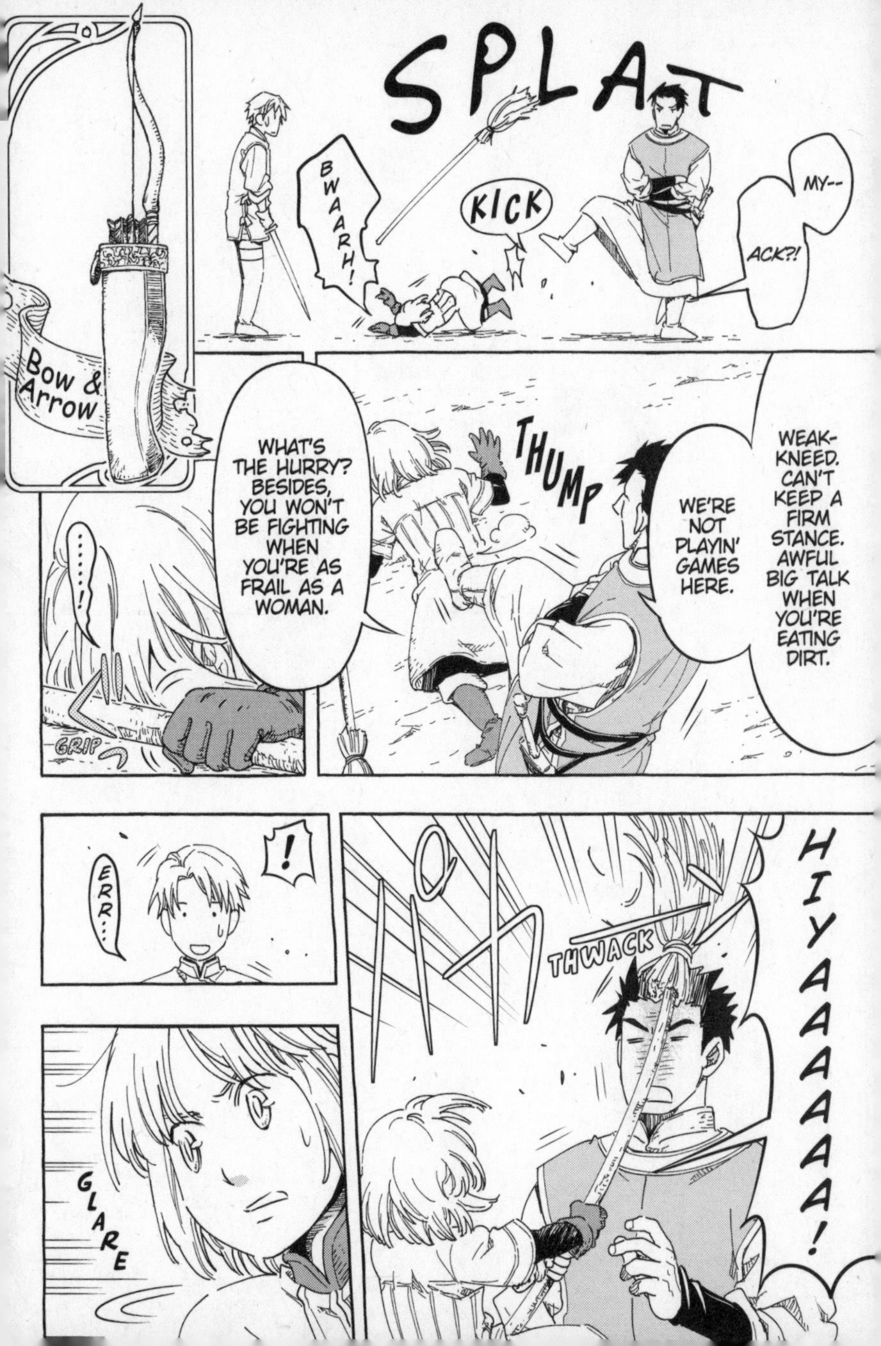

MY-- ACK?!
SPLAT
KICK
BWAARH!
Bow & Arrow
WEAK-KNEED. CAN'T KEEP A FIRM STANCE. AWFUL BIG TALK WHEN YOU'RE EATING DIRT.
WE'RE NOT PLAYIN' GAMES HERE.
THUMP
WHAT'S THE HURRY? BESIDES, YOU WON'T BE FIGHTING WHEN YOU'RE AS FRAIL AS A WOMAN.
......!
GRIP
HIYAAAAAAAA!
THWACK
!
ERR...
GLARE

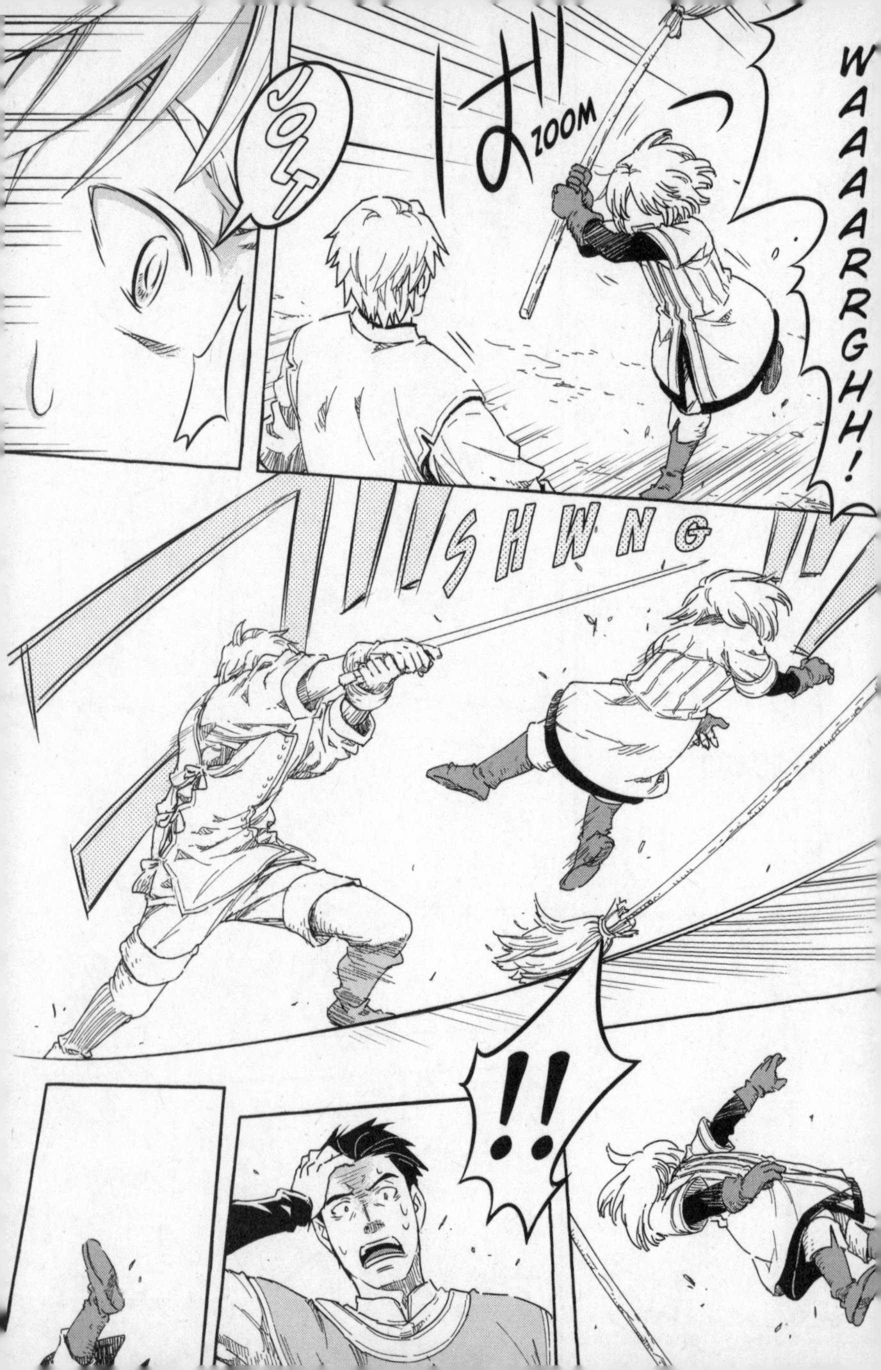
WAAAARRGHH!
ZOOM
JOLT
SHWNG
!!

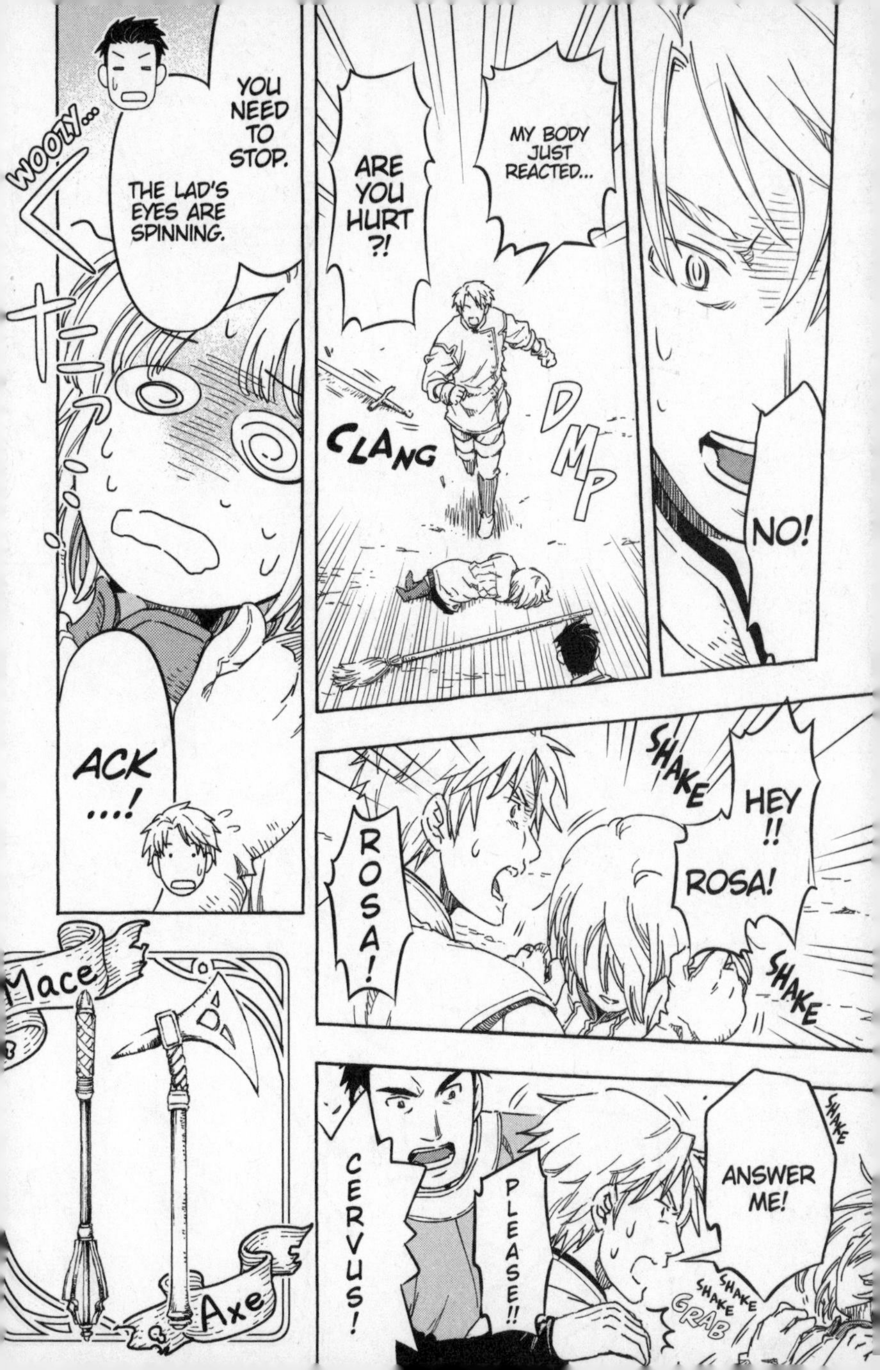
NO!
MY BODY JUST REACTED...
ARE YOU HURT?!
DMP
CLANG
SHAKE
HEY!!
ROSA!
SHAKE
ROSA!
SHAKE
ANSWER ME!
CERVUS!
PLEASE!!
SHAKE
SHAKE
GRAB
WOOZY...
YOU NEED TO STOP.
THE LAD'S EYES ARE SPINNING.
ACK...!
Mace
Axe

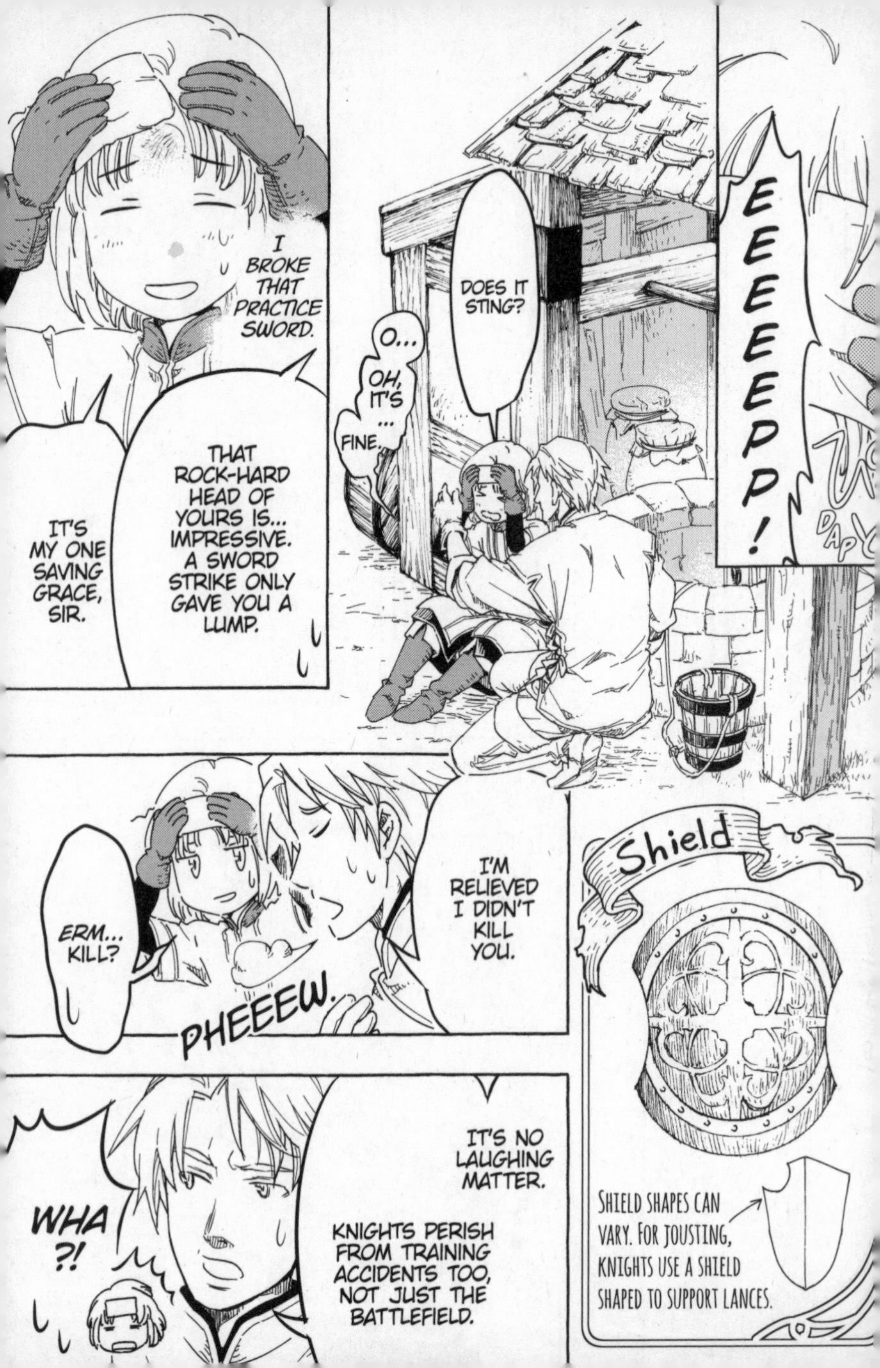
EEEEEEEP!
DAP
DOES IT STING?
O...
OH, IT'S... FINE.
I BROKE THAT PRACTICE SWORD.
THAT ROCK-HARD HEAD OF YOURS IS... IMPRESSIVE. A SWORD STRIKE ONLY GAVE YOU A LUMP.
IT'S MY ONE SAVING GRACE, SIR.
Shield
SHIELD SHAPES CAN VARY. FOR JOUSTING, KNIGHTS USE A SHIELD SHAPED TO SUPPORT LANCES.
I'M RELIEVED I DIDN'T KILL YOU.
ERM... KILL?
PHEEEW.
IT'S NO LAUGHING MATTER.
KNIGHTS PERISH FROM TRAINING ACCIDENTS TOO, NOT JUST THE BATTLEFIELD.
WHA?!

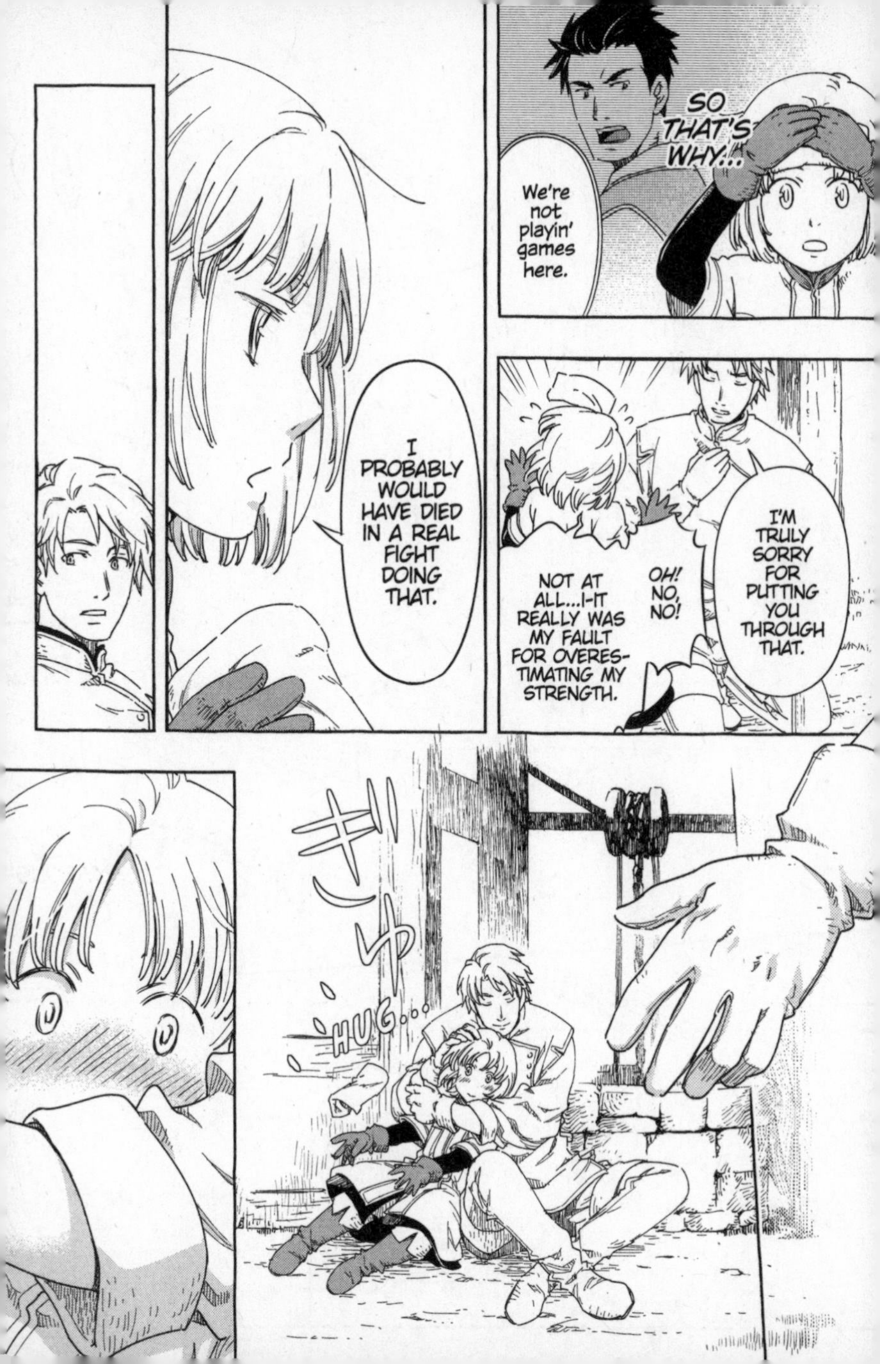
SO THAT'S WHY...
We're not playin' games here.
I'M TRULY SORRY FOR PUTTING YOU THROUGH THAT.
OH! NO, NO!
NOT AT ALL...I-IT REALLY WAS MY FAULT FOR OVERES-TIMATING MY STRENGTH.
I PROBABLY WOULD HAVE DIED IN A REAL FIGHT DOING THAT.
HUG...

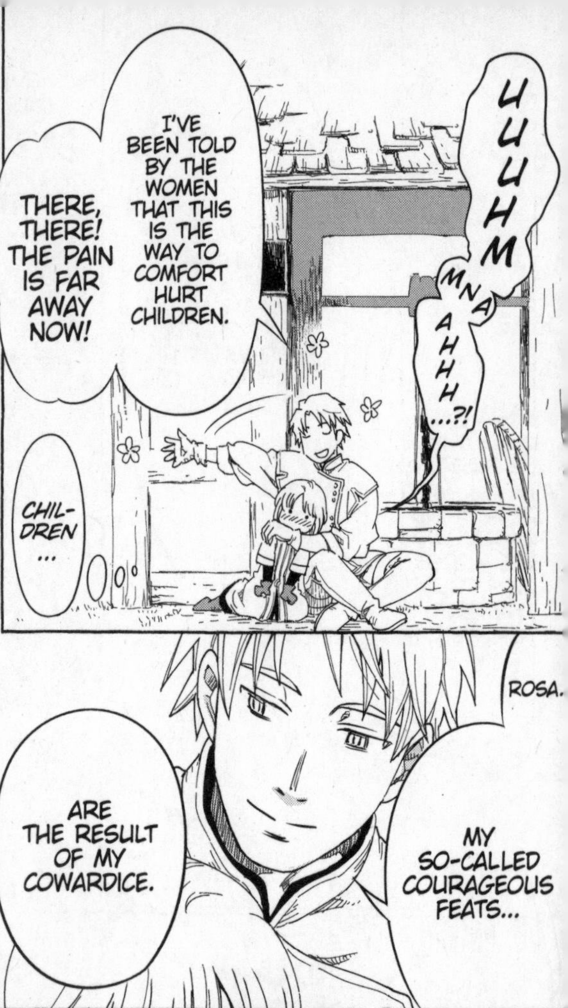
UUUHM
MNA
AHHH...?!
I'VE BEEN TOLD BY THE WOMEN THAT THIS IS THE WAY TO COMFORT HURT CHILDREN.
THERE, THERE! THE PAIN IS FAR AWAY NOW!
CHIL-DREN...
ROSA.
MY SO-CALLED COURAGEOUS FEATS...
ARE THE RESULT OF MY COWARDICE.

BONUS
Spurs

AS MOUNTED UNITS, CANDIDATES RECEIVING KNIGHTHOOD ARE GIVEN A SWORD AS WELL AS A PAIR OF SPURS.

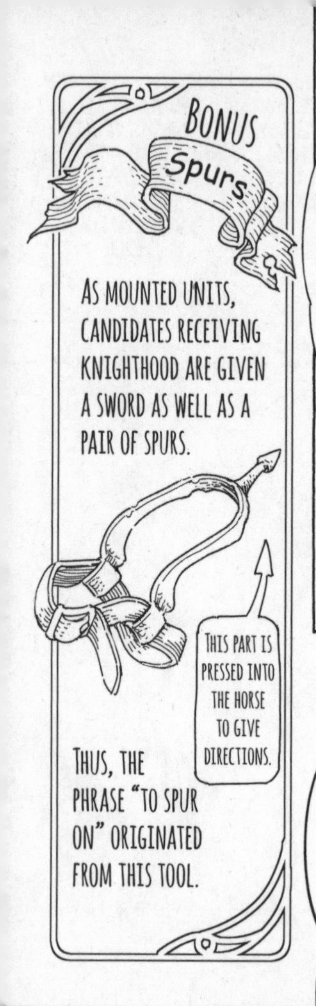
THIS PART IS PRESSED INTO THE HORSE TO GIVE DIRECTIONS.

THUS, THE PHRASE "TO SPUR ON" ORIGINATED FROM THIS TOOL.

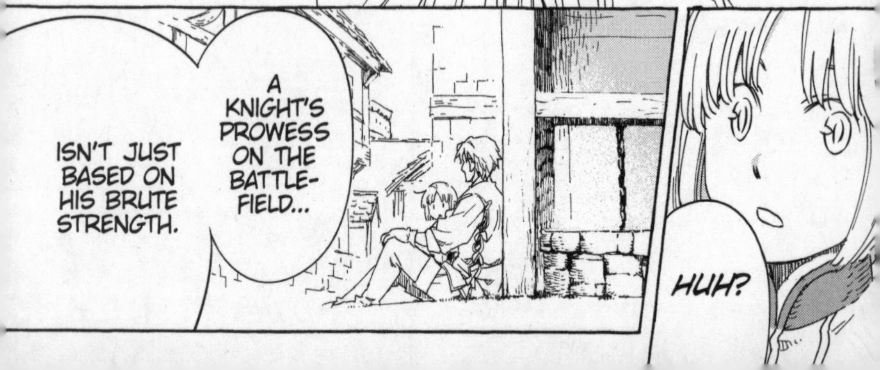
HUH?
A KNIGHT'S PROWESS ON THE BATTLE-FIELD...
ISN'T JUST BASED ON HIS BRUTE STRENGTH.

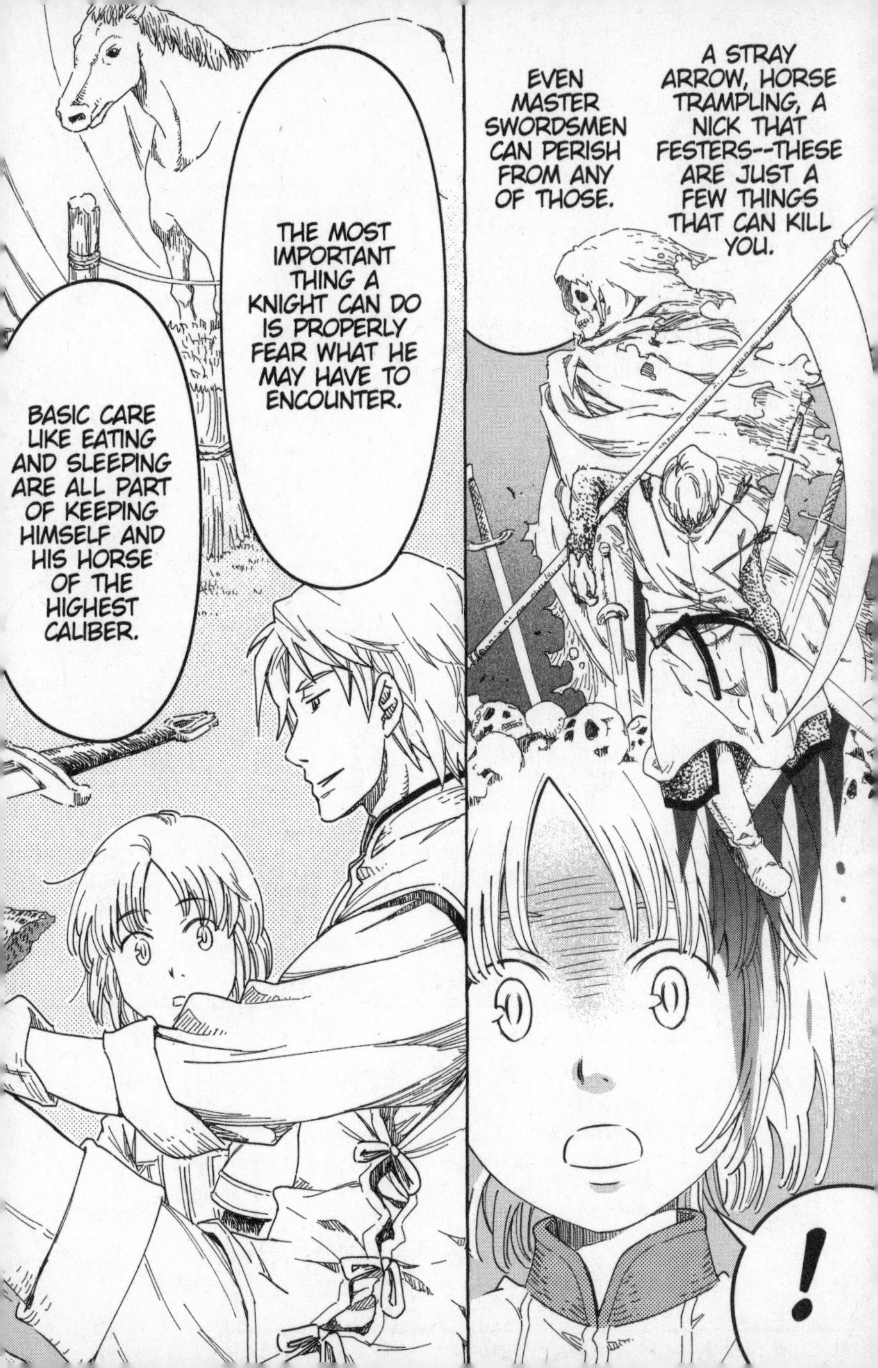
A STRAY ARROW, HORSE TRAMPLING, A NICK THAT FESTERS--THESE ARE JUST A FEW THINGS THAT CAN KILL YOU.
EVEN MASTER SWORDSMEN CAN PERISH FROM ANY OF THOSE.
!
THE MOST IMPORTANT THING A KNIGHT CAN DO IS PROPERLY FEAR WHAT HE MAY HAVE TO ENCOUNTER.
BASIC CARE LIKE EATING AND SLEEPING ARE ALL PART OF KEEPING HIMSELF AND HIS HORSE OF THE HIGHEST CALIBER.

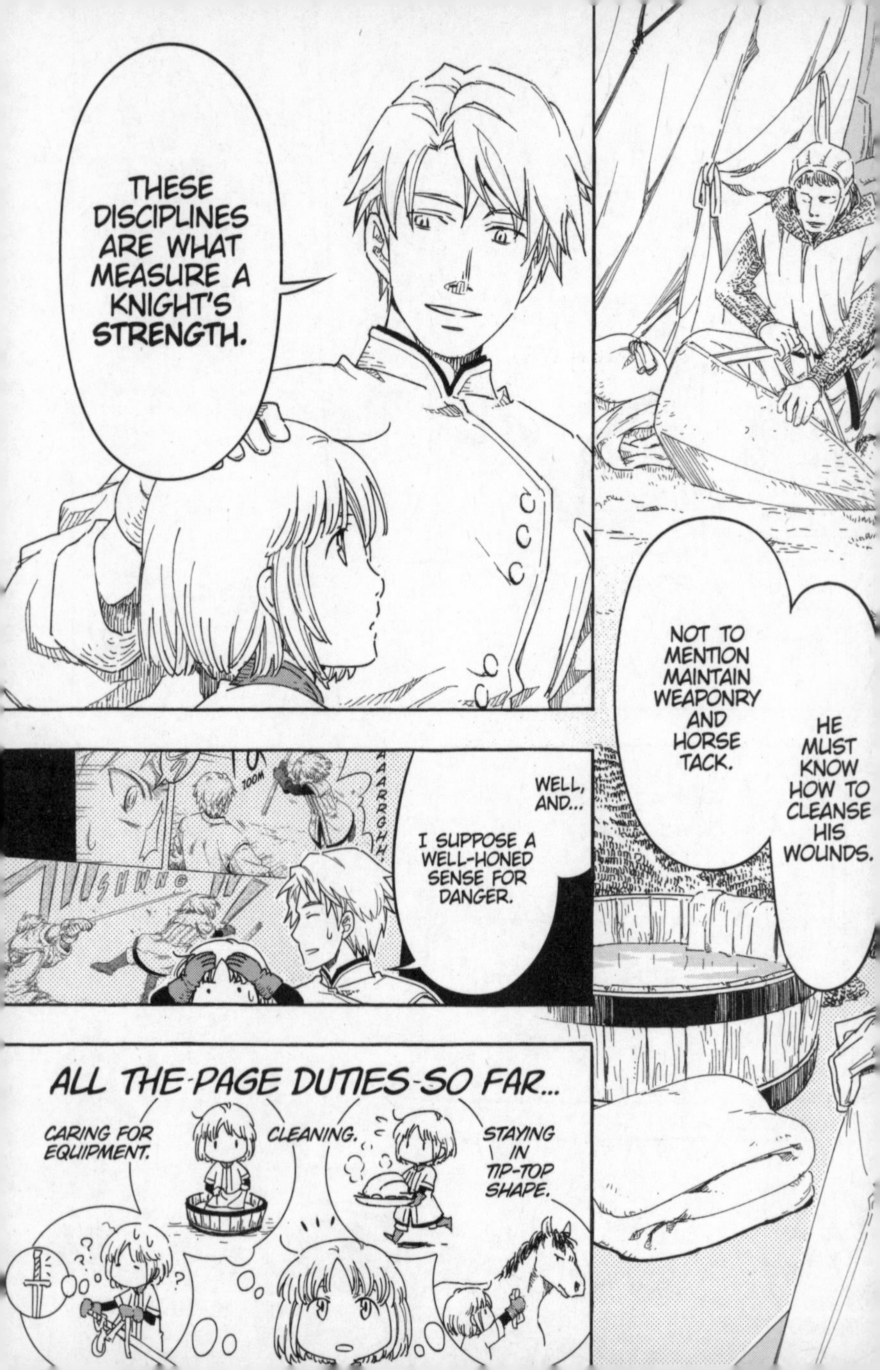

NOT TO MENTION MAINTAIN WEAPONRY AND HORSE TACK.
HE MUST KNOW HOW TO CLEANSE HIS WOUNDS.
THESE DISCIPLINES ARE WHAT MEASURE A KNIGHT'S STRENGTH.
WELL, AND...
I SUPPOSE A WELL-HONED SENSE FOR DANGER.
AAARRGHH
ZOOM
SHWNG
ALL THE-PAGE DUTIES-SO FAR...
STAYING IN TIP-TOP SHAPE.
CLEANING.
CARING FOR EQUIPMENT.

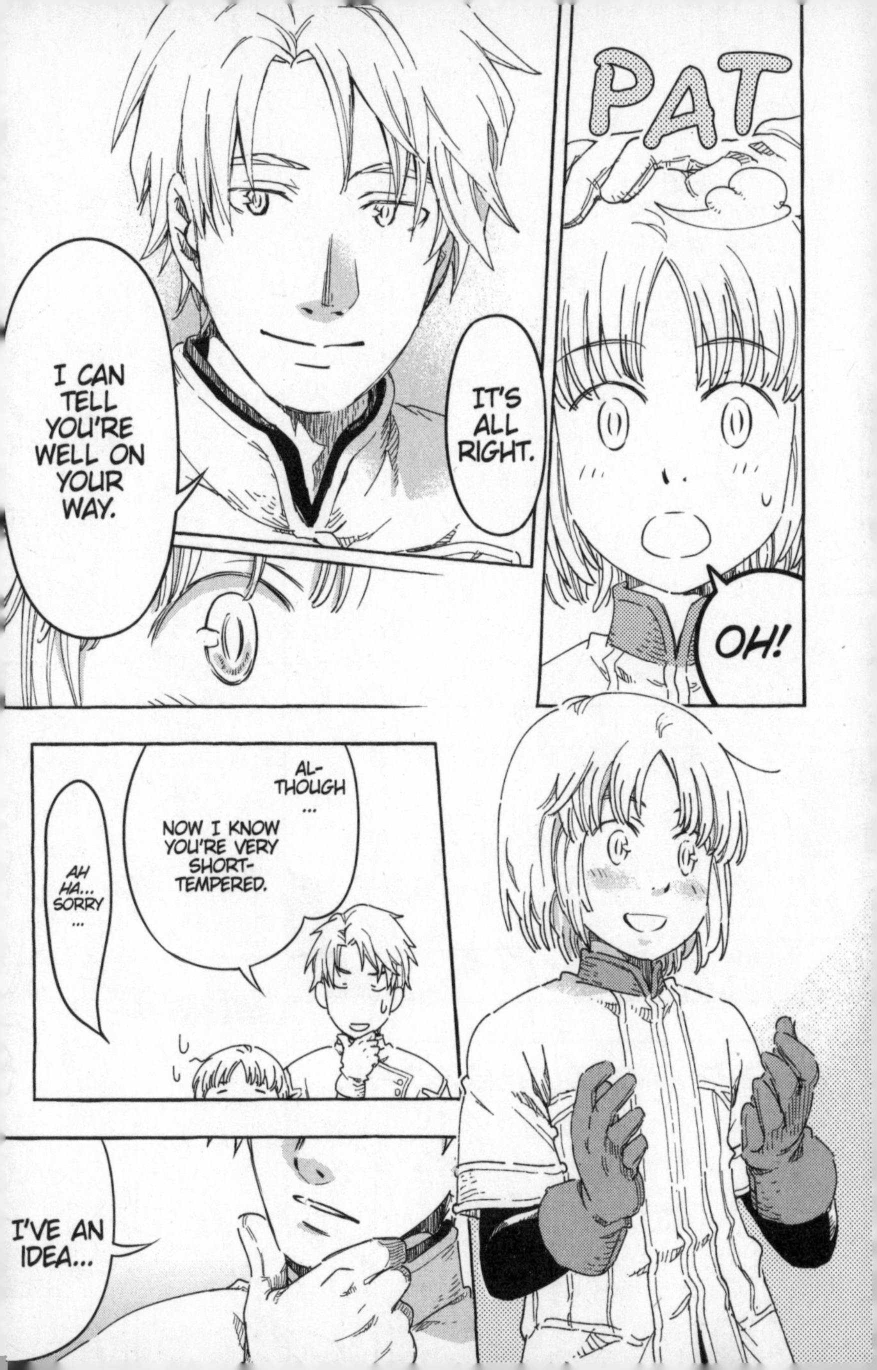
PAT
OH!
IT'S ALL RIGHT.
I CAN TELL YOU'RE WELL ON YOUR WAY.
AL-THOUGH ...
NOW I KNOW YOU'RE VERY SHORT-TEMPERED.
AH HA... SORRY ...
I'VE AN IDEA...

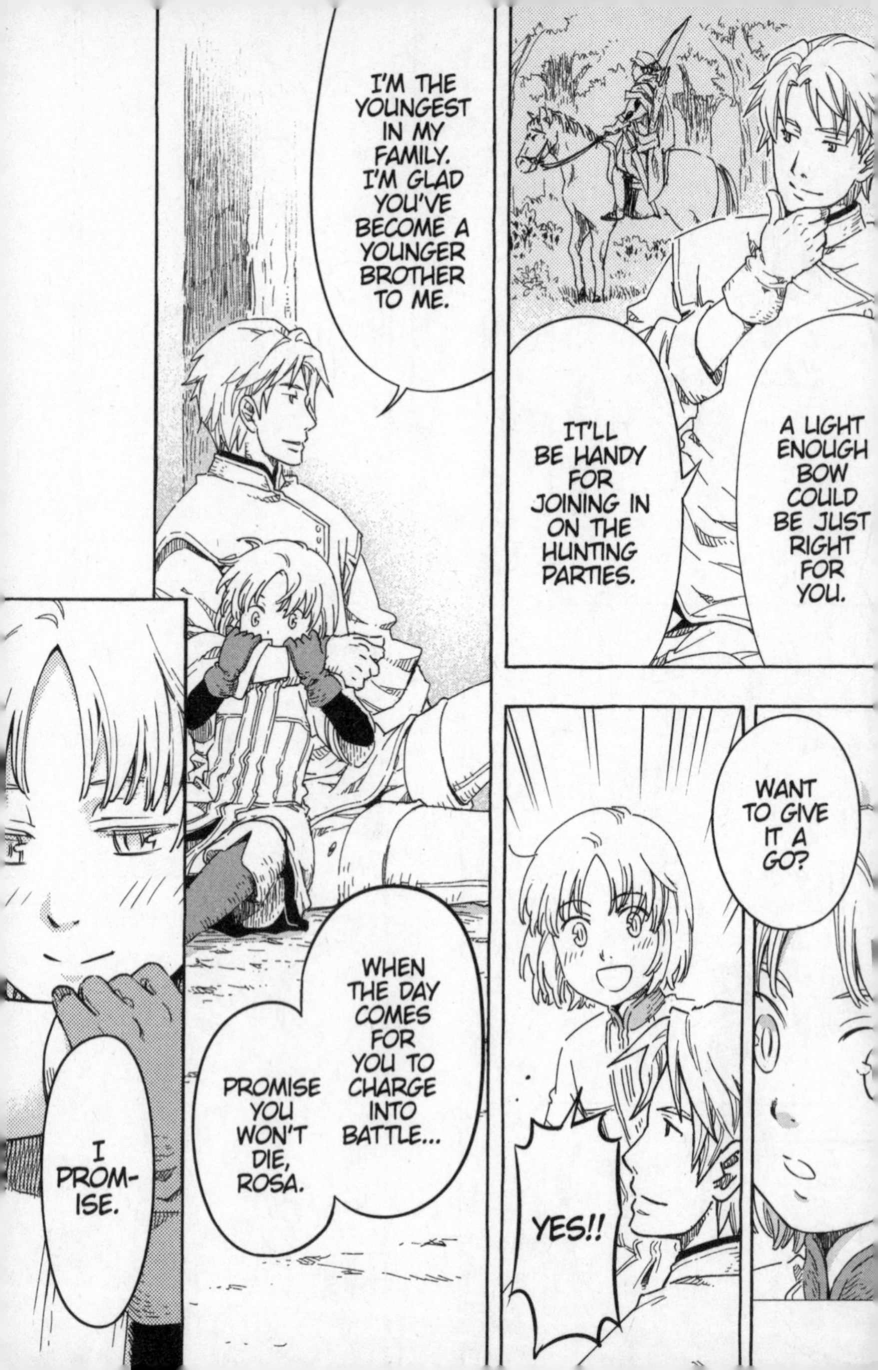
A LIGHT ENOUGH BOW COULD BE JUST RIGHT FOR YOU.
IT'LL BE HANDY FOR JOINING IN ON THE HUNTING PARTIES.
WANT TO GIVE IT A GO?
YES!!
I'M THE YOUNGEST IN MY FAMILY. I'M GLAD YOU'VE BECOME A YOUNGER BROTHER TO ME.
WHEN THE DAY COMES FOR YOU TO CHARGE INTO BATTLE...
PROMISE YOU WON'T DIE, ROSA.
I PROM-ISE.

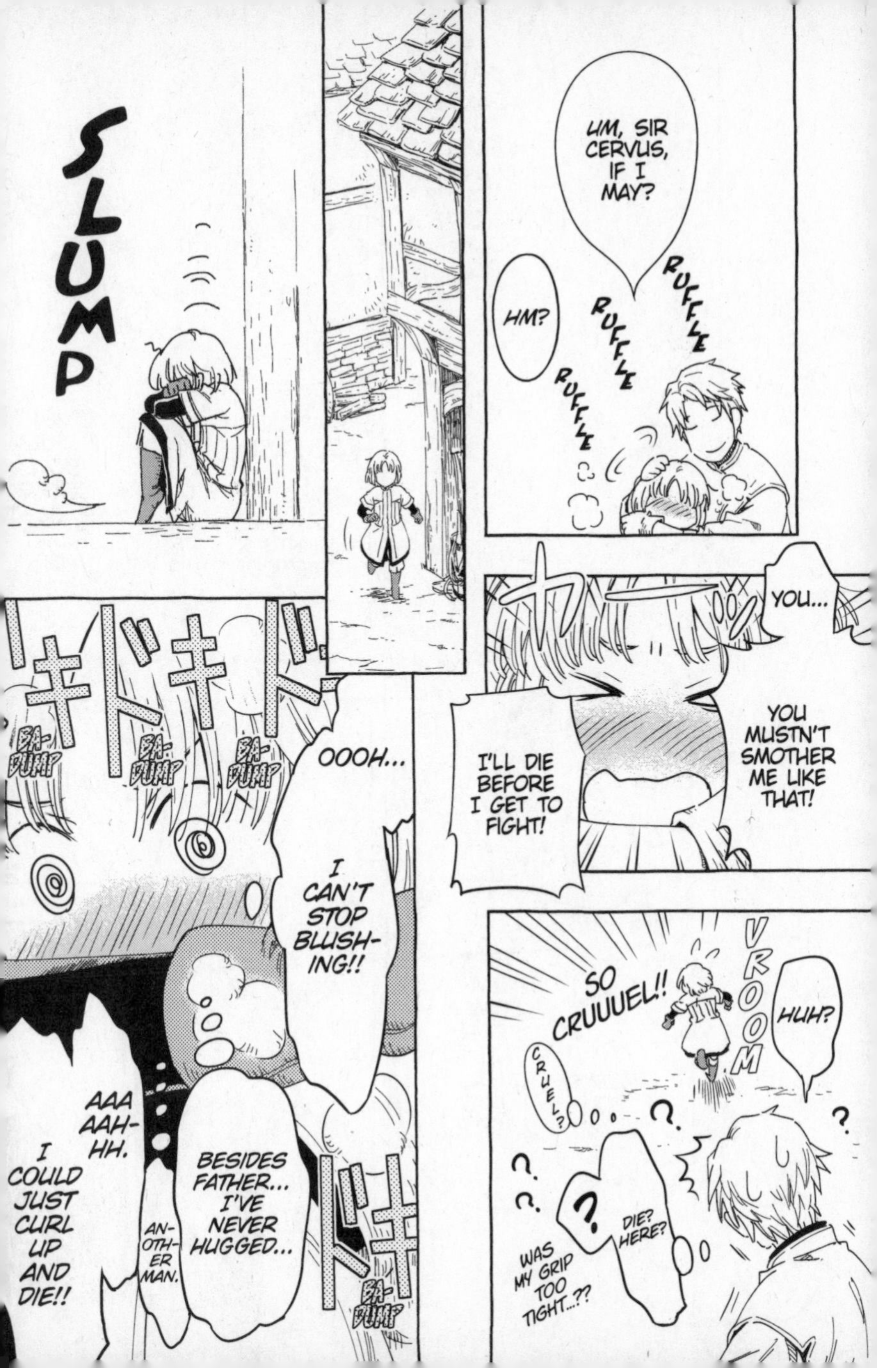
UM, SIR CERVUS, IF I MAY?
RUFFLE
RUFFLE
RUFFLE
HM?
YOU...
YOU MUSTN'T SMOTHER ME LIKE THAT!
I'LL DIE BEFORE I GET TO FIGHT!
SO CRUUUEL!!
VROOM
HUH?
CRUEL?
DIE? HERE?
WAS MY GRIP TOO TIGHT...??
SLUMP
ドキドキドキ
BA-DUMP
BA-DUMP
BA-DUMP
OOOH...
I CAN'T STOP BLUSHING!!
BESIDES FATHER... I'VE NEVER HUGGED...
AN-OTH-ER MAN.
ドキ
BA-DUMP
AAA AAH-HH.
I COULD JUST CURL UP AND DIE!!

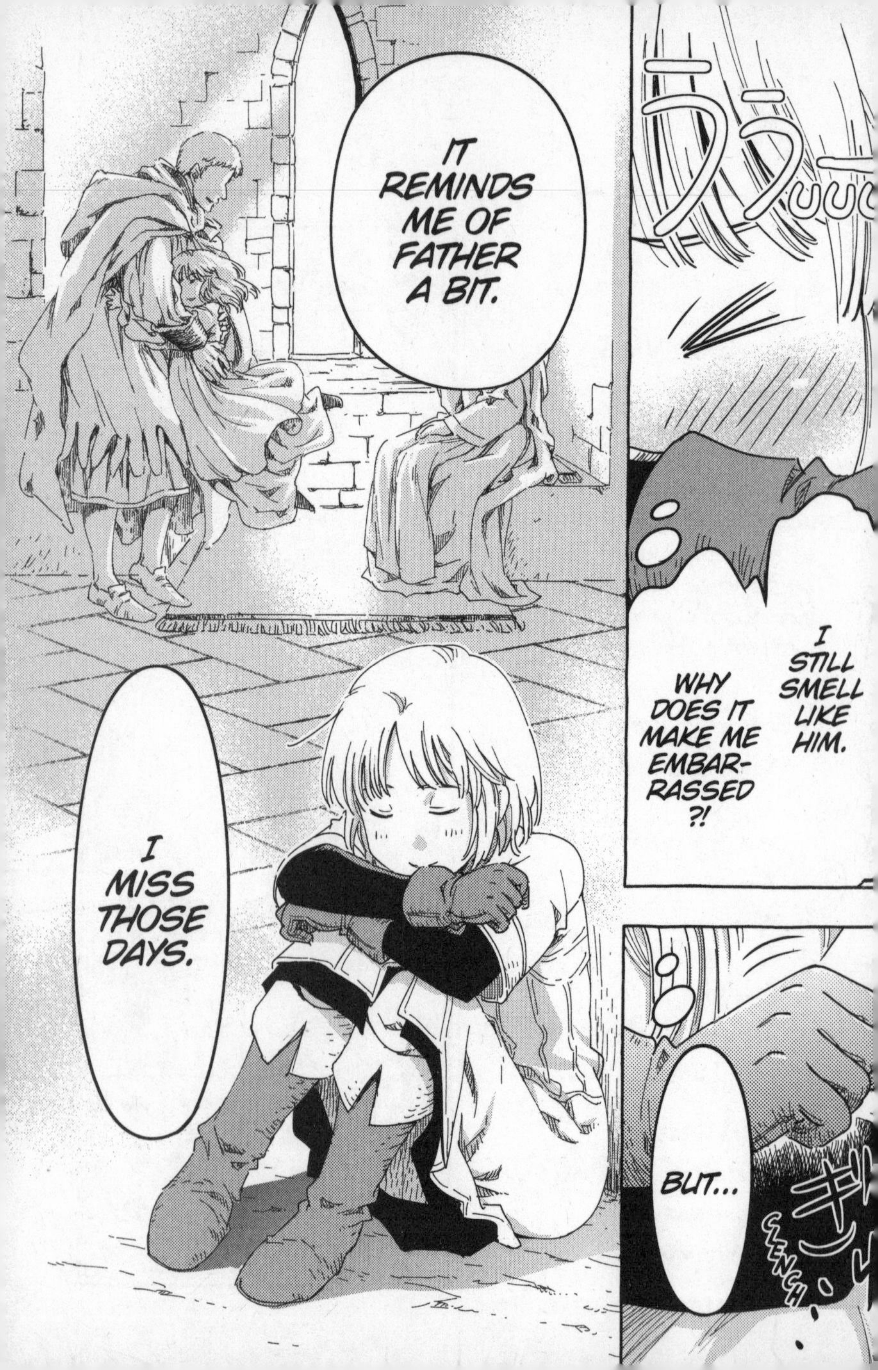
I STILL SMELL LIKE HIM.
WHY DOES IT MAKE ME EMBARRASSED?!
BUT...
CLENCH
IT REMINDS ME OF FATHER A BIT.
I MISS THOSE DAYS.

Cervus

A knight who serves at Castle Claustra. Cordial and handsome, Cervus' many skills make him an exemplary knight. Best described as hard-working rather than naturally talented.

- Favorite Foods
  White Bread

- Least Favorite Foods
  Cheese
  Strong acidic foods

- Talents
  Needs little sleep
  Hunting

- Weaknesses
  Slender physique
  Tone-deaf
  (unaware of it)

Cervus

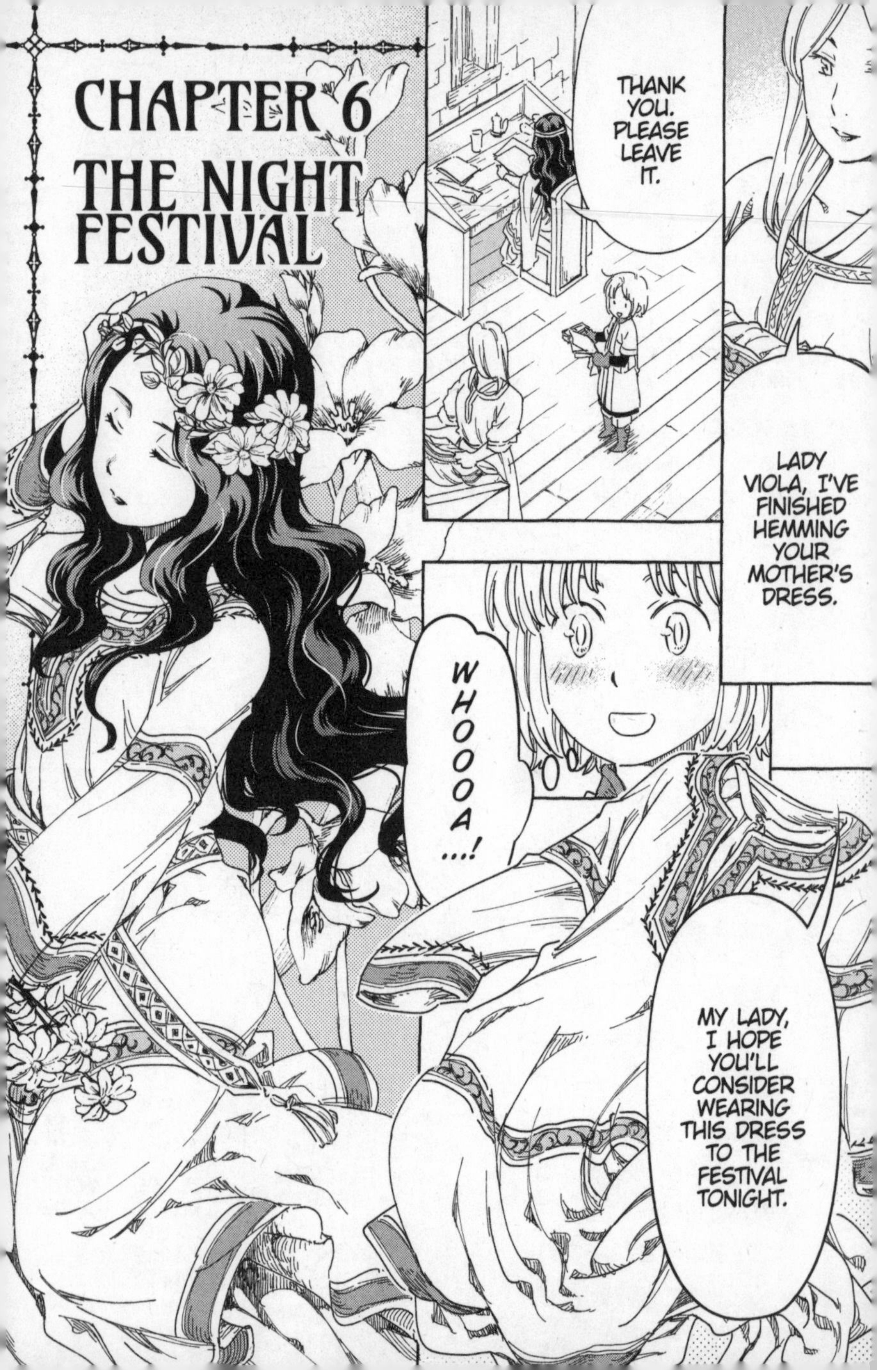
LADY VIOLA, I'VE FINISHED HEMMING YOUR MOTHER'S DRESS.
THANK YOU. PLEASE LEAVE IT.
MY LADY, I HOPE YOU'LL CONSIDER WEARING THIS DRESS TO THE FESTIVAL TONIGHT.
WHOOOOA...!
CHAPTER 6
THE NIGHT FESTIVAL

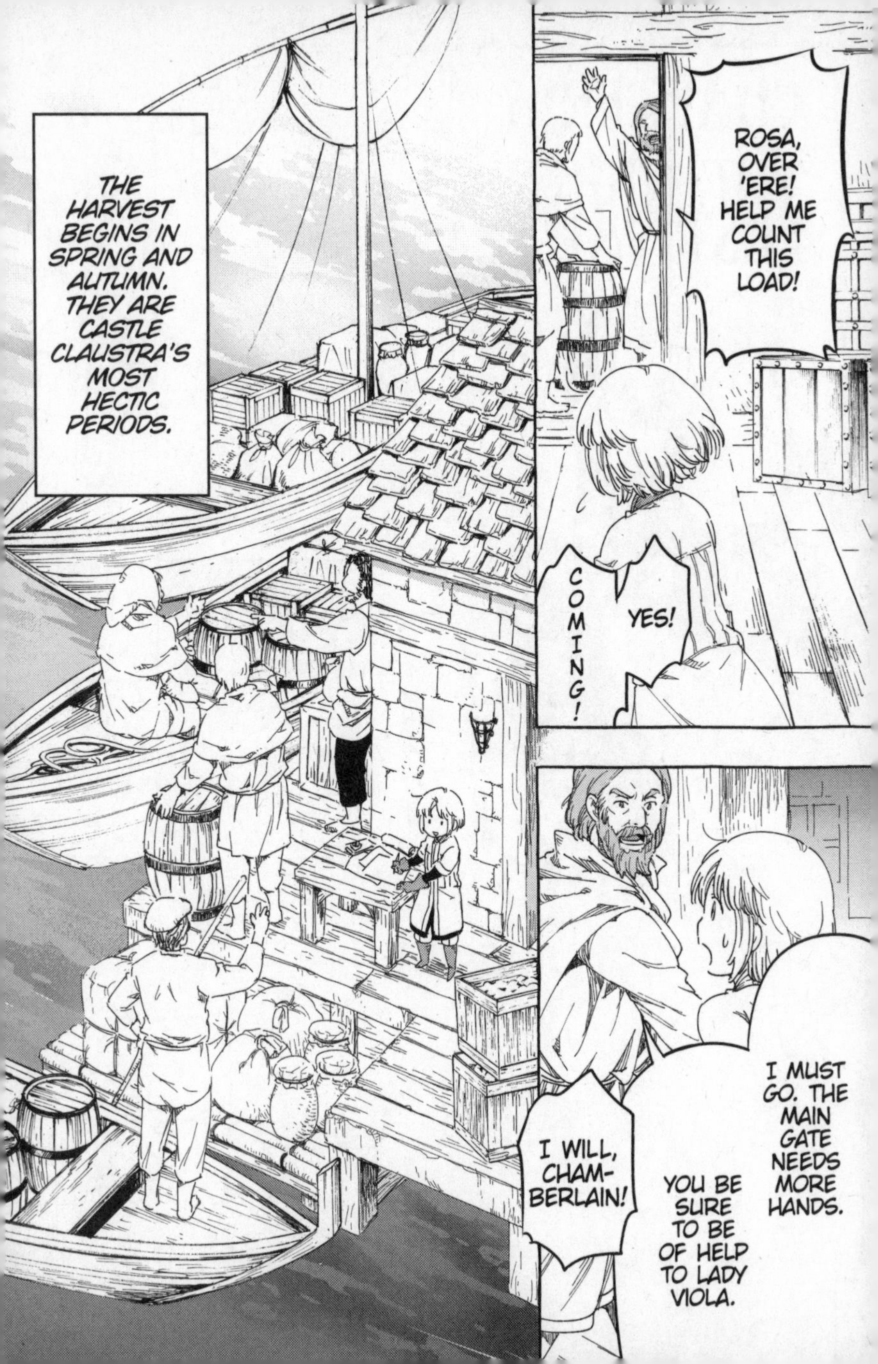
ROSA, OVER 'ERE! HELP ME COUNT THIS LOAD!
YES!
COMING!
I MUST GO. THE MAIN GATE NEEDS MORE HANDS.
YOU BE SURE TO BE OF HELP TO LADY VIOLA.
I WILL, CHAMBERLAIN!
THE HARVEST BEGINS IN SPRING AND AUTUMN. THEY ARE CASTLE CLAUSTRA'S MOST HECTIC PERIODS.

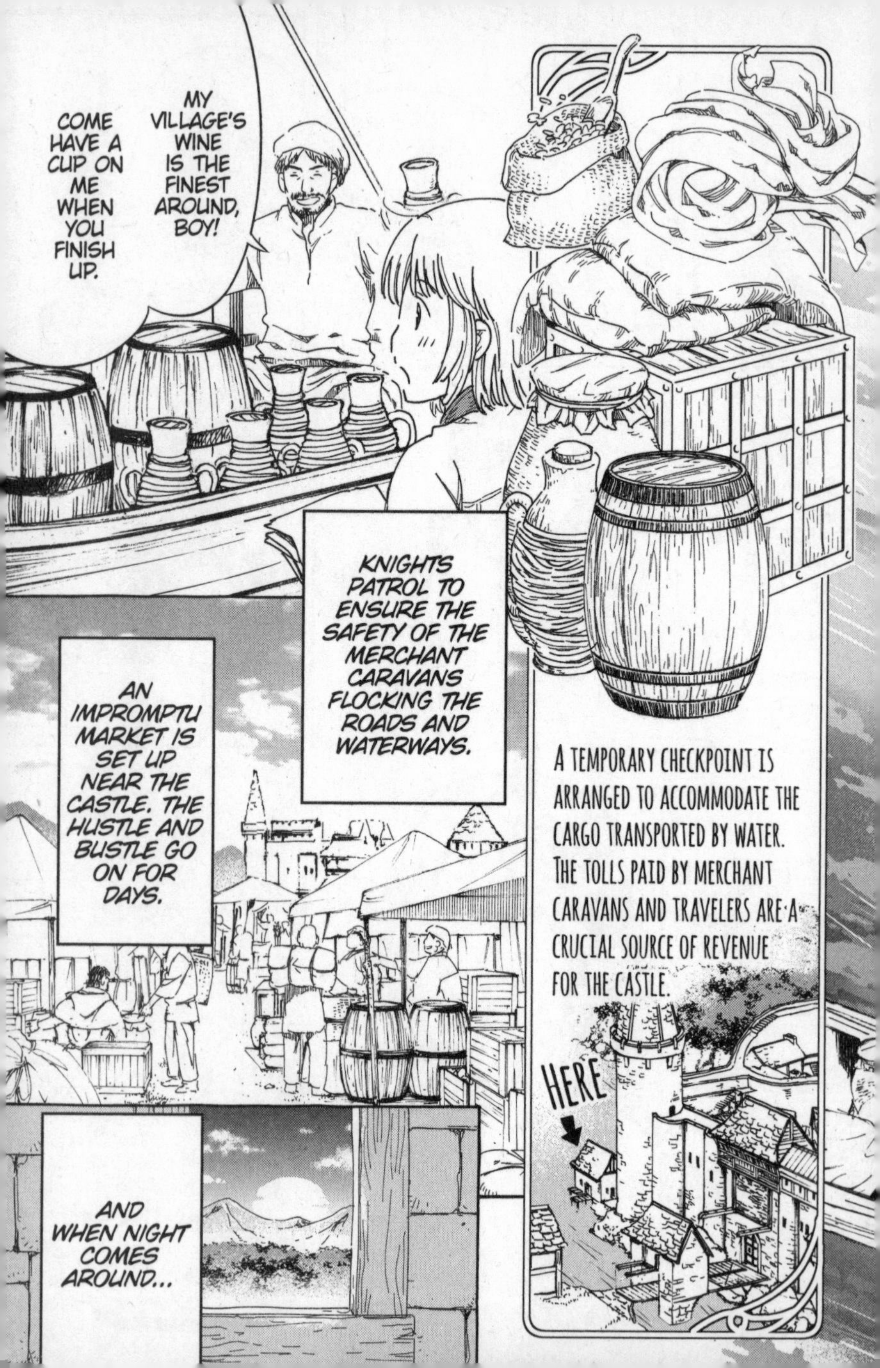
A TEMPORARY CHECKPOINT IS ARRANGED TO ACCOMMODATE THE CARGO TRANSPORTED BY WATER. THE TOLLS PAID BY MERCHANT CARAVANS AND TRAVELERS ARE A CRUCIAL SOURCE OF REVENUE FOR THE CASTLE.
HERE
MY VILLAGE'S WINE IS THE FINEST AROUND, BOY!
COME HAVE A CUP ON ME WHEN YOU FINISH UP.
KNIGHTS PATROL TO ENSURE THE SAFETY OF THE MERCHANT CARAVANS FLOCKING THE ROADS AND WATERWAYS.
AN IMPROMPTU MARKET IS SET UP NEAR THE CASTLE. THE HUSTLE AND BUSTLE GO ON FOR DAYS.
AND WHEN NIGHT COMES AROUND...

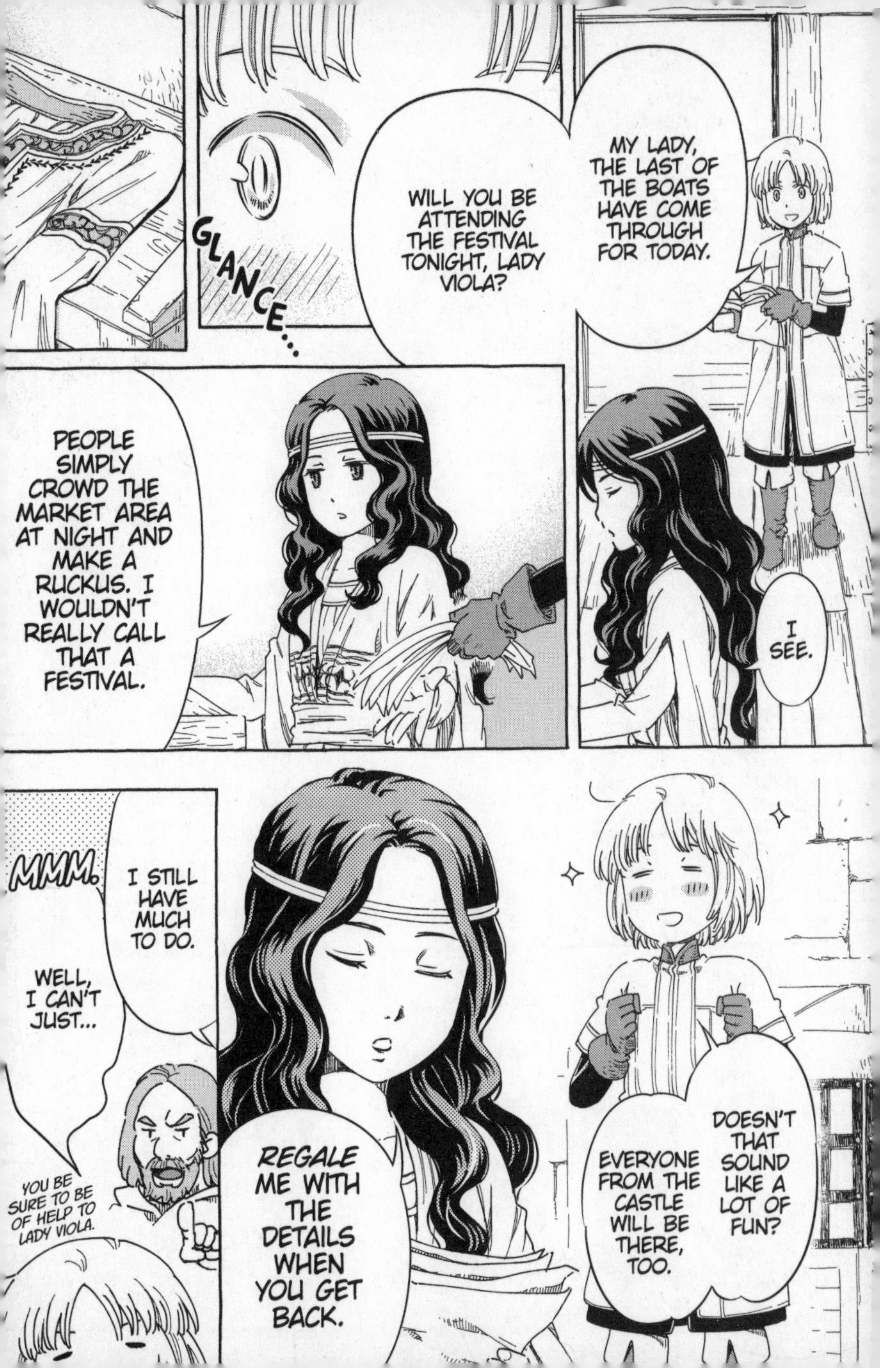
MY LADY, THE LAST OF THE BOATS HAVE COME THROUGH FOR TODAY.
I SEE.
WILL YOU BE ATTENDING THE FESTIVAL TONIGHT, LADY VIOLA?
GLANCE...
PEOPLE SIMPLY CROWD THE MARKET AREA AT NIGHT AND MAKE A RUCKUS. I WOULDN'T REALLY CALL THAT A FESTIVAL.
DOESN'T THAT SOUND LIKE A LOT OF FUN?
EVERYONE FROM THE CASTLE WILL BE THERE, TOO.
REGALE ME WITH THE DETAILS WHEN YOU GET BACK.
MMM.
I STILL HAVE MUCH TO DO.
WELL, I CAN'T JUST...
YOU BE SURE TO BE OF HELP TO LADY VIOLA.

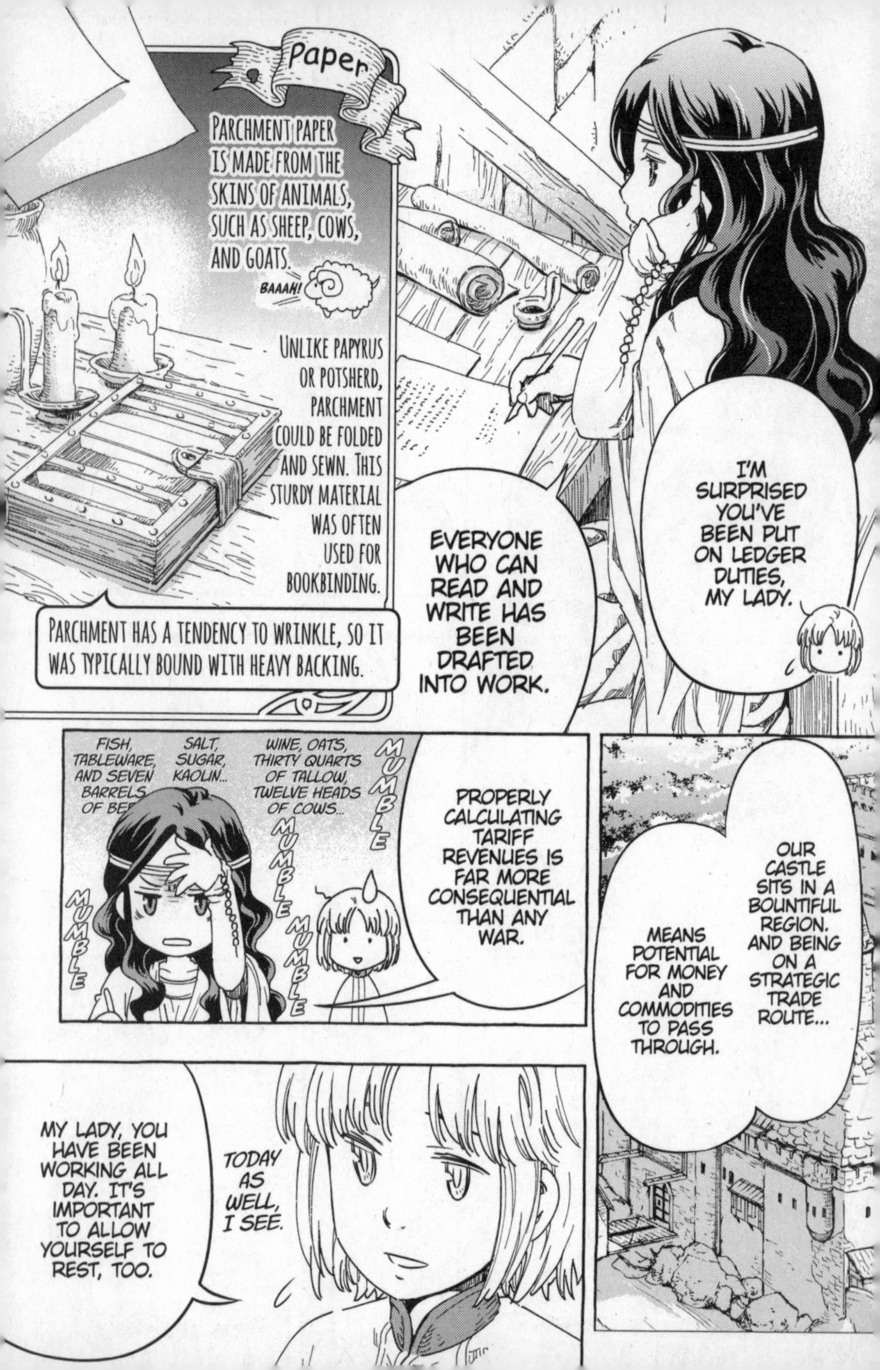
I'M SURPRISED YOU'VE BEEN PUT ON LEDGER DUTIES, MY LADY.
EVERYONE WHO CAN READ AND WRITE HAS BEEN DRAFTED INTO WORK.
Paper
PARCHMENT PAPER IS MADE FROM THE SKINS OF ANIMALS, SUCH AS SHEEP, COWS, AND GOATS.
BAAAH!
UNLIKE PAPYRUS OR POTSHERD, PARCHMENT COULD BE FOLDED AND SEWN. THIS STURDY MATERIAL WAS OFTEN USED FOR BOOKBINDING.
PARCHMENT HAS A TENDENCY TO WRINKLE, SO IT WAS TYPICALLY BOUND WITH HEAVY BACKING.
OUR CASTLE SITS IN A BOUNTIFUL REGION. AND BEING ON A STRATEGIC TRADE ROUTE...
MEANS POTENTIAL FOR MONEY AND COMMODITIES TO PASS THROUGH.
PROPERLY CALCULATING TARIFF REVENUES IS FAR MORE CONSEQUENTIAL THAN ANY WAR.
MUMBLE
WINE, OATS, THIRTY QUARTS OF TALLOW, TWELVE HEADS OF COWS...
SALT, SUGAR, KAOLIN...
FISH, TABLEWARE, AND SEVEN BARRELS OF BE
MUMBLE
MUMBLE
MUMBLE
TODAY AS WELL, I SEE.
MY LADY, YOU HAVE BEEN WORKING ALL DAY. IT'S IMPORTANT TO ALLOW YOURSELF TO REST, TOO.

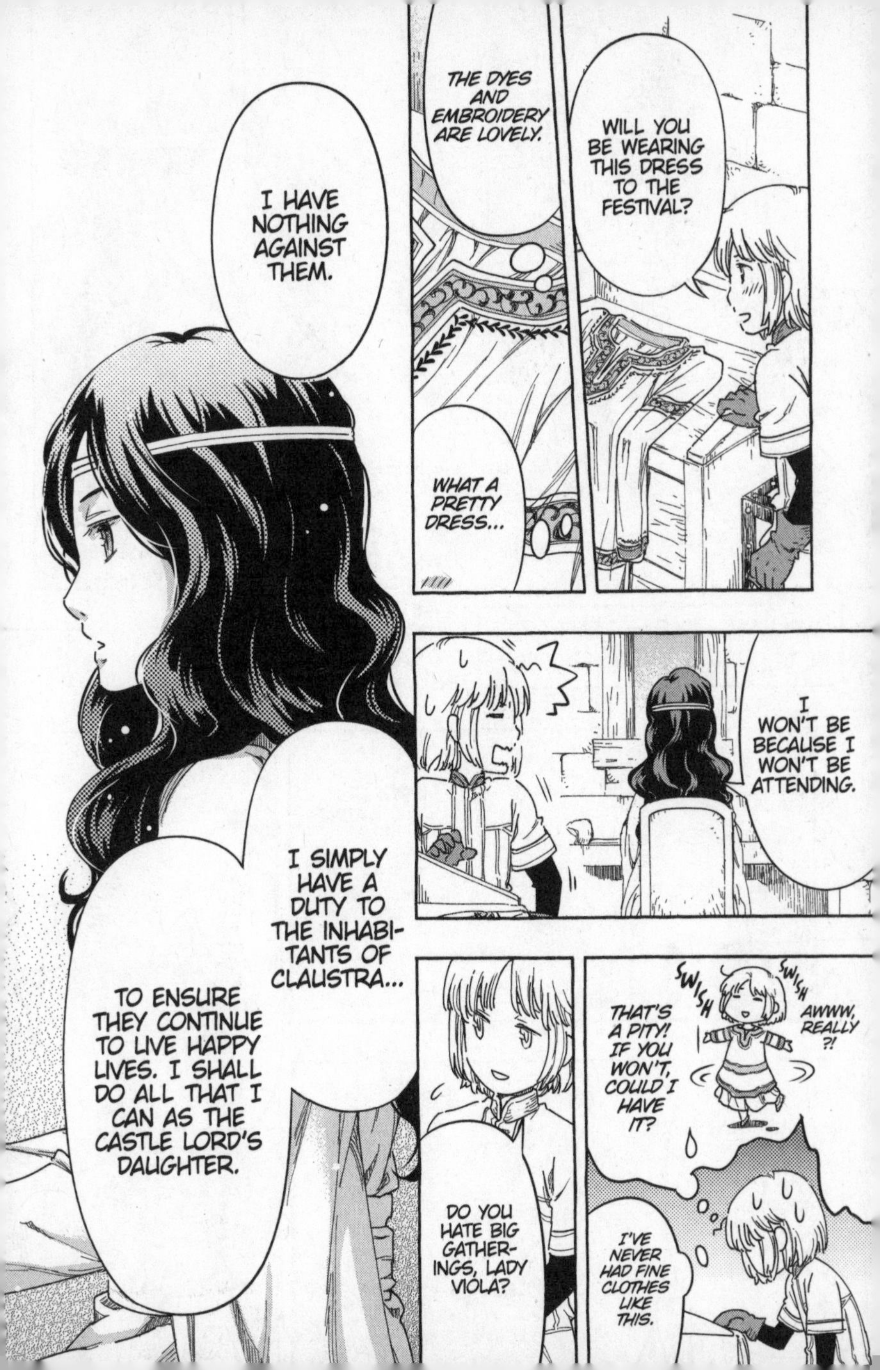
WILL YOU BE WEARING THIS DRESS TO THE FESTIVAL?
THE DYES AND EMBROIDERY ARE LOVELY.
WHAT A PRETTY DRESS...
I WON'T BE BECAUSE I WON'T BE ATTENDING.
SWISH
SWISH
AWWW, REALLY ?!
THAT'S A PITY! IF YOU WON'T, COULD I HAVE IT?
I'VE NEVER HAD FINE CLOTHES LIKE THIS.
DO YOU HATE BIG GATHER-INGS, LADY VIOLA?
I HAVE NOTHING AGAINST THEM.
I SIMPLY HAVE A DUTY TO THE INHABI-TANTS OF CLAUSTRA...
TO ENSURE THEY CONTINUE TO LIVE HAPPY LIVES. I SHALL DO ALL THAT I CAN AS THE CASTLE LORD'S DAUGHTER.

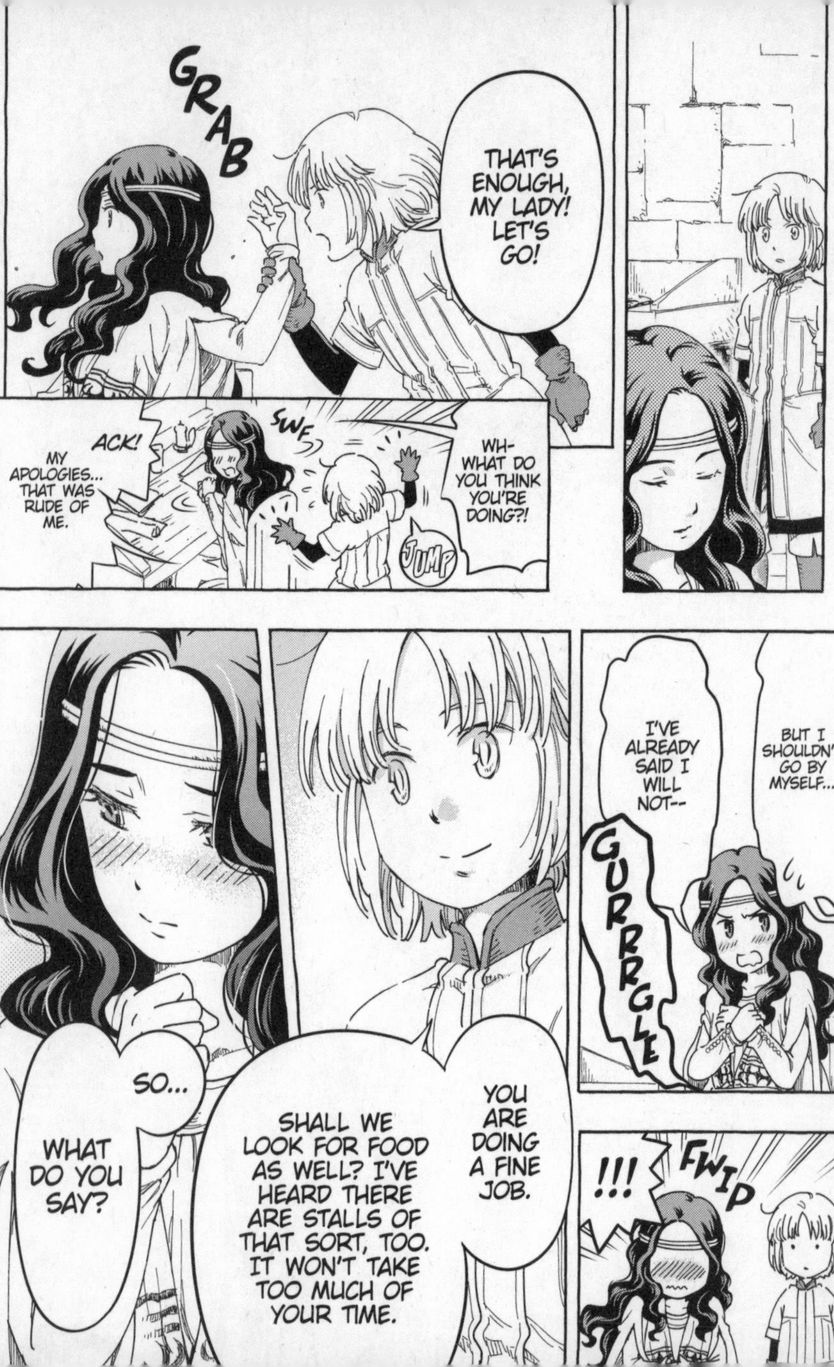
GRAB
THAT'S ENOUGH, MY LADY! LET'S GO!
WH- WHAT DO YOU THINK YOU'RE DOING?!
JUMP
SWF
ACK!
MY APOLOGIES... THAT WAS RUDE OF ME.
BUT I SHOULDN'T GO BY MYSELF...
I'VE ALREADY SAID I WILL NOT--
GURRRGLE
FWIP
!!!
YOU ARE DOING A FINE JOB.
SHALL WE LOOK FOR FOOD AS WELL? I'VE HEARD THERE ARE STALLS OF THAT SORT, TOO. IT WON'T TAKE TOO MUCH OF YOUR TIME.
SO...
WHAT DO YOU SAY?

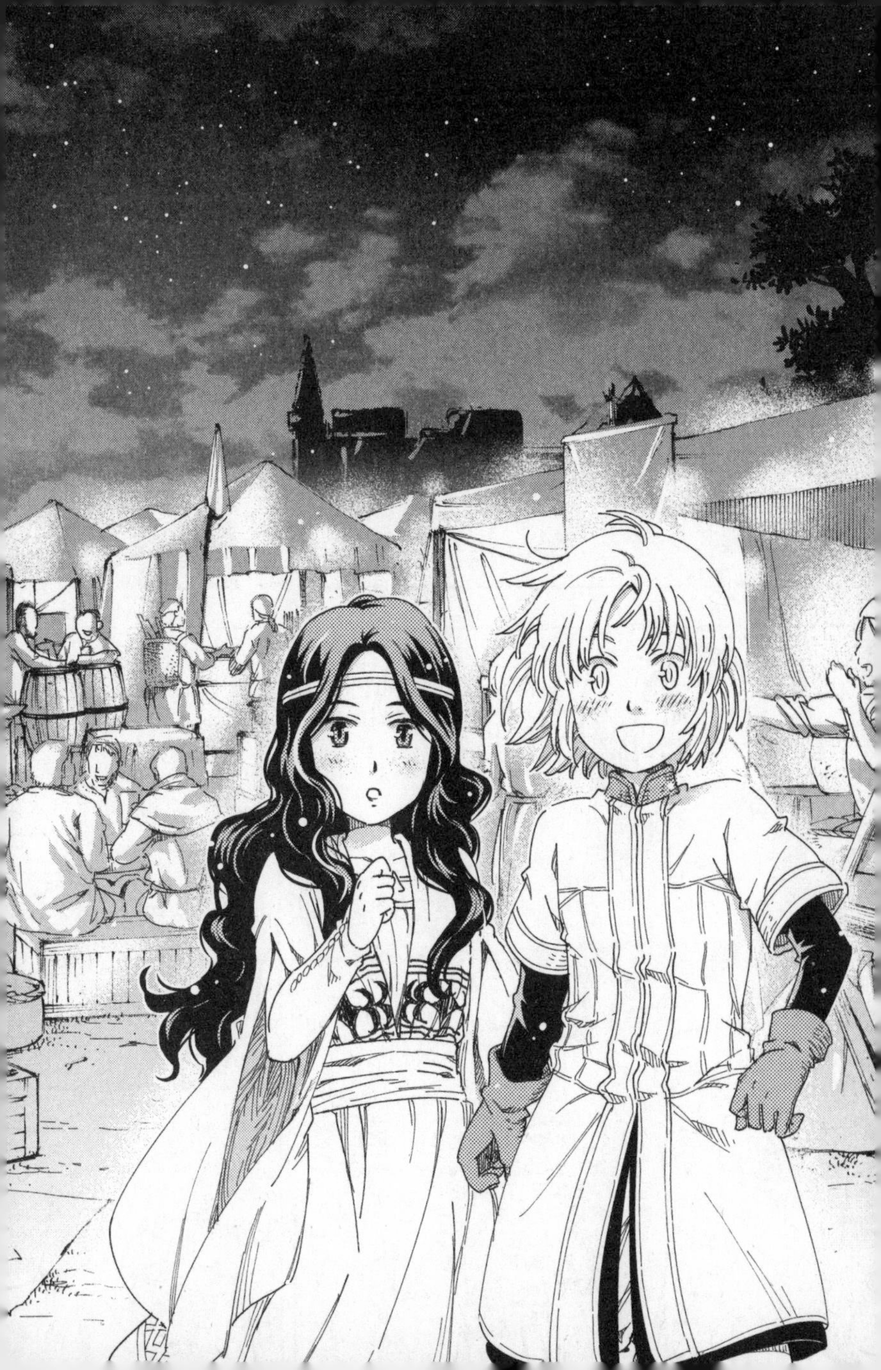

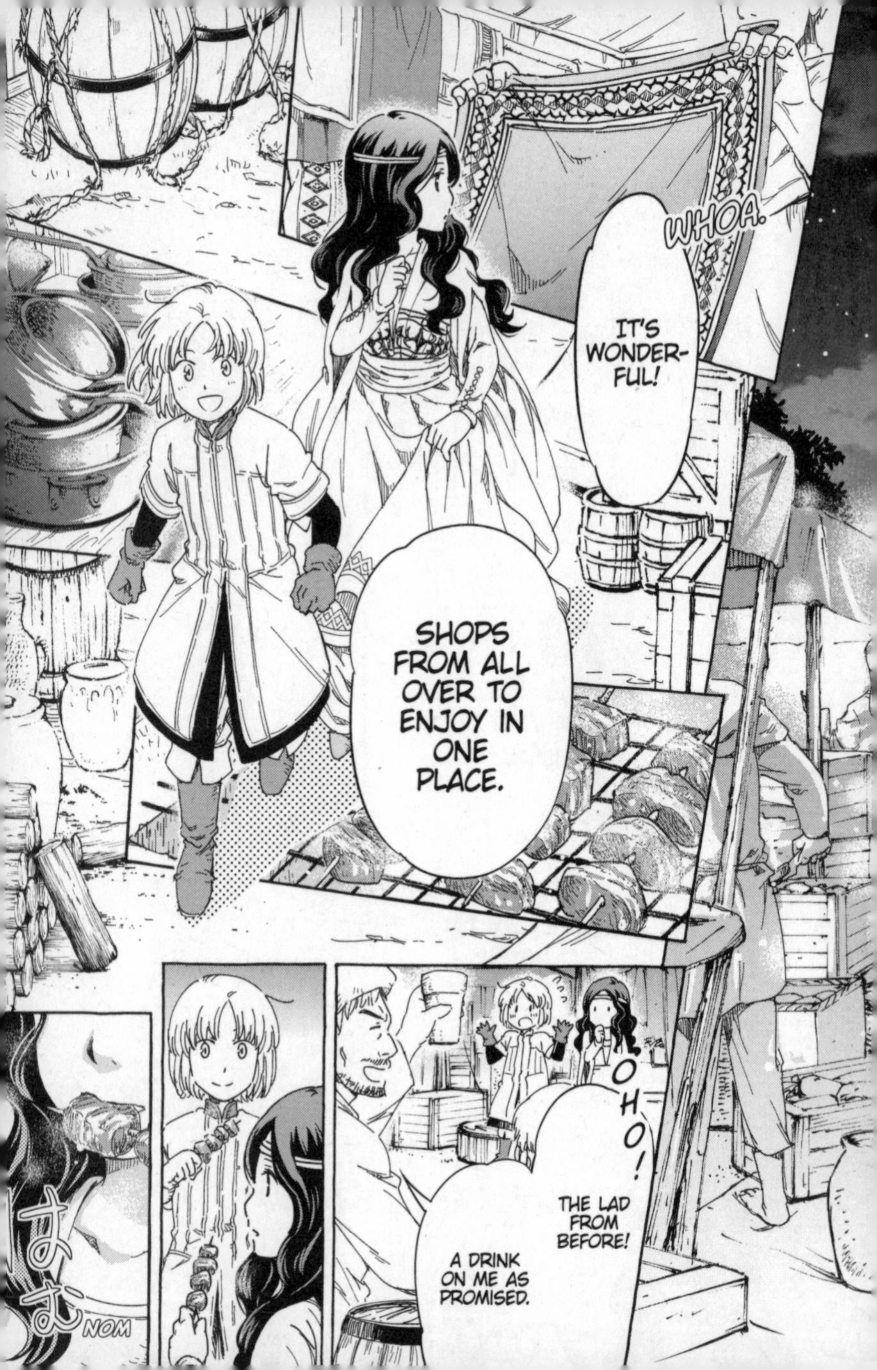
WHOA.
IT'S WONDERFUL!
SHOPS FROM ALL OVER TO ENJOY IN ONE PLACE.
OHOHO!
THE LAD FROM BEFORE!
A DRINK ON ME AS PROMISED.
NOM

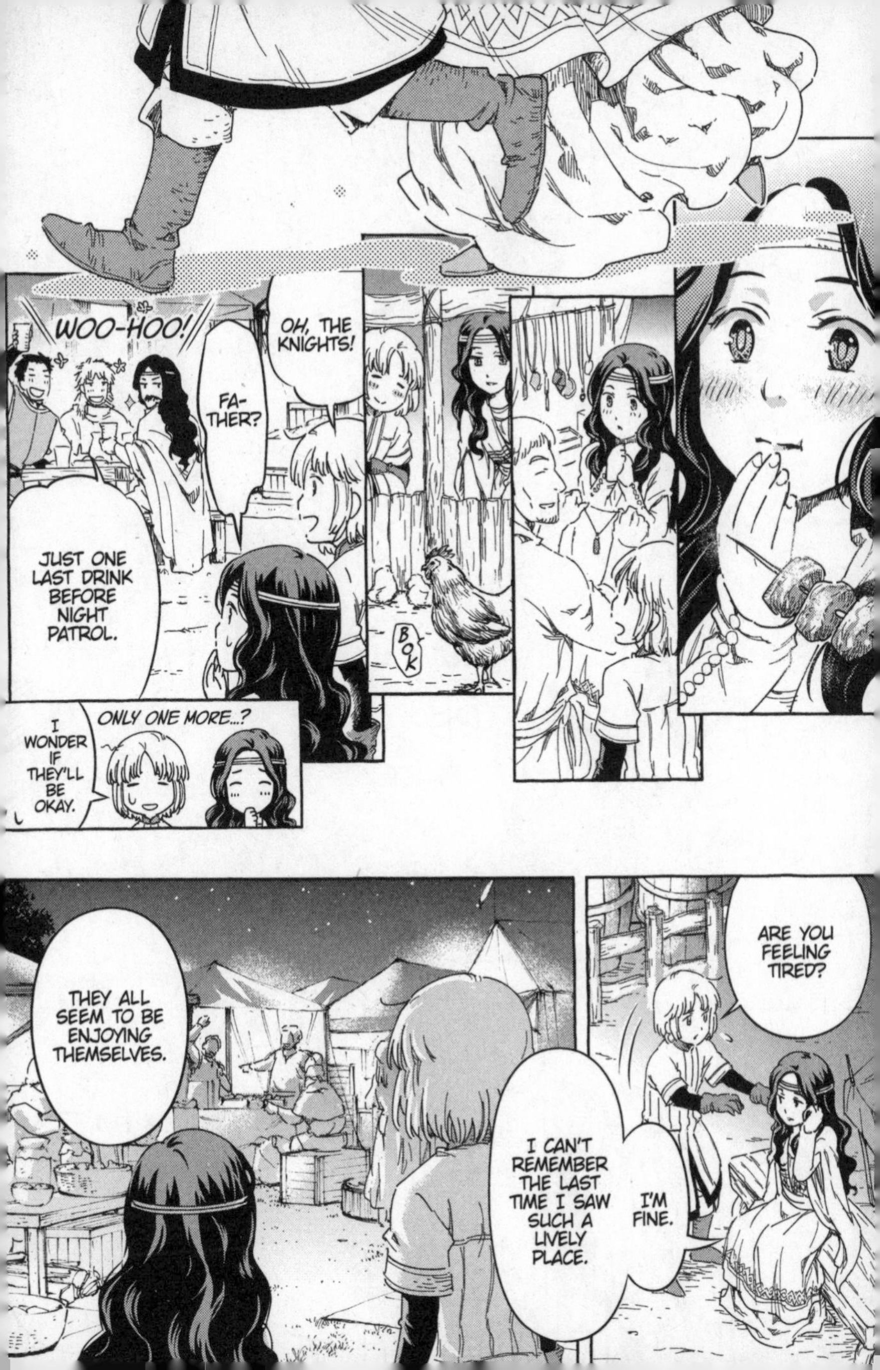
OH, THE KNIGHTS!
FA-THER?
BOK
WOO-HOO!
JUST ONE LAST DRINK BEFORE NIGHT PATROL.
ONLY ONE MORE...?
I WONDER IF THEY'LL BE OKAY.
ARE YOU FEELING TIRED?
I'M FINE.
THEY ALL SEEM TO BE ENJOYING THEMSELVES.
I CAN'T REMEMBER THE LAST TIME I SAW SUCH A LIVELY PLACE.

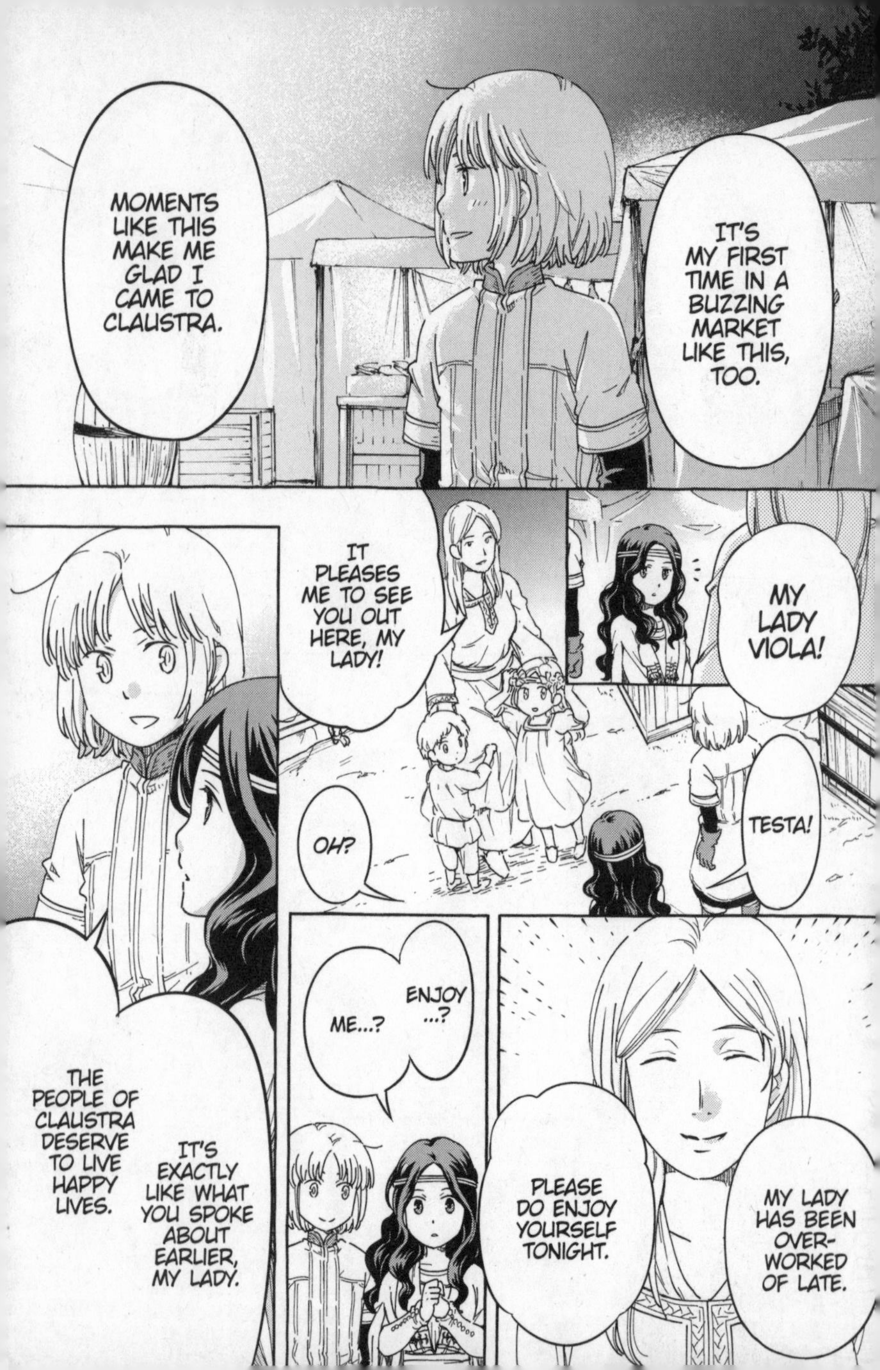
IT'S MY FIRST TIME IN A BUZZING MARKET LIKE THIS, TOO.
MOMENTS LIKE THIS MAKE ME GLAD I CAME TO CLAUSTRA.
MY LADY VIOLA!
IT PLEASES ME TO SEE YOU OUT HERE, MY LADY!
TESTA!
OH?
MY LADY HAS BEEN OVER-WORKED OF LATE.
PLEASE DO ENJOY YOURSELF TONIGHT.
ENJOY ...?
ME...?
IT'S EXACTLY LIKE WHAT YOU SPOKE ABOUT EARLIER, MY LADY.
THE PEOPLE OF CLAUSTRA DESERVE TO LIVE HAPPY LIVES.

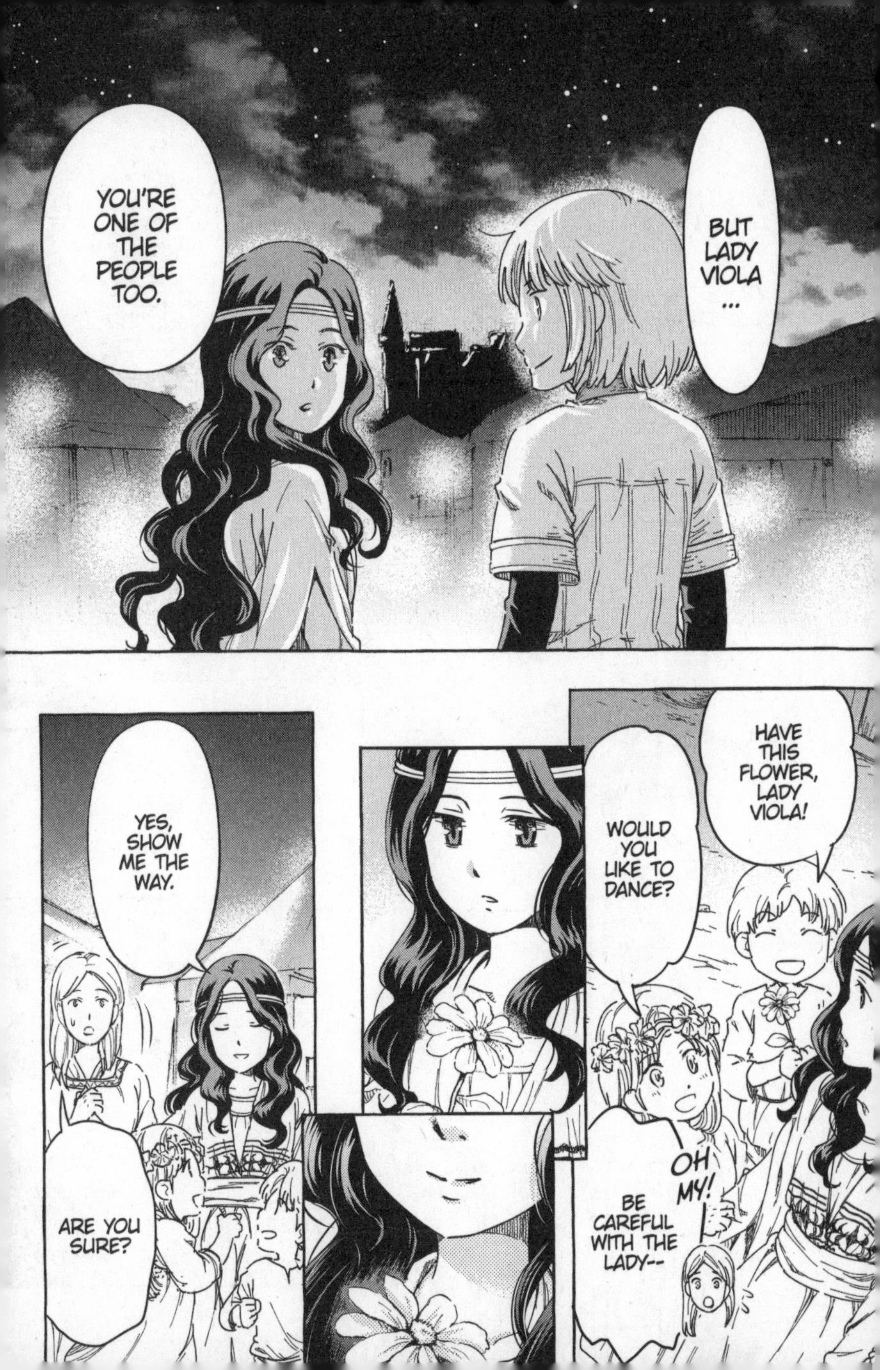
BUT LADY VIOLA ...
YOU'RE ONE OF THE PEOPLE TOO.
HAVE THIS FLOWER, LADY VIOLA!
WOULD YOU LIKE TO DANCE?
OH MY!
BE CAREFUL WITH THE LADY--
YES, SHOW ME THE WAY.
ARE YOU SURE?

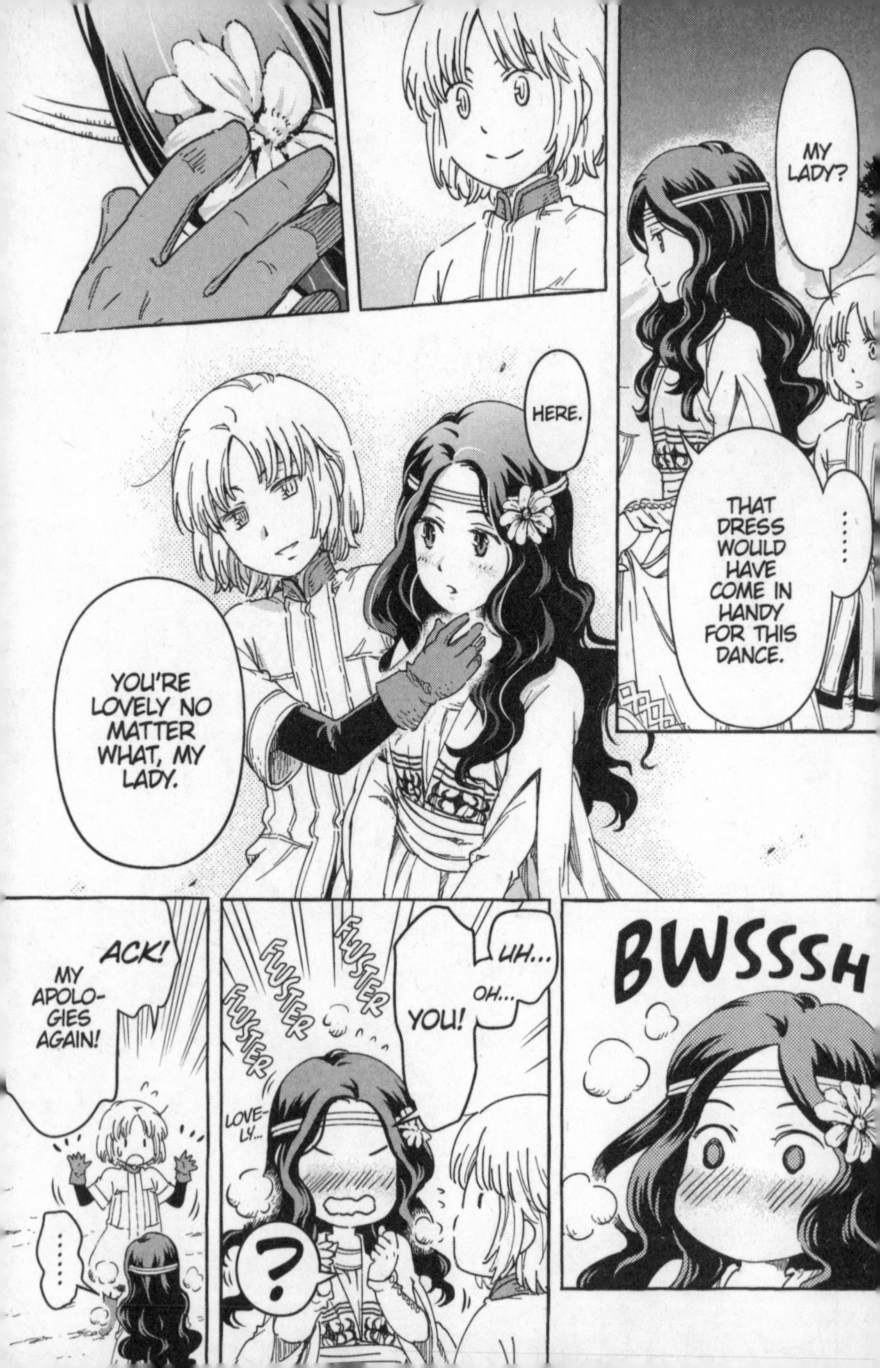
MY LADY?
THAT DRESS WOULD HAVE COME IN HANDY FOR THIS DANCE.
......
HERE.
YOU'RE LOVELY NO MATTER WHAT, MY LADY.
BWSSSH
UH... OH... YOU!
FLUSTER FLUSTER FLUSTER
LOVELY...
?
ACK! MY APOLOGIES AGAIN!
......

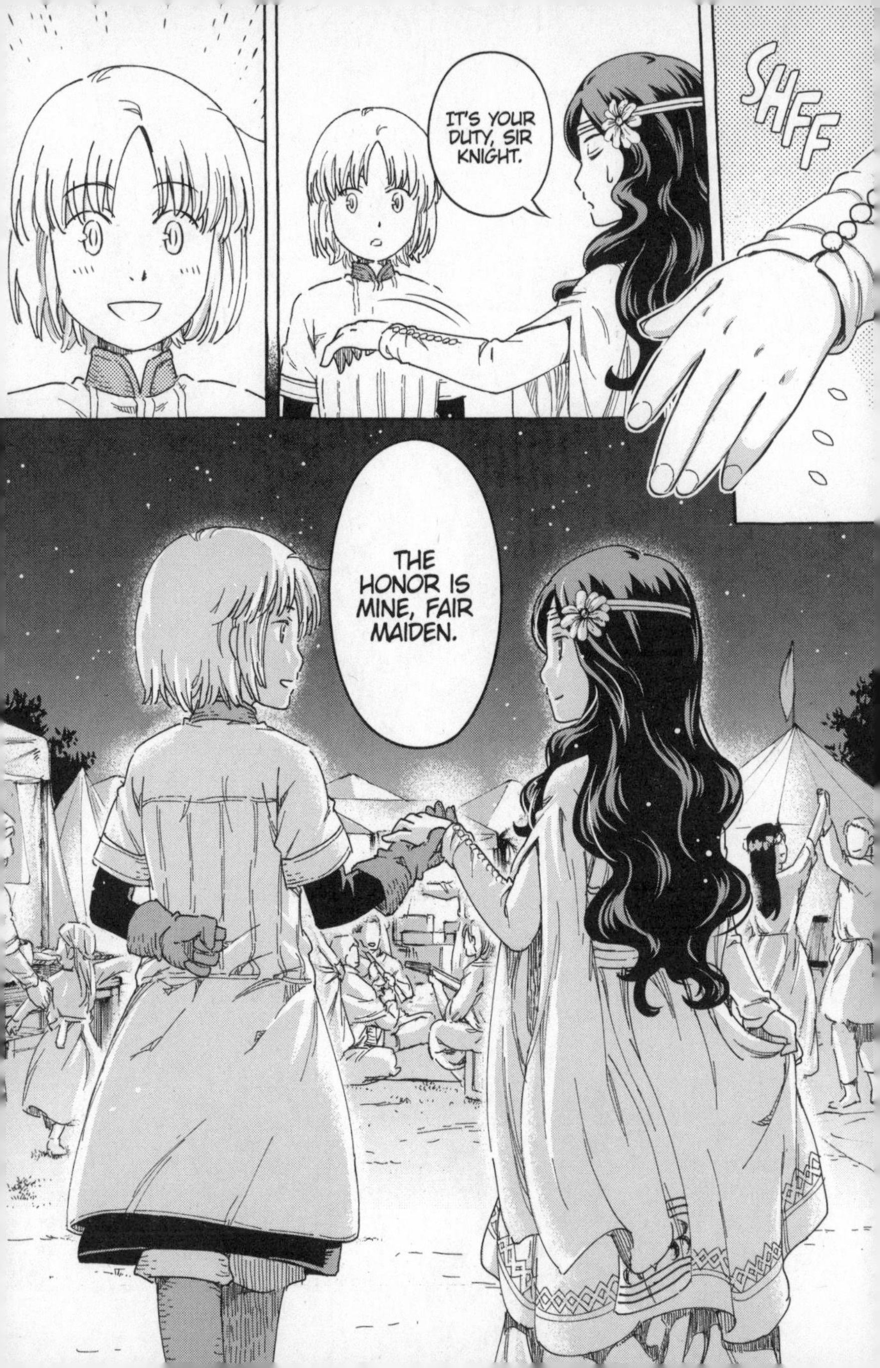
SHFF
IT'S YOUR DUTY, SIR KNIGHT.
THE HONOR IS MINE, FAIR MAIDEN.

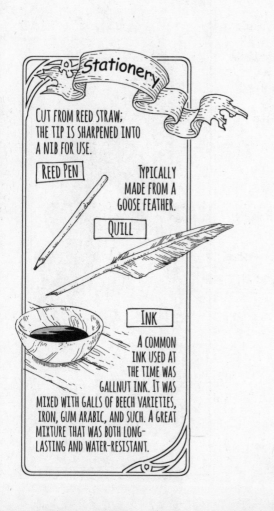

Stationery

CUT FROM REED STRAW; THE TIP IS SHARPENED INTO A NIB FOR USE.

Reed Pen

TYPICALLY MADE FROM A GOOSE FEATHER.

Quill

Ink

A COMMON INK USED AT THE TIME WAS GALLNUT INK. IT WAS MIXED WITH GALLS OF BEECH VARIETIES, IRON, GUM ARABIC, AND SUCH. A GREAT MIXTURE THAT WAS BOTH LONG-LASTING AND WATER-RESISTANT.

Viola Claustra

Daughter of Lord Clavis. Viola has taken over of her mother's duties while she recovers from an illness. She's a reliable and wise young lady, devoted to supporting her father.

- Favorite Foods
  Honey
- Least Favorite Foods
  Meat
  Strong-scented foods
  Many others...
- Talents
  Mental math
  Taking pride in
    inheriting her
    father's hair
- Weaknesses
  Small appetite,
  weak constitution
  Being reserved

Viola

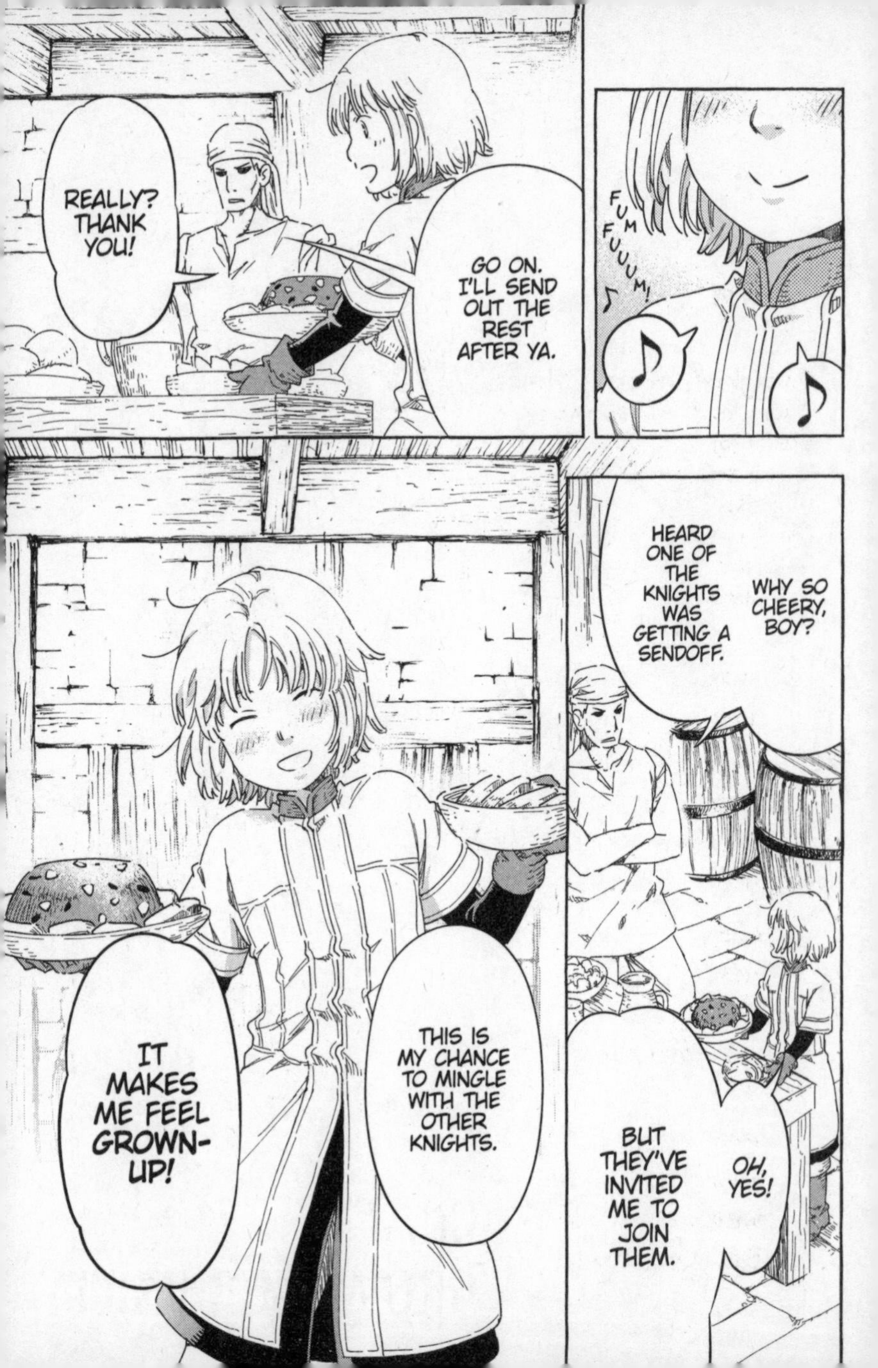

FUM FUUUUM!
♪
♪
GO ON. I'LL SEND OUT THE REST AFTER YA.
REALLY? THANK YOU!
WHY SO CHEERY, BOY?
HEARD ONE OF THE KNIGHTS WAS GETTING A SENDOFF.
OH, YES!
BUT THEY'VE INVITED ME TO JOIN THEM.
THIS IS MY CHANCE TO MINGLE WITH THE OTHER KNIGHTS.
IT MAKES ME FEEL GROWN-UP!

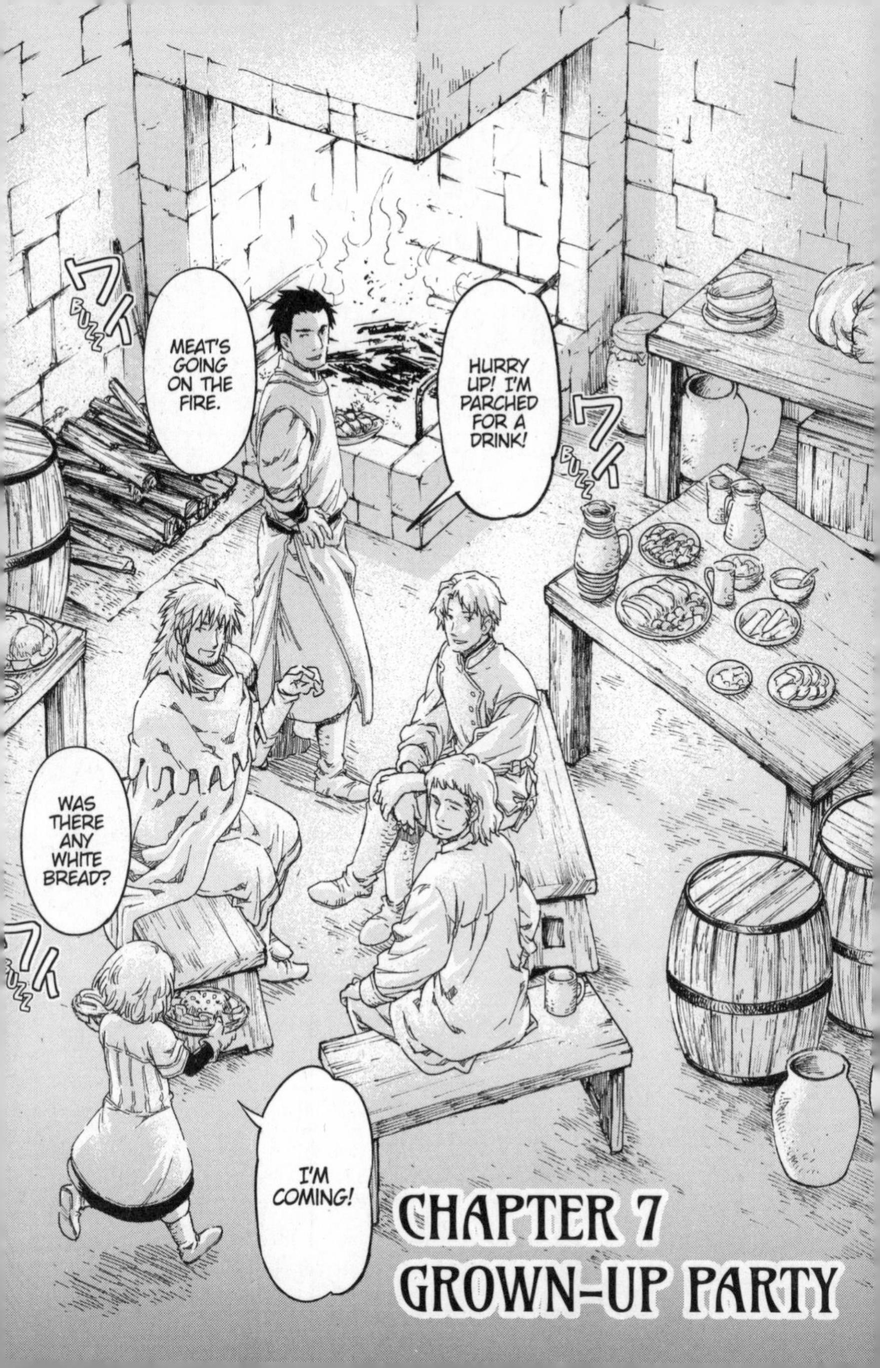
BUZZ
HURRY UP! I'M PARCHED FOR A DRINK!
MEAT'S GOING ON THE FIRE.
BUZZ
WAS THERE ANY WHITE BREAD?
BUZZ
I'M COMING!
CHAPTER 7
GROWN-UP PARTY

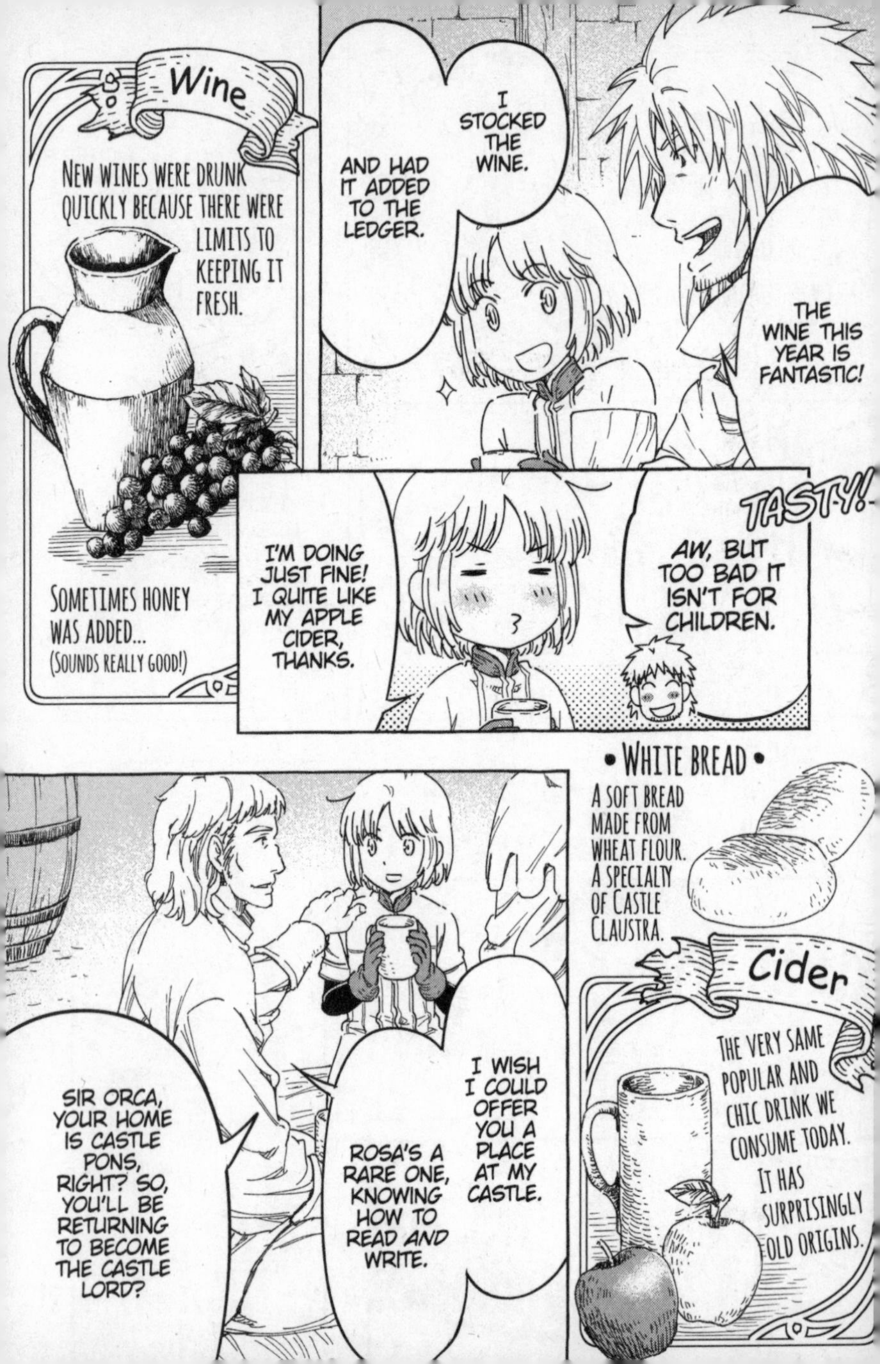

THE WINE THIS YEAR IS FANTASTIC!
I STOCKED THE WINE.
AND HAD IT ADDED TO THE LEDGER.
TASTY!
AW, BUT TOO BAD IT ISN'T FOR CHILDREN.
I'M DOING JUST FINE! I QUITE LIKE MY APPLE CIDER, THANKS.
Wine
NEW WINES WERE DRUNK QUICKLY BECAUSE THERE WERE LIMITS TO KEEPING IT FRESH.
SOMETIMES HONEY WAS ADDED...
(SOUNDS REALLY GOOD!)
• WHITE BREAD •
A SOFT BREAD MADE FROM WHEAT FLOUR. A SPECIALTY OF CASTLE CLAUSTRA.
Cider
THE VERY SAME POPULAR AND CHIC DRINK WE CONSUME TODAY. IT HAS SURPRISINGLY OLD ORIGINS.
I WISH I COULD OFFER YOU A PLACE AT MY CASTLE.
ROSA'S A RARE ONE, KNOWING HOW TO READ AND WRITE.
SIR ORCA, YOUR HOME IS CASTLE PONS, RIGHT? SO, YOU'LL BE RETURNING TO BECOME THE CASTLE LORD?

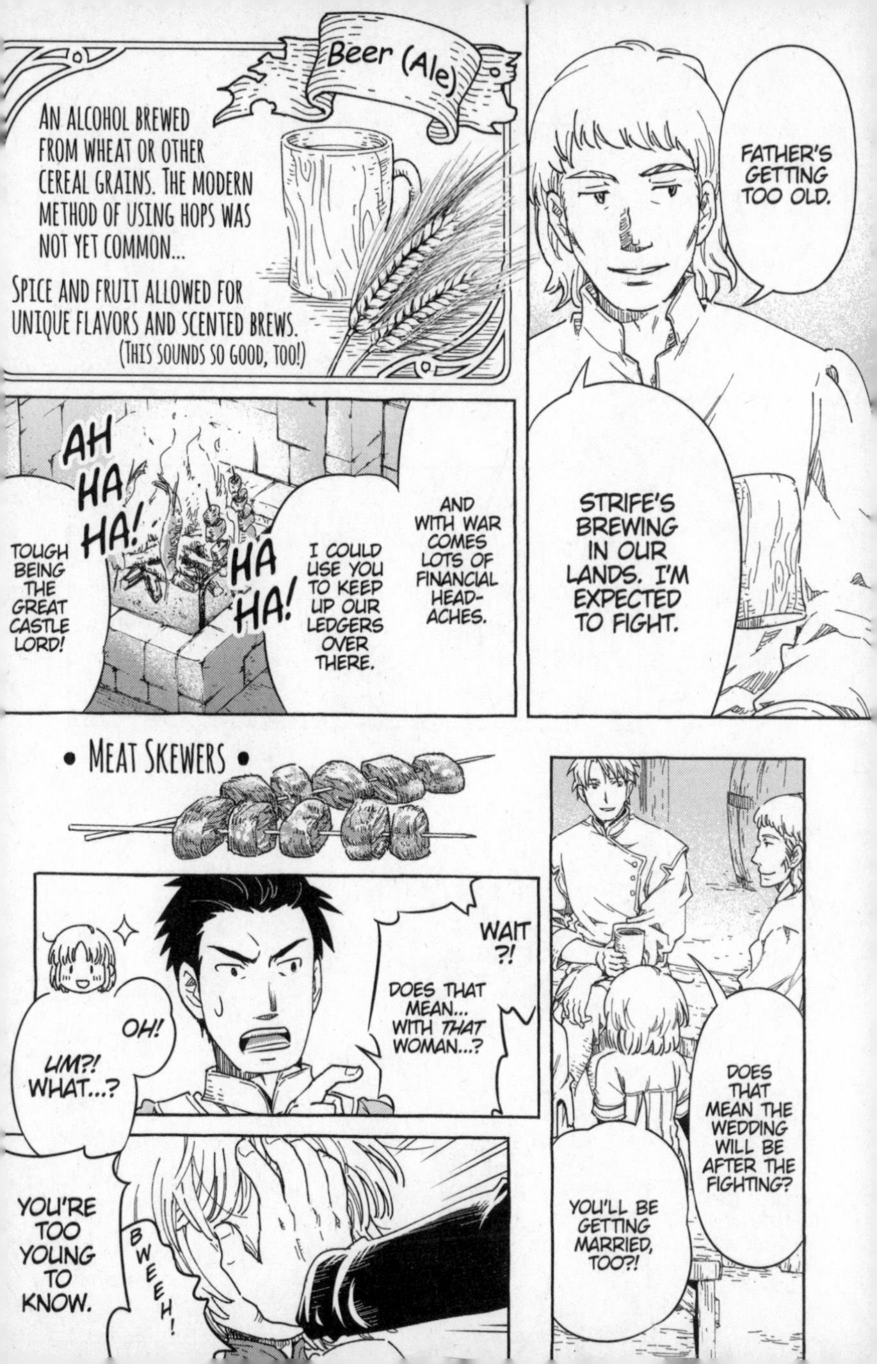

FATHER'S GETTING TOO OLD.
STRIFE'S BREWING IN OUR LANDS. I'M EXPECTED TO FIGHT.
Beer (Ale)
AN ALCOHOL BREWED FROM WHEAT OR OTHER CEREAL GRAINS. THE MODERN METHOD OF USING HOPS WAS NOT YET COMMON...
SPICE AND FRUIT ALLOWED FOR UNIQUE FLAVORS AND SCENTED BREWS.
(THIS SOUNDS SO GOOD, TOO!)
AND WITH WAR COMES LOTS OF FINANCIAL HEAD-ACHES.
I COULD USE YOU TO KEEP UP OUR LEDGERS OVER THERE.
HA HA!
AH HA HA!
TOUGH BEING THE GREAT CASTLE LORD!
• MEAT SKEWERS •
DOES THAT MEAN THE WEDDING WILL BE AFTER THE FIGHTING?
YOU'LL BE GETTING MARRIED, TOO?!
WAIT?!
DOES THAT MEAN... WITH *THAT* WOMAN...?
OH!
UM?! WHAT...?
BWEEH!
YOU'RE TOO YOUNG TO KNOW.

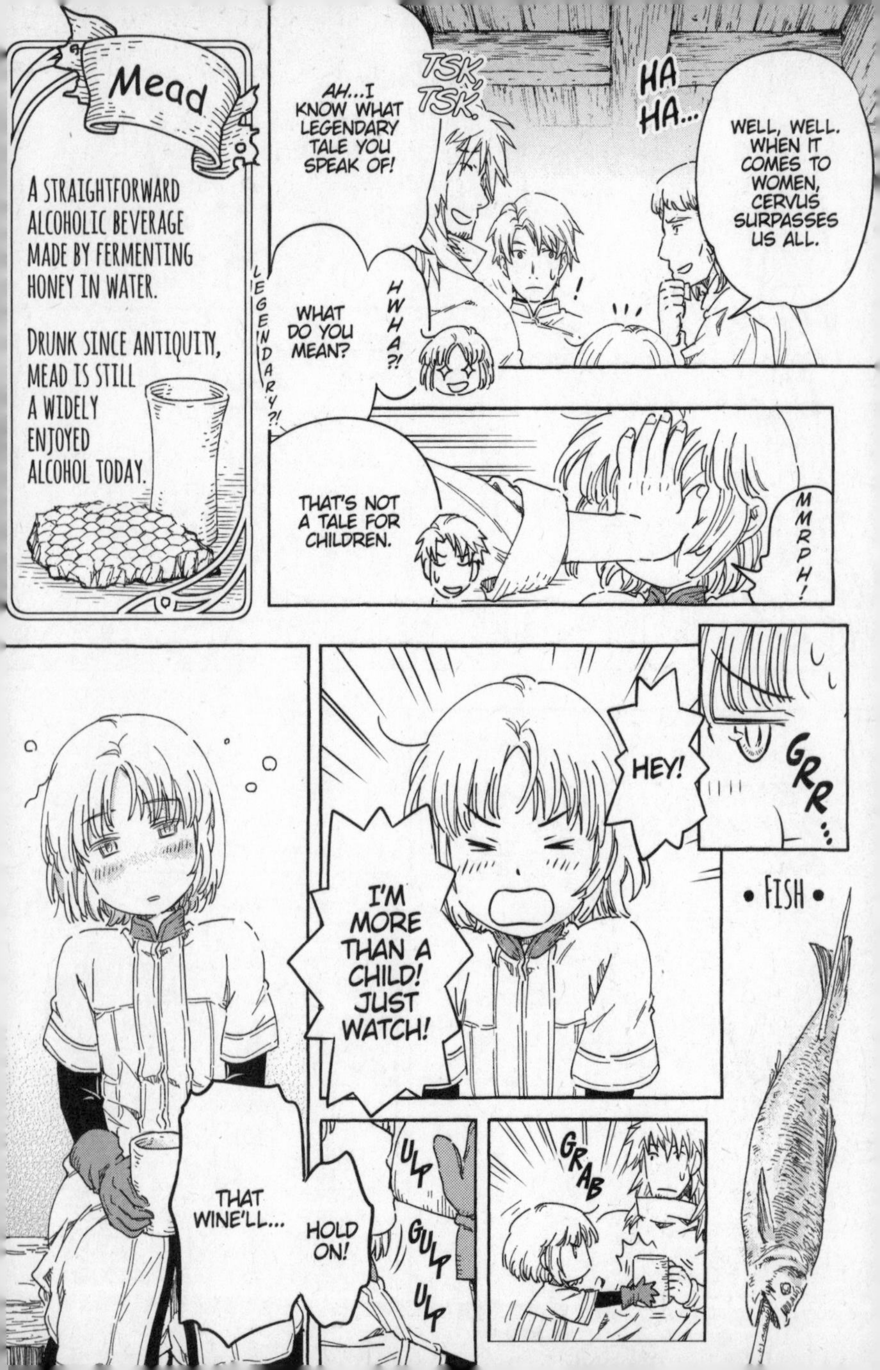
HA HA...
WELL, WELL. WHEN IT COMES TO WOMEN, CERVUS SURPASSES US ALL.
TSK, TSK.
AH...I KNOW WHAT LEGENDARY TALE YOU SPEAK OF!
!
HWHA?!
WHAT DO YOU MEAN?
LEGENDARY?!
MMRPH!
THAT'S NOT A TALE FOR CHILDREN.
Mead
A STRAIGHTFORWARD ALCOHOLIC BEVERAGE MADE BY FERMENTING HONEY IN WATER.
DRUNK SINCE ANTIQUITY, MEAD IS STILL A WIDELY ENJOYED ALCOHOL TODAY.
• FISH •
GRR...
HEY!
I'M MORE THAN A CHILD! JUST WATCH!
GRAB
ULP
GULP
ULP
HOLD ON!
THAT WINE'LL...

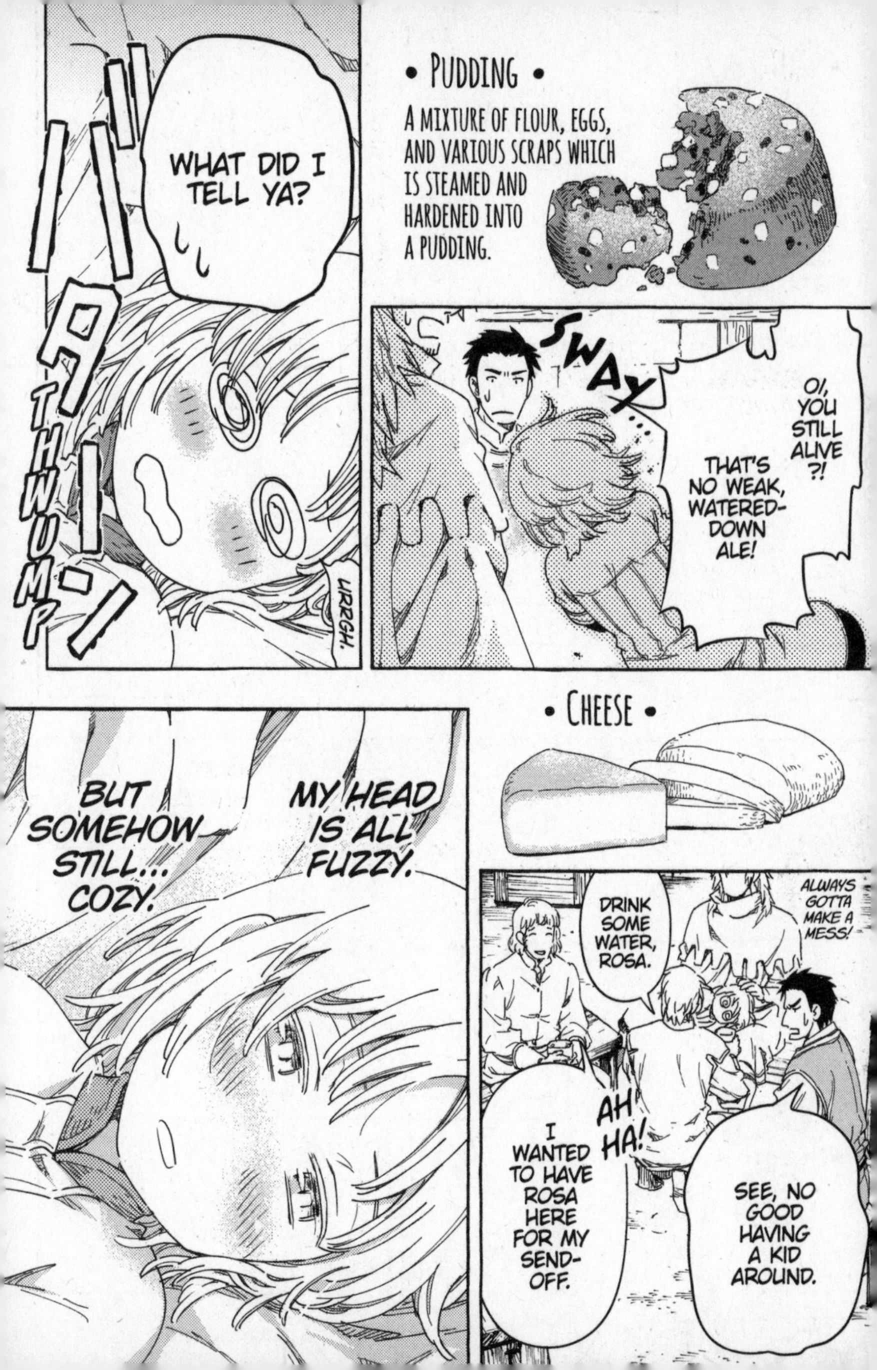
• PUDDING •
A MIXTURE OF FLOUR, EGGS, AND VARIOUS SCRAPS WHICH IS STEAMED AND HARDENED INTO A PUDDING.
SWAY...
OI, YOU STILL ALIVE?!
THAT'S NO WEAK, WATERED-DOWN ALE!
WHAT DID I TELL YA?
THWUMP
URRGH.
• CHEESE •
ALWAYS GOTTA MAKE A MESS!
DRINK SOME WATER, ROSA.
AH HA!
SEE, NO GOOD HAVING A KID AROUND.
I WANTED TO HAVE ROSA HERE FOR MY SEND-OFF.
MY HEAD IS ALL FUZZY.
BUT SOMEHOW STILL... COZY.

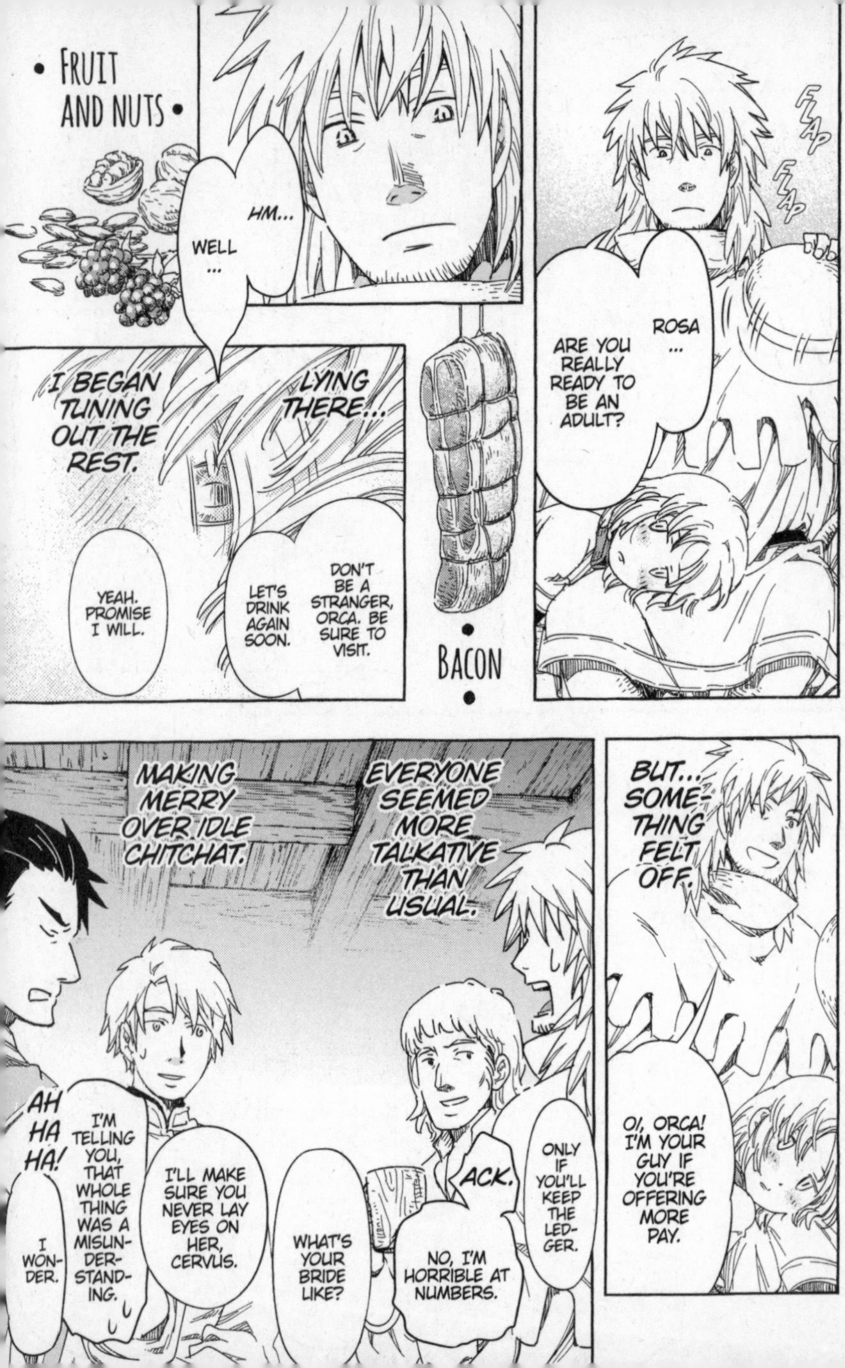
FLAP
FLAP
ROSA ...
ARE YOU REALLY READY TO BE AN ADULT?
HM...
WELL ...
• FRUIT AND NUTS •
LYING THERE...
I BEGAN TUNING OUT THE REST.
DON'T BE A STRANGER, ORCA. BE SURE TO VISIT.
LET'S DRINK AGAIN SOON.
YEAH. PROMISE I WILL.
• BACON •
BUT... SOME-THING FELT OFF.
OI, ORCA! I'M YOUR GUY IF YOU'RE OFFERING MORE PAY.
EVERYONE SEEMED MORE TALKATIVE THAN USUAL.
MAKING MERRY OVER IDLE CHITCHAT.
ONLY IF YOU'LL KEEP THE LED-GER.
ACK.
NO, I'M HORRIBLE AT NUMBERS.
WHAT'S YOUR BRIDE LIKE?
I'LL MAKE SURE YOU NEVER LAY EYES ON HER, CERVUS.
I'M TELLING YOU, THAT WHOLE THING WAS A MISUN-DER-STAND-ING.
AH HA HA!
I WON-DER.

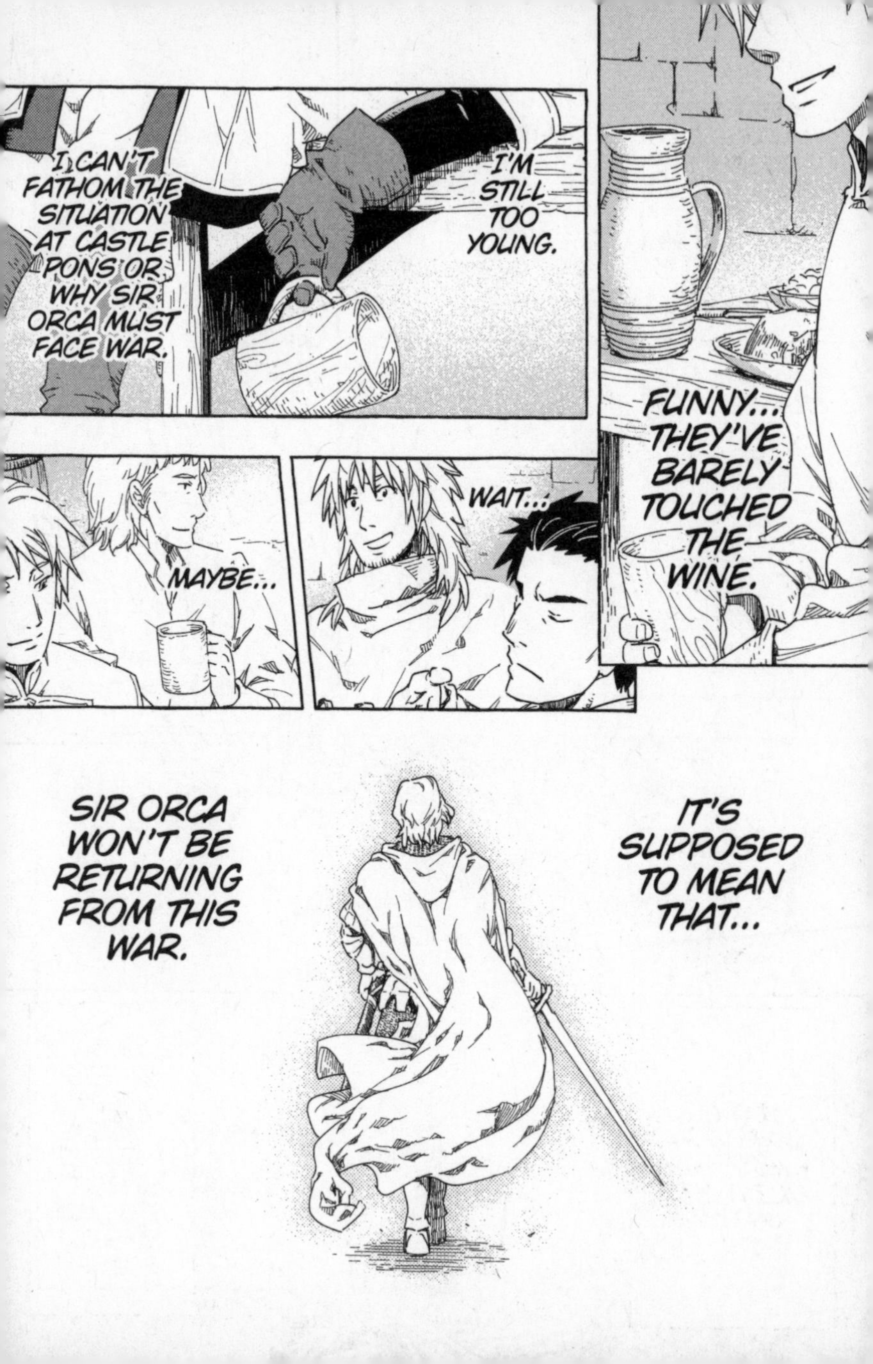
FUNNY... THEY'VE BARELY TOUCHED THE WINE.
I'M STILL TOO YOUNG.
I CAN'T FATHOM THE SITUATION AT CASTLE PONS OR WHY SIR ORCA MUST FACE WAR.
WAIT...
MAYBE...
IT'S SUPPOSED TO MEAN THAT...
SIR ORCA WON'T BE RETURNING FROM THIS WAR.

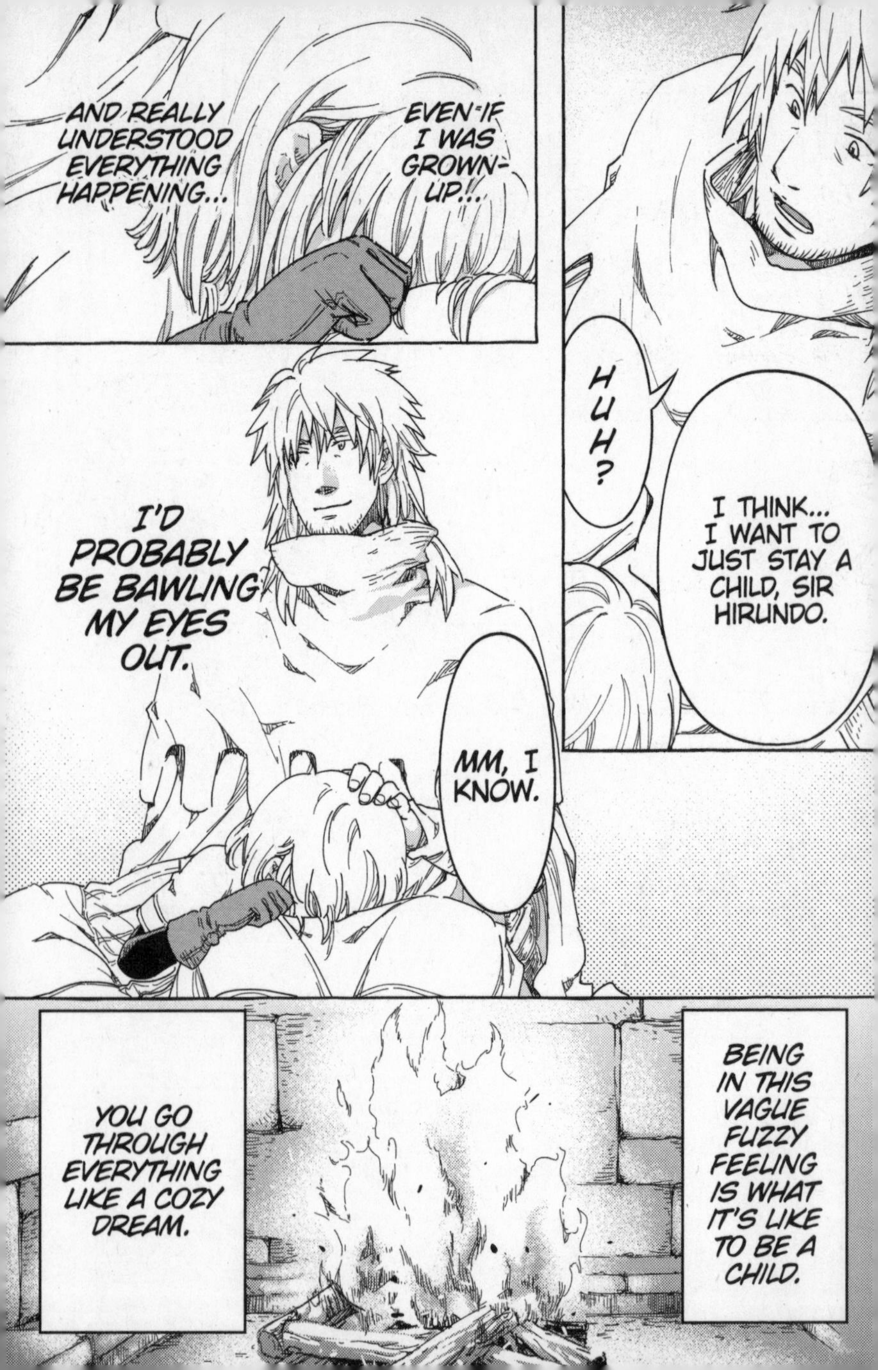
HUH?
I THINK... I WANT TO JUST STAY A CHILD, SIR HIRUNDO.
EVEN IF I WAS GROWN-UP...
AND REALLY UNDERSTOOD EVERYTHING HAPPENING...
MM, I KNOW.
I'D PROBABLY BE BAWLING MY EYES OUT.
BEING IN THIS VAGUE FUZZY FEELING IS WHAT IT'S LIKE TO BE A CHILD.
YOU GO THROUGH EVERYTHING LIKE A COZY DREAM.

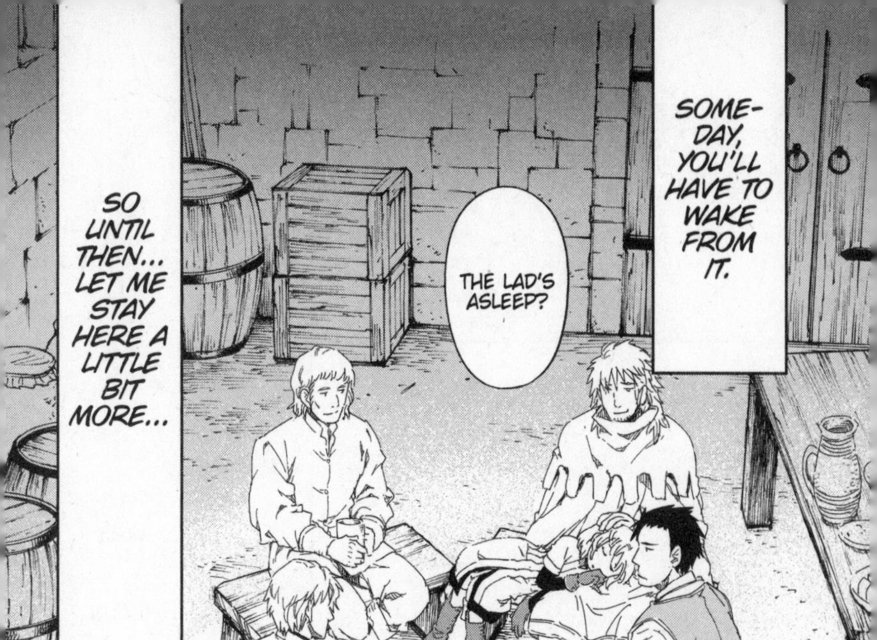
SOME-DAY, YOU'LL HAVE TO WAKE FROM IT.
THE LAD'S ASLEEP?
SO UNTIL THEN... LET ME STAY HERE A LITTLE BIT MORE...
STILL A SNOT-NOSED KID.

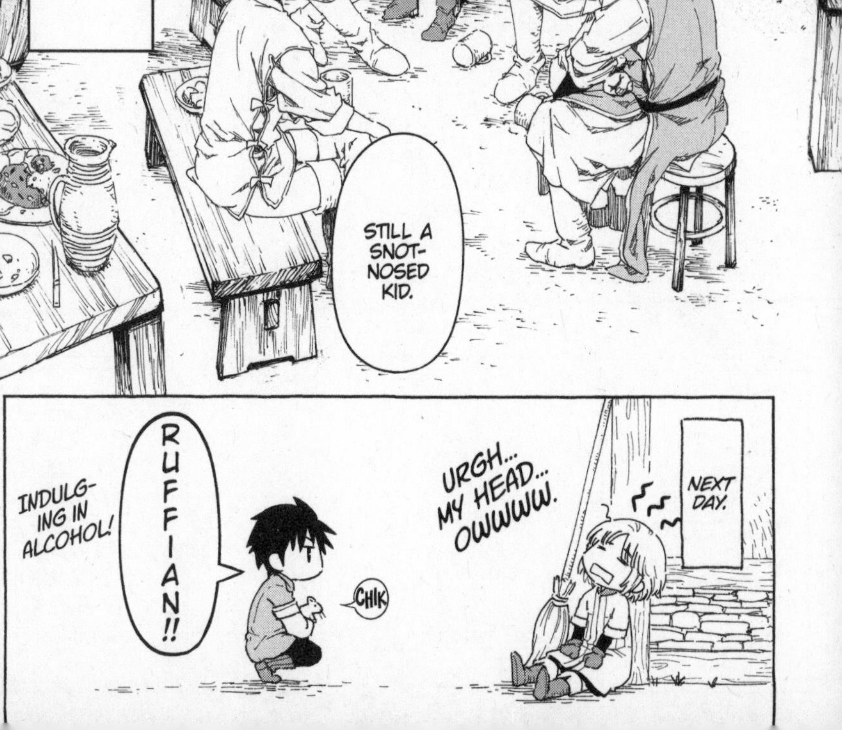
NEXT DAY.
URGH... MY HEAD... OWWWW.
RUFFIAN!!
INDULG-ING IN ALCOHOL!
CHIK

On Alcohol

Perhaps you've been imagining a clear liquid like *sake* whenever alcohol was mentioned so far. However, it's much closer to *amazake*, which is to say a cloudy and unfiltered type of drink.

It was high in nutrients and often an accompaniment with meals. Children were even given watered-down alcohol daily, too.

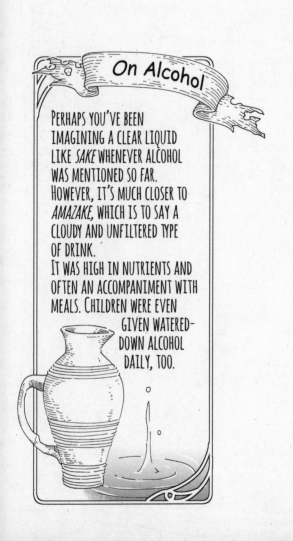

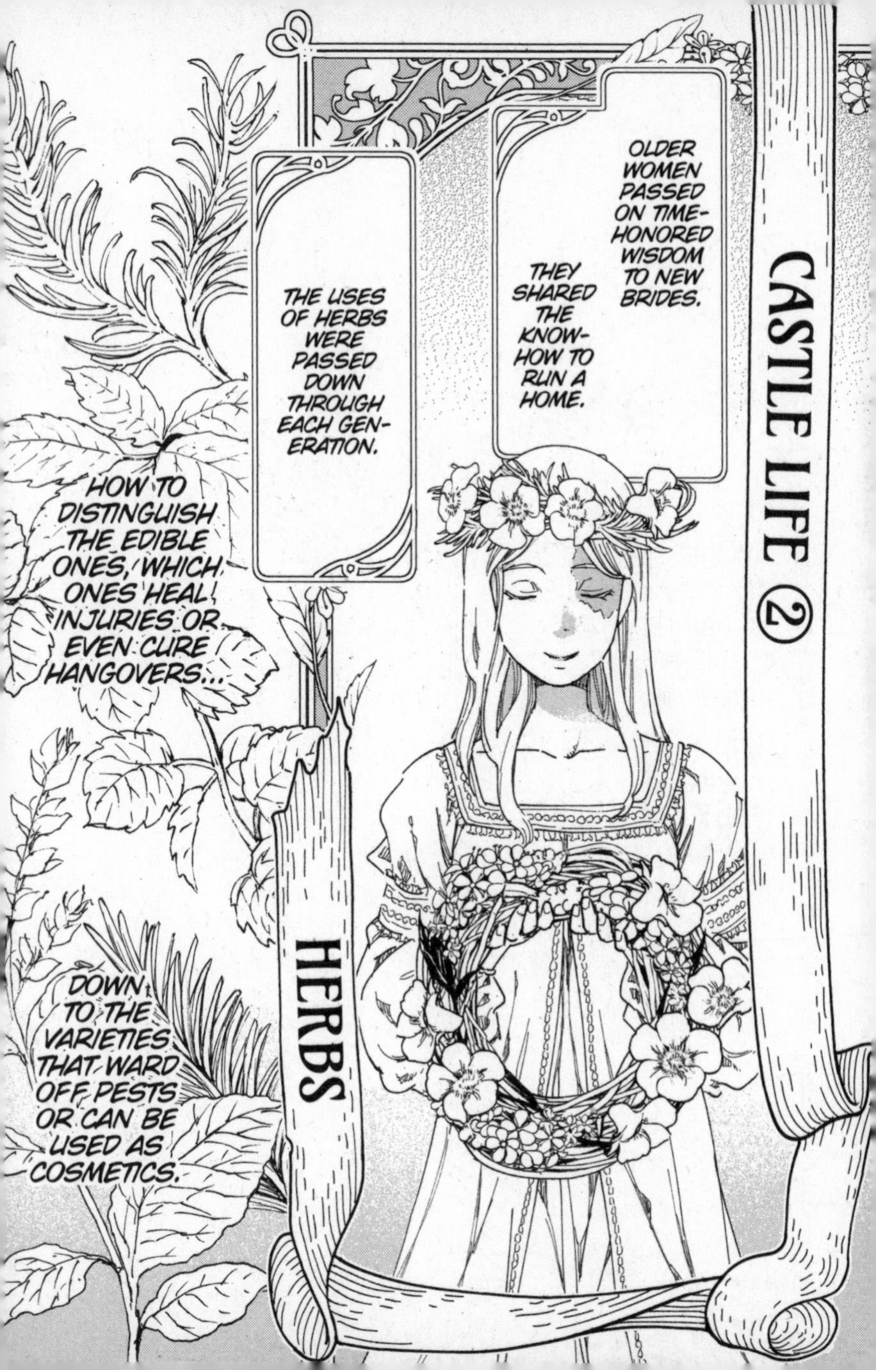
CASTLE LIFE ②
HERBS
OLDER WOMEN PASSED ON TIME-HONORED WISDOM TO NEW BRIDES.
THEY SHARED THE KNOW-HOW TO RUN A HOME.
THE USES OF HERBS WERE PASSED DOWN THROUGH EACH GEN-ERATION.
HOW TO DISTINGUISH THE EDIBLE ONES, WHICH ONES HEAL INJURIES OR EVEN CURE HANGOVERS...
DOWN TO THE VARIETIES THAT WARD OFF PESTS OR CAN BE USED AS COSMETICS.

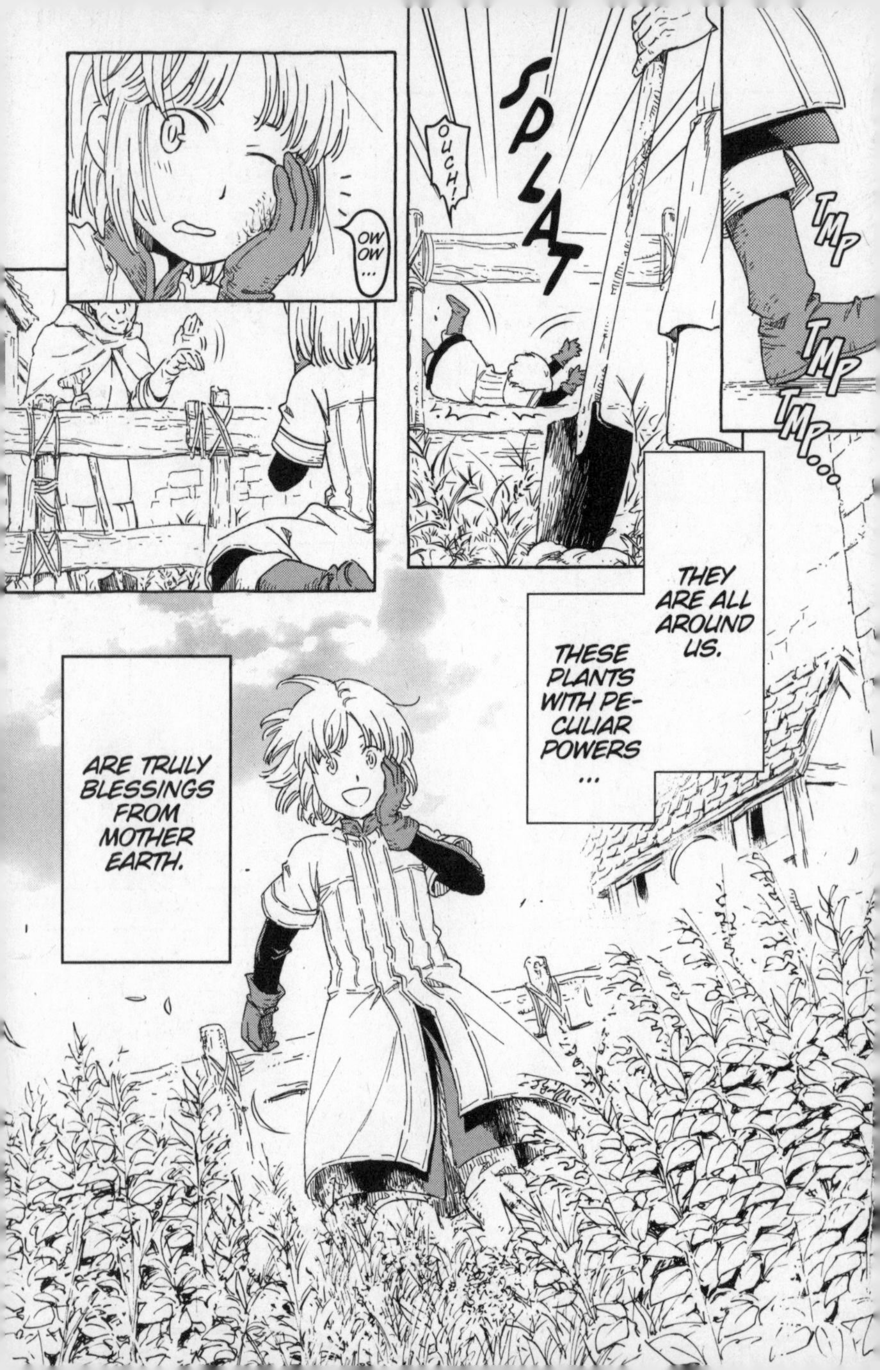
TMP
TMP
TMP...
SPLAT
OUCH!
OW OW...
THEY ARE ALL AROUND US.
THESE PLANTS WITH PE-CULIAR POWERS...
ARE TRULY BLESSINGS FROM MOTHER EARTH.

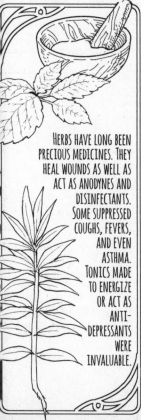

HERBS HAVE LONG BEEN PRECIOUS MEDICINES. THEY HEAL WOUNDS AS WELL AS ACT AS ANODYNES AND DISINFECTANTS. SOME SUPPRESSED COUGHS, FEVERS, AND EVEN ASTHMA. TONICS MADE TO ENERGIZE OR ACT AS ANTI-DEPRESSANTS WERE INVALUABLE.

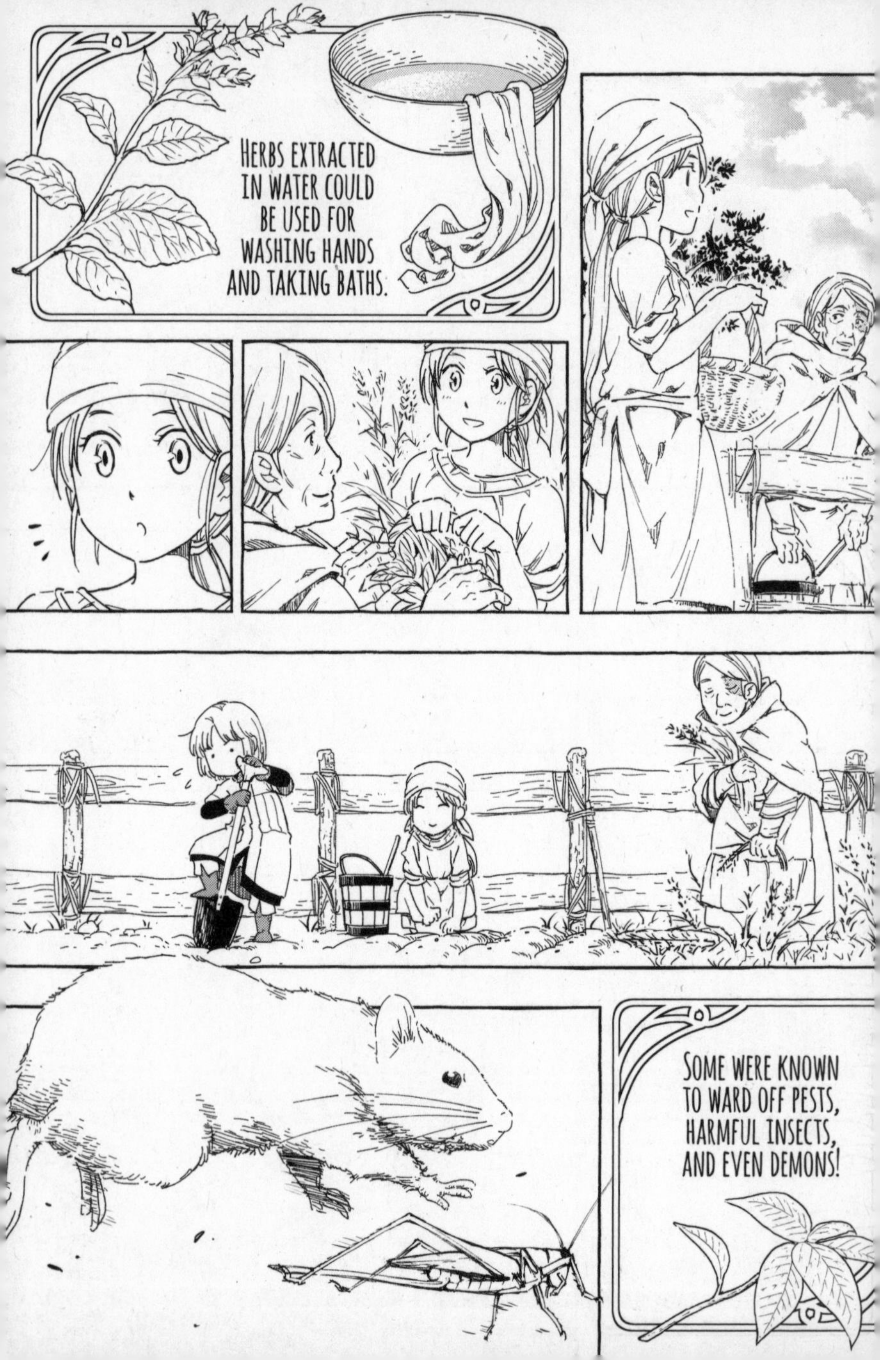
HERBS EXTRACTED IN WATER COULD BE USED FOR WASHING HANDS AND TAKING BATHS.
SOME WERE KNOWN TO WARD OFF PESTS, HARMFUL INSECTS, AND EVEN DEMONS!

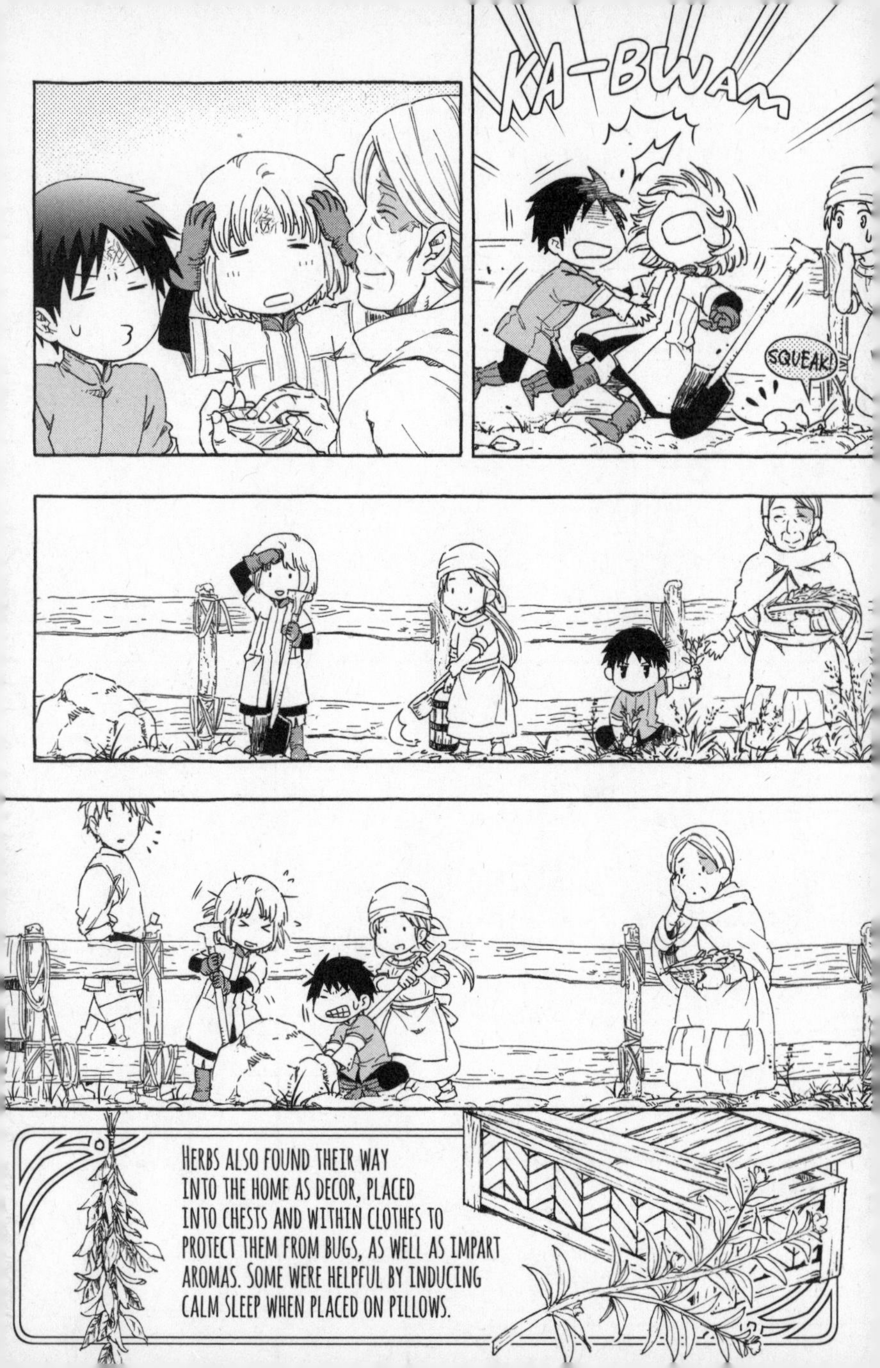
KA-BWAM
SQUEAK!
HERBS ALSO FOUND THEIR WAY INTO THE HOME AS DECOR, PLACED INTO CHESTS AND WITHIN CLOTHES TO PROTECT THEM FROM BUGS, AS WELL AS IMPART AROMAS. SOME WERE HELPFUL BY INDUCING CALM SLEEP WHEN PLACED ON PILLOWS.

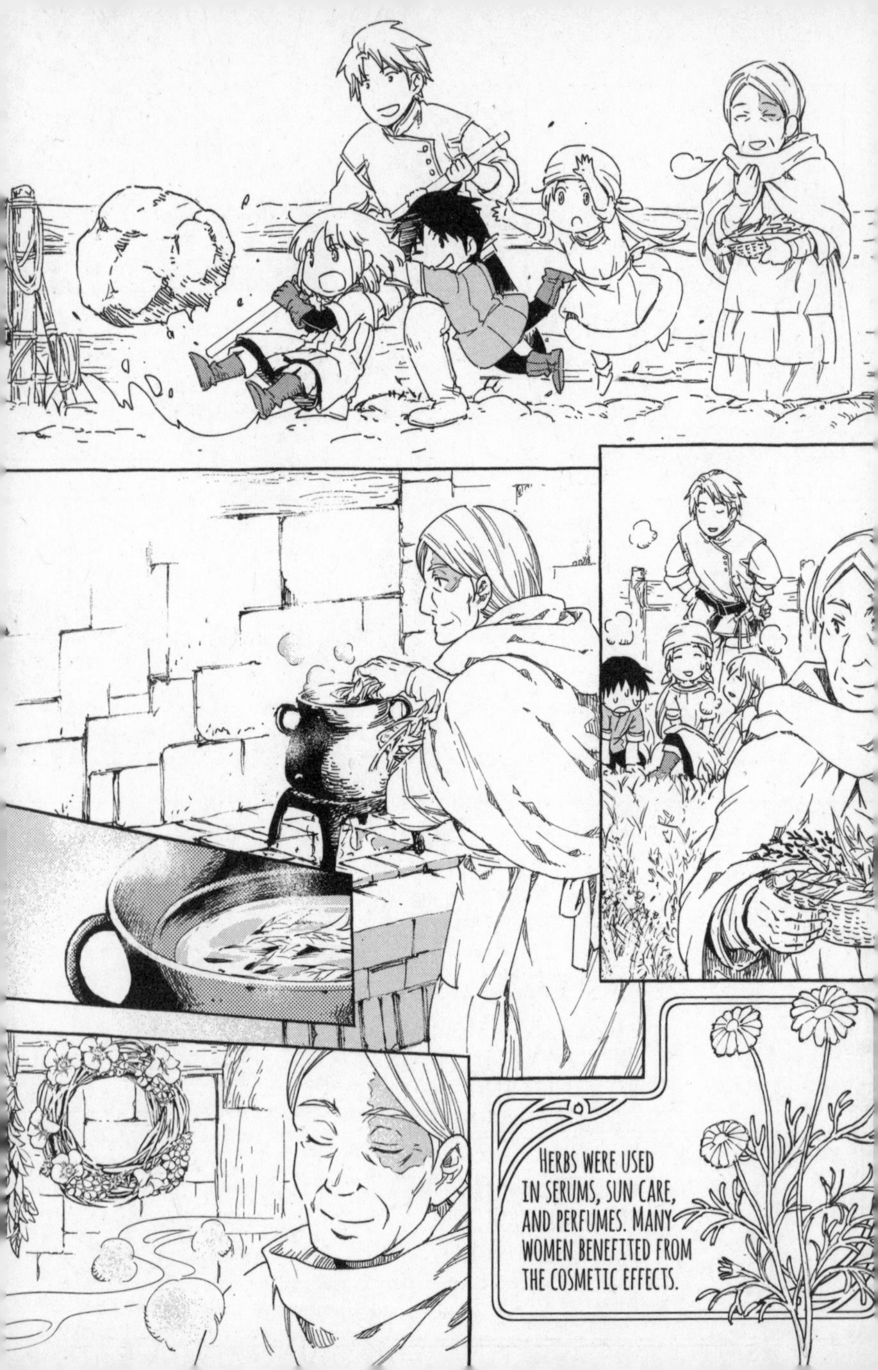
HERBS WERE USED IN SERUMS, SUN CARE, AND PERFUMES. MANY WOMEN BENEFITED FROM THE COSMETIC EFFECTS.

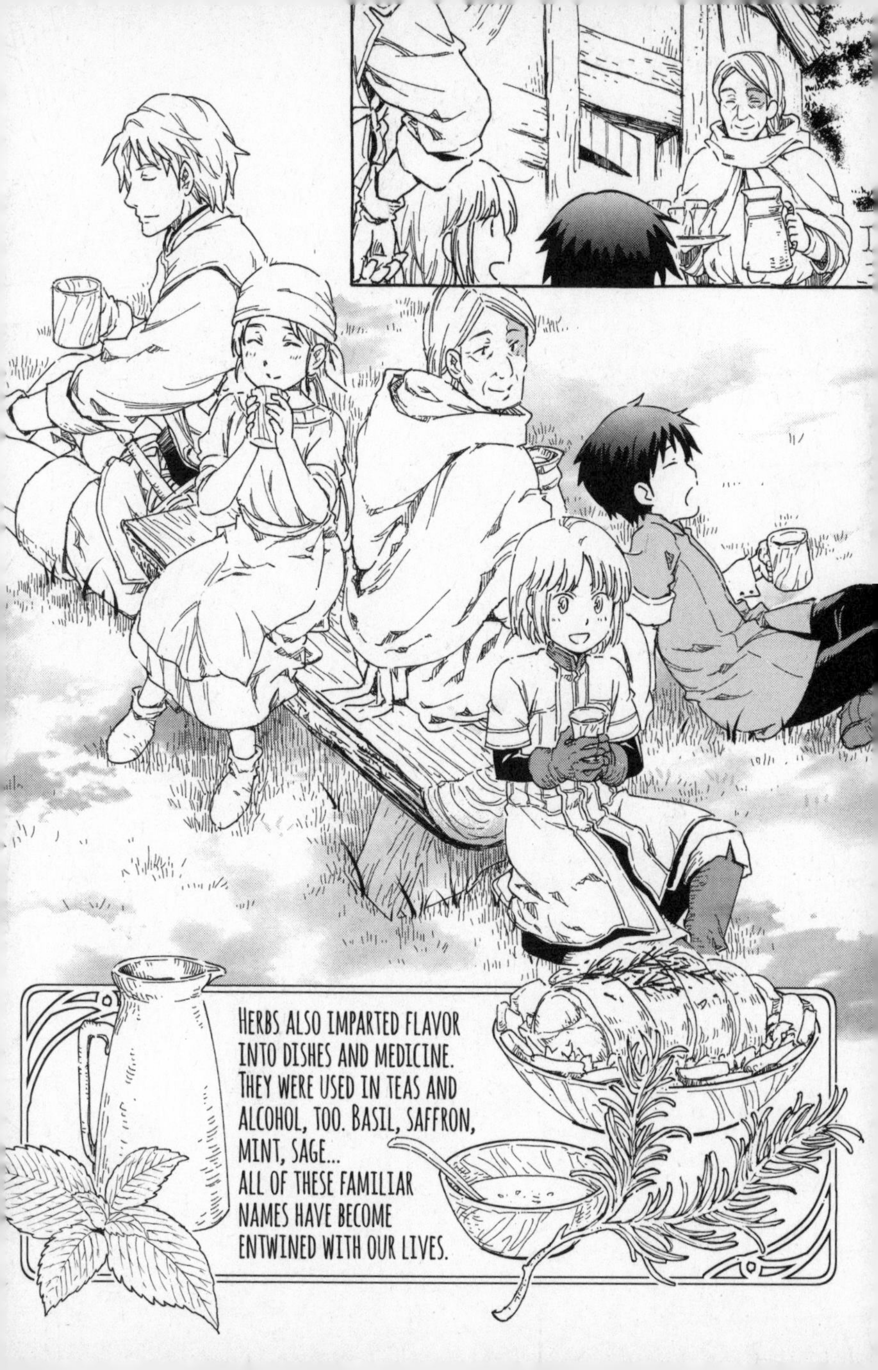
HERBS ALSO IMPARTED FLAVOR INTO DISHES AND MEDICINE. THEY WERE USED IN TEAS AND ALCOHOL, TOO. BASIL, SAFFRON, MINT, SAGE... ALL OF THESE FAMILIAR NAMES HAVE BECOME ENTWINED WITH OUR LIVES.

CHAPTER 8

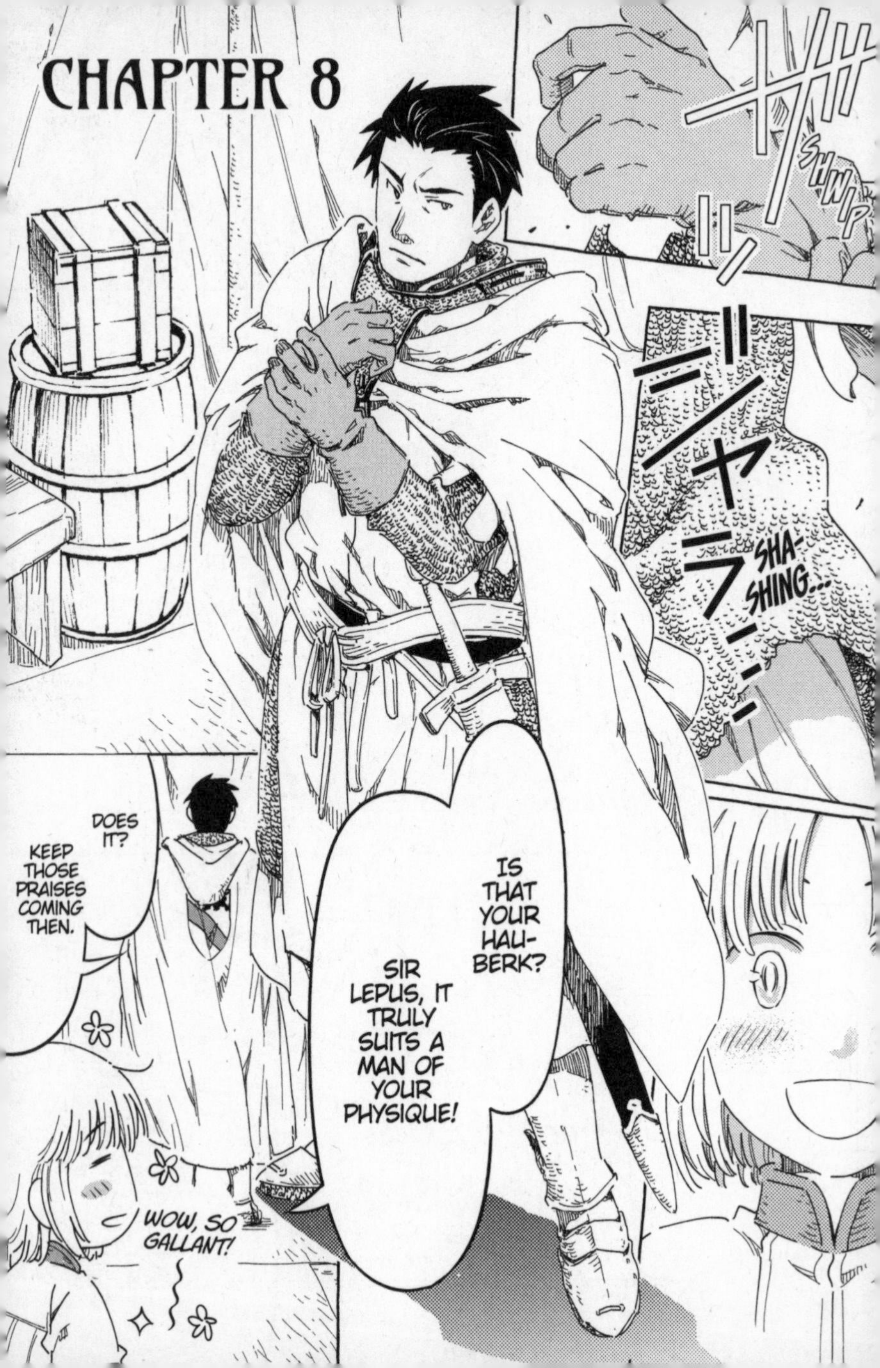
SHWIP
SHA-SHING...
IS THAT YOUR HAUBERK?
SIR LEPUS, IT TRULY SUITS A MAN OF YOUR PHYSIQUE!
DOES IT?
KEEP THOSE PRAISES COMING THEN.
WOW, SO GALLANT!

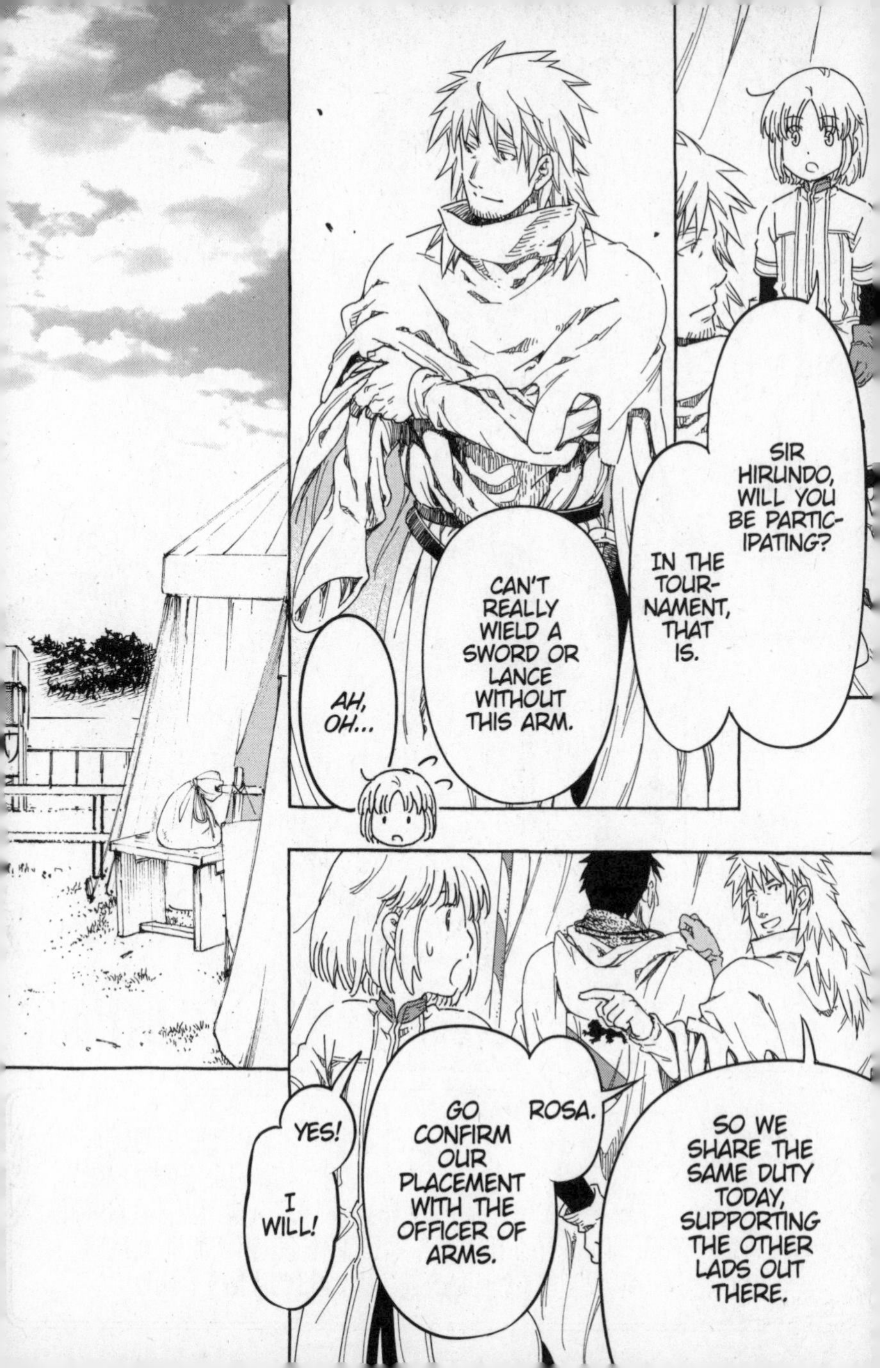
SIR HIRUNDO, WILL YOU BE PARTICIPATING?
IN THE TOURNAMENT, THAT IS.
CAN'T REALLY WIELD A SWORD OR LANCE WITHOUT THIS ARM.
AH, OH...
SO WE SHARE THE SAME DUTY TODAY, SUPPORTING THE OTHER LADS OUT THERE.
ROSA.
GO CONFIRM OUR PLACEMENT WITH THE OFFICER OF ARMS.
YES!
I WILL!

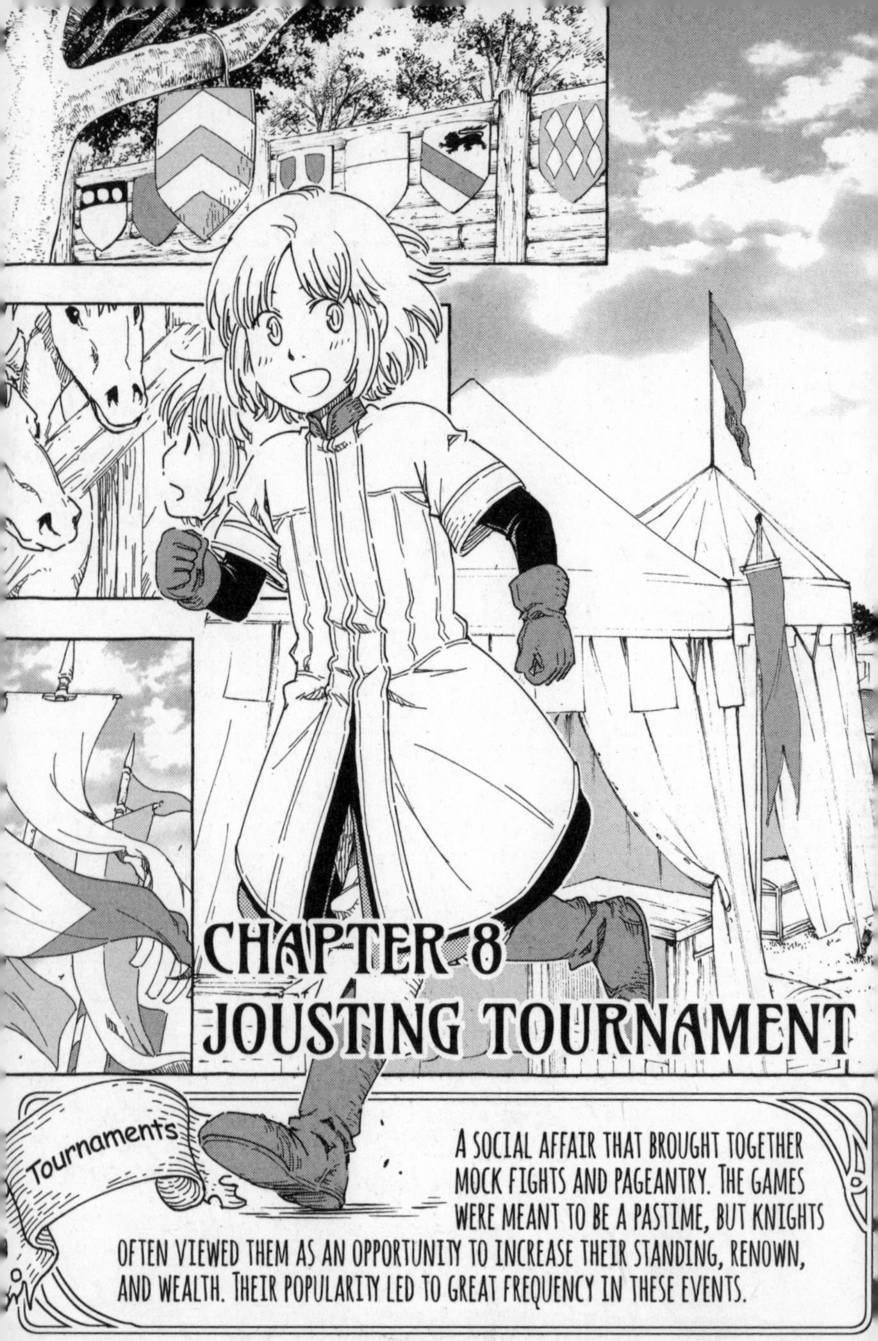
CHAPTER 8
JOUSTING TOURNAMENT

Tournaments

A SOCIAL AFFAIR THAT BROUGHT TOGETHER MOCK FIGHTS AND PAGEANTRY. THE GAMES WERE MEANT TO BE A PASTIME, BUT KNIGHTS OFTEN VIEWED THEM AS AN OPPORTUNITY TO INCREASE THEIR STANDING, RENOWN, AND WEALTH. THEIR POPULARITY LED TO GREAT FREQUENCY IN THESE EVENTS.

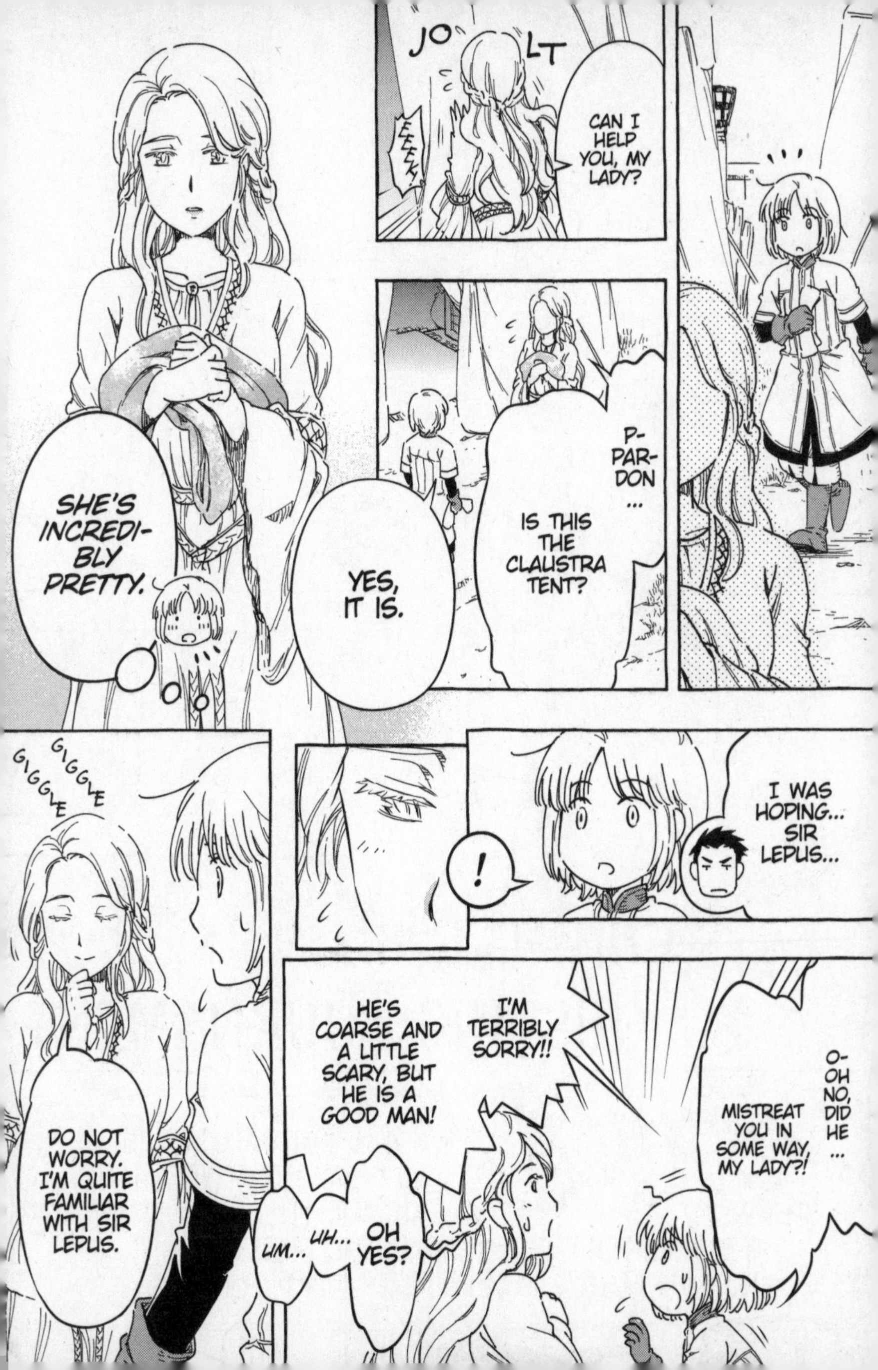
...
JOLT
EEEEK
CAN I HELP YOU, MY LADY?
P-PARDON...
IS THIS THE CLAUSTRA TENT?
YES, IT IS.
SHE'S INCREDIBLY PRETTY.
I WAS HOPING... SIR LEPUS...
!
O-OH NO, DID HE...
MISTREAT YOU IN SOME WAY, MY LADY?!
I'M TERRIBLY SORRY!!
HE'S COARSE AND A LITTLE SCARY, BUT HE IS A GOOD MAN!
OH YES?
UH...
UM...
GIGGLE GIGGLE
DO NOT WORRY. I'M QUITE FAMILIAR WITH SIR LEPUS.

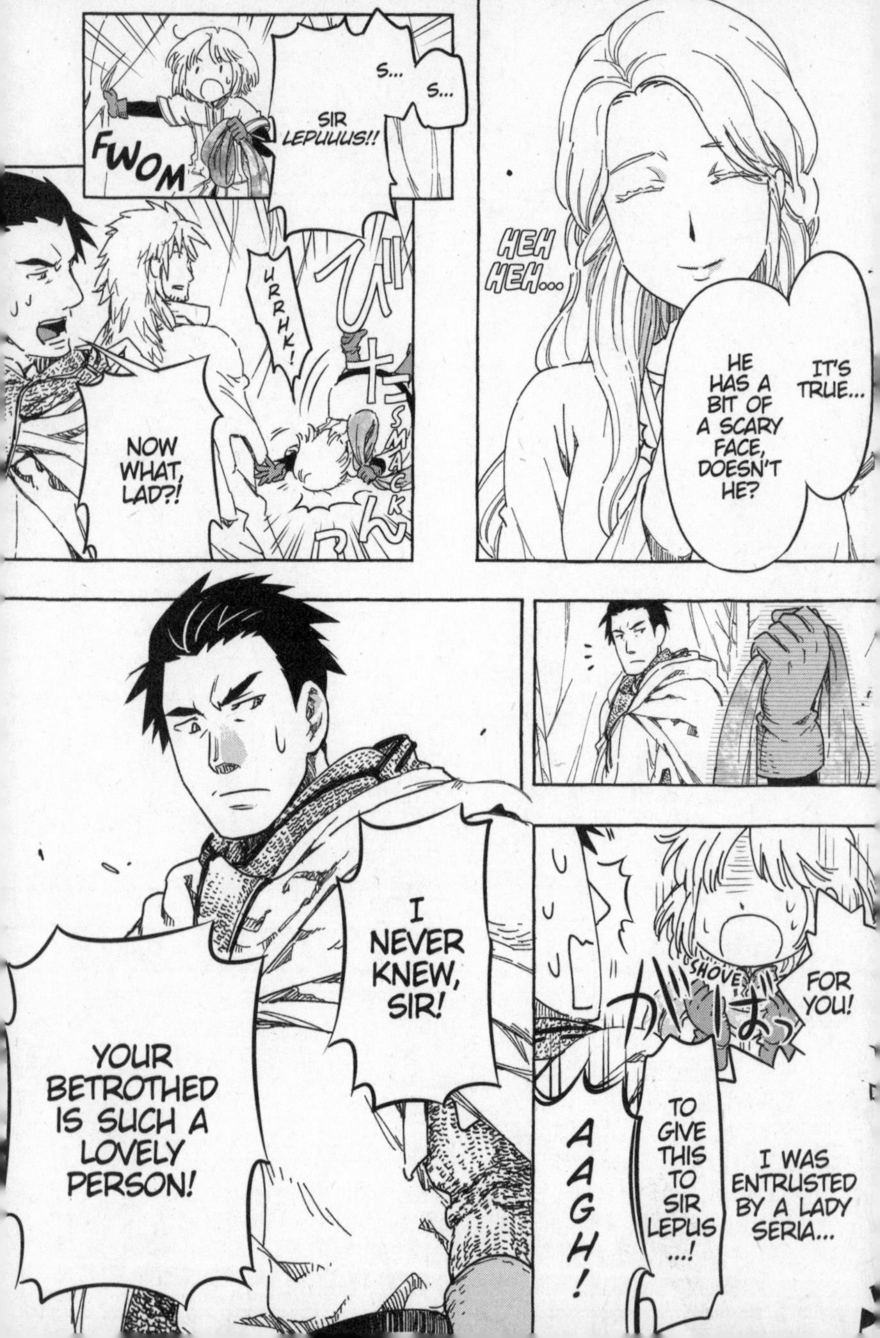
HEH HEH...
IT'S TRUE...
HE HAS A BIT OF A SCARY FACE, DOESN'T HE?
S...
S...
SIR LEPUUUS!!
FWOM
URRHK!
SMACK
NOW WHAT, LAD?!
FOR YOU!
SHOVE
I WAS ENTRUSTED BY A LADY SERIA...
TO GIVE THIS TO SIR LEPUS...!
AAGH!
I NEVER KNEW, SIR!
YOUR BETROTHED IS SUCH A LOVELY PERSON!

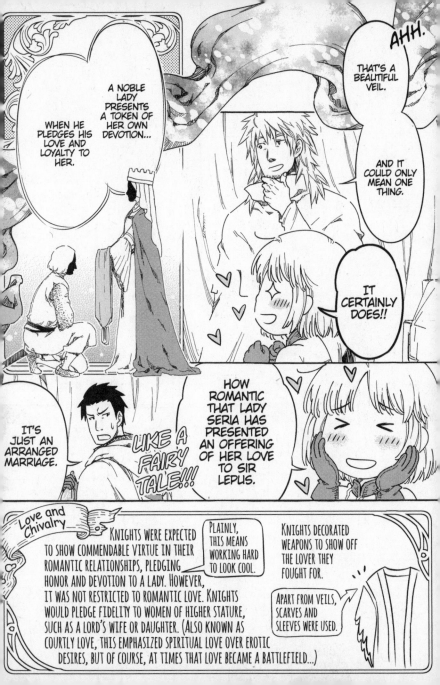

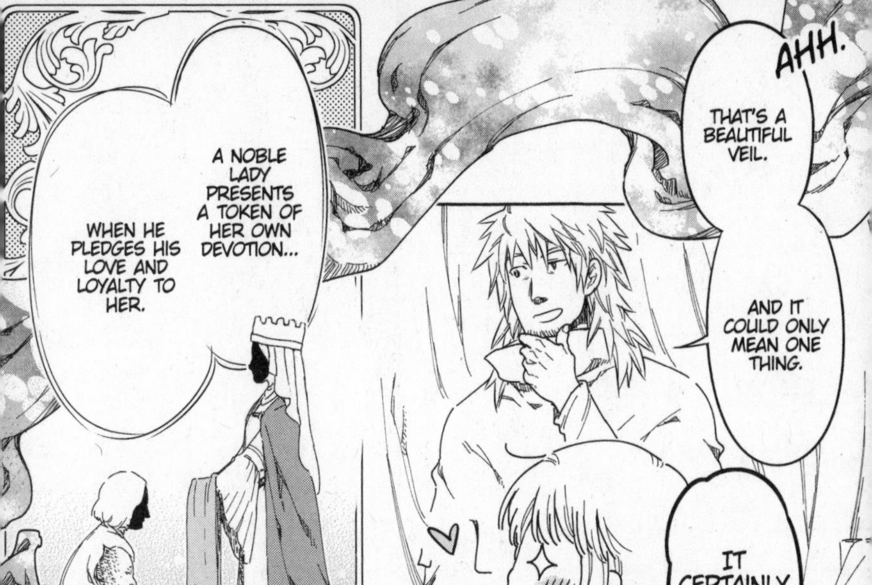
AHH.
THAT'S A BEAUTIFUL VEIL.
AND IT COULD ONLY MEAN ONE THING.
IT CERTAINLY DOES!!
A NOBLE LADY PRESENTS A TOKEN OF HER OWN DEVOTION...
WHEN HE PLEDGES HIS LOVE AND LOYALTY TO HER.
HOW ROMANTIC THAT LADY SERIA HAS PRESENTED AN OFFERING OF HER LOVE TO SIR LEPUS.
LIKE A FAIRY TALE!!!
IT'S JUST AN ARRANGED MARRIAGE.

Love and Chivalry

Knights were expected to show commendable virtue in their romantic relationships, pledging honor and devotion to a lady. However, it was not restricted to romantic love. Knights would pledge fidelity to women of higher stature, such as a lord's wife or daughter. (Also known as courtly love, this emphasized spiritual love over erotic desires, but of course, at times that love became a battlefield...)

Plainly, this means working hard to look cool.

Knights decorated weapons to show off the lover they fought for.

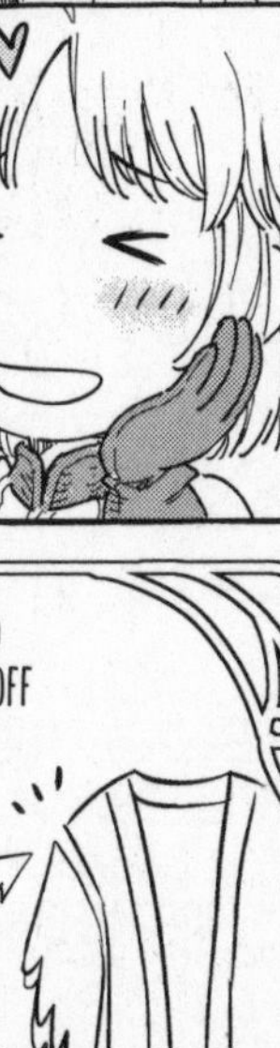

Apart from veils, scarves and sleeves were used.

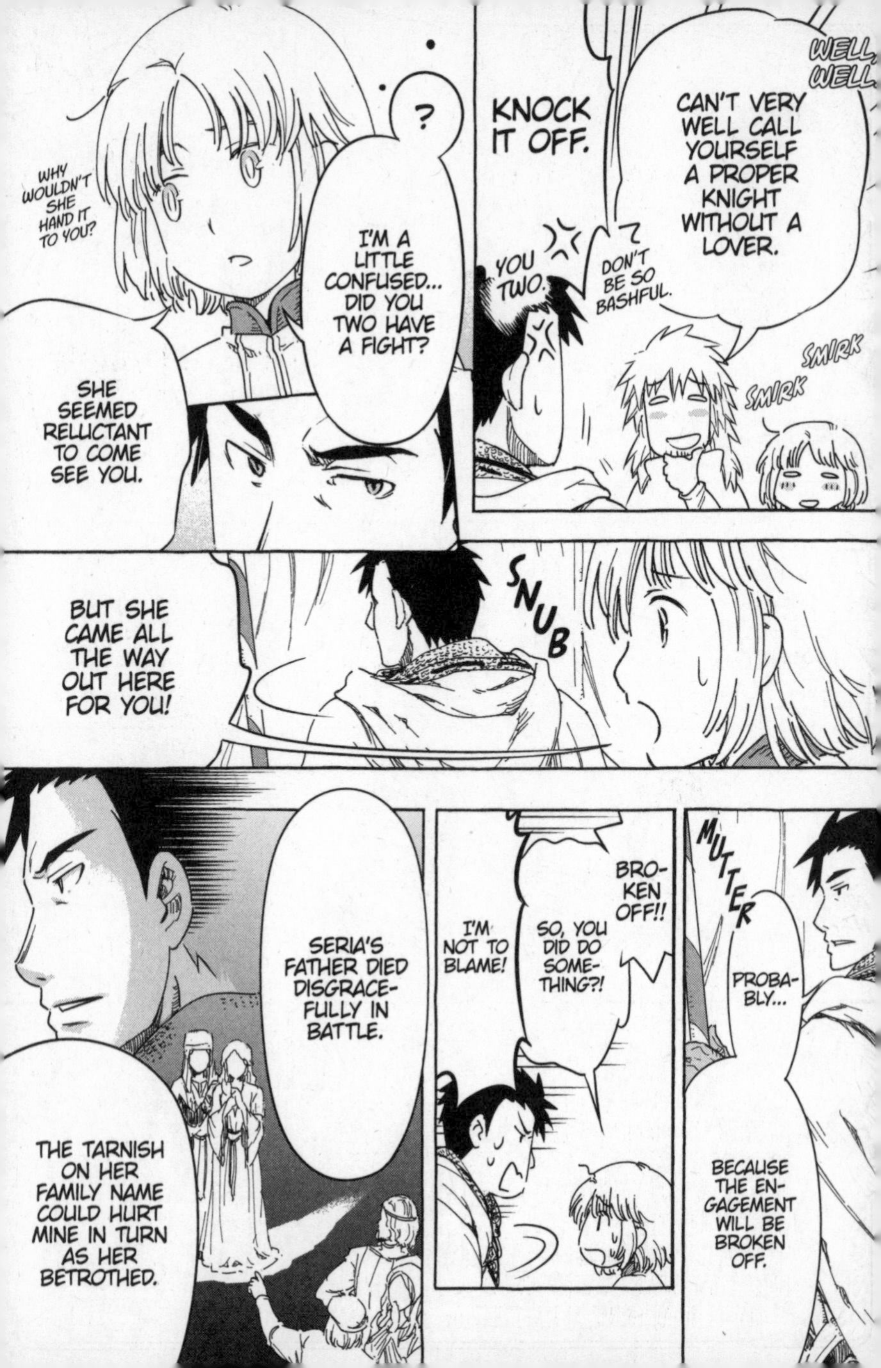

WELL, WELL
CAN'T VERY WELL CALL YOURSELF A PROPER KNIGHT WITHOUT A LOVER.
SMIRK
SMIRK
DON'T BE SO BASHFUL.
YOU TWO.
KNOCK IT OFF.
?
I'M A LITTLE CONFUSED... DID YOU TWO HAVE A FIGHT?
WHY WOULDN'T SHE HAND IT TO YOU?
SHE SEEMED RELUCTANT TO COME SEE YOU.
SNUB
BUT SHE CAME ALL THE WAY OUT HERE FOR YOU!
MUTTER
PROBABLY...
BECAUSE THE ENGAGEMENT WILL BE BROKEN OFF.
BROKEN OFF!!
SO, YOU DID DO SOMETHING?!
I'M NOT TO BLAME!
SERIA'S FATHER DIED DISGRACEFULLY IN BATTLE.
THE TARNISH ON HER FAMILY NAME COULD HURT MINE IN TURN AS HER BETROTHED.

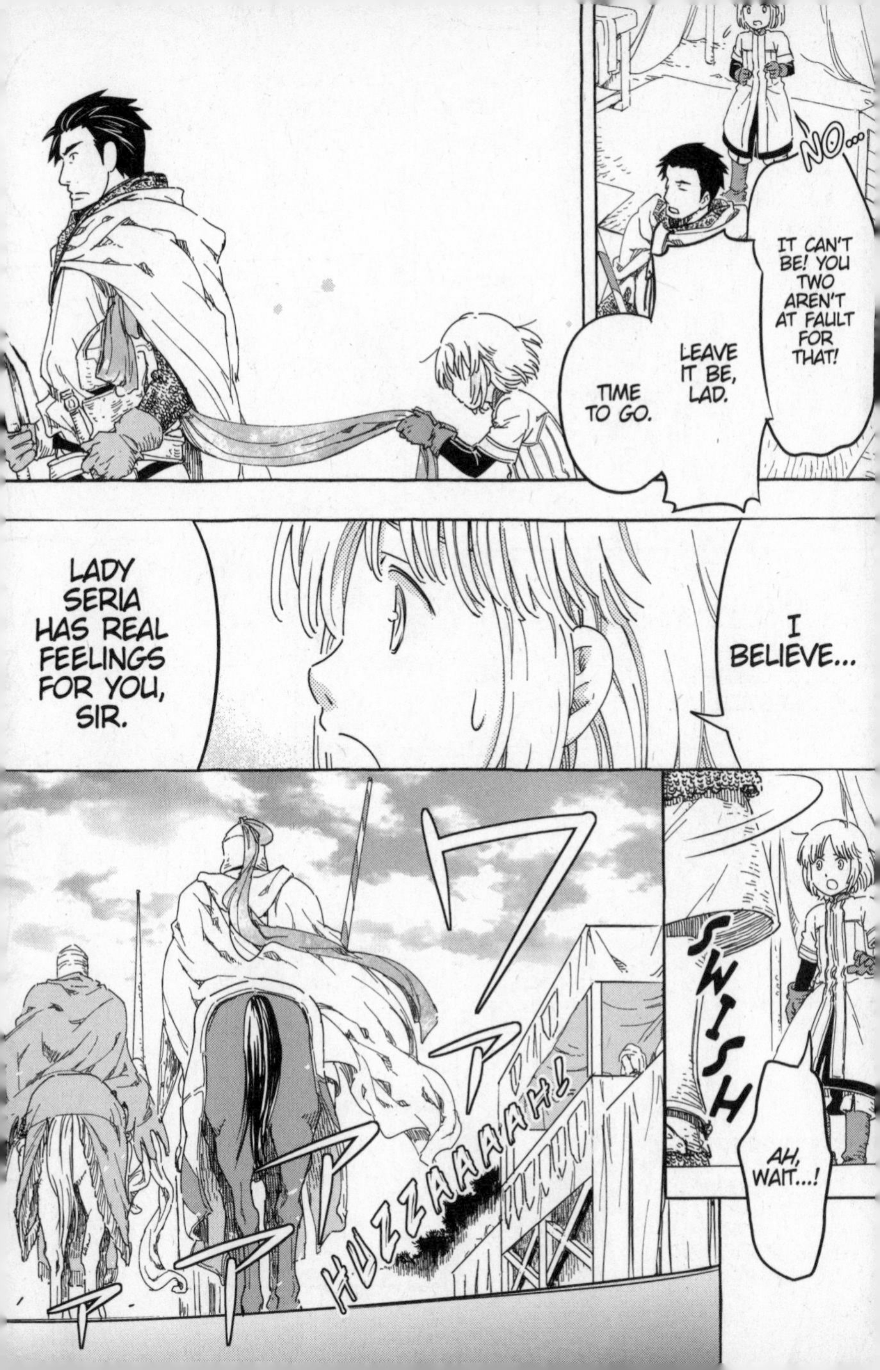
NO...
IT CAN'T BE! YOU TWO AREN'T AT FAULT FOR THAT!
LEAVE IT BE, LAD.
TIME TO GO.
I BELIEVE...
LADY SERIA HAS REAL FEELINGS FOR YOU, SIR.
SWISH
AH, WAIT...!
HUZZAAAAAH!

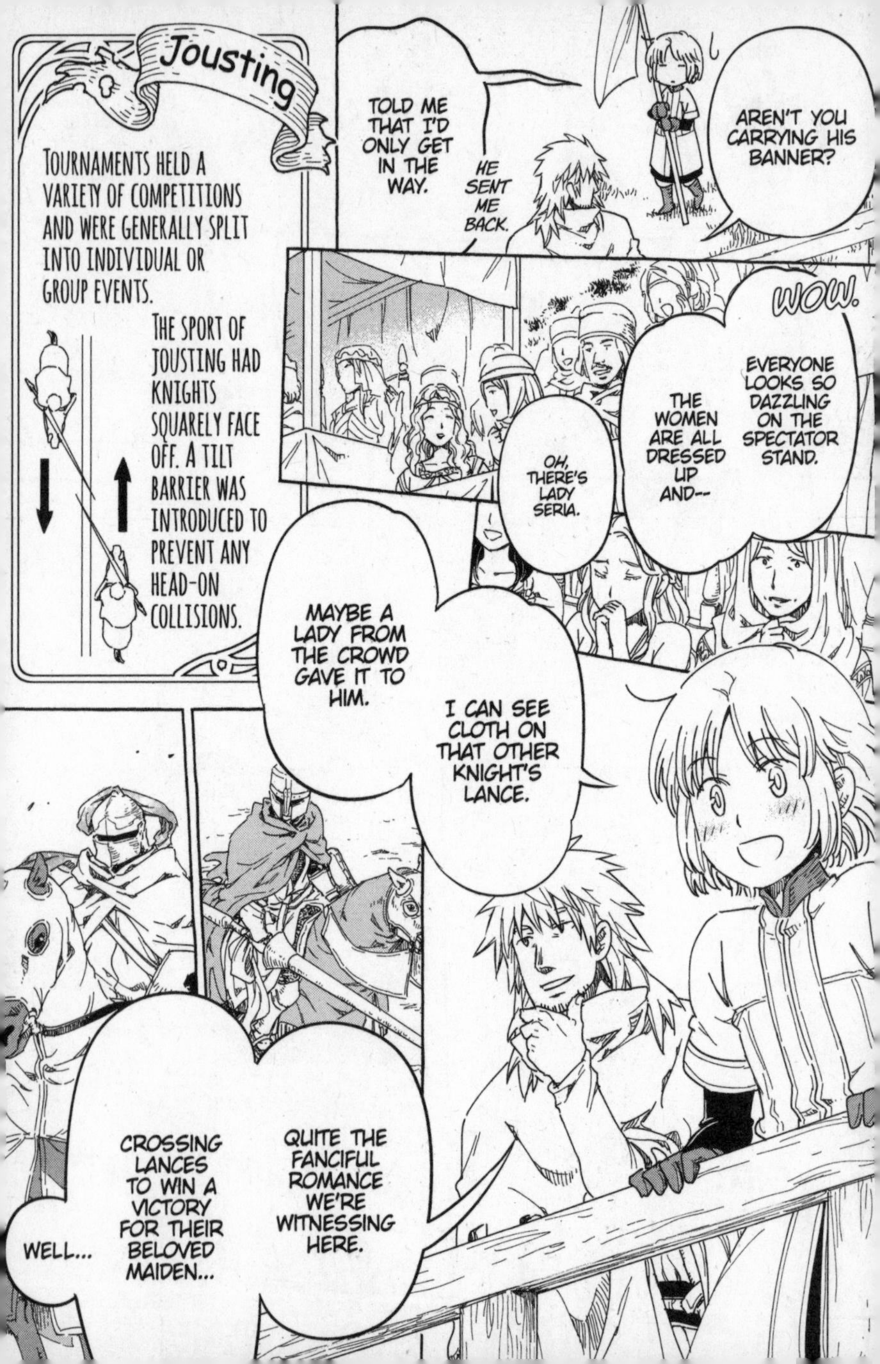
AREN'T YOU CARRYING HIS BANNER?
HE SENT ME BACK.
TOLD ME THAT I'D ONLY GET IN THE WAY.
Jousting
TOURNAMENTS HELD A VARIETY OF COMPETITIONS AND WERE GENERALLY SPLIT INTO INDIVIDUAL OR GROUP EVENTS.
THE SPORT OF JOUSTING HAD KNIGHTS SQUARELY FACE OFF. A TILT BARRIER WAS INTRODUCED TO PREVENT ANY HEAD-ON COLLISIONS.
WOW.
EVERYONE LOOKS SO DAZZLING ON THE SPECTATOR STAND.
THE WOMEN ARE ALL DRESSED UP AND--
OH, THERE'S LADY SERIA.
I CAN SEE CLOTH ON THAT OTHER KNIGHT'S LANCE.
MAYBE A LADY FROM THE CROWD GAVE IT TO HIM.
QUITE THE FANCIFUL ROMANCE WE'RE WITNESSING HERE.
CROSSING LANCES TO WIN A VICTORY FOR THEIR BELOVED MAIDEN...
WELL...

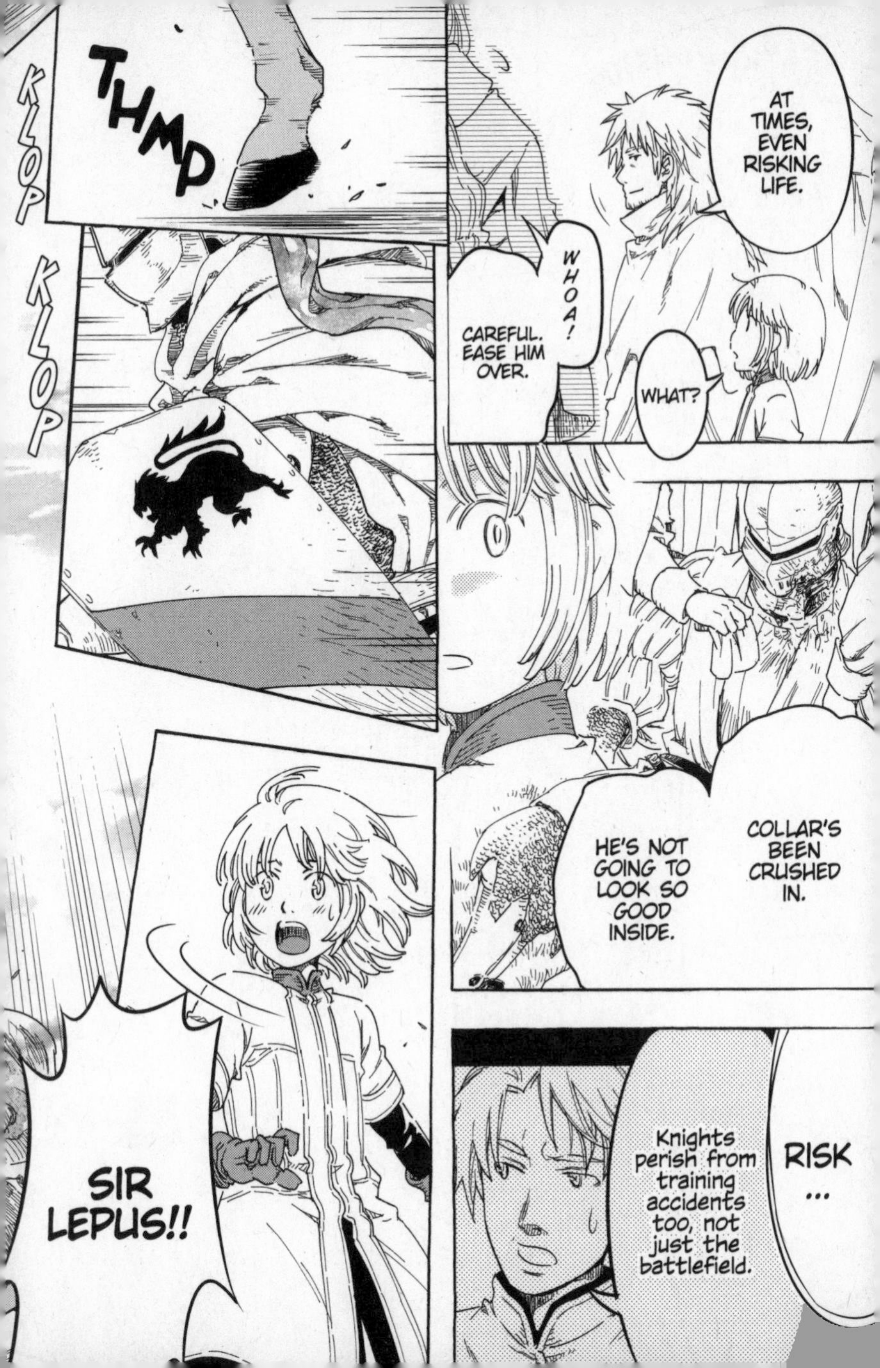
AT TIMES, EVEN RISKING LIFE.
WHOA!
WHAT?
CAREFUL. EASE HIM OVER.
THMP
KLOP KLOP KLOP
COLLAR'S BEEN CRUSHED IN.
HE'S NOT GOING TO LOOK SO GOOD INSIDE.
SIR LEPUS!!
RISK...
Knights perish from training accidents too, not just the battlefield.

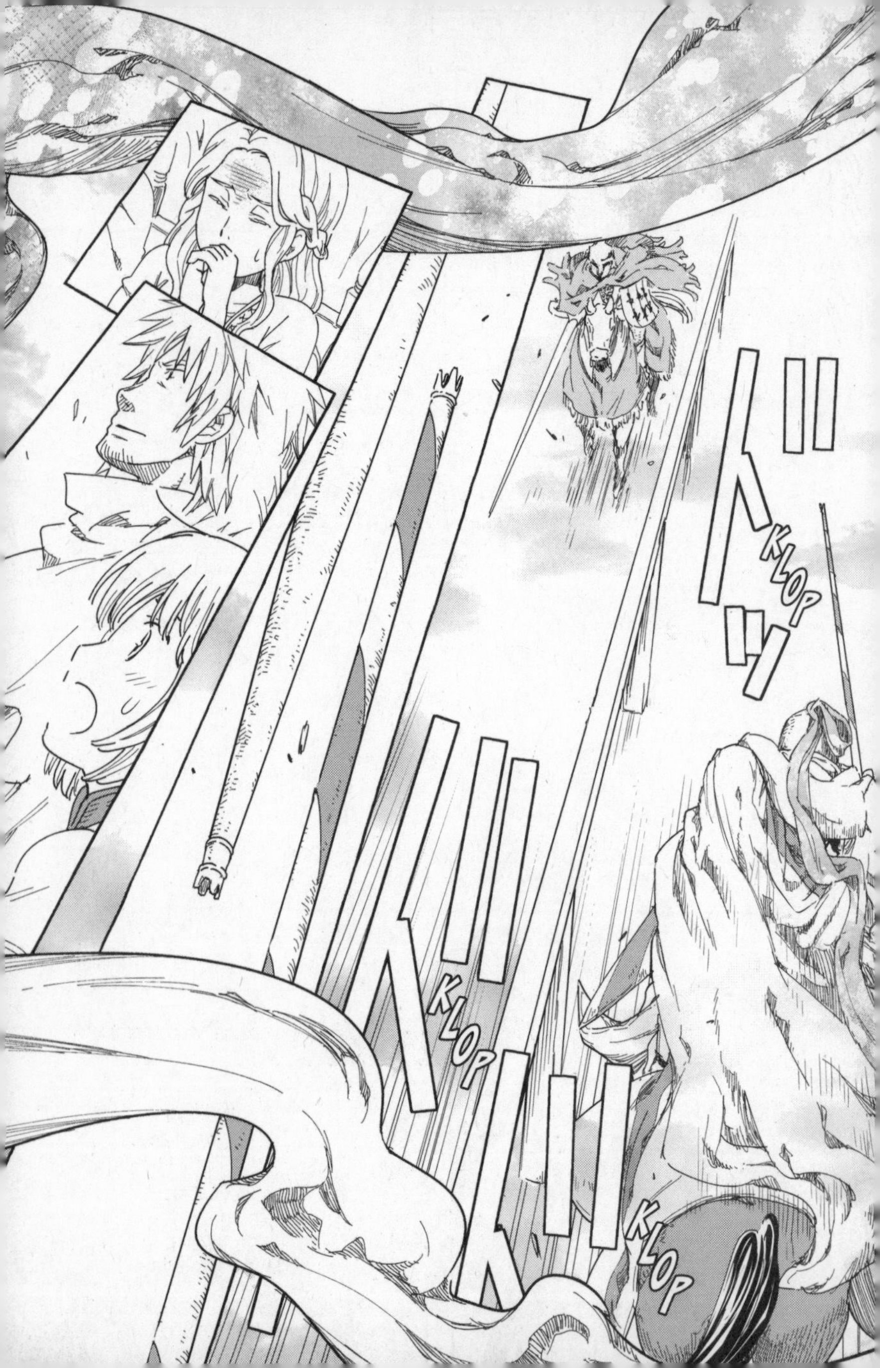
KLOP
KLOP
KLOP

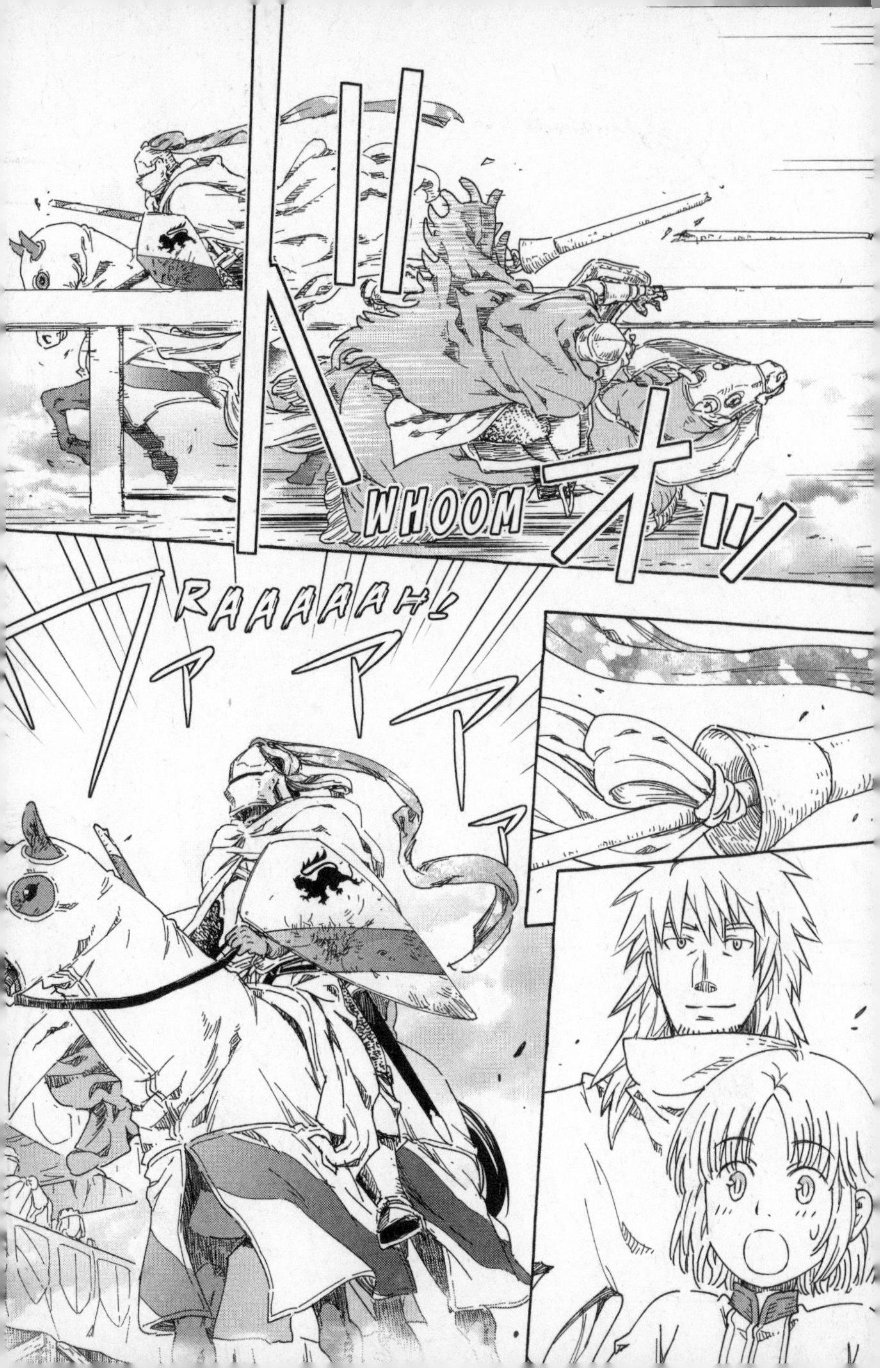
ドオッ
WHOOM
RAAAAAH!

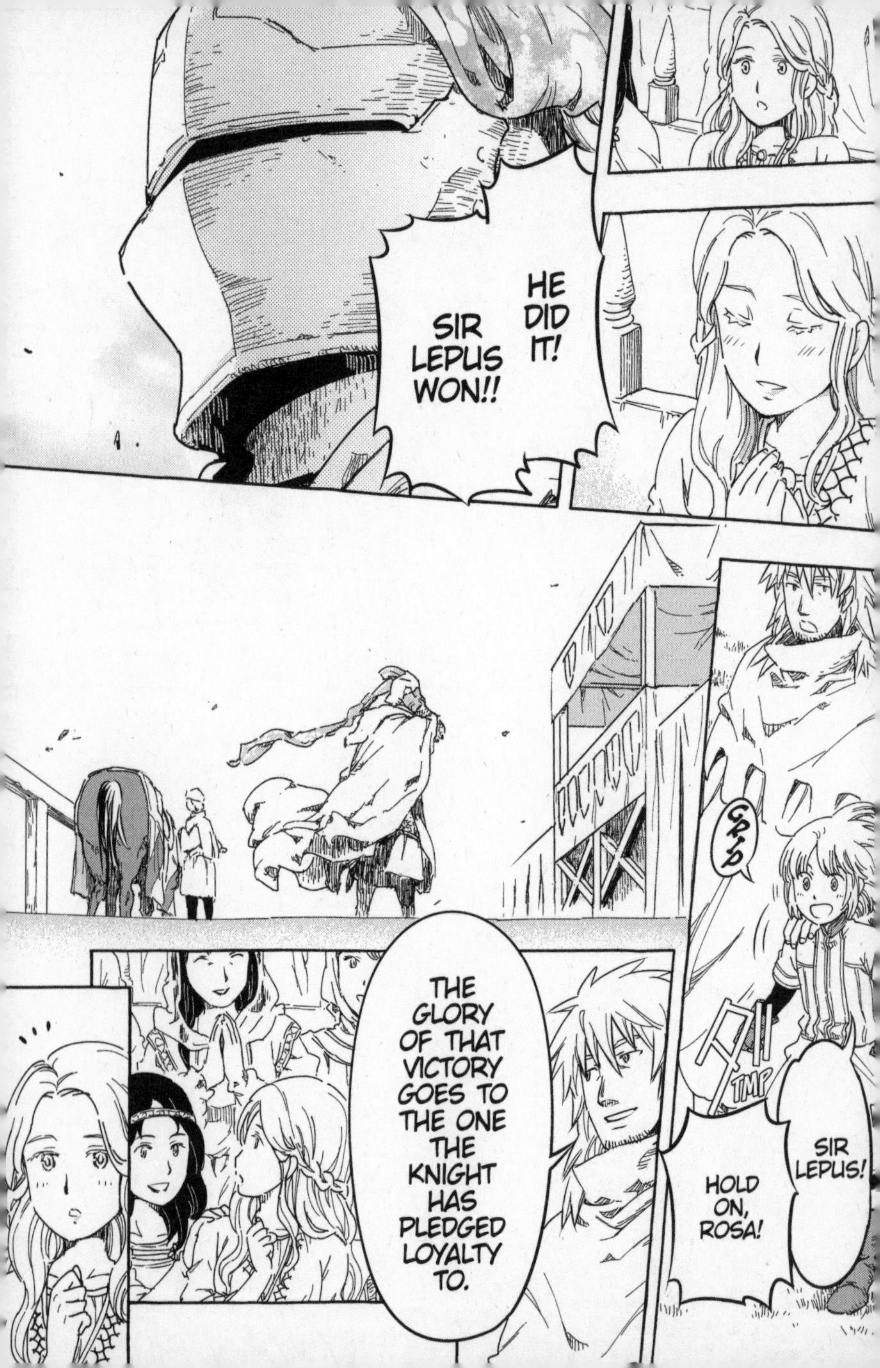
HE DID IT! SIR LEPUS WON!!
GRIP
TMP
SIR LEPUS!
HOLD ON, ROSA!
THE GLORY OF THAT VICTORY GOES TO THE ONE THE KNIGHT HAS PLEDGED LOYALTY TO.
...

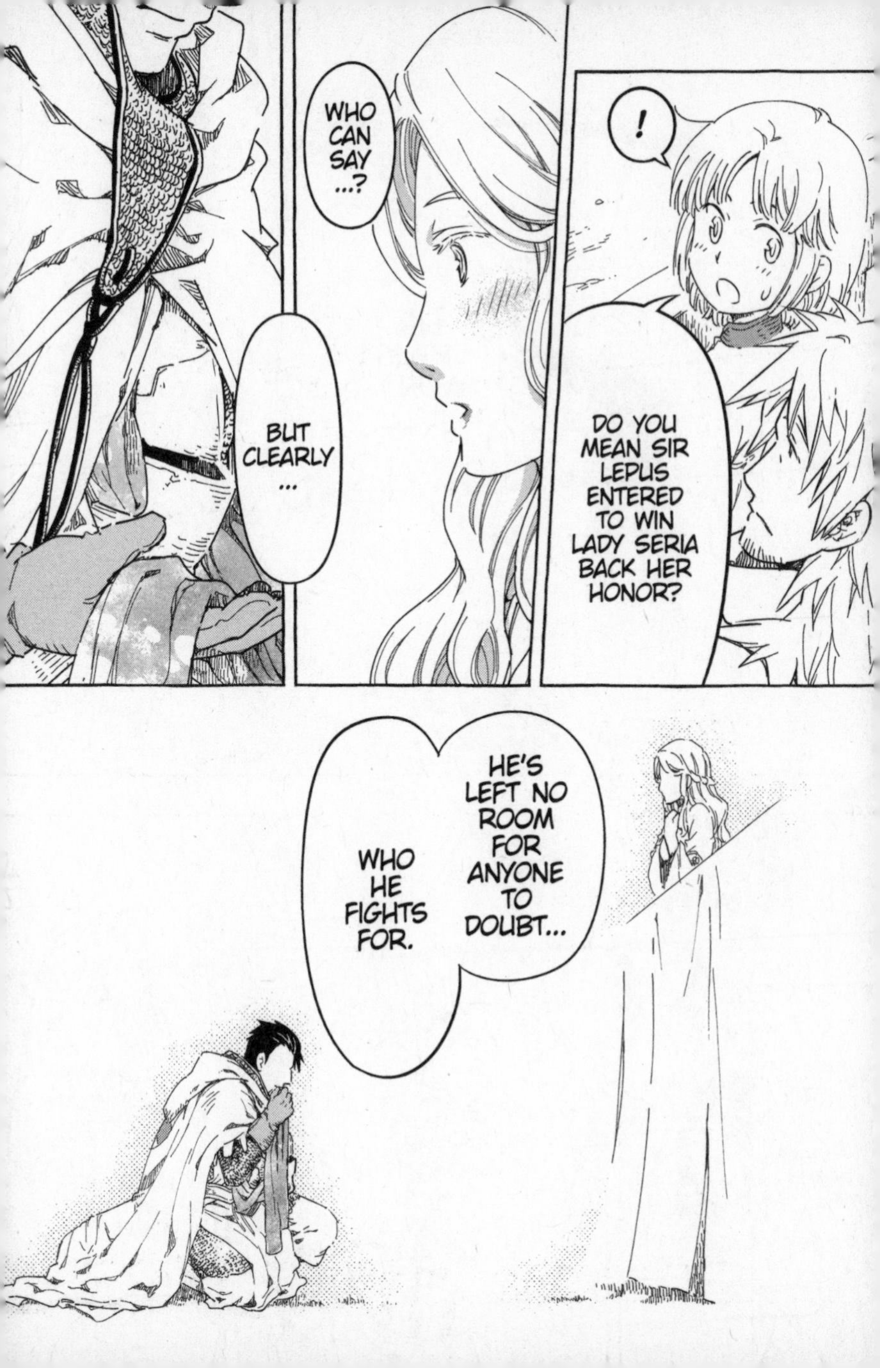
!
DO YOU MEAN SIR LEPUS ENTERED TO WIN LADY SERIA BACK HER HONOR?
WHO CAN SAY ...?
BUT CLEARLY ...
HE'S LEFT NO ROOM FOR ANYONE TO DOUBT...
WHO HE FIGHTS FOR.

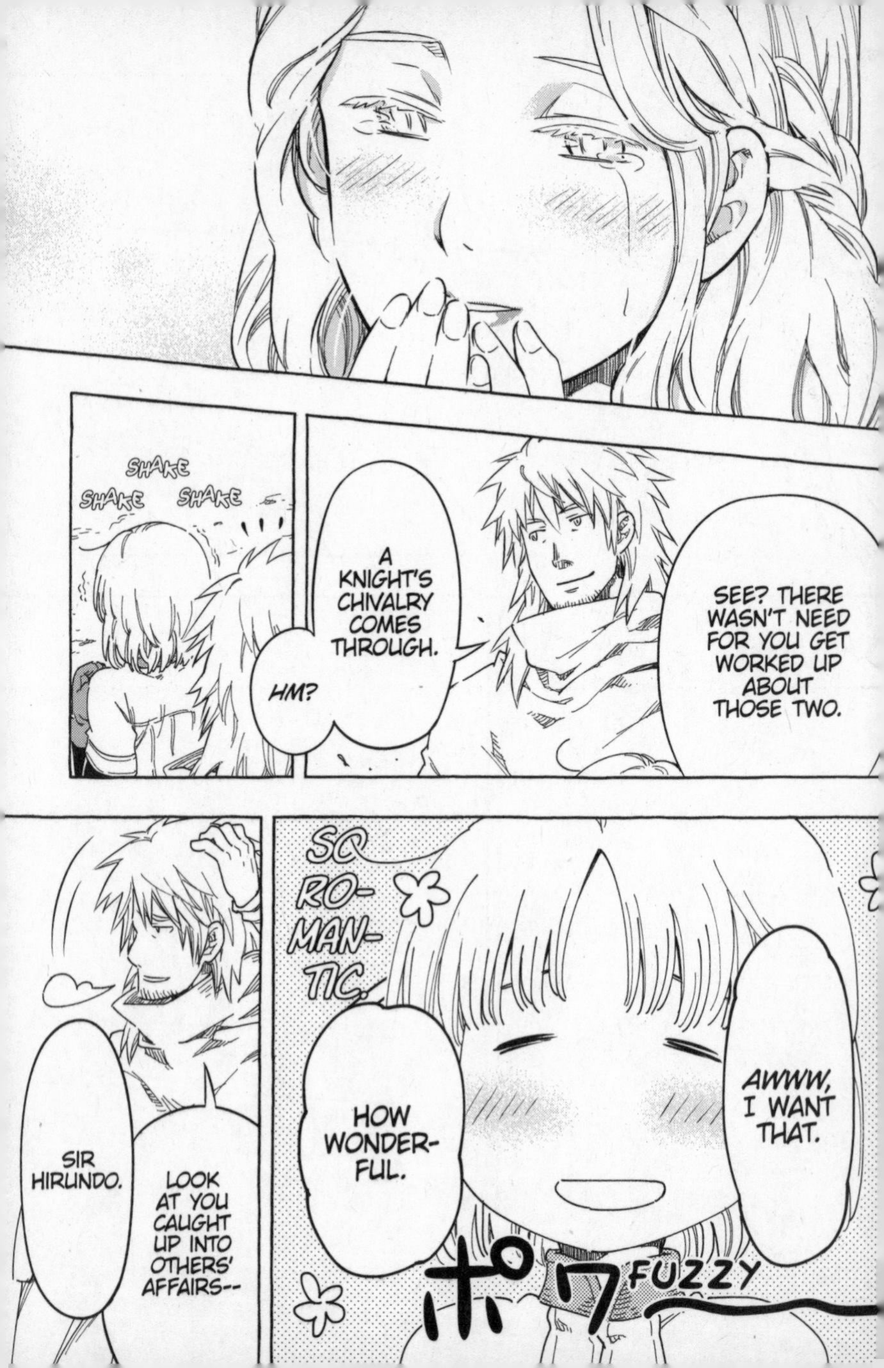
SEE? THERE WASN'T NEED FOR YOU GET WORKED UP ABOUT THOSE TWO.
A KNIGHT'S CHIVALRY COMES THROUGH.
HM?
SHAKE
SHAKE
SHAKE
AWWW, I WANT THAT.
HOW WONDER-FUL.
SO RO-MAN-TIC.
ポワ FUZZY
LOOK AT YOU CAUGHT UP INTO OTHERS' AFFAIRS--
SIR HIRUNDO.

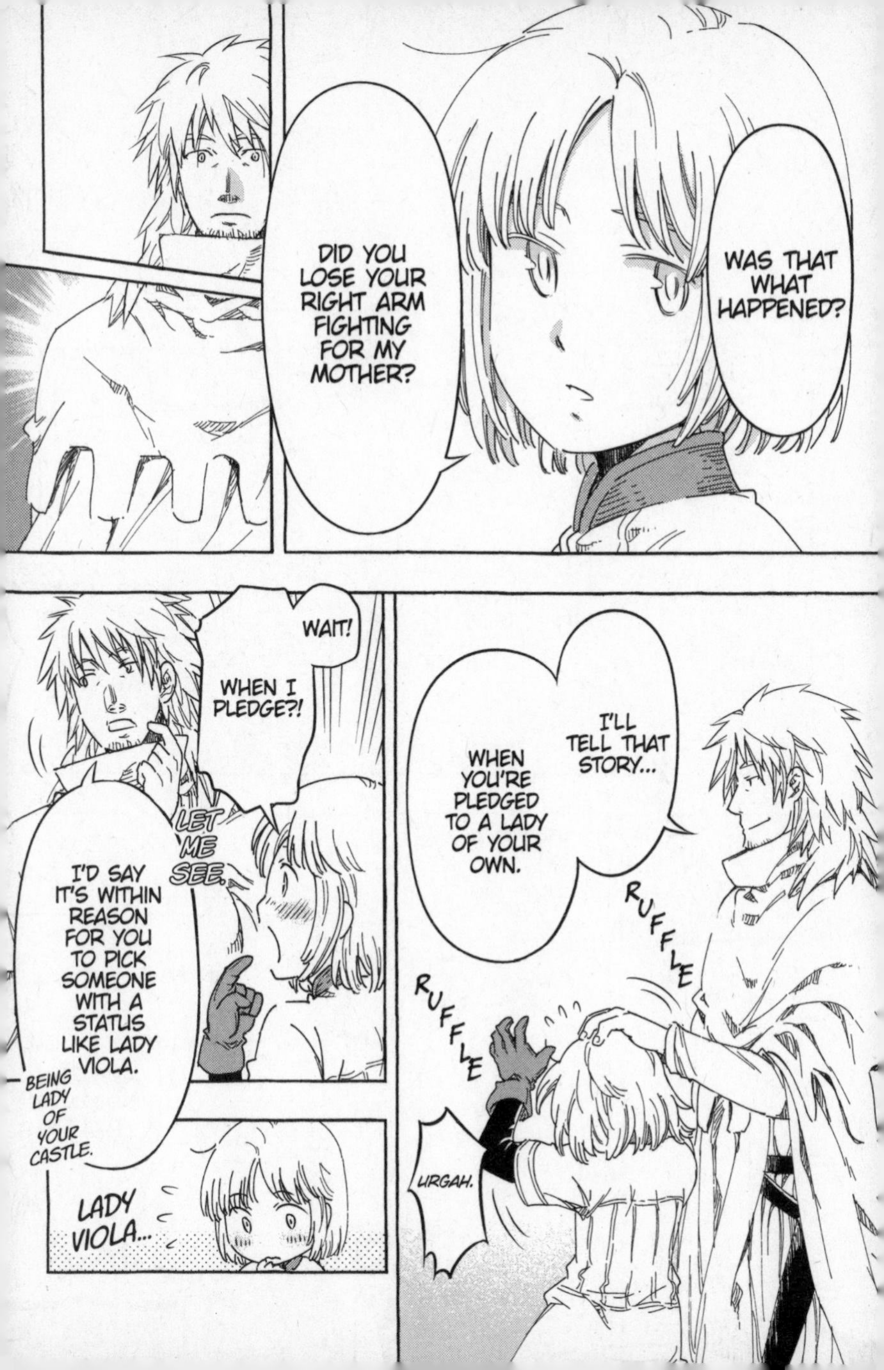
DID YOU LOSE YOUR RIGHT ARM FIGHTING FOR MY MOTHER?
WAS THAT WHAT HAPPENED?
I'LL TELL THAT STORY...
WHEN YOU'RE PLEDGED TO A LADY OF YOUR OWN.
RUFFLE
RUFFLE
URGAH.
WAIT!
WHEN I PLEDGE?!
LET ME SEE.
I'D SAY IT'S WITHIN REASON FOR YOU TO PICK SOMEONE WITH A STATUS LIKE LADY VIOLA.
BEING LADY OF YOUR CASTLE.
LADY VIOLA...

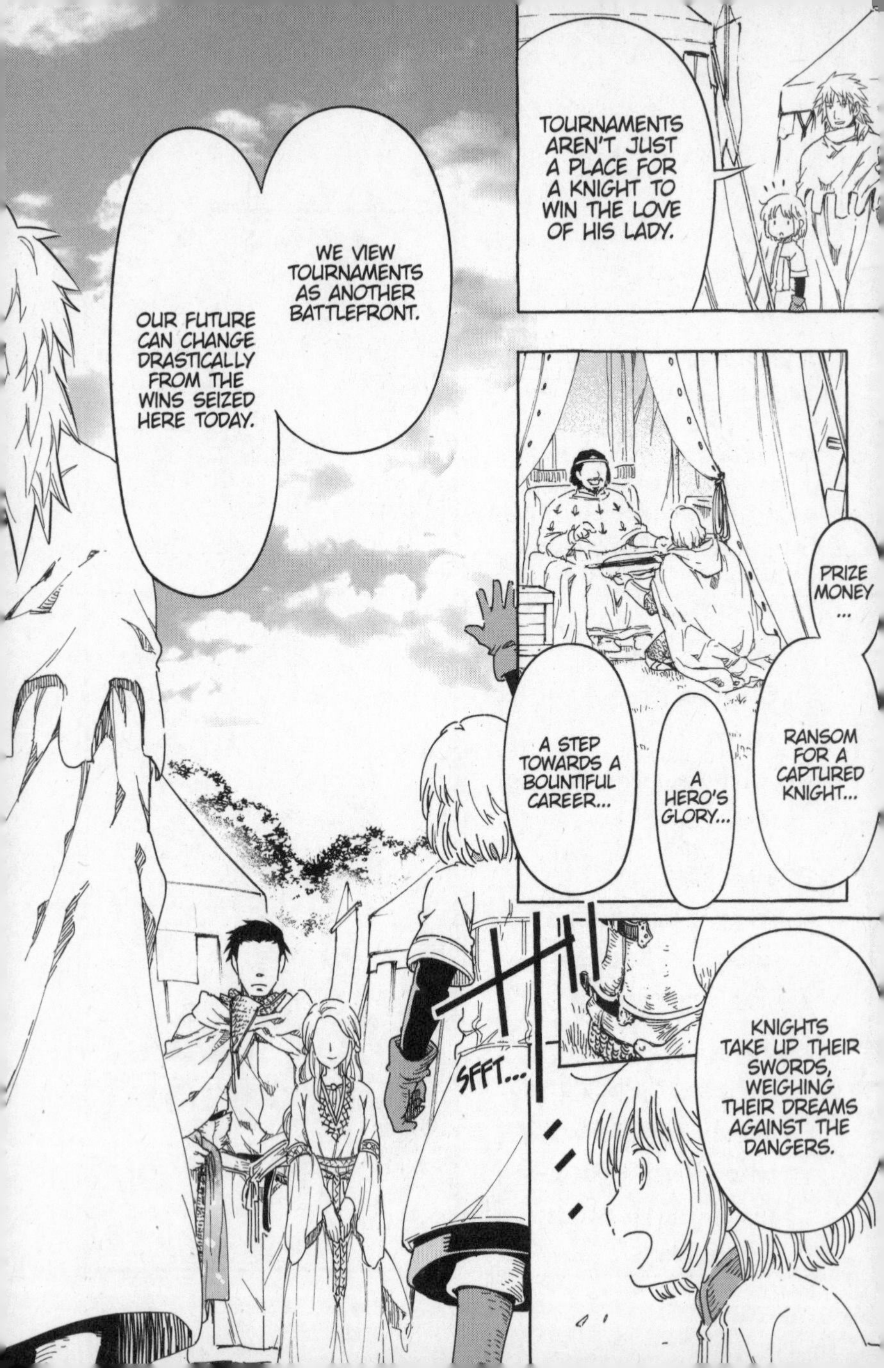
TOURNAMENTS AREN'T JUST A PLACE FOR A KNIGHT TO WIN THE LOVE OF HIS LADY.
PRIZE MONEY ...
RANSOM FOR A CAPTURED KNIGHT...
A HERO'S GLORY...
A STEP TOWARDS A BOUNTIFUL CAREER...
KNIGHTS TAKE UP THEIR SWORDS, WEIGHING THEIR DREAMS AGAINST THE DANGERS.
WE VIEW TOURNAMENTS AS ANOTHER BATTLEFRONT.
OUR FUTURE CAN CHANGE DRASTICALLY FROM THE WINS SEIZED HERE TODAY.
SFFT...

Lepus

A knight who serves Castle Claustra. At first glance, he is brusque and coarse, but shows a strong sense of duty and uprightness. Surprisingly also known to show a caring side for others.

- Favorite Foods
  Salt pork
  Pears

- Least Favorite Foods
  Cabbage

- Talents
  Easily winning a dog's affection
  Ration cooking

- Weaknesses
  For good or bad, an overly serious man who often causes children to burst into tears.

Lepus

CHAPTER 9
A NEW HOME

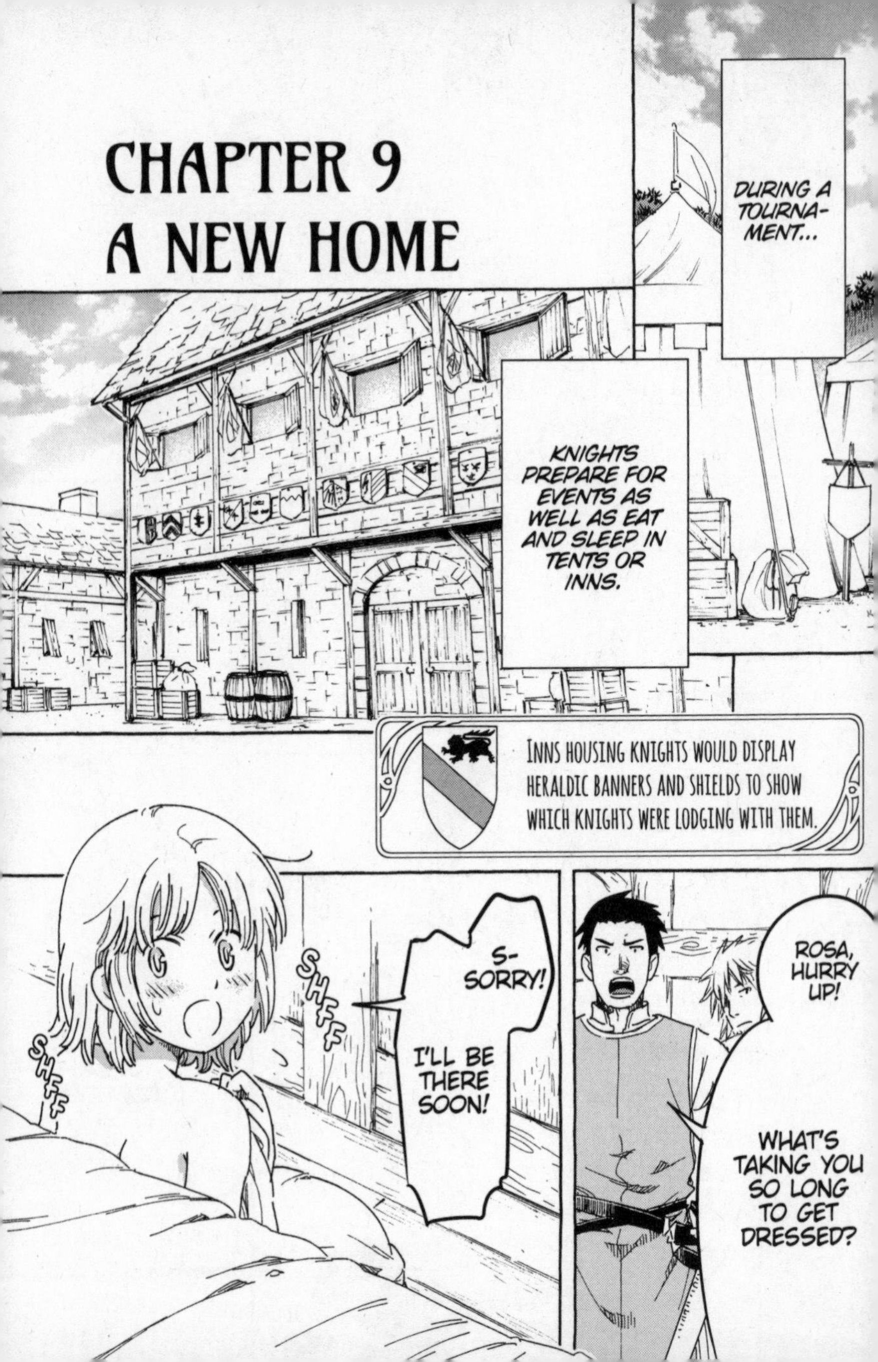
DURING A TOURNAMENT...
KNIGHTS PREPARE FOR EVENTS AS WELL AS EAT AND SLEEP IN TENTS OR INNS.
INNS HOUSING KNIGHTS WOULD DISPLAY HERALDIC BANNERS AND SHIELDS TO SHOW WHICH KNIGHTS WERE LODGING WITH THEM.
ROSA, HURRY UP!
WHAT'S TAKING YOU SO LONG TO GET DRESSED?
S-SORRY!
I'LL BE THERE SOON!
SHFF
SHFF

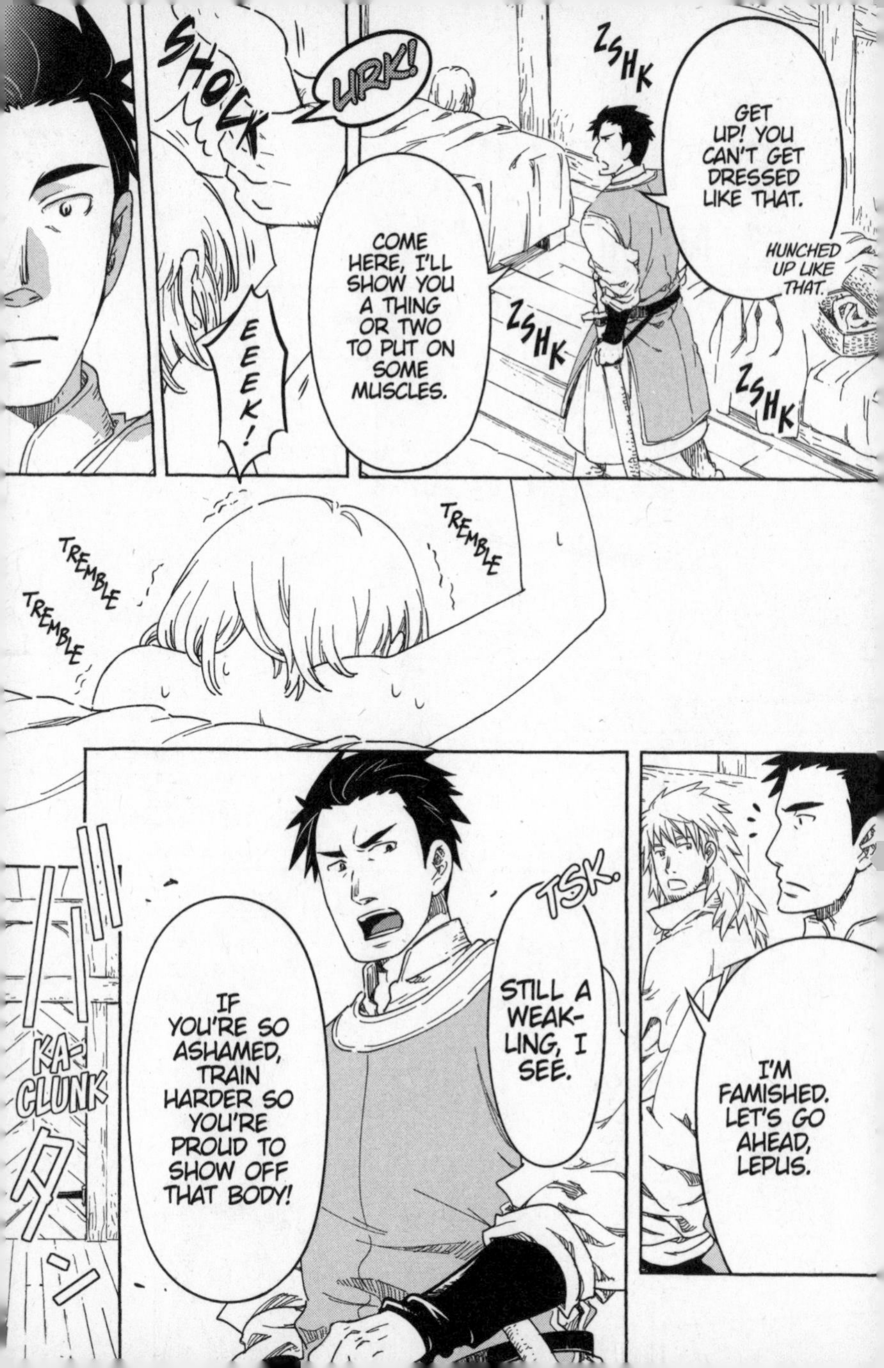
GET UP! YOU CAN'T GET DRESSED LIKE THAT.
HUNCHED UP LIKE THAT.
ZSHK
ZSHK
ZSHK
COME HERE, I'LL SHOW YOU A THING OR TWO TO PUT ON SOME MUSCLES.
SHOVK
URK!
EEEK!
TREMBLE
TREMBLE
TREMBLE
I'M FAMISHED. LET'S GO AHEAD, LEPUS.
TSK.
STILL A WEAK-LING, I SEE.
IF YOU'RE SO ASHAMED, TRAIN HARDER SO YOU'RE PROUD TO SHOW OFF THAT BODY!
KA-CLUNK
タン

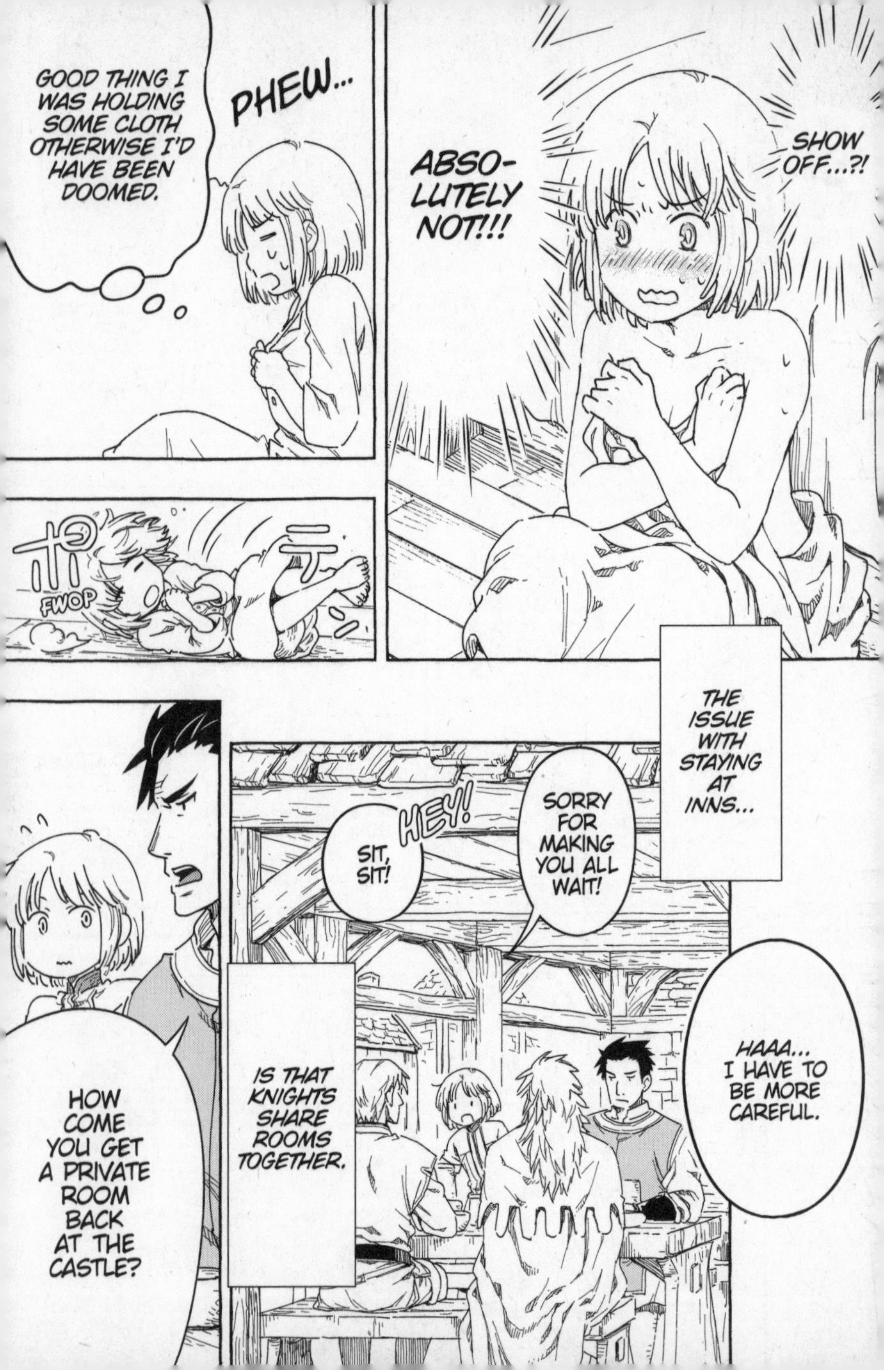
SHOW OFF...?!
ABSO-LUTELY NOT!!!
PHEW...
GOOD THING I WAS HOLDING SOME CLOTH OTHERWISE I'D HAVE BEEN DOOMED.
ポ
テ
FWOP
THE ISSUE WITH STAYING AT INNS...
SORRY FOR MAKING YOU ALL WAIT!
HEY!
SIT, SIT!
IS THAT KNIGHTS SHARE ROOMS TOGETHER.
HAAA... I HAVE TO BE MORE CAREFUL.
HOW COME YOU GET A PRIVATE ROOM BACK AT THE CASTLE?

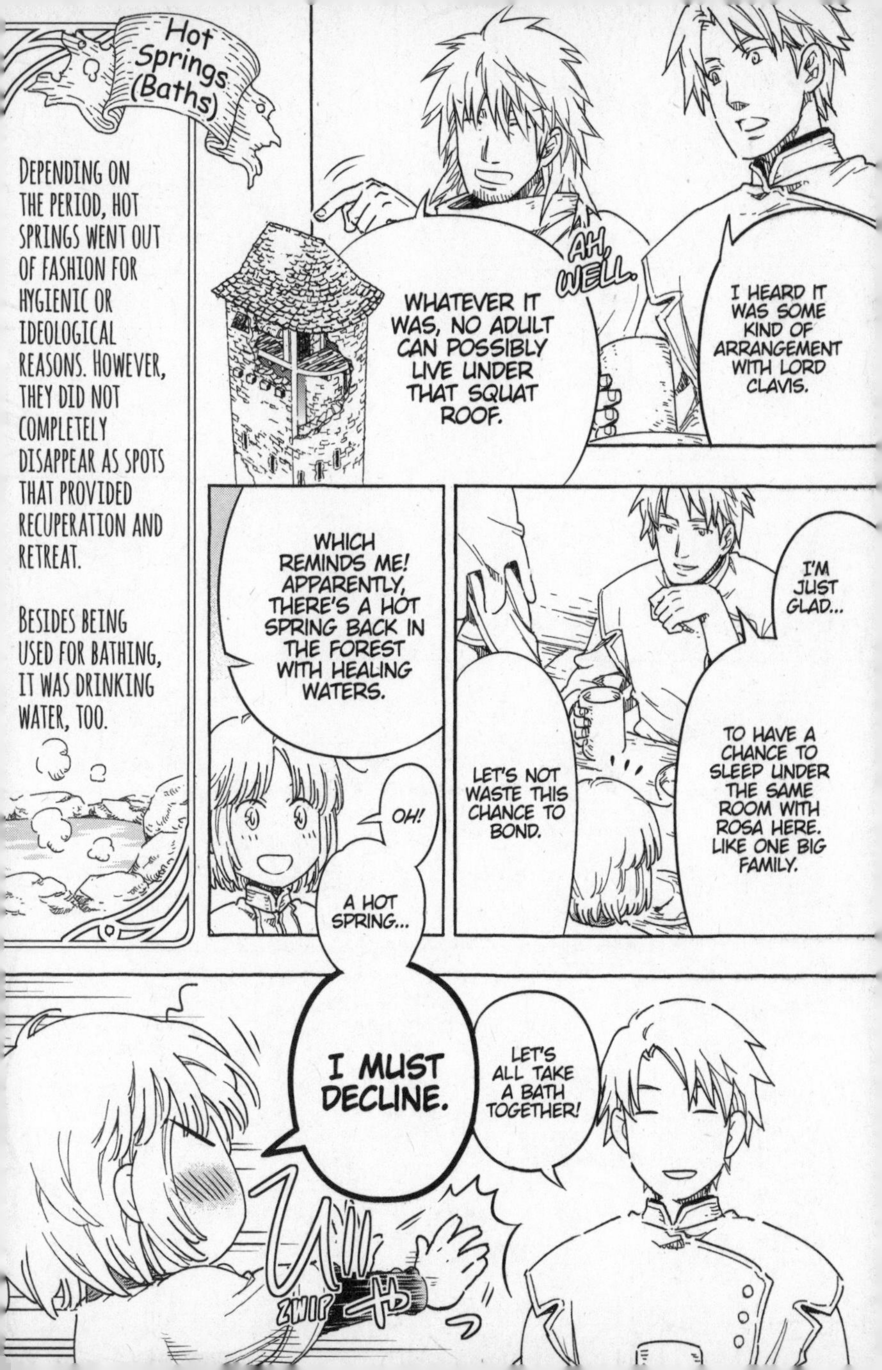
I HEARD IT WAS SOME KIND OF ARRANGEMENT WITH LORD CLAVIS.
AH, WELL.
WHATEVER IT WAS, NO ADULT CAN POSSIBLY LIVE UNDER THAT SQUAT ROOF.
I'M JUST GLAD...
TO HAVE A CHANCE TO SLEEP UNDER THE SAME ROOM WITH ROSA HERE. LIKE ONE BIG FAMILY.
LET'S NOT WASTE THIS CHANCE TO BOND.
WHICH REMINDS ME! APPARENTLY, THERE'S A HOT SPRING BACK IN THE FOREST WITH HEALING WATERS.
OH!
A HOT SPRING...
Hot Springs (Baths)
DEPENDING ON THE PERIOD, HOT SPRINGS WENT OUT OF FASHION FOR HYGIENIC OR IDEOLOGICAL REASONS. HOWEVER, THEY DID NOT COMPLETELY DISAPPEAR AS SPOTS THAT PROVIDED RECUPERATION AND RETREAT.
BESIDES BEING USED FOR BATHING, IT WAS DRINKING WATER, TOO.
LET'S ALL TAKE A BATH TOGETHER!
I MUST DECLINE.
ZWIP

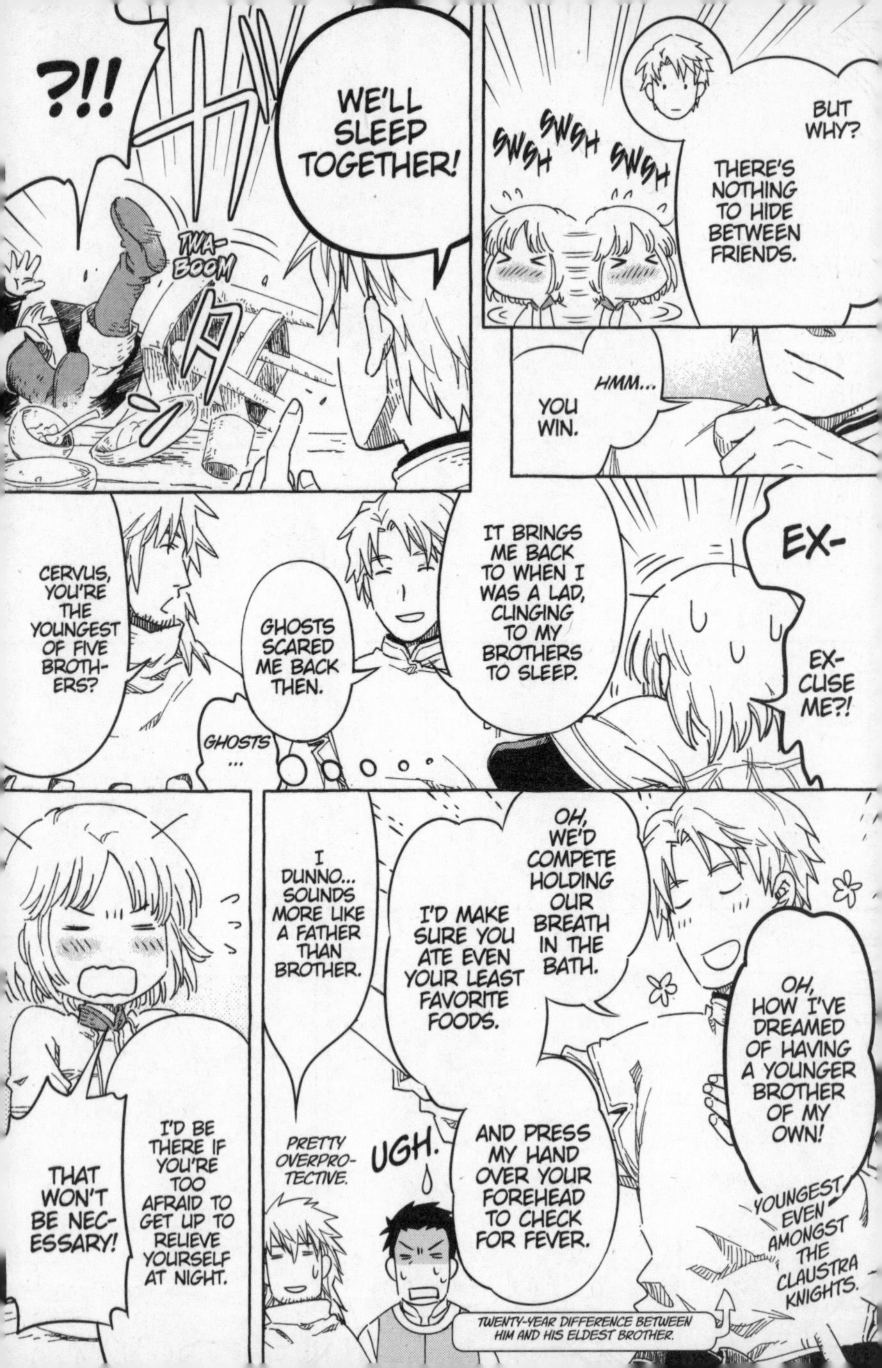
SWSH SWSH SWSH
BUT WHY?
THERE'S NOTHING TO HIDE BETWEEN FRIENDS.
HMM...
YOU WIN.
WE'LL SLEEP TOGETHER!
?!!
TWA-BOOM
EX-
EX-CUSE ME?!
IT BRINGS ME BACK TO WHEN I WAS A LAD, CLINGING TO MY BROTHERS TO SLEEP.
GHOSTS SCARED ME BACK THEN.
GHOSTS...
CERVUS, YOU'RE THE YOUNGEST OF FIVE BROTH-ERS?
OH, HOW I'VE DREAMED OF HAVING A YOUNGER BROTHER OF MY OWN!
YOUNGEST EVEN AMONGST THE CLAUSTRA KNIGHTS.
TWENTY-YEAR DIFFERENCE BETWEEN HIM AND HIS ELDEST BROTHER.
OH, WE'D COMPETE HOLDING OUR BREATH IN THE BATH.
I'D MAKE SURE YOU ATE EVEN YOUR LEAST FAVORITE FOODS.
AND PRESS MY HAND OVER YOUR FOREHEAD TO CHECK FOR FEVER.
I DUNNO... SOUNDS MORE LIKE A FATHER THAN BROTHER.
UGH.
PRETTY OVERPRO-TECTIVE.
I'D BE THERE IF YOU'RE TOO AFRAID TO GET UP TO RELIEVE YOURSELF AT NIGHT.
THAT WON'T BE NEC-ESSARY!

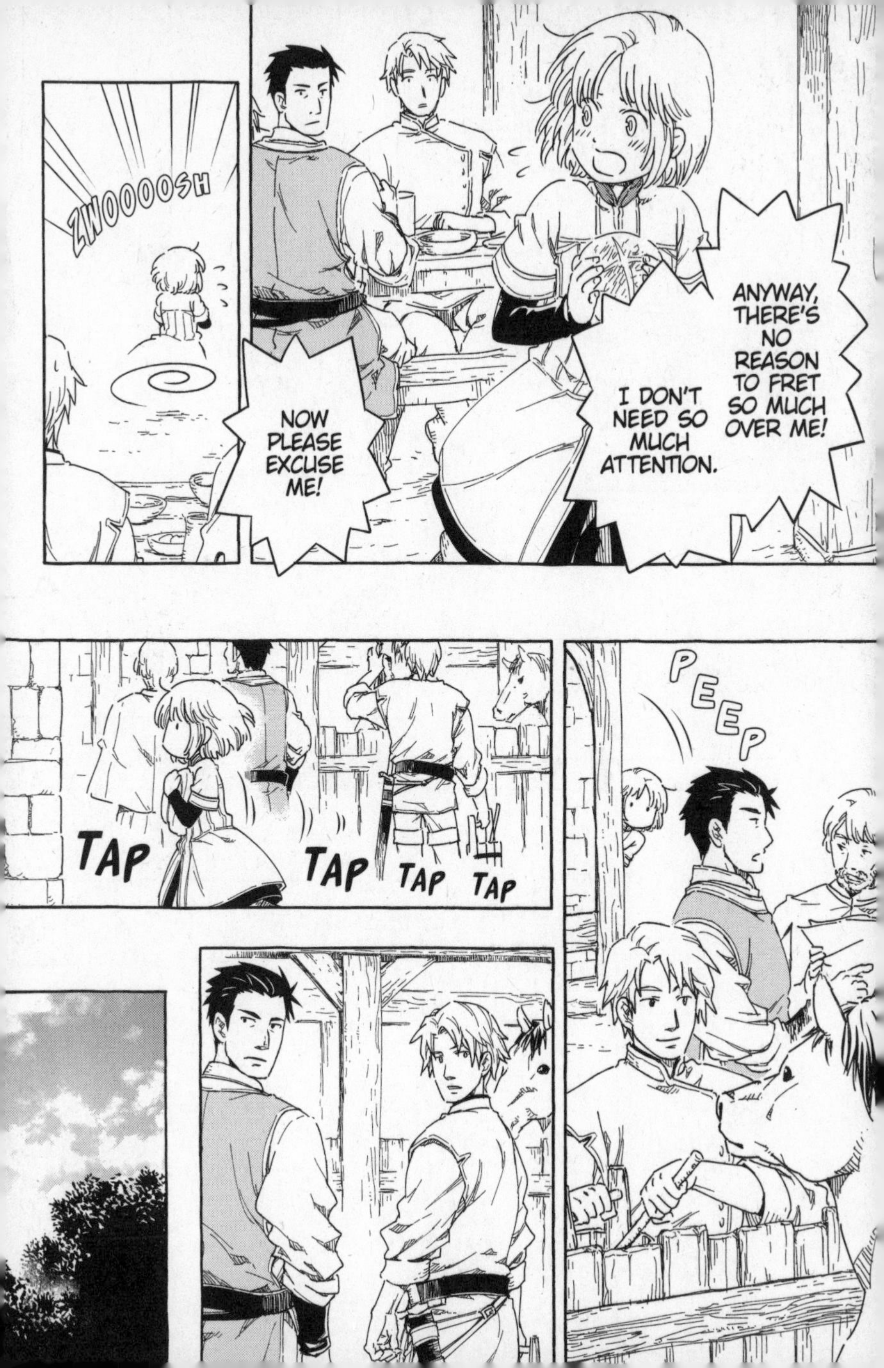
ANYWAY, THERE'S NO REASON TO FRET SO MUCH OVER ME!
I DON'T NEED SO MUCH ATTENTION.
NOW PLEASE EXCUSE ME!
ZWOOOOSH
PEEP
TAP
TAP
TAP
TAP

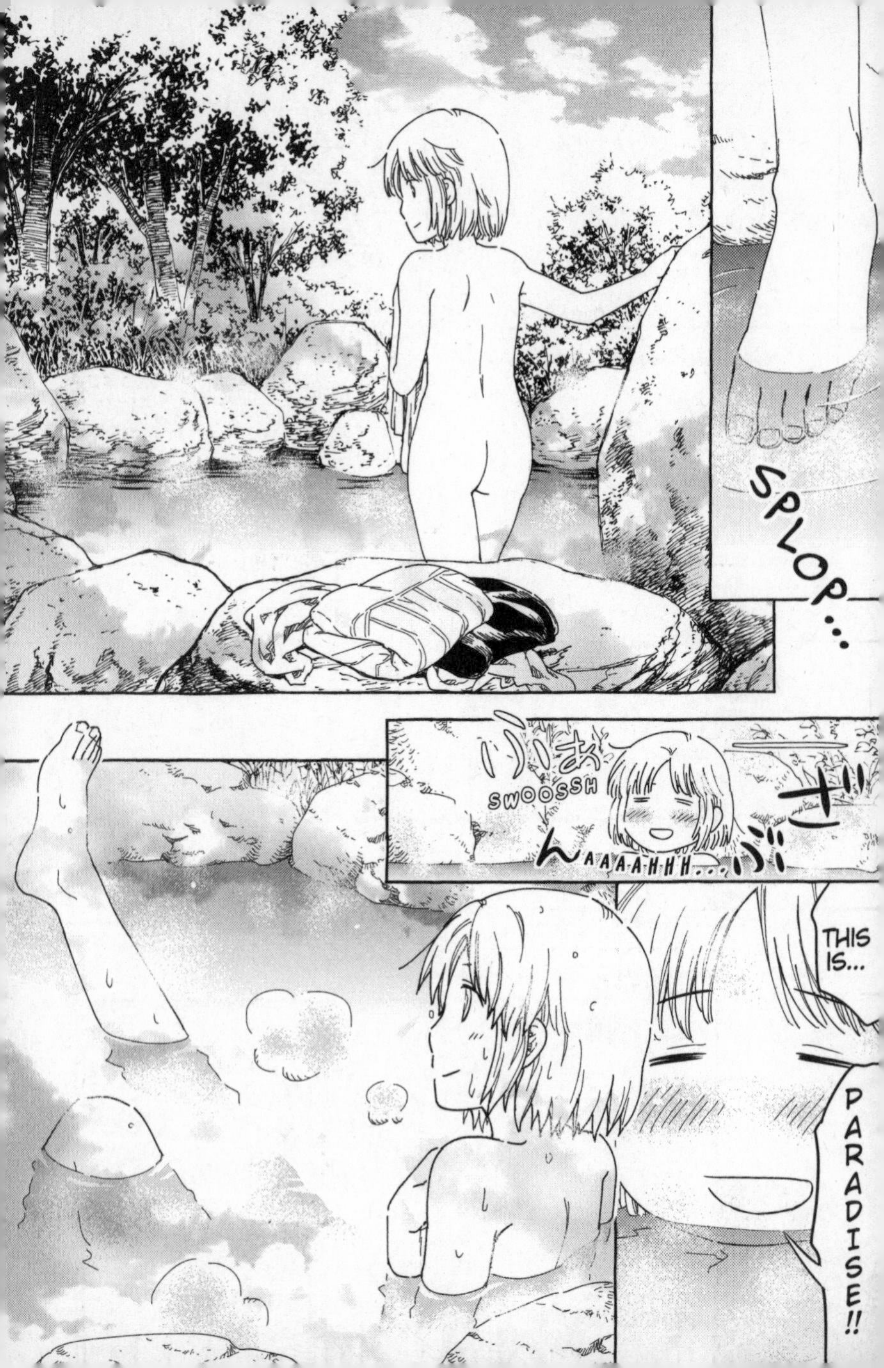
SPLOP...
ざぶ
SWOOSSH
ふぁ
んAAAAHHH...
THIS IS...
PARADISE!!

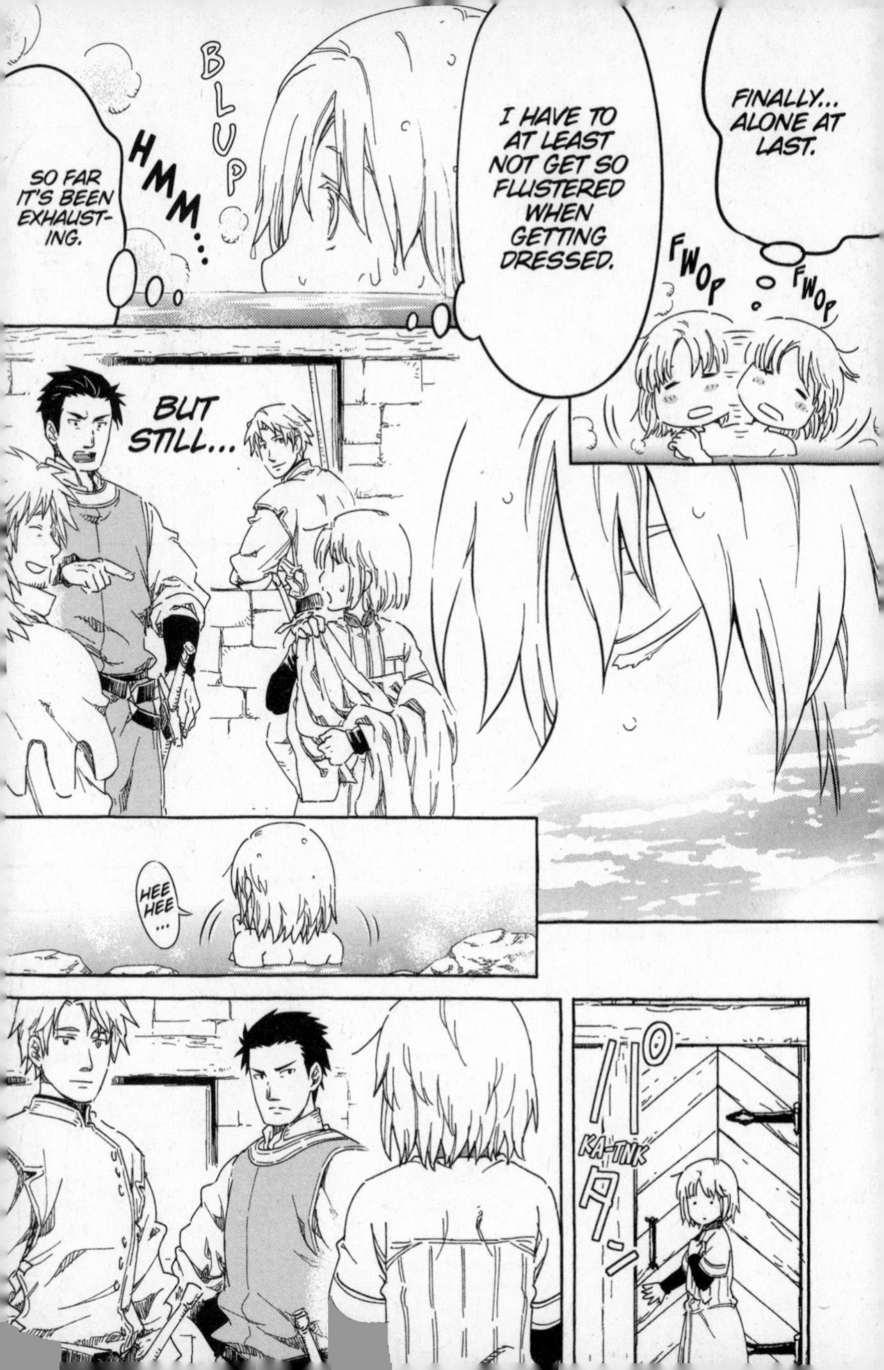
FINALLY... ALONE AT LAST.
FWOP
FWOP
I HAVE TO AT LEAST NOT GET SO FLUSTERED WHEN GETTING DRESSED.
BLUP
HMM...
SO FAR IT'S BEEN EXHAUST-ING.
BUT STILL...
HEE HEE...
KA-TNK

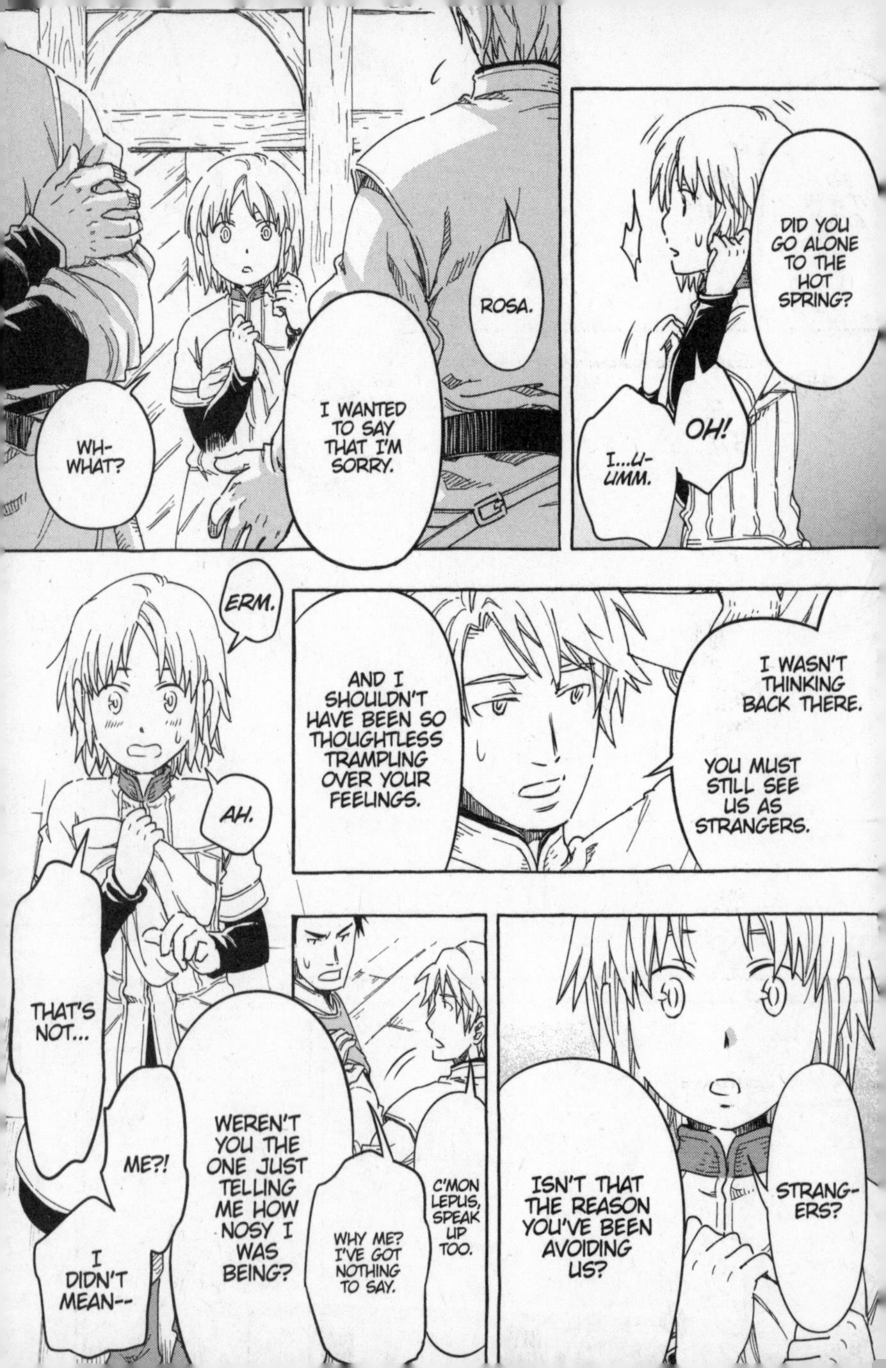
DID YOU GO ALONE TO THE HOT SPRING?
OH!
I...U-UMM.
ROSA.
I WANTED TO SAY THAT I'M SORRY.
WH-WHAT?
I WASN'T THINKING BACK THERE.
YOU MUST STILL SEE US AS STRANGERS.
AND I SHOULDN'T HAVE BEEN SO THOUGHTLESS TRAMPLING OVER YOUR FEELINGS.
STRANGERS?
ISN'T THAT THE REASON YOU'VE BEEN AVOIDING US?
C'MON LEPUS, SPEAK UP TOO.
WHY ME? I'VE GOT NOTHING TO SAY.
WEREN'T YOU THE ONE JUST TELLING ME HOW NOSY I WAS BEING?
ME?!
ERM.
AH.
THAT'S NOT...
I DIDN'T MEAN--

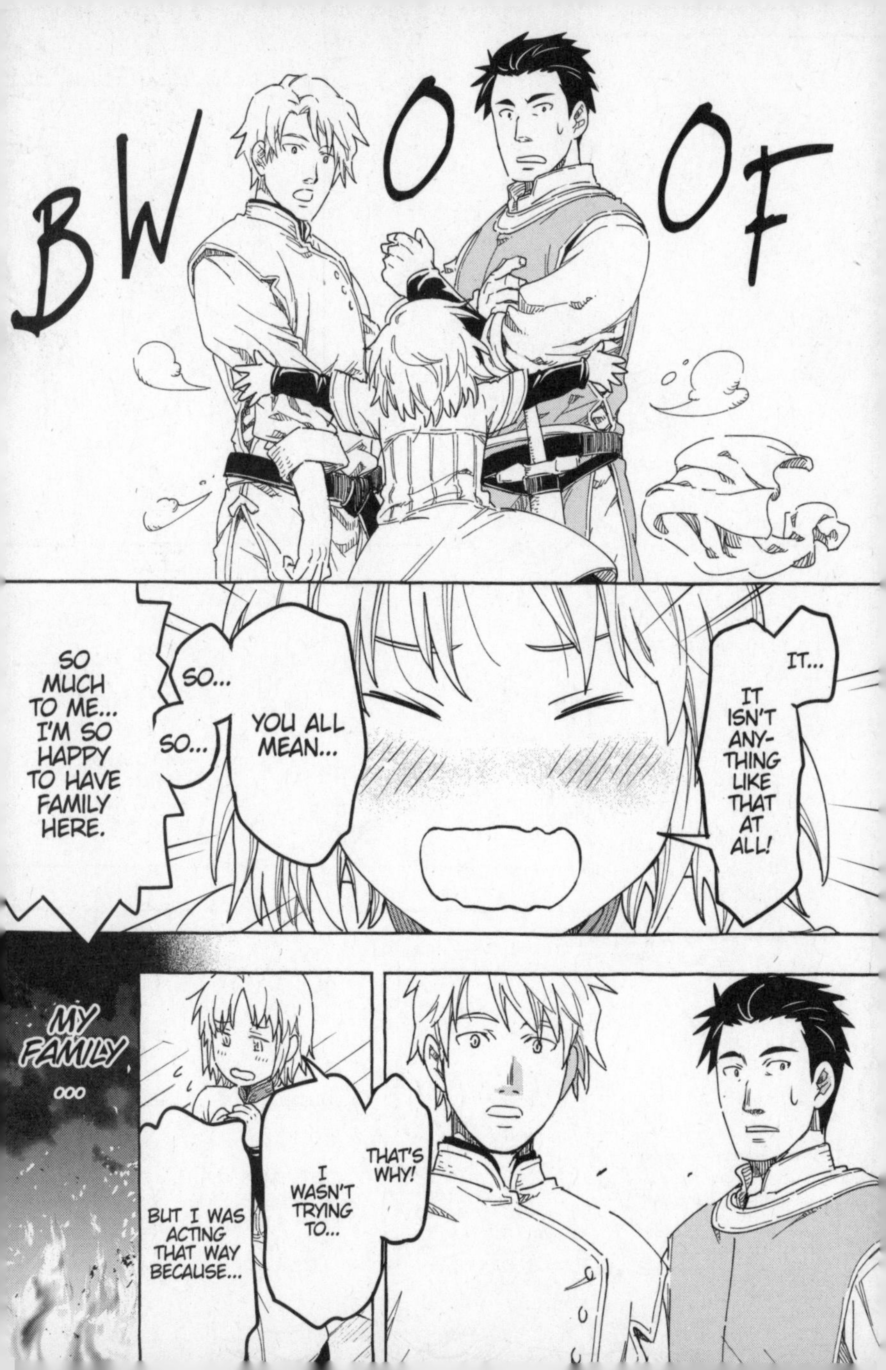
BWOOF
IT...
IT ISN'T ANYTHING LIKE THAT AT ALL!
YOU ALL MEAN...
SO...
SO...
SO MUCH TO ME... I'M SO HAPPY TO HAVE FAMILY HERE.
THAT'S WHY!
I WASN'T TRYING TO...
BUT I WAS ACTING THAT WAY BECAUSE...
MY FAMILY...

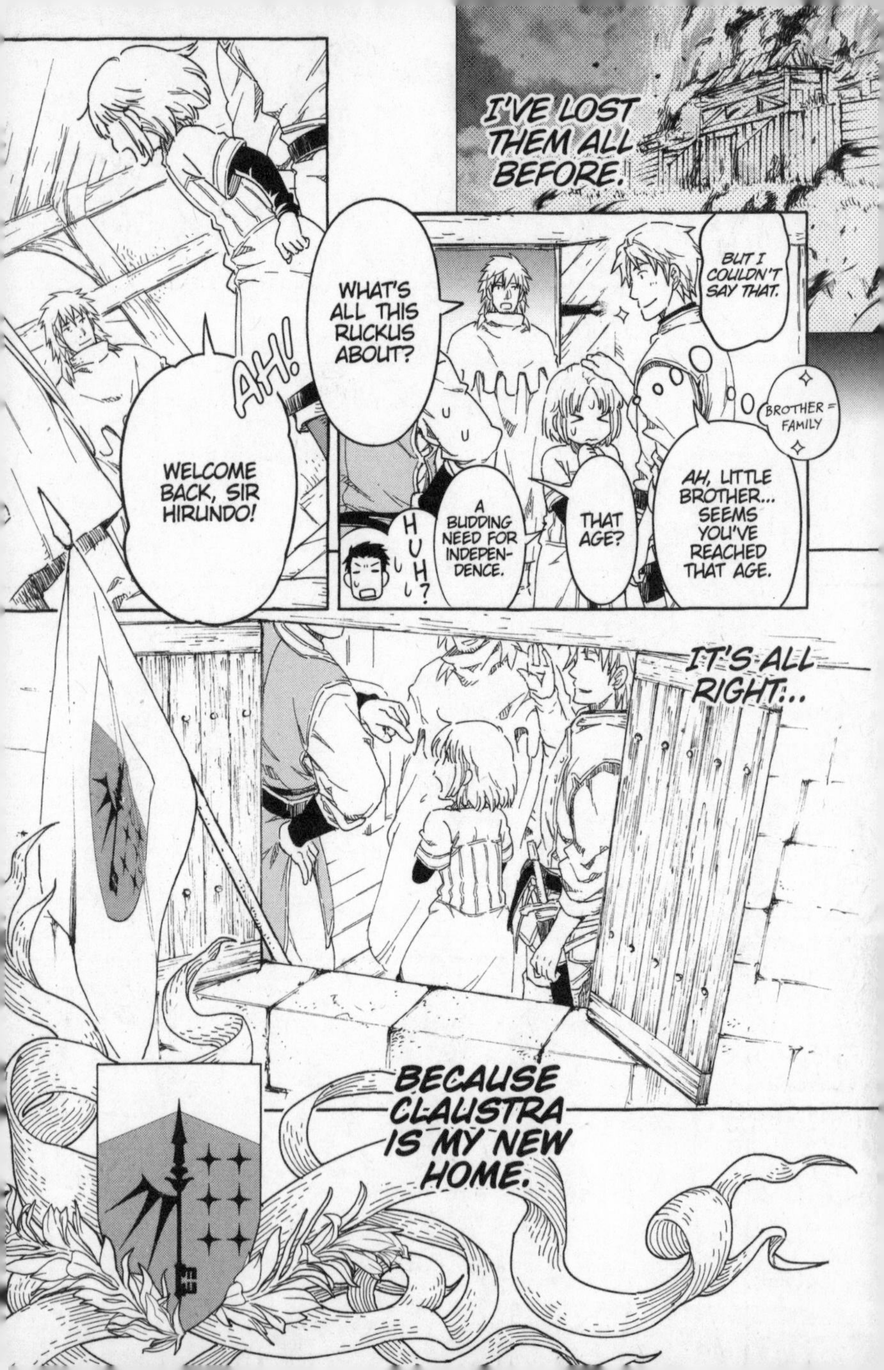
I'VE LOST THEM ALL BEFORE.
BUT I COULDN'T SAY THAT.
BROTHER = FAMILY
AH, LITTLE BROTHER... SEEMS YOU'VE REACHED THAT AGE.
THAT AGE?
A BUDDING NEED FOR INDEPENDENCE.
HUH?
WHAT'S ALL THIS RUCKUS ABOUT?
AH!
WELCOME BACK, SIR HIRUNDO!
IT'S ALL RIGHT...
BECAUSE CLAUSTRA IS MY NEW HOME.

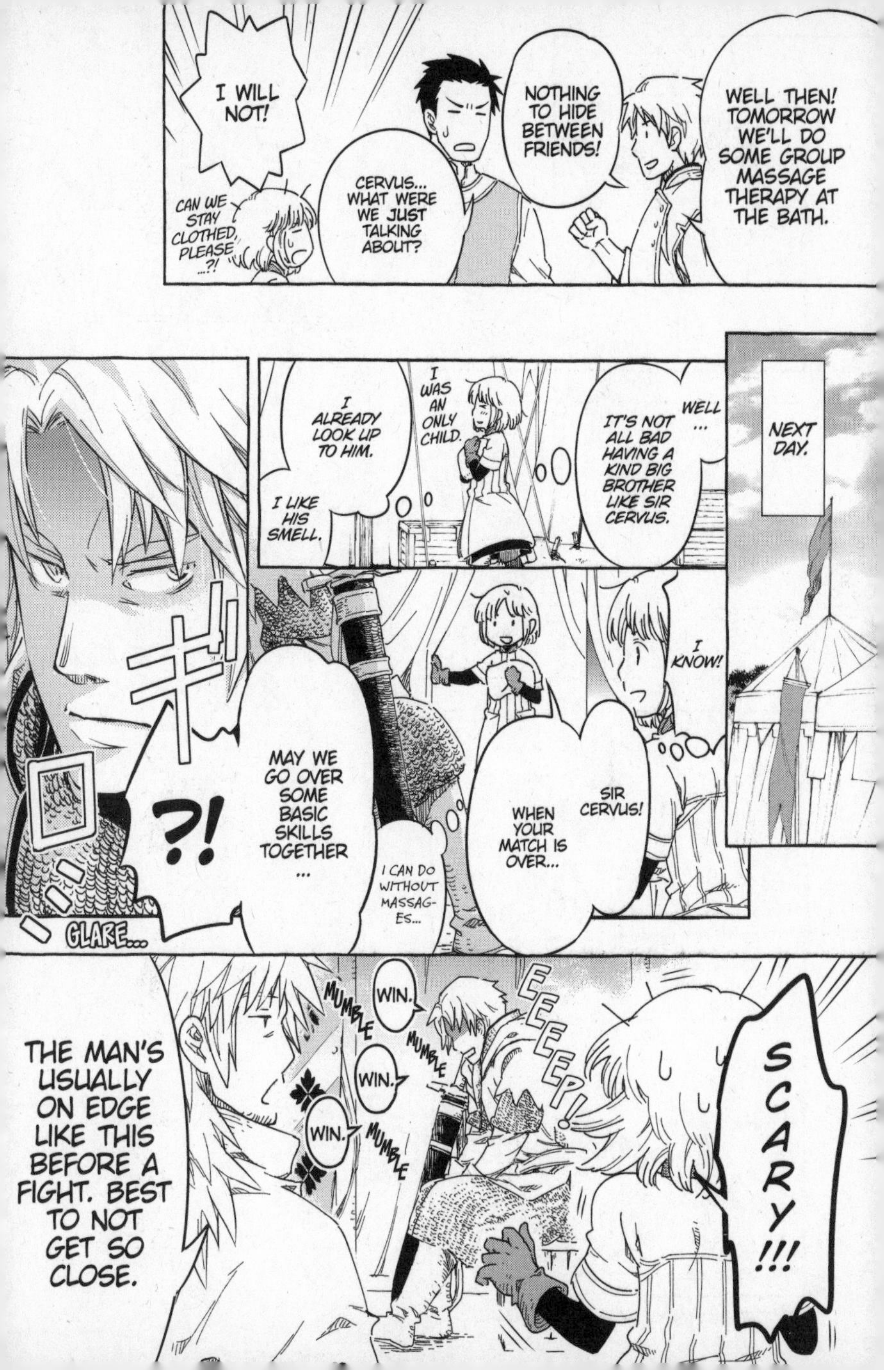
WELL THEN! TOMORROW WE'LL DO SOME GROUP MASSAGE THERAPY AT THE BATH.
NOTHING TO HIDE BETWEEN FRIENDS!
CERVUS... WHAT WERE WE JUST TALKING ABOUT?
I WILL NOT!
CAN WE STAY CLOTHED, PLEASE ...?!
NEXT DAY.
WELL ...
IT'S NOT ALL BAD HAVING A KIND BIG BROTHER LIKE SIR CERVUS.
I WAS AN ONLY CHILD.
I ALREADY LOOK UP TO HIM.
I LIKE HIS SMELL.
I KNOW!
SIR CERVUS!
WHEN YOUR MATCH IS OVER...
MAY WE GO OVER SOME BASIC SKILLS TOGETHER ...
I CAN DO WITHOUT MASSAG-ES...
?!
GLARE...
SCARY!!!
EEEEP!
WIN.
MUMBLE
WIN.
MUMBLE
WIN.
MUMBLE
THE MAN'S USUALLY ON EDGE LIKE THIS BEFORE A FIGHT. BEST TO NOT GET SO CLOSE.